SALTWATER GAMEFISHING

OFFSHORE AND ONSHORE

SALTWATER GAMEFISHING

OFFSHORE AND ONSHORE

PETER GOADBY

F*or my family, my fishing friends*
and the great saltwater gamefish

PHOTOGRAPHS APPEARING ON PRELIMINARY PAGES

HALF TITLE: *Hippolytus Salvianus,* Aquatilium animalium
historiae, *Rome, 1554.*

TITLE PAGE: *Stand up angler Ms Marsha Bierman tangles with
a Costa Rican sailfish. Photo: Darrell Jones.*

*First published in the United States of America in 1992
by International Marine Publishing Company
An imprint of TAB Books
Tab Books is a division of McGraw-Hill, Inc.*

*International Marine Publishing
P.O. Box 220,
Camden, Maine 04843*

*by arrangement with CollinsAngus&Robertson
Publishers Pty Limited, Sydney, Australia*

*First published in 1991 in Australia by
CollinsAngus&Robertson Publishers Pty Limited (ACN 009 913 517)
A division of HarperCollinsPublishers (Australia) Pty Limited
4 Eden Park, 31 Waterloo Road, North Ryde,
NSW 2113, Australia*

Copyright © Peter Goadby 1991

ISBN 0-87742-323-7

*TAB books offers software for sale. For information and a
catalog, please contact TAB Software Department, Blue Ridge
Summit, PA 17294-0850.*

*Cover photograph: Darrell Jones
Typeset in Australia by Midland Typesetters, Victoria
Printed in Australia by Griffin Press*

FOREWORD

In 1970, Peter Goadby's first gamefishing book, *Big Fish and Blue Water*, was published and instantly accepted by the saltwater fishing community. Five editions and several reprints later, it is regarded not only as a fishing classic, but as the definitive work on gamefishing in the Pacific.

In Peter's new book, *Saltwater Gamefishing*, he has expanded beyond the Pacific to cover all gamefishing areas of the world. The work is again a blend of authoritative text and graphics ranging from quality photographs to drawings and paintings that will provide pleasure as well as information.

Charles M. Cooke III of Maui, an avid and successful pioneering angler himself, summed it up in the foreword of *Big Fish and Blue Water* when he noted: 'Of all the sportfishermen of the great Pacific Ocean, no one is more knowledgeable of his subject than Peter Goadby.' Charlie was the first chief judge of the world class Hawaiian International Billfish Tournament. The second and only other person to hold that position is Peter Goadby who has served as chief judge since 1970. His influence on the integrity of that tournament has been substantial.

Having fished with Peter in the waters of many countries, under diverse conditions, I have personally experienced the expertise referred to by Charlie as well as his ability to impart his knowledge both verbally and in the written word. The only present day analogy that comes to mind would be playing golf with Jack Nicklaus. If there were a professional anglers' association, I know Peter would be similarly regarded by those who pursue the sport of saltwater angling.

Since his earliest published works, Peter has used his abiding thirst for fishing history and knowledge to build a worldwide exposure to fish, tackle, tournaments and tactics. This is all shared with the reader in *Saltwater Gamefishing*. The contents cover the spectrum of gamefishing from giant tuna and billfish to the smaller gamefish of estuaries and flats as well as the international developments of tag and release, lure fishing for billfish, and night fishing for broadbill.

More than twenty years in the making, *Saltwater Gamefishing* packs into its pages Peter's years of travelling and fishing the world listening, sharing, judging and lecturing. The result is a book that will be a constant companion in your quest for tight lines. Enjoy it.

Cheers and Aloha,

PETER S. FITHIAN
TRUSTEE, INTERNATIONAL GAME FISH ASSOCIATION
CHAIRMAN, HAWAIIAN INTERNATIONAL BILLFISH ASSOCIATION
HONOLULU, HAWAII

CONTENTS

SUGGESTED READING
AND VIEWING

BOOKS

Aflalo, F. G., *Sunshine and Sport in Florida and the West Indies*, Geo. W. Jacobs, Philadelphia, 1907

Bass, A. J., D'Aubrey, J. D., and Kistnasamy, N., *Sharks of the East Coast of Southern Africa*, Parts I, II, III, Oceanographic Research Institute, Durban, 1975
Bickerdyke, J. H., and others, *Sea Fishing*, Longman Green, London, 1895
Big Game Fishing Club of France, *Game Fish*, Big Game Fishing Club of France, Paris, 1985
Bird, E. ('Chilo') A., *Fishing Off Puerto Rico*, Barnes & Co., New York, 1956
Bloch, M. E., *Allgemeine Naturgeschichte der Fische*, Berlin, 1782–1795
Brooks, J., *Salt Water Fly Fishing*, G. J. Putman's Sons, New York, 1950
Brooks, J., *Salt Water Game Fishing*, Harper & Row, New York, 1968

Caunter, J., *Shark Angling in Great Britain*, George Allen & Unwin, London, 1961
Chapralis, J., *Pan Anglers' World Guide to Fly Fishing*, Pan Angling Publishing, Chicago, 1987
Clostermann, Pierre, *Des Poissons se Grands*, Flammarion, Paris, 1969
Connett, Eugene V. (ed.), *American Big Game Fishing*, Derrydale, New York, 1935
Coppleson, V. and Goadby, P., *Shark Attack*, Angus and Robertson, Sydney, 1988
Cuvier and Valenciennes, *Histoire Natural des Poissons*, Paris, 1829–1849

Davie, P. S., *Pacific Marlins—Anatomy and Physiology*, Massey University Printery, Palmerston North, 1990
Davis, C. II, *California Salt Water Fishing*, A. S. Barnes & Co., New York, 1949
Davis, C. III, *Hook-up*, Outdoor Empire Publishing, Seattle, 1977
Dimock, A. W., *The Book of the Tarpon*, Outing Publishing, New York, 1911
D'Ombrain, A., *Game Fishing Off the Australian Coast*, Angus & Robertson, Sydney, 1959
Dunaway, V., *Complete Book of Baits, Rigs and Tackle*, STD Publications, Miami, 1971

Earp, A., and Wildeman, W. J., *The Blue Water Bait Book*, Little, Brown & Co., Boston, 1974
Evanoff, V., *Fishing Secrets of the Experts*, Doubleday & Co., New York, 1962

FAO Species Catalogues, 'Billfish', 'Scombrids of the World', 'Sharks of the World', FAO Rome, 1984
Farrington, Chisie, *Women can fish*, Coward McCann Inc., New York, 1951
Farrington, S. Kip Jnr, *Atlantic Game Fishing*, Kennedy Bros Inc., New York, 1937
Farrington, S. Kip Jnr, *Fishing the Atlantic Offshore and On*, Coward McCann, New York, 1949

Farrington, S. Kip Jnr, *Fishing the Pacific Offshore and On*, Coward McCann, New York, 1953
Farrington, S. Kip Jnr, *Fishing with Hemingway and Glassell*, David McKay, New York, 1971
Farrington, S. Kip Jnr, *Pacific Game Fishing*, Coward McCann, New York, 1942
Farrington, S. Kip Jnr, *The Trail of the Sharp Cup*, Dodd Mead & Co., New York, 1974

Garrick, J. A. F., *Sharks of the Genus Carcharhinus*, NOAA and NMFS, Washington, 1982
Gifford, T., *Anglers and Muscleheads*, E. P. Dutton, New York, 1960
Gilbert, P., *Sharks and Survival*, D. C. Heath, Boston, 1963
Goadby, P., *Big Fish and Blue Water*, Angus and Robertson, Sydney, 1970
Goadby, P., *Sharks & Other Predatory Fish*, Jacaranda Press, Brisbane, 1957
Goode, G. B., *Materials for a History of the Swordfishes*, Government Printing Office, Washington DC, 1883
Grey, R. C., *Adventures of a Deep-Sea Angler*, Harper Bros, New York, 1930
Grey, Romer, *The Cruise of the Fisherman*, Harper Bros, New York, 1930
Grey, Romer, *The Fishermen under the Southern Cross*, Harper Bros, New York, 1928
Grey, Zane, *An American Angler in Australia*, Harper Bros, New York, 1937
Grey, Zane, *Angler's El Dorado in the South Pacific*, Angus and Robertson, Sydney, 1982
Grey, Zane, *Tales from a Fisherman's Log*, Hodder & Stoughton, Auckland, 1978
Grey, Zane, *Tales of Fishes*, Harper Bros, New York, 1919
Grey, Zane, *Tales of Fishing Virgin Seas*, Harper Bros, New York, 1925
Grey, Zane, *Tales of Swordfish and Tuna*, Grossett & Dunlap, New York, 1925
Grey, Zane, *Tales of Tahitian Waters*, Harper Bros, New York, 1931
Grey, Zane, *Tales of the Angler's El Dorado New Zealand*, Harper Bros, New York, 1926

Heilner, Van Campen, *Salt Water Fishing*, Penn Publishing, Philadelphia, 1937
Heilner, Van Campen, and Stick, F., *The Call of the Surf*, Doubleday Page, New York, 1920
Hemingway, Ernest, *The Old Man and the Sea*, Jonathon Cape, London, 1952
Holder, C. F., *Big Game at Sea*, The Outing Publishing Company, New York, 1908
Holden, C. F., *The Log of a Sea Angler*, Houghton Mifflin & Co., Boston, 1906
Horne, C., *Big Game Fishing in South Africa*, Howard Timmins, Cape Town, 1959
Hosaka, E. V., *Sport Fishing in Hawaii*, Bonds, Honolulu, 1944
Housby, T., *Big Game Fishing*, Priory Press, Dorset, 1985

IGFA, *World Record Game Fishes*, published annually by IGFA Fort Lauderdale, from 1978

Illingworth, Neil, *Fighting Fins*, W. H. and A. W. Reed, Wellington, 1961

Jean, Ruben, *Fishing in the Caribbean*, Editorial Arte, Caracas, 1964

Jordan, D. S., and Evermann, B. W., *American Food & Game Fishes*, Doubleday, Page & Co., New York, 1902

Joseph, J., Klawe, W., and Murphy, P., *Tuna & Billfish*, IATTC, La Jolla, 1979

Kreh, Lefty, *Fly Fishing in Salt Water*, Crown Publishers, New York, 1974

Kreh, Lefty, and Sosin, M., *Practical Fishing Knots*, Crown Publishers, New York, 1972

Lacapede, B. G. E., *Histoire naturelle des Poissons* (5 vols), Plassen, Paris, 1798–1803

LaMonte, F. R., *North American Game Fishes*, Doubleday and Co. Inc., New York, 1958

Linnaeus, C., *Systems naturae . . . etc*, 1758

Lyman, H., *Bluefishing*, A. S. Barnes & Co., New York, 1955

McClane, A. J., *Standard Fishing Encyclopaedia*, Holt, Rinehart & Winston, New York, 1965

McCristal, V., *The Rivers & the Sea*, A. H. & A. W. Reed, Sydney, 1974

Major, H., *Salt Water Fishing Tackle*, Funk & Wagnalls Co., New York, 1939

Marron, E., *Albacora*, Random House, New York, 1957

Mather, C. O., *Billfish*, Saltaire Publishing Ltd, Sidney, British Columbia, 1976

Mitchell-Hedges, F. A., *Battles with Giant Fish*, Duckworth & Co., London, 1923

Mitchell-Henry, L., *Tunny Fishing—At Home and Abroad*, London, 1934

Moss, F. T., *Successful Ocean Game Fishing*, International Marine, Maine, 1971

Real del Sarte, G., *Technique des Grands Poissons*, Creppin Leblond, Paris, 1969

Reiger, G., *Profiles in Salt Water Angling*, Prentice-Hall Inc., Englewood Cliffs, 1972

Richard, Marc, *L'Aventure de la Grande Peche Sportive*, Poseidon, Zurich, 1979

Rizzuto, J., *Fishing Hawaiian Style*, Vols I, II, III, Hawaiian Fishing News, 1983–1990

Rizzuto, J., *Modern Hawaiian Gamefishing*, The University Press of Hawaii, 1977

Samson, Jack, *Line Down!*, Winchester Press, 1973

Shaw, G., and Nodder, F. P., *Naturalists' Miscellany*, Royal Society, London, 1770–1799

Shomura, R., and Williams, F. (eds), *Proceedings of International Billfish Symposium*, Parts 1, 2, 3, Kona, Hawaii, NOAA/NMFS, 1975

Sosin, M., *Anglers' Bible*, Stoeger Publishing Co., Chicago, 1975

Sosin, M., *Practical Light Tackle Fishing*, Doubleday, New York, 1979

Sosin, M., and Kreh, L., *Fishing the Flats*, Winchester Press, Piscataway, 1983

Starling, S., *The Australian Fishing Book*, A. H. & A. W. Reed, Sydney, 1986

Stroud, R. (ed.), *Planning the Future of Billfishes, Second International Billfish Symposium*, Parts 1, 2, Kona, Hawaii, 1988

Stroud, R. (ed.), *World Angling Resources and Challenges*, IGFA, Fort Lauderdale, 1985

Suga, Yasanori, *Esprit of World's Game Fishermen*, Zin Hatten Shiyo, Tokyo, 1988

Taylor, R., Taylor, V., Goadby, P., Pepperell, Dr J., and others, *Sharks*, Readers Digest, Sydney, 1978

Thomas, George C. Jnr, and Thomas, George C. III, *Gamefish of the Pacific (Southern Californian and Mexican)*, J. B. Lippincott Co., Philadelphia, 1930

Tinsley, J. B., *The Sailfish—Swashbuckler of the Open Sea*, University of Florida Press, Gainesville, 1964

Trycare T., and Cagner, E., *Fishing the Complete Book*, David & Charles Newton Abbot, London, 1976

Ulrich, H., *How the Experts catch Trophy Fish*, A. S. Barnes, Brunswick, 1969

Vesey-Fitzgerald, B., and La Monte, F., *Game Fish of the World*, London, 1949

Waterman, C. F., *Modern Fresh & Saltwater Fly Fishing*, Winchester House, 1972

Wilkins, F., and Sale, E. V., *Saltwater Gamefishing in New Zealand*, A. H. & A. W. Reed, Wellington, 1982

Williams, T., and Underwood, J., *Fishing the Big Three*, Simon & Schuster, New York, 1982

Wisner, W., and Mundus, F., *Sportfishing for Sharks*, Macmillan, New York, 1971

Woolner, F., *Modern Salt-Water Sport Fishing*, Crown, New York, 1972

Wylie, P., *Crunch and Des: Stories of Florida Fishing*, Rinehart, New York, 1948

Wylie, P., *The Big Ones Get Away*, Farrah & Rinehart, New York, 1934

VIDEOS

Murray Brothers (Murray Brothers Productions)
Fresh Bait Rigging; Release; How to Rig Artificial Lures; Tuna Mania; Marlin Mania—1, 2, 3; How to Use a Fighting Chair.

Malcolm Florence (Dorado Video)
Of Tigers, Sails and Crocodiles; Great White; Black Marlin; Sailfish; Away from it all; The Great Reef Exploration—Parts 1 & 2.

Scotty
Pacific Ocean Salmon Fishing

Vidmark Heritage Collection
Fishing Tuna.

Lefty Kreh (Outdoor Safaris International)
All New Flycasting Technique; Light Tackle Tips; Exciting World of Saltwater Fly Fishing.

Pesca and Exploration with Mark Sosin
Fishing Pacific Panama.

INTRODUCTION

The twenty-odd years since the first publication of *Big Fish and Blue Water* have been a period of challenge and change in saltwater gamefishing. The major change has been the acceptance of tag and release, of assistance to science and understanding of the need to conserve and manage the stocks and resources of the great ocean predators, as well as their bait. There is growing awareness of the need for knowledge, not only to improve fishing technique, but to help manage the resources of the sea for this and future generations. There is awareness that modern fishing puts great pressure on fish stocks with the danger that some species and populations may be fished beyond recovery.

In the 1990s, recreational fishermen benefit from the refinements of tackle and technique that were just beginning in the 1970s. They may also take advantage of increased knowledge, not only contributed by other fishermen, skippers and crews, and authors of fishing books, but by scientists and fisheries managers. Fishermen, scientists and managers have moved closer together, partly by participating in successful co-operative tag and release programs and also from joint involvement in seminars or symposiums.

Since 1945, it has been my good fortune to meet and fish with many of the world's great and pioneering anglers and skippers, crews and fish scientists in many places and on more than a thousand boats. It is a privilege to collate, gather and pass on information on the sport

A *black marlin jumping close to the boat for angler John Johnston. Photo: Peter Goadby.*

of saltwater gamefishing as it approaches its hundredth birthday. There is an unprecedented moving together and acceptance of techniques right around the world as well as great recognition of the use and benefits of the various tackle categories and line classes. Many world records are now being routinely set, broken and rebroken in salt water on tackle designed and built for the generally acknowledged smaller, less powerful and less violent species found in fresh water. The International Game Fish Association (IGFA), the world rule and record keeping organization, now grants records of fresh as well as saltwater species on line classes as light as 2-lb (1-kg) class, with specific rules and records for fly fishing in fresh and salt water.

Saltwater fly fishing is a fast growing facet of saltwater fishing. Its master devotees not only fish with great skill, but through their writings and photographs have given anglers another sport with its own tradition, rules, ethics and techniques. Fly fishing, along with the quest for big fish on bait-casting and spin-fishing tackle, give fishermen every chance to fish for big fish with tackle similar or identical to that used in their home fishing.

Saltwater gamefishing is no longer predominantly boat fishing on troll, drift or anchor. Gamefish are fished with all types of tackle and in all environments (from shore and on headlands), as well as the long-established traditional offshore locations.

International Game Fish Association, Pacific Ocean Research Foundation, National Coalition for Marine Conservation and the Sport Fishing Institute in USA, as well as the gamefishing bodies of most nations, are concerned with conservation. These organizations and others such as the Hawaiian International Billfish Association and Club Nautico de San Juan in Puerto Rico work with scientists, with fish managers and government to ensure that the sport of saltwater gamefishing can continue to be enjoyed by our children and future generations.

There is growing awareness of the necessity of adhering to the fishing rules and ethics. The first rules drafted by the Tuna Club of Avalon, Santa Catalina, along with rules of the British Tunny Club, Gamefish Association of Australia and other long-established and ethical fishing organizations, formed the basis of the first rules published by the International Game Fish Association. These 1938 world rules have been modified to reflect the changes in fishing, in the species of fish sought, and tackle.

There has also been an amazing proliferation of saltwater fishing tournaments since Kip Farrington conceived and organized the world's first tournament, the International Tuna Cup Match at Nova Scotia, the world's fifth oldest international sporting competition. Ethical tournaments attract an increasing number of competitors and interest. For many, tournament fishing is an additional challenge, it is not just a matter of 'gone fishing'. Tactics involving the fish and the other competitors and teams, add to the interest and competition. There are, of course, many who do not like or react well to tournament pressure, as officials, skippers, crews or anglers, but tournaments and participation are here to stay. There is no doubt tournaments add to the benefits from fishing, particularly in simply meeting people and in increasing knowledge and learning.

This book is very much a team effort, like fishing and indeed living. It has been my good fortune to have received generous assistance from many people in bringing a dream to reality. The encouragement and confidence of the many people who have contributed information, photographs, drawings, time, skills and involvement in many ways is gratefully acknowledged. *Saltwater Gamefishing* would not have been possible without Sandra, whose long hours at the word processor keys and in just putting up with this fisherman are appreciated beyond words.

Thanks also go to Elwood K. Harry, Chairman and President of IGFA, who has not only been encouraging over the years, but who has given me access to IGFA photographic reference files, particularly the Michael Lerner and Joe Brooks collections. The advice and support of John O'Brien MBE and Claude (Gus) Fay, Trustees of the Australian Fishing Museum, and Peter Fithian, Chairman of the Hawaiian International Billfish Association and Pacific Ocean Research Foundation, are sincerely acknowledged. The natural bait fishing information has been improved by the co-operation and input of skilled riggers from the Atlantic and Pacific fisheries, particularly Florida's Split Tail Charley Hayden and Cairns's Billy Fairbairn.

Fisheries science is an important factor in modern fishing as well as management. The assistance of Australia's Dr Julian Pepperell and Hawaii's Dr David Grobecker, Dr Kim Holland and Dr Richard Brill is greatly appreciated.

No fishing book is complete without paintings, photographs and drawings of the great saltwater gamefish in action. In his *Profiles in Saltwater Angling* George Reiger mentioned van Campen Heilner's classic *Salt Water Fishing* and the involvement of US artist Bill Goadby Lawrence in it. He noted, 'In the fall of 1972, angling writer Peter (*Big Fish and Blue Water*) Goadby went to Nova Scotia to captain the Australian Tuna Team in the Wedgeport competition. On his way home, he stopped off to visit his "distant cousin", William Goadby Lawrence, who now lives in Edgecomb, Maine. The two hope to collaborate on a book at some future date.' This prediction has now come true, and William Goadby Lawrence's superb paintings adorn this book. The other paintings are from the pen and brush of ichthyologist, fisherman and artist Dr Guy Harvey of Jamaica, whose work is in great demand as art and whose classic action fish paintings, worn around the world on golf and T shirts, have revolutionized fishing clothing.

The drawings of Val Osborn, Mike Fox, Les Byrom and Anthony Burke clarify and enhance the words of the text.

Every fishing book needs photographs to illustrate the color and action normally seen only by a few. Photographs from above and below the surface by many of the world's outstanding fish and fishing photographers show fish action from Arctic waters, where giant bluefin are fished alongside icebergs, to the tropics, where the sun triggers the life cycle of many of the great gamefish species. Photographers who have helped beyond thanks include Darrell Jones, Gilbert Keech, Captain Paul Murray, Al Pfleuger, Biff Lampton, Bill Harrison, Charles Perry, Jacquie Acheson, James Watts, Charley Davis, Vic Dunaway, Graham Farmer, Sadu Frehm, Syd Kraul, Kim Holland, Mike Kenyon, Gayl Henze, Jim Witten, Bob Valente, Frank Moss, Peter Hoogs, John Jordan, Greg Finney, Tudor Collins, Lyndon Rea, G. Angus, Didier van der Veeken, Simon Cassetarri, Sandra Clarry, Andrew Taulerman, Vic McCristal, Tim Simpson, John Blumenthal, Greg Edwards, Andy Hurst, George Mayson, John McIntyre, Alex Julius, Shaun Wallace, Bob Bury, David Rogers, Campbell Bridges, Julian Pepperell, Scott Mitchell, Andy Hurst, Mark Deeney and others credited in the photographs in the book.

My thanks go also to the management of Walkers Cay and Captain Billy Black of *Duchess II*, and to the management of Hotel Palmilla, David Liles and the captains of the Palmilla Innovator boats, and Captain James Bass of *Blowout* for their help and co-operation.

Thanks go also to the many other top captains and crews who have made it easy for me to fish in many parts of the world.

Sincere thanks go to Kim Anderson, Publisher Non-fiction, Ruth Sheard, editor, and Leonie Bremer-Kamp, designer, at CollinsAngus&Robertson, whose skill and professionalism have helped bring *Saltwater Gamefishing* to life.

Saltwater Gamefishing brings back memories of not only some of the world's most prolific fishing locations, but of the generous co-operation of hotel managements, captains, crews, tournament organizers and anglers.

One of the moving and enduring benefits of game-fishing in salt water is that fishermen experience a bond that extends beyond friendship to family. It has been my privilege to fish with many of the world's best anglers and captains over a long period. My thanks go to Ted Naftzger of California, Claude (Gus) Fay of Sydney, Jack Anderson of Palm Beach, the late Sir William (Alf) Stevenson of Auckland, and Norman Gow and John Wilson of Brisbane for their friendship and understanding.

Every locality is different, yet fish and people make every fishing trip memorable and very special. The anticipation of other locations not yet visited, of other great fish not yet tried, provides incentive and interest for the future.

Fishing brings together people from all parts of the world. It is reassuring to watch people of different nations, creeds and languages, bonded by a common interest and involvement with the sport. This is one of the reasons why many of the hardest-working and greatest achievers of fishing administration are top fishermen.

For some, fishing is not just a sport, it is a way of life, integral in their lives. They spend much of their time in assisting others enjoy ethical sport and in helping conservation and management. They are proud to be bonded with the title 'fisherman'.

The question of the ingredients for success in salt-water gamefishing can be briefly summed up. A mix of preparation, concentration and perspiration, to which is added a little luck, will ensure success. Even though the necessary proportions may vary with the type of fish, the first three are most necessary. The experience factor can be offset to some degree by communication and coaching from skipper, crew or other experienced angler. One of these assisting is enough. Participation by all creates possible confusion.

Finally, *don't give up*. Fish every day and every hook-up to its ultimate conclusion. You never know what may happen until the time is up. It is not over 'Till the whistle blows for the end of the game'.

It is my hope this book helps spread information about saltwater gamefishing and helps in recognition of the beauty and power of fish and of nature itself.

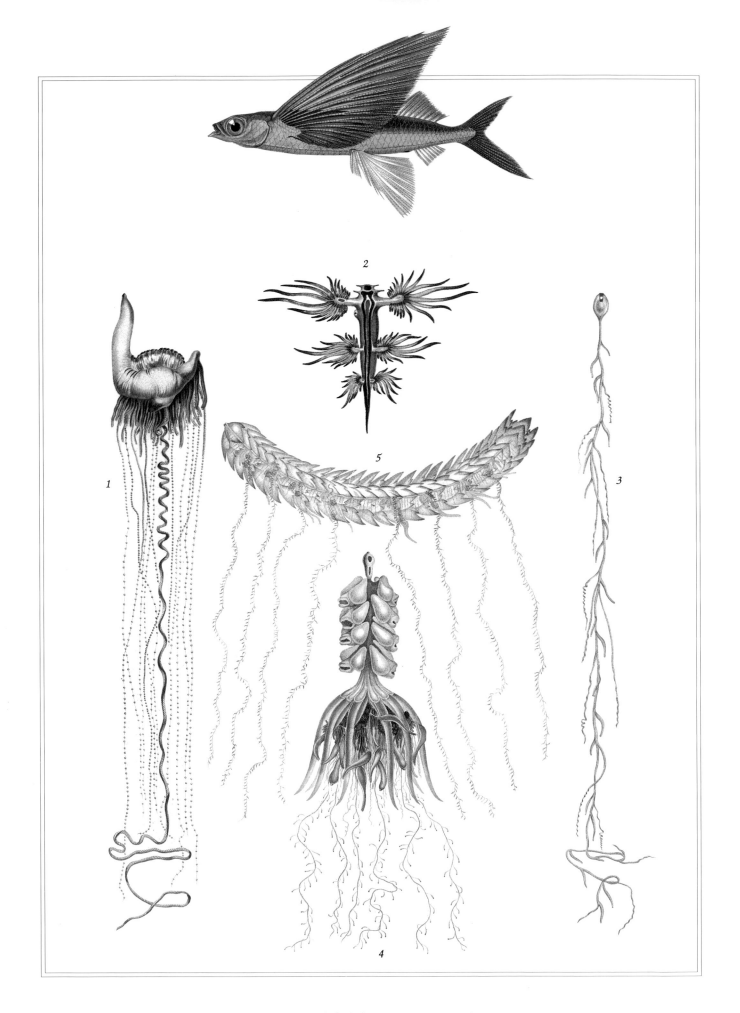

THE OCEAN CURRENTS

OCEAN CURRENTS

From the earliest times, navigators and traders knew the characteristics, direction and importance of the ocean currents. Today, satellites, with their specialised sensors and camera eyes, give unprecedented views of the currents, counter currents, drifts, eddies, temperatures and the current edges that are so important to the saltwater fisherman everywhere. Possessing an understanding of the currents and being able to identify them, makes the difference between success and failure in fishing offshore.

Currents are recognised by their colour: beautiful shades of transparent dark blue for the warm currents and solid dark green shades for the cooler to cold currents. The position of the currents over the sea bottom configuration, and the position of the current edges, the upwellings and meetings, tell fishermen where to spend time and effort.

The warm currents that are a magnet to sport fishermen are home to animals of beautiful colours and often weird configurations and unusual habits (some of which are illustrated on the opposite page). These include fish that live in drifting, stinging tentacles; and vivid blue fish that were believed to fly, but which are now known to glide on fragile transparent wings. Flying fish and other bait school fish are food for predators of various sizes, from billfish to mahi mahi (dolphin fish).

The ocean currents, particularly the warm rivers in the sea and their attendant inhabitants, offer yet another reason to go on in search of the edges, the weed lines and flotsam, around which the life in the currents congregate.

The map below shows the locations of the currents and counter currents of the world.

Opposite: Flying fish, A. C. V. D'Orbigny, Dictionnaire Universal D'Histoire Naturelle, Paris, 1841–1849; 1. Physalia; 2. Glaucus; 3. Rizophysa; 4. Physsophora; 5. Stephanomia—all from F. E. Peron and L. Freycinet, Voyage è Decouvetes aux Terres Australes, Paris, 1812.

The following key relates to the maps on pages 8-63.

⬅— Migration ░░░ Occurrence

⬛➤ Established recreational fishing areas

For the map below: ⬅— Warm currents

⬅— Cool currents

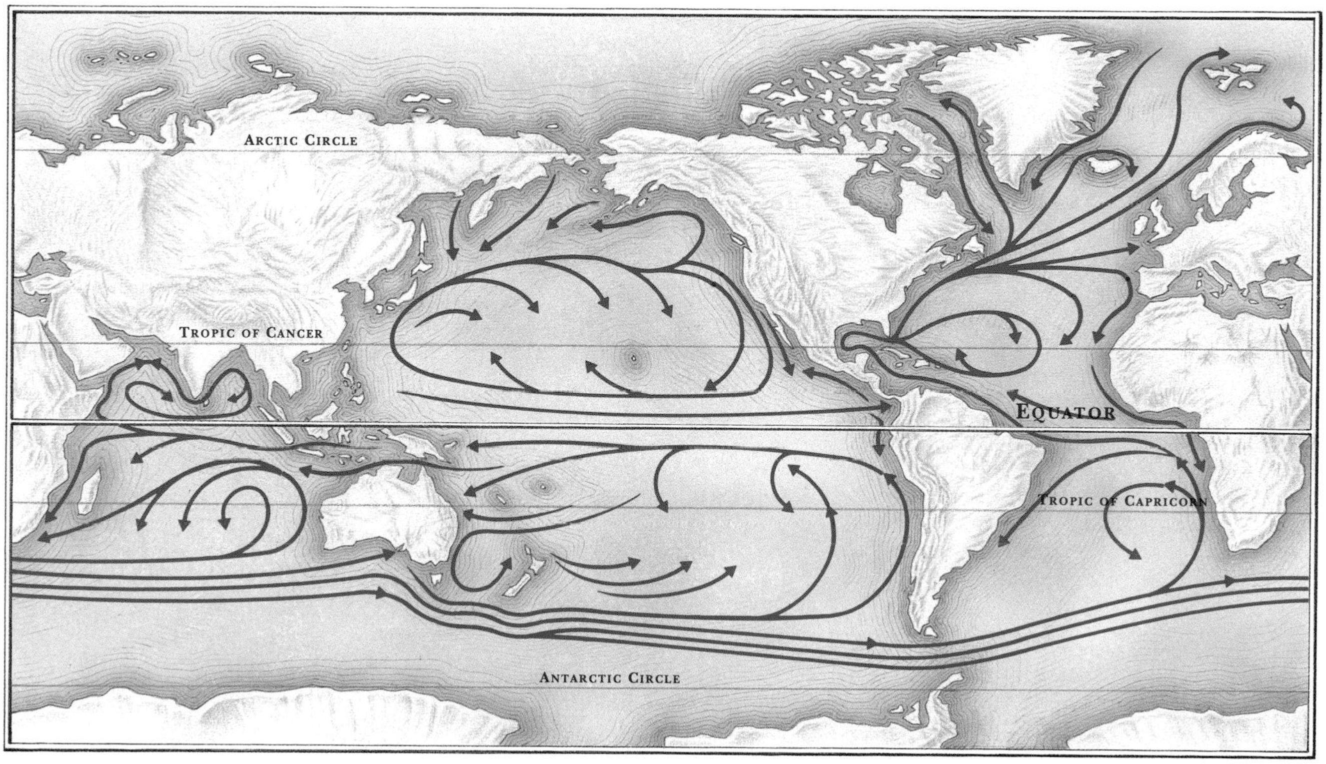

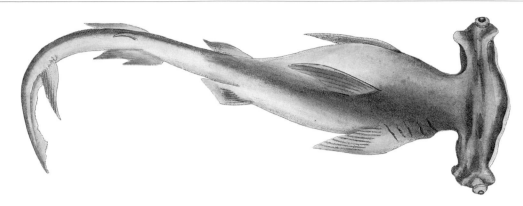

Hammerhead shark, G. Shaw and F. P. Nodder, THE NATURALIST'S MISCELLANY, *London, 1790–1813.*

Indo-Pacific sailfish, G. Shaw and F. P. Nodder, THE NATURALIST'S MISCELLANY, *London, 1790–1813.*

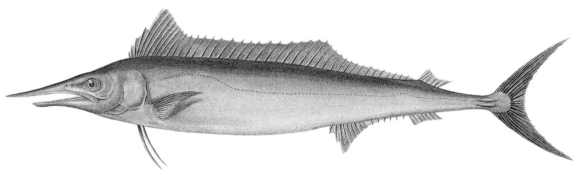

Shortbill spearfish, G. L. Cuvier, LE RÈGNE ANIMAL, *Disciples edition, Paris, 1836–1849.*

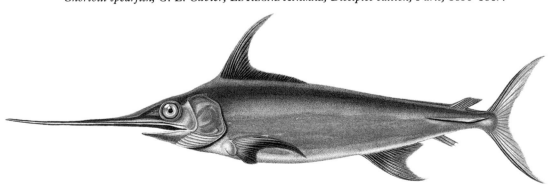

Broadbill swordfish, A. C. V. D'Orbigny, DICTIONNAIRE UNIVERSAL D'HISTOIRE NATURELLE, *Paris, 1841–1849.*

SECTION II

CLASSIFICATION AND IDENTIFICATION

BILLFISH

Broadbill swordfish
Atlantic blue marlin
Black marlin
Indo-Pacific blue marlin
Striped marlin
White marlin
Longbill and Mediterranean spearfish
Shortbill spearfish
Atlantic sailfish
Pacific sailfish

SHARKS

Blue shark
Hammerhead sharks
Mako sharks
Porbeagle sharks
Thresher sharks
Tiger shark
White shark
Requiem (whaler) sharks
Tope

THE FUN FISH

Chub mackerel
Wahoo
Mahi mahi (dolphin fish)
Cobia
Bluefish
Barramundi
Amberjack
Permit
Barracuda
Snook
Roosterfish
Bonefish
Queenfish
Tarpon
Garrick
Threadfin salmon
Salmon
Atlantic Caribbean jacks and trevallies
Indo-Pacific jacks and trevallies
Yellowtail

TUNA

Bluefin tuna
Longtail tuna
Blackfin tuna
Albacore
Skipjack tuna
Dog tooth tuna
Yellowfin tuna
Big eye tuna
Southern bluefin tuna
Bonitos
Little tuna—kawa kawa, little tunny, black skipjack

MACKEREL

Tanguigue

King mackerel

Atlantic and Caribbean spotted and Spanish mackerels

Indo-Pacific spotted and Spanish mackerels

Seerfish—Papuan, Chinese, Streaked, Korean

Scaley mackerel

BROADBILL SWORDFISH

XIPHIAS GLADIUS
LINNAEUS 1758

Other common names Swordfish, broadbill.

Identifying features Upper body dark blue, often with bronze coloration, lower body silvery white, colors merge to light brown. Maximum weight 680 kg (1500 lb). Long flat bill. High, rigid sickle dorsal, equal in height and similar in shape to upper caudal lobe. Straight lower jaw. No visible lateral line. Fixed sickle pectoral. Wide single body keel at junction of body and tail.

Expected temperature range 13°C–22°C (55°F–72°F).

Typical location Open water deeper than 110 m (60 fathoms) to 1850 m (1000 fathoms) or more, over canyons and submarine peaks and banks, cruising to reoxygenate along current lines.

Fishing methods In daylight, presenting trolled baits of squid, barracuda or chub mackerel, striped tuna or small tuna to broadbill cruising on surface with dorsal and tail clear of surface. Drifting at night with live or dead squid, spotted mackerel, small tuna, bonito or bottom fish species obtained from commercial trawlers. Eating quality is excellent.

Typical fighting characteristics Regarded as the king of fishes, broadbill are dogged deep and mid water fighters that occasionally jump in a spectacular fashion. At night they often run to the surface immediately after hook-up. Use of a light stick shows the position and depth of swordfish in night fighting. The soft mouth and body flesh and skin dictates that these fish be fought with maximum 10-kg (22-lb) brake. 24-kg (50-lb) and 37-kg (80-lb) tackle is balanced for most broadbill, with 60-kg (130-lb) for the superfish.

Major sportfishing areas Chile, Peru, Panama, Ecuador, Mexico, north-east coast USA, Florida, Venezuela, Portugal, New Zealand, Australia, South Africa, Hawaii.

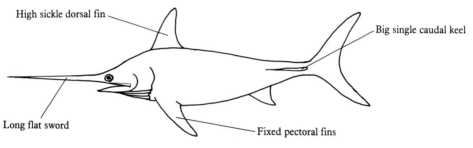

High sickle dorsal fin

Big single caudal keel

Long flat sword

Fixed pectoral fins

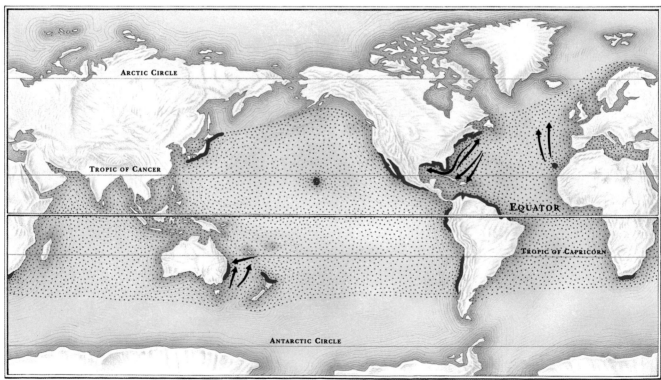

ARCTIC CIRCLE

TROPIC OF CANCER

TROPIC OF CANCER

EQUATOR

TROPIC OF CAPRICORN

ANTARCTIC CIRCLE

ATLANTIC BLUE MARLIN

MAKAIRA NIGRICANS

LACEPEDE 1802

Other common names Blue marlin.

Identifying features Back dark blue with light blue stripes of dots and bars, belly silvery white. In life, fins and tail electric blue. Maximum weight 900 kg (2000 lb). Start of second dorsal behind start of second anal fin. Pectoral fins fold flat. Lateral line generally does not show in adults. When scales or skin are removed the lateral line shows as multiple, up to four, chain loops. Bill medium long. Lower jaw turns down slightly at tip. Dorsal fin and anal fin pointed and medium height.

Expected temperature range 21°C–30°C (70°F–86°F).

Typical location Open ocean along continental shelf drop-off over deeper canyons along 110-m (60-fathom) reefs and submarine mountains and peaks and ledges, along current lines, around bait schools of tuna, mahi mahi (dolphin fish), squid, around logs, weed lines.

Fishing methods Trolling lures of hard and soft plastic, trolling dead baits, tuna, mullet, Spanish mackerel, squid, trolling live baits, drifting with live or dead baits. Eating quality good.

Typical fighting characteristics Whether in the Caribbean, the Atlantic or the Indo-Pacific, blue marlin are the heavyweights, very fast tough fighters and spectacular jumpers that tend to fish deeper than black or striped marlin.

Major sportfishing areas Puerto Rico, Walker's Cay, Bimini, Virgin Islands, Jamaica, Bermuda and other east Atlantic and Caribbean Islands, Costa Rica, North and South Carolina, Florida, Gulf of Mexico, Mexico, Venezuela, Brazil, Azores, Canary Islands, Cape Verde Islands, Ivory Coast of Africa.

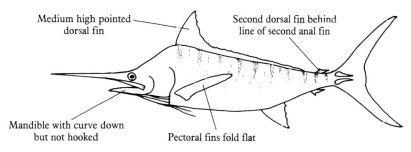

Medium high pointed dorsal fin

Second dorsal fin behind line of second anal fin

Mandible with curve down but not hooked

Pectoral fins fold flat

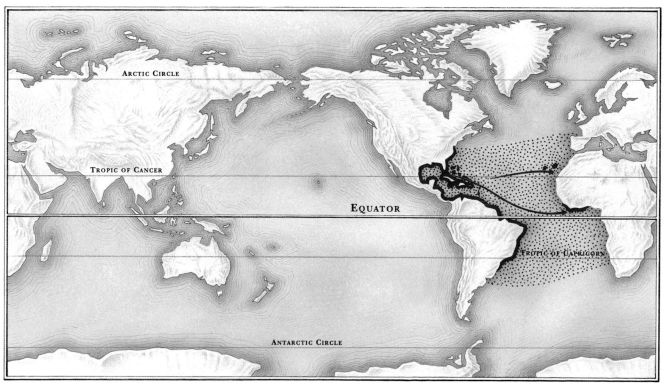

ARCTIC CIRCLE

TROPIC OF CANCER

EQUATOR

TROPIC OF CAPRICORN

ANTARCTIC CIRCLE

BLACK MARLIN

MAKAIRA INDICA

CUVIER 1832

Other common names White marlin (in Japan, possibly from color of flesh), giant black marlin, silver marlin.

Identifying features Temperate waters: Back and fins dark slatey blue or black, belly silvery white. Tropical waters: Back dark blue, sometimes with light blue stripes that fade after death, belly silver, dorsal fin lavender, other fins and tails electric blue, sometimes spots on dorsal. Maximum weight 863 kg (1900 lb). Start of second dorsal forward of start of second anal fin. Fixed pectoral fins in marlin in excess of 50 kg (110 lb). In black marlin less than 50 kg (110 lb) the pectorals can often be moved despite *rigor mortis*, but will not fold flat against body. Short lower jaw curved down. Short heavy round bill.

Expected temperature range 21°C–30°C (70°F–86°F).

Typical location Along current lines. Open ocean around schools of bait species and small tuna, along reefs, along continental shelf dropoff 182 m (100 fathoms) and submarine peaks, along shore where warm currents are running, around logs. A few 'local' fish on reefs, even in cooler waters off-season. Juveniles move in schools of similar age and class along coast and islands.

Fishing methods Adults: Trolling tuna, Spanish mackerel, mullet. Trolling lures of hard and soft plastic. Drifting or anchor live and dead bait. Juveniles: Trolling mullet, ballyhoo (garfish), chub mackerel, strips often in combination with plastic squid, feather jigs. Trolling live baits, skipjack and other small tuna, kawa kawa, trevally. Fly fishing after teasing occasionally from rocky headland with live bait. Trolling small lures, spoons, konaheads, knuckleheads, big and bibless minnows, plastic squid.

Typical fighting characteristics A dogged deep fighter and aerial performer that usually mixes jumping, fast runs with deep fighting characteristics. Will jump at any time during fight, and right alongside boat when leader is in hand.

Major sportfishing areas East and west coast of Australia, Panama, Peru, Costa Rica, Mexico, Ecuador, Tahiti, Papua New Guinea, Pacific islands, southern Asia, New Zealand, Fiji, Mauritius, Mozambique, East Africa.

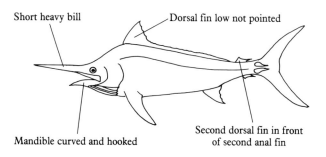

Short heavy bill — Dorsal fin low not pointed

Mandible curved and hooked — Second dorsal fin in front of second anal fin

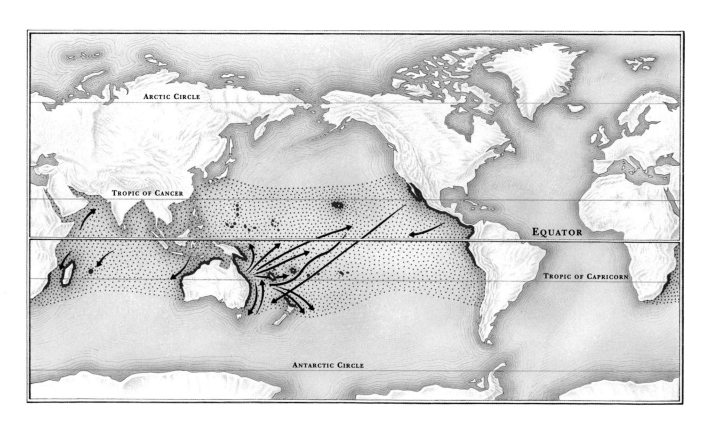

ARCTIC CIRCLE

TROPIC OF CANCER

EQUATOR

TROPIC OF CAPRICORN

ANTARCTIC CIRCLE

INDO-PACIFIC BLUE MARLIN

MAKAIRA MAZARA

JORDAAN & SNYDER 1901

Other common names Pacific blue marlin, blue marlin.

Identifying features Back dark blue with light blue stripes of dots and bars, belly silvery white. In life fins and tail are electric blue. Maximum weight 1181 kg (2600 lb). Start of second dorsal behind start of second anal. Pectoral fins fold flat. Lateral line generally does not show in adults, but with scales or skin removed is single line of chain. Bill medium and long. Lower jaw turns down slightly at tip. Dorsal fin and anal fin pointed and medium height.

Expected temperature range 21°C–30°C (70°F–86°F).

Typical location Open ocean along continental shelf drop-off. Over deeper canyons along current lines. Along 110-m (60-fathom) reefs, submarine mountains and peaks and ledges, weed line, around bait schools of tuna, mahi mahi (dolphin fish), squid, and around logs.

Fishing methods Trolling lures of hard and soft plastic, trolling dead baits of tuna, mullet, Spanish mackerel, trolling live baits, drifting and at anchor with live and dead baits.

Typical fighting characteristics At all weights a very tough fighter and spectacular jumper that tends to fight deeper than black or striped marlin. Will spin and reverse direction when jumping and greyhounding, a tactic that often causes cut or broken lines. The first run will sometimes spool the reel.

Major sportfishing areas Hawaii, Tahiti, Fiji, Guam, other Pacific islands, Mexico, Panama, Ecuador, Costa Rica, east and west coast of Australia, New Zealand, Papua New Guinea, Mauritius, southern Asia, East Africa, Mozambique.

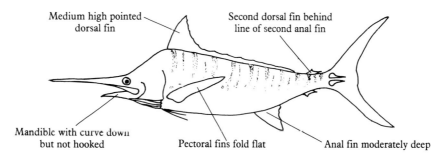

Medium high pointed dorsal fin

Second dorsal fin behind line of second anal fin

Mandible with curve down but not hooked

Pectoral fins fold flat

Anal fin moderately deep

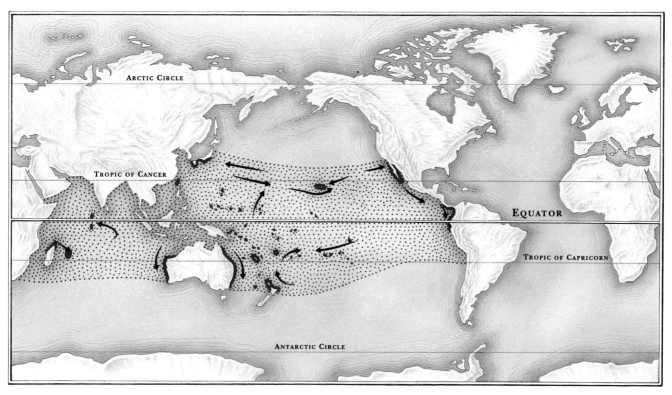

ARCTIC CIRCLE

TROPIC OF CANCER

EQUATOR

TROPIC OF CAPRICORN

ANTARCTIC CIRCLE

STRIPED MARLIN

Tetrapturus audax

PHILLIPI 1887

Other common names Striper, stripey.

Identifying features Upper body dark with powder blue, cobalt or lavender stripes, lower body silvery white. Maximum weight 250 kg (550 lb). High dorsal fin in which three high rays are of almost equal height. Single prominent lateral line. Pectoral fins fold in against body. Start of second dorsal behind start of second anal fin. Tail veed, cuts away at tip of each lobe of tail. Anal fin high. Bill long and slender. Lower jaw straight.

Expected temperature range 20°C–26°C (68°F–79°F).

Typical location Around bait schools, chub mackerel, sardines, pilchards, anchovies, small tuna, squid.

Fishing methods Trolling dead baits, chub mackerel, kahawai, yellowtail, squid. Trolling strip baits sometimes with plastic squid in combination. Trolling live bait, chub mackerel, small tuna, kahawai. Trolling lures, hard and soft plastic lures, minnows, plastic fish or squid replicas. Casting live bait, chub mackerel, yellowtail scad, sardines, anchovies. Drifting with live bait, kahawai, small tuna, yellowtail, chub mackerel. Eating quality good. Excellent for sashimi.

Typical fighting characteristics Exciting jumper, a greyhounding and tailwalking fighter that gives long runs and sounds deep. The marlin that is a challenge on tackle of all weights up to 37 kg (80 lb). In many areas is an ideal opponent on 13.6-kg (30-lb) tackle.

Major sportfishing areas California, Mexico, Panama, Costa Rica, Ecuador, Chile, New Zealand, east and west coast of Australia, east Africa, Kenya, Japan, Okinawa, Hawaii and other Pacific islands, Indian Ocean islands, Western Arabian sea.

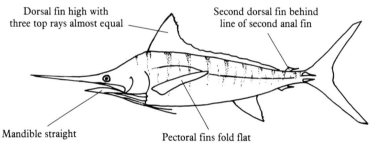

Dorsal fin high with three top rays almost equal

Second dorsal fin behind line of second anal fin

Mandible straight

Pectoral fins fold flat

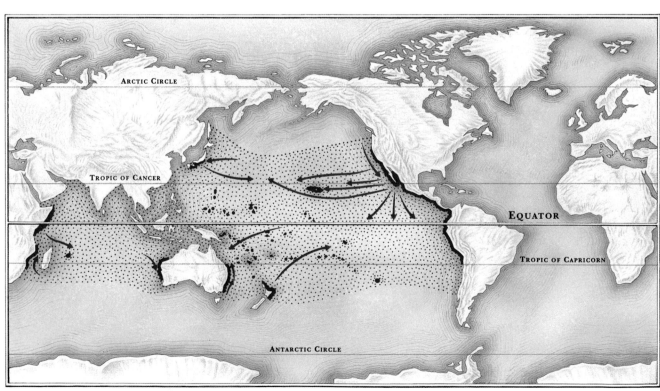

ARCTIC CIRCLE

TROPIC OF CANCER

EQUATOR

TROPIC OF CAPRICORN

ANTARCTIC CIRCLE

WHITE MARLIN

TETRAPTURUS ALBIDUS

POEY 1860

Other common names Atlantic white marlin.

Identifying features Back dark blue, belly silvery white, light stripes along body, dorsal fin dark blue with spots. Maximum weight 90 kg (200 lb). Dorsal, anal and pectoral fins rounded at tips. Single lateral line. Dorsal fin high and rounded. Slender bill. Slender straight lower jaw. Second dorsal starts forward of start of second anal fin. Pelvic fins long.

Expected temperature range 20°C–29°C (68°F–84°F).

Typical location Open water around bait schools (ballyhoo, mullet squid, flying fish). Over deep reefs, canyons, dropoffs and holes in the sea bed. Along current lines and weed lines.

Fishing methods Trolling dead bait (ballyhoo, mullet, squid, chub mackerel, eel). Often rigged with plastic squid or feather jigs. Trolling with small hard and soft plastic lures. Trolling with live bait, ballyhoo, chub mackerel. Spin casting live bait. Eating quality good.

Typical fighting characteristics This aggressive ocean acrobat is a most spectacular jumper, with all the surface tricks punctuated with long runs and sounding to depths. Ideal for light tackle up to 15 kg (30 lb).

Major sportfishing areas Bahamas, Walker's Cay, Cat Cay, Bimini, Chub Key, Puerto Rico, St Thomas, Gulf of Mexico, Florida, east coast of USA north to Hudson Canyon, Bermuda, Mexico, Costa Rica, Venezuela, Brazil, Cuba.

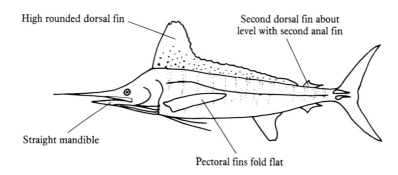

High rounded dorsal fin

Second dorsal fin about level with second anal fin

Straight mandible

Pectoral fins fold flat

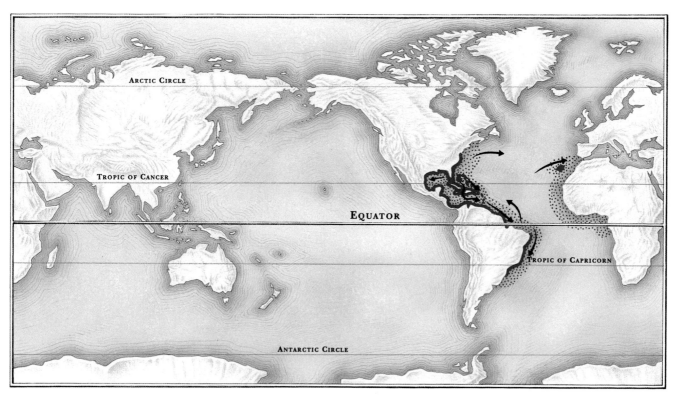

SPEARFISH

LONGBILL
TETRAPTURUS PFLEUGERI
ROBINS & de SYLVA 1963

MEDITERRANEAN
T. BELONE
RAFINESQUE 1810

Other common names Long-nosed spearfish, Atlantic spearfish.

Identifying features *Longbill spearfish:* Bill longer than head length, lower jaw straight and slender, long pelvic fin. Long wide rounded pectoral fins, prominent single lateral line, dorsal fin high and wide and if not, curved as it tapers to body. Distance between anus and anal fin nearly equal to depth of anal fin. Tail veed. *Mediterranean spearfish:* Bill shorter than head length, lower jaw straight and slender. Prominent single lateral line, short tapered pectoral fins, long pelvic fins. High dorsal rounded at front, dorsal curved as it tapers to body. Distance between anus and anal fin nearly equal to depth of anal fin. Tail veed. Maximum weight both species 40 kg (90 lb).

Expected temperature range 21°C–30°C (70°F–86°F).

Typical location Open ocean along current lines, over dropoffs and ledges, around flotsam and logs.

Fishing methods Trolling hard or soft plastic lures, trolling small baits, ballyhoo (mullet), squid sometimes in combination with small plastic squid or feather jigs. Usually taken by accident when trolling for other billfish, tuna or current-dwelling species. Eating quality excellent.

Typical fighting characteristics Billfish lightweights with splashing jumps·and long surface runs if tackle allows. Ideal on light tackle, unable to show their real fighting ability on heavier tackle on which they are usually taken.

Major sportfishing areas *Longbill spearfish:* Bahamas, Venezuela, Portugal, Azores, Florida. *Mediterranean spearfish:* Open Mediterranean. Not common anywhere.

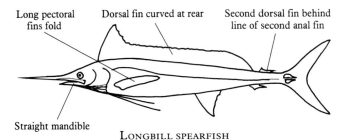

Long pectoral fins fold — Dorsal fin curved at rear — Second dorsal fin behind line of second anal fin

Straight mandible

LONGBILL SPEARFISH

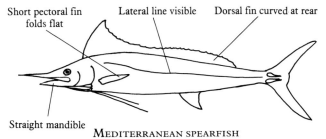

Short pectoral fin folds flat — Lateral line visible — Dorsal fin curved at rear

Straight mandible

MEDITERRANEAN SPEARFISH

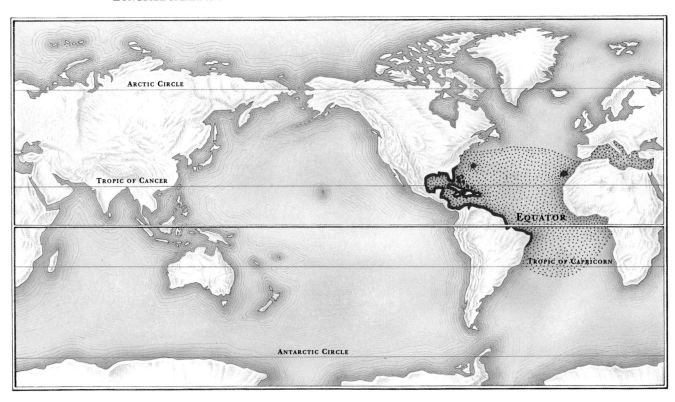

SHORTBILL SPEARFISH

Tetrapturus angustirostris

TANAKA 1915

Other common names Short-nose spearfish, Pacific spearfish.

Identifying features Back dark blue, belly silvery. Life colors bright electric blue and silver, rarely show stripes. Maximum size up to 45 kg (100 lb). Very short bill, almost equal to length of lower jaw. Prominent single lateral line. Straight slender lower jaw. Pectoral fins narrow and short. Long pelvic fins. Dorsal fin high in front, curves before joining body. Distance between anus and anal fin nearly equal to height of anal fin. Anal fin pointed.

Expected temperature range 21°C–30°C (70°F–86°F).

Typical location Open ocean along current lines, over dropoffs and ledges, around logs and flotsam.

Fishing methods Trolling hard or soft plastic lures. Trolling small baits—ballyhoo (garfish), mullet. Trolling strips sometimes squid, chub mackerel in combination with mostly squid and scad. Usually taken accidentally when trolling for other billfish, tuna or current-dwelling species. Eating quality excellent.

Typical fighting characteristics Has characteristics of billfish and mackerels (splashing jumps and surface runs). Ideal on light tackle, unable to show their real fighting ability on the heavier tackle on which they are usually taken.

Major sportfishing areas Hawaii (believed to be a spawning area). Sporadically in the Indian and Pacific Oceans' sportfishing areas. Apart from Hawaii not commonly encountered.

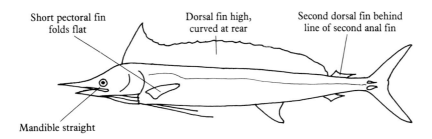

Short pectoral fin folds flat

Dorsal fin high, curved at rear

Second dorsal fin behind line of second anal fin

Mandible straight

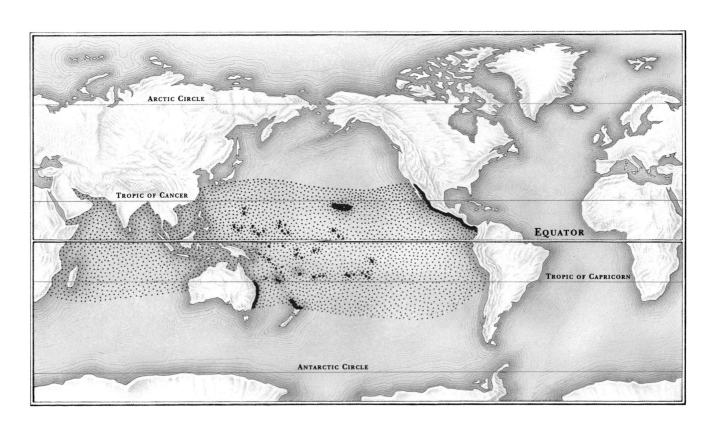

ARCTIC CIRCLE

TROPIC OF CANCER

EQUATOR

TROPIC OF CAPRICORN

ANTARCTIC CIRCLE

ATLANTIC SAILFISH

ISTIOPHORUS ALBICANS

LATREILLE 1804

Other common names Sailfish.

Identifying features Upper body and sail dorsal spotted with dark and light blue spots, lower body silvery white, body spots in vertical rows, bright colors in life. Maximum weight 60 kg (130 lb). Very high dorsal fin highest in centre, tail veed. Very long pelvic fins with membrane. Prominent single lateral line. Slender straight lower jaw. Long slender bill.

Expected temperature range 21°C–30°C (70°F–86°F).

Typical location Open water around bait schools of small bait fish—ballyhoo (garfish), mullet, small sea toads, squid, flying fish. Along reefs where warm currents are close inshore. Over deep reefs and canyons.

Fishing methods Trolling with dead bait, ballyhoo (garfish), mullet, goggle eye, chub mackerel, often rigged in combination with plastic squid or feather jigs. Fly casting after teasing. Trolling strip bait. Trolling or drifting with live baits—ballyhoo (garfish), mullet, goggle eye, chub mackerel, blue runner. Trolling small lures. Spin casting live bait. Occasionally from rocky headlands with drifting live bait. Kite fishing live baits. Deep trolling baits or lures. Eating quality poor. Improved by smoking.

Typical fighting characteristics A spectacular jumping jack whose aerial performances and fast surface runs have established its reputation as a top sport fish, particularly on light tackle up to 10 kg (20 lb). Really big sailfish, those in excess of 70 kg (150 lb) warrant the use of 15-kg (30-lb) and 24-kg (50-lb) tests.

Major sportfishing areas Florida, Mexico, Venezuela, Brazil, Senegal, Angola, Gulf of Mexico. Most records are held in Senegal and Angola.

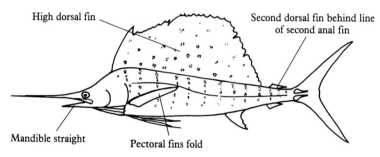

High dorsal fin

Second dorsal fin behind line of second anal fin

Mandible straight

Pectoral fins fold

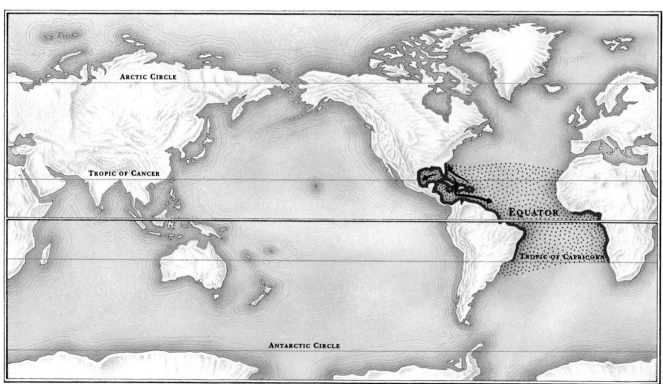

ARCTIC CIRCLE

TROPIC OF CANCER

EQUATOR

TROPIC OF CAPRICORN

ANTARCTIC CIRCLE

PACIFIC SAILFISH

ISTIOPHORUS PLATYPTERUS

SHAW & NODDER 1792

Other common names Indo-Pacific sailfish, sailfish.

Identifying features Body and sail dorsal spotted with dark and light blue spots, body spots in vertical rows, bright colors in life, brighter than those of the Atlantic species. Maximum weight 120 kg (260 lb). Very high dorsal fin, highest in centre, tail veed, very long pelvic fins with membrane, prominent single lateral line, slender straight lower jaw, long slender bill.

Expected temperature range 21°C–30°C (70°F–86°F).

Typical location Open water around bait schools of small bait fish, ballyhoo (garfish), mullet, small sea toads, squid, flying fish. Reefs where warm currents are close inshore.

Fishing methods Trolling with dead baits, ballyhoo (garfish), mullet, goggle eye (yellowtail scad), chub mackerel, often rigged in combination with plastic squid or feather lures. Trolling strip baits. Trolling or drifting live baits, ballyhoo (garfish), mullet, yellowtail scad, chub mackerel. Trolling small lures. Fly casting after teasing. Occasionally from rocky headlands with drifting live baits. Spincasting live bait. Kite fishing live bait. Deep trolling baits or lures.

Typical fighting characteristics Spectacular jumper whose aerial performance and fast surface runs have established its reputation as a top sport fish, particularly on light tackle. Sailfish over 45 kg (100 lb) are tough fighters.

Major sportfishing areas Galapagos Islands, Ecuador, Costa Rica, Mexico, Panama, Fiji, Tahiti, Philippines, all Pacific and Indian Ocean islands, north-east and west coast tropical Australia, Southern Asia, East African coast, Kenya. Most records are held in Mexico, Panama, Ecuador, Australia and Fiji.

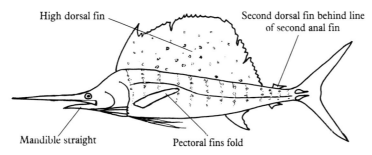

High dorsal fin

Second dorsal fin behind line of second anal fin

Mandible straight

Pectoral fins fold

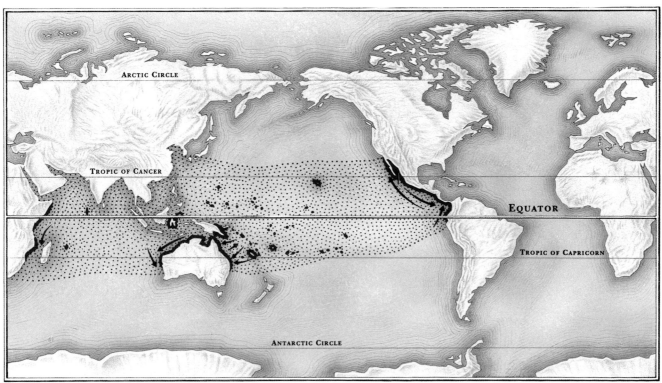

ARCTIC CIRCLE

TROPIC OF CANCER

EQUATOR

TROPIC OF CAPRICORN

ANTARCTIC CIRCLE

B L U E F I N   T U N A

THUNNUS THYNNUS
LINNAEUS 1758

Other common names Northern bluefin tuna, giant bluefin.

Identifying features Upper body blue-black, lower body silvery white, finlets dark yellow edged in black, caudal keel black. Maximum weight 820 kg (1800 lb). Short second dorsal and anal fins, very short pectoral fins less than 80 per cent of head length.

Expected temperature range 10°C-28°C (50°F-82°F).

Typical location In cold water, around herring and mackerel schools, along current and temperature lines. In warm water, over Bahamas Bank, particularly when wind and current are opposed.

Fishing methods Cold water: Trolling natural baits, daisy-chain, swimming bait, skip bait, herring, chub mackerel.

Drifting or at anchor, herring, mackerel, whiting with bunker and other small fish, chum and chunked mackerel. Warm water: Spotting school and presenting bait of mackerel, mullet or squid. Eating quality excellent, for top-grade sashimi.

Typical fighting characteristics Fast surface runs followed by deep diving, circling. In cold water, fight anti-clockwise. In warm water (Bahamas) boat must be maneuvered to keep tuna in shallow water away from deep water or dropoff, otherwise sharks could mutilate the hooked tuna.

Major sportfishing areas Nova Scotia, Prince Edward Island, Newfoundland, Canary Islands, Cat Cay, Bimini, Bahamas, Mediterranean, California, occasionally Australia and New Zealand.

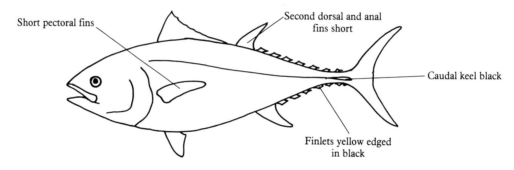

Short pectoral fins

Second dorsal and anal fins short

Caudal keel black

Finlets yellow edged in black

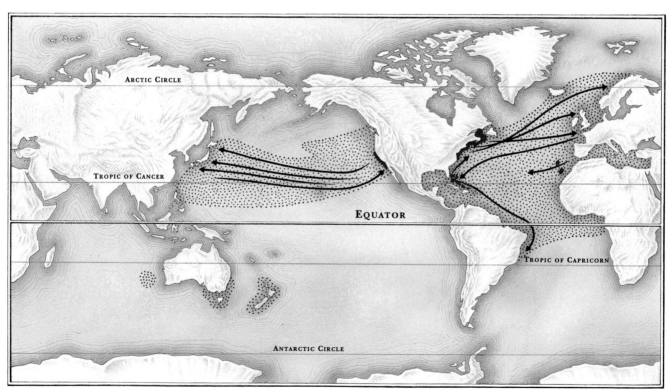

ARCTIC CIRCLE

TROPIC OF CANCER

EQUATOR

TROPIC OF CAPRICORN

ANTARCTIC CIRCLE

LONGTAIL TUNA

Thunnus tonggol

BLEEKER 1851

Other common names Northern bluefin (Australia).

Identifying features Upper body black and dark blue, lower body silvery white, caudal keel dark, finlets yellow with grey edges. Maximum weight 40 kg (90 lb). Pectoral fins short, shorter than length of head. Second dorsal and anal fin short. Tail with long upper and lower lobes.

Expected temperature range 20°C–30°C (66°F–86°F).

Typical location A shallow water inshore species, close within 16 km (10 miles) of shoreline, bays and estuaries. Around bait schools of small fish, occasionally taken offshore in deep water along current lines and over reefs.

Fishing methods Natural baits and strip baits, sometimes with plastic squid or feather jigs. Trolling small lures, feathers, squid and minnows. Drifting when trawlers are clearing trash fish. Casting live or dead bait. Casting small metal lures, minnows and poppers. Fly casting in chum.

Typical fighting characteristics Tough deep dogged fighter that never gives up. Appears faster than other tunas, particularly as it is usually hooked in shallow water.

Major sportfishing areas Northern Australia, Papua New Guinea through to Asia and Arabian Sea.

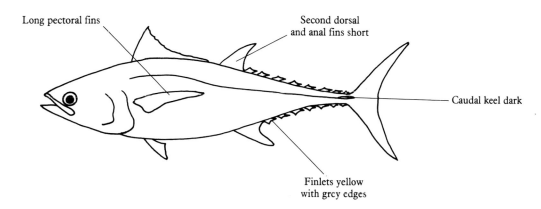

Long pectoral fins

Second dorsal and anal fins short

Caudal keel dark

Finlets yellow with grey edges

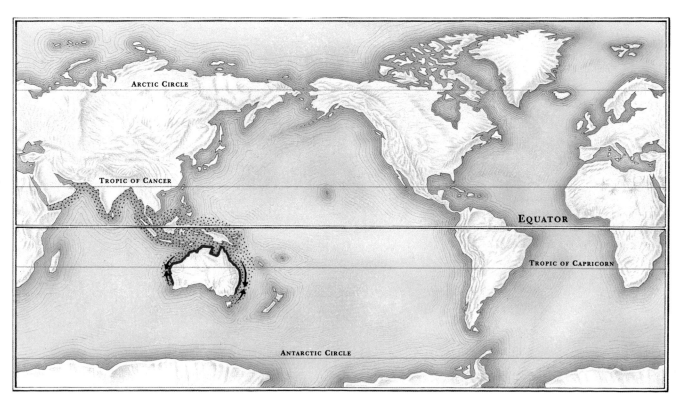

ARCTIC CIRCLE

TROPIC OF CANCER

EQUATOR

TROPIC OF CAPRICORN

ANTARCTIC CIRCLE

BLACKFIN TUNA

THUNNUS ATLANTICUS

LESSON 1830

Other common names Blackfin albacore.

Identifying features Upper body dark blue, lower body silvery white, finlets dark with yellowish tinge, second dorsal and anal fin dark. Maximum weight 24 kg (50 lb). Pectoral fins equal to line of start of second dorsal.

Expected temperature range 20°C–30°C (68°F–86°F).

Typical location Open ocean along current lines over reefs and banks.

Fishing methods Trolling lures, feathers, squid. Trolling small natural bait, ballyhoo, mullet, squid strips, often in conjunction with plastic squid or feather lure, small minnows. Casting small lures. Drifting or anchor with chum and small bait (chunks or cubes of chum add to success as does floating chum). Fly casting with chum. Eating quality is good.

Typical fighting characteristics Tough fast deep fighting tuna. Light tackle up to 10 kg (20 lb) class.

Major sportfishing areas USA coast, Carolinas, Gulf of Mexico, Florida, Bermuda, Cuba, Bahamas, Virgin Islands, Venezuela, Brazil.

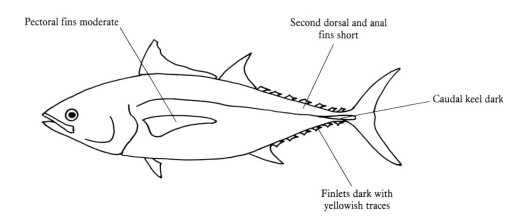

Pectoral fins moderate

Second dorsal and anal fins short

Caudal keel dark

Finlets dark with yellowish traces

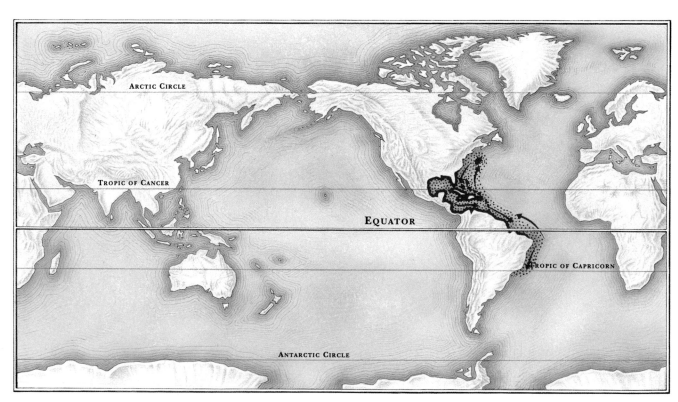

ARCTIC CIRCLE

TROPIC OF CANCER

EQUATOR

TROPIC OF CAPRICORN

ANTARCTIC CIRCLE

ALBACORE

THUNNUS ALALUNGA

BONNATERRE 1788

Other common names Longfin tunny, longfin tuna, albacora.

Identifying features Upper body black (live fish have a light blue iridescent stripe running along the body), lower body silvery white without spots or striations, white strip at rear of tail, finlets dark. Maximum size 45 kg (100 lb). Pectoral fins that extend past second dorsal and position of anal fin. Pectoral fins may not reach anal fins in juveniles. Flesh white.

Expected temperature range 12°C–25°C (59°F–77°F).

Typical location In excess of 110 m (60 fathoms). Open ocean along continental dropoff and outside dropoff over submarine banks, open water along temperature changes. Often found well offshore in trans-ocean migrations.

Fishing methods Trolling with lures, hexheads, feather lures, nylon jigs, Christmas trees, small minnows. Trolling small natural baits. Drifting or slow troll with live chum, anchovies or sardines may be used as bait. Lures cast with live and dead bait. Fly fishing with chum. Eating quality excellent.

Typical fighting characteristics Fast surface runs and deep dives typical of tuna, plus the chance of multiple hook-ups and stand-up fights make albacore interesting and challenging. Line class up to 10 kg (20 lb) is generally used. Many albacore are taken on lures trolled on heavier tackle for other species in the blue water.

Major sportfishing areas California, Oregon, north-east coast USA, Bermuda, South Africa, Japan, Italy, Canary Islands, Australia, New Zealand, Hawaii, Japan, Chile.

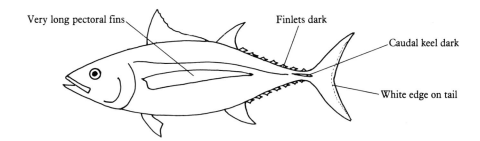

Very long pectoral fins — Finlets dark — Caudal keel dark — White edge on tail

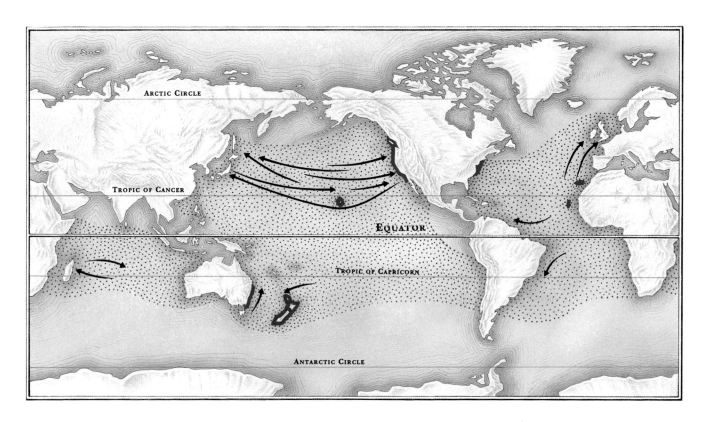

ARCTIC CIRCLE

TROPIC OF CANCER

EQUATOR

TROPIC OF CAPRICORN

ANTARCTIC CIRCLE

SKIPJACK TUNA

KATSUWONUS PELAMIS

LINNAEUS 1758

Other common names Striped tuna, oceanic bonito, bonito.

Identifying features Upper body dark purplish blue on back sometimes with vertical lavender blotches, lower body silver with the four to six conspicuous dark long bands. Maximum weight 35 kg (80 lb). Barred body, four to six wavy stripes on lower body below lateral line.

Expected temperature range 15°C–30°C (59°F–86°F).

Typical location Most often found in open ocean over ledges, dropoff along canyons and along variations in surface temperature. Over upwellings, around bait schools of small fish, pilchards, sardines, squid. Around flotsam often with other tuna.

Fishing methods Trolling small lures, feathers, plastic squid, nylon jigs, small spoons, small knuckleheads, small minnows. Trolling small dead baits. Casting shiny metal lures. Fly casting with chum. Eating quality excellent for sashimi.

Typical fighting characteristics A fast deep plugging fighter that never gives up. Pound for pound one of the hardest fighters in the sea. An excellent light tackle opponent on lines up to 9 kg (20 lb). The occasional giants of this species give a tough fight on 13.6 kg (30 lb) tackle. Hooks can be ripped through mouth if too much pressure is applied.

Major sportfishing areas In all tropical and temperate waters of open ocean.

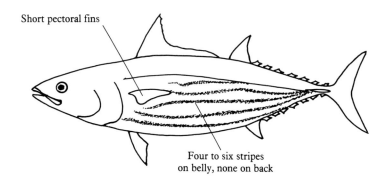

Short pectoral fins

Four to six stripes on belly, none on back

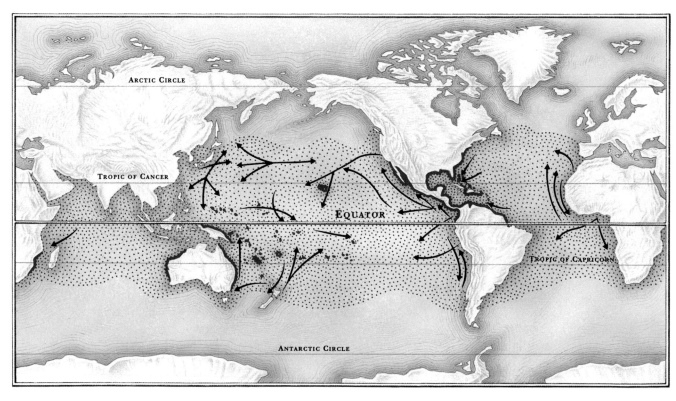

DOG TOOTH TUNA

GYMNOSARDA UNICOLOR

RUPPELL 1838

Other common names Scaleless tuna, peg tooth tuna.

Identifying features Upper body purplish blue–black, lower body silver. Maximum size 135 kg (300 lb). Big, round teeth. Body without scales. Prominent lateral line. Large eye.

Expected temperature range 25°C–30°C (77°F–86°F).

Typical location In reef openings, passes and reef edge dropoffs, over ridges and sea bed outside reefs in open ocean.

Fishing methods Trolling baits, kawa kawa, oceanic bonito, mackerel, scad, mullet, ballyhoo (garfish). Trolling lures, hard and soft head plastic, spoons and big minnows. Eating quality excellent.

Typical fighting characteristics A tough deep fighter that dives for reef and obstructions, swims with a jerky tail beat. Often hooked on heavy tackle rigged for big marlin. A superb medium tackle opponent.

Major sportfishing areas Tahiti, East Africa, Madagascar, Mozambique, Fiji, Philippines, tropical Australia, Okinawa.

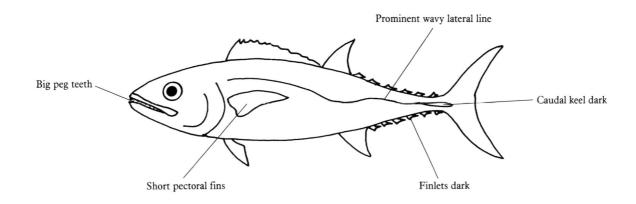

Prominent wavy lateral line

Big peg teeth

Caudal keel dark

Short pectoral fins

Finlets dark

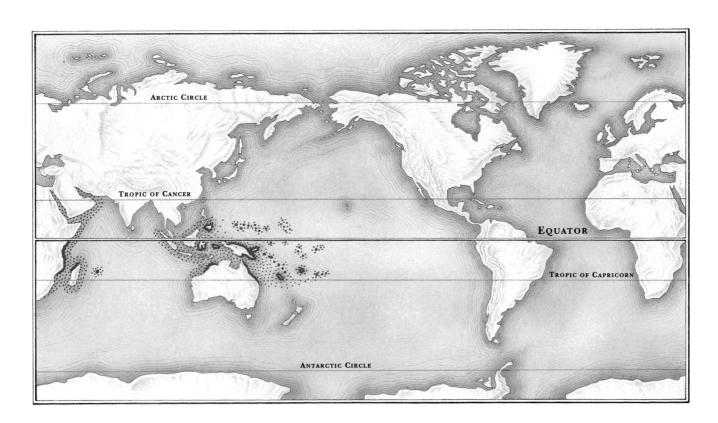

ARCTIC CIRCLE

TROPIC OF CANCER

EQUATOR

TROPIC OF CAPRICORN

ANTARCTIC CIRCLE

YELLOWFIN TUNA

THUNNUS ALBACARES
BONNATERRE 1788

Other common names Ahi, yellowfin.

Identifying features Upper body black with greenish blue overtones, yellow stripe along body, tail keel dark, finlets yellow with black edge, striations on belly. Maximum weight 175 kg (400 lb). In adult fish second dorsal and anal fin are elongated. Pectoral fin long—reaches back to line of start of second dorsal.

Expected temperature range 18°C–30°C (64°F–86°F).

Typical location Open ocean along temperature changes, upwelling over peaks and submarine ridges.

Fishing methods Trolling lures, hard and soft head plastic, minnows, feather lures. Trolling natural and strip baits, may be rigged with plastic skirts or squid. Drifting or at anchor. Live baits with chum, strip baits with chum, casting live bait with chum, casting lures with chum.

Trolling live bait. In some areas trolling in front of dolphin schools. Fly fishing with chum. Occasionally from shore with live bait. Eating quality excellent for sashimi.

Typical fighting characteristics One of the world's finest opponents. A fast determined deep fighter. The biggest yellow fin (135 kg; 300 lb plus) are caught at night by long-range boats anchored near the islands wide offshore from Mexico. The lights attract other bait species and the yellowfin to give the angler a chance at a giant yellowfin, which are often taken quickly in contrast to the daytime hook-ups. Circles anti-clockwise.

Major sportfishing areas Mexico offshore islands, Mexico, Costa Rica, Ecuador, Venezuela, Bermuda, Bahamas, Azores, Canary Islands, Hawaii, Tahiti, Fiji and all Pacific islands, New Zealand, Australia, South Africa, Mauritius, Kenya.

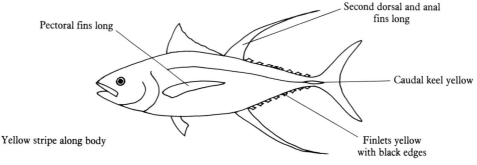

Pectoral fins long

Second dorsal and anal fins long

Caudal keel yellow

Yellow stripe along body

Finlets yellow with black edges

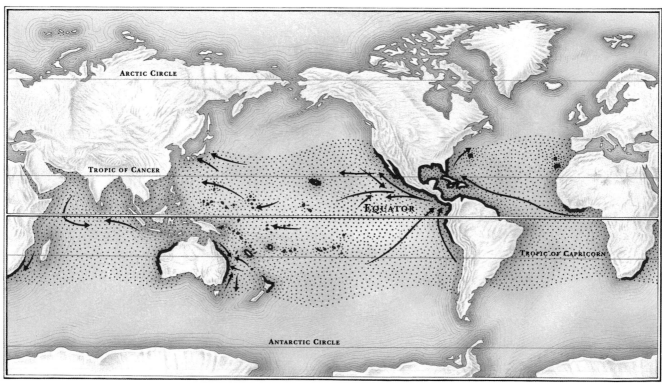

ARCTIC CIRCLE

TROPIC OF CANCER

EQUATOR

TROPIC OF CAPRICORN

ANTARCTIC CIRCLE

BIG EYE TUNA

THUNNUS OBESUS
LOWE 1839

Other common names Atlantic big eye tuna, Pacific big eye tuna.

Identifying features Upper body blackish blue, lower body silvery white, first dorsal deep yellow, finlets yellow edged in black. Maximum size 218 kg (480 lb). Short second dorsal and anal fin. Long pectoral equal to length of head.

Expected temperature range 13°C–28°C (55°F–82°F).

Typical location Open ocean—110 m (60 fathoms) and deeper. Along current and temperature changes. Over continental shelf and canyon dropoff. Over submarine peaks. Small big eye may school around buoys and FADs.

Fishing methods Trolling hard and soft plastic lures early morning, late afternoon. Deep drifting with live and dead baits with cube chum. Eating quality excellent, for top-grade sashimi.

Typical fighting characteristics One of the toughest and deepest fighters. Circle anti-clockwise after initial run. For juvenile school fish, use tackle up to 10 kg (20 lb), for adult fish use tackle up to 60 kg (130 lb).

Major sportfishing areas Canary Islands, north-east USA, Maryland, New York, North Carolina, California, Ivory Coast, Ecuador, Mexico, California, Peru, Hawaii.

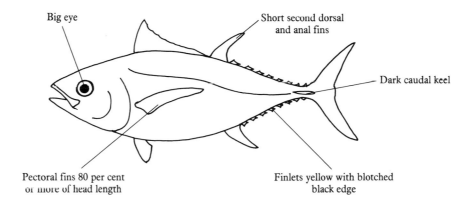

Big eye

Short second dorsal and anal fins

Dark caudal keel

Pectoral fins 80 per cent or more of head length

Finlets yellow with blotched black edge

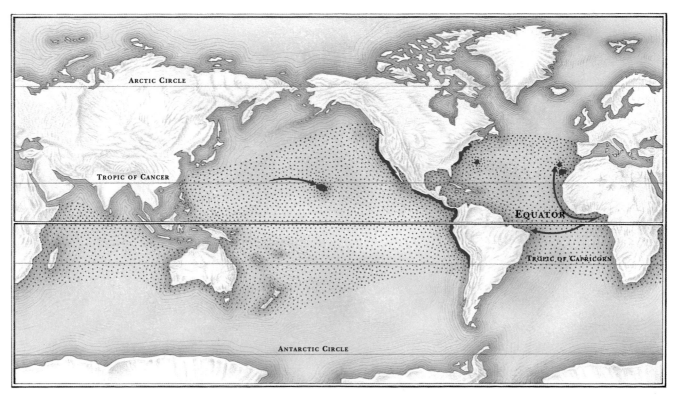

SOUTHERN BLUEFIN TUNA

THUNNUS MACCOYII

CASTELNAU 1872

Other common names Southern tunny.

Identifying features Upper body black to very dark blue, lower body silvery white, caudal keel at body and tail yellow, finlets yellow edged with black. Maximum weight 164 kg (360 lb). Pectoral fins short, less than 80 per cent of head length, never reaches the space between dorsal fins.

Expected temperature range 10°C–20°C (50°F–68°F).

Typical location Open ocean along current lines and temperature changes. Working around schools of saury, squid, anchovies, pilchards.

Fishing methods Trolling with lures, hard and soft plastic, plastic squid, konahead types, feathers, knuckleheads, metal-headed jigs with plastic tails, metal and plastic tuna jigs. Eating quality excellent—often used for top-quality sashimi.

Typical fighting characteristics Fast surface and deep fighter that circles anti-clockwise as it tires.

Major sportfishing areas Southern Australia including Tasmania, New Zealand, South Africa.

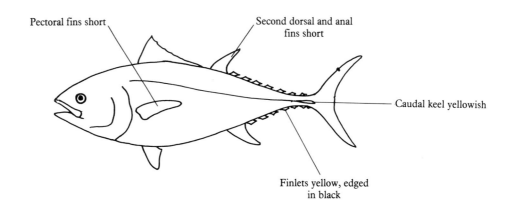

Pectoral fins short

Second dorsal and anal fins short

Caudal keel yellowish

Finlets yellow, edged in black

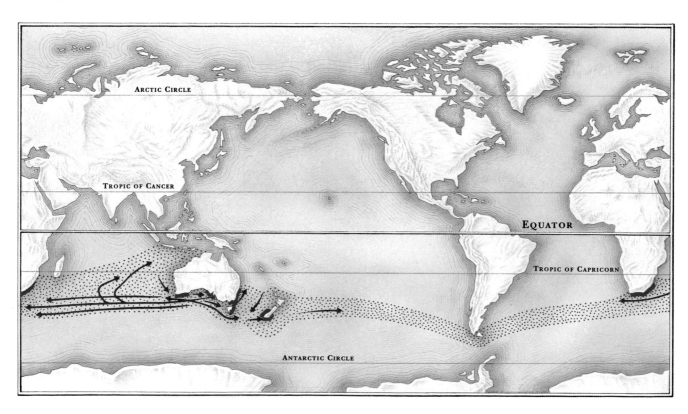

ARCTIC CIRCLE

TROPIC OF CANCER

EQUATOR

TROPIC OF CAPRICORN

ANTARCTIC CIRCLE

BONITOS

AUSTRALIAN
SARDA AUSTRALIS
MACLEAY 1880

EASTERN PACIFIC
S. CHILIENSIS
CURVIER 1831

STRIPED
S. ORIENTALIS
TEMMINCK & SCHLEGEL 1844

ATLANTIC
S. SARDA
BLOCH 1793

Other common names *Striped bonito:* horse mackerel, little bonito; *eastern Pacific bonito:* Chilean bonito.

Identifying features Upper body blue-grey with darker stripes, lower body silver. Maximum weight 11 kg (25 lb). Slim body with stripes along the top of body and down past lateral line. Small round teeth, prominent lateral line.

Expected temperature range 15°C–25°C (59°F–77°F).

Typical location Within 80 km (50 miles) of coast of continents and major islands, often close along rocky shores and inshore islands, around schools of small bait species.

Fishing methods Trolling small lures, feather and nylon jigs, spoons and Christmas trees, small tuna jigs, small knuckleheads, small minnows, casting small flashy metal lures. Fly casting. Casting onshore with high-speed metal lures.

Typical fighting characteristics Fast surface runs. Ideal light tackle opponents on lines up to 8 kg (16 lb).

Major sportfishing areas *Australian:* South-east Australia, northern New Zealand. *Eastern Pacific bonito:* Western Canada, California, Baja, Chile, Peru. *Striped bonito (S. orientalis):* East Africa, Asia, Western Australia, Pacific Central America. *Atlantic bonito:* East coast USA, Venezuela, Brazil, Western Africa, British Isles. These species overlap to cover most of the shoreline of the continents in the Indo-Pacific and Atlantic oceans, Europe, east and west coast Africa, central America, east coast USA, Papua New Guinea, Indonesia, Philippines to Asia.

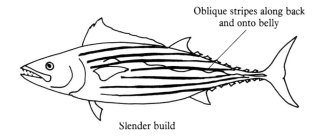

Oblique stripes along back and onto belly

Slender build

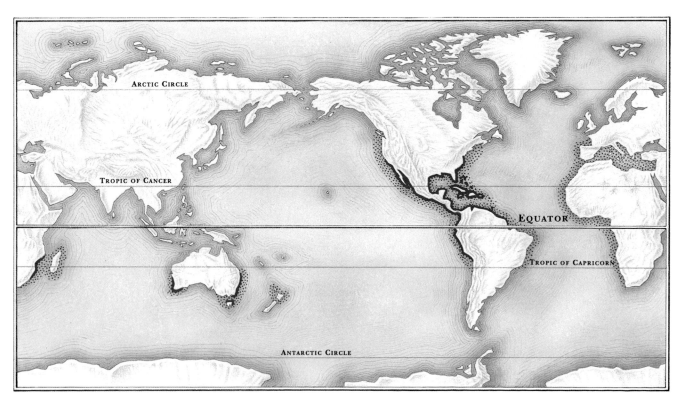

LITTLE TUNA

KAWA KAWA
EUTHYNNUS AFFINIS
CANTOR 1848

LITTLE TUNNY
E. ALLETTERATUS
RAFINESQUE 1810

BLACK SKIPJACK
E.LINEATUS
KISHINOUYE 1920

Other common names *Kawa kawa:* bonito, mackerel tuna; *little tunny:* bonito, false albacore; *black skipjack:* bonito.

Identifying features *Kawa kawa, little tunny:* Upper body green-blue with stripes of same color, lower body silver with blotched spots near pectoral fins. Broken wavy oblique stripes above lateral line with up to five indistinct spots near pectoral fins. Maximum weights kawa kawa 15 kg (35 lb), little tunny 12 kg (25 lb). *Black skipjack:* Upper body blue with darker stripes, lower body silver with blotched spots near pectoral fins. Maximum weight 12 kg (25 lb).

Expected temperature range 21°C–30°C (70°F–86°F).

Typical location Coastal waters, bays, estuaries and reef openings and open water up to 400 km (250 miles) offshore. Around schools of small bait species, anchovies, pilchards, sardines, chub mackerel.

Fishing methods Trolling with small lures, feathers, Christmas trees, knuckleheads, minnows, spoons. Trolling with small baits. Spin and casting small shiny lures and spoons. Drifting and at anchor with small bait fish and chum. Fly fishing with chum. Eating quality fair. As sashimi, flesh very red.

Typical fighting characteristics Dogged deep fighters that make repeated runs and sound often. Often difficult to get to strike. A number one light and ultra-light tackle opponent.

Major sportfishing areas *Kawa kawa:* Indo-Pacific to Hawaii, east Africa, Papua New Guinea, Philippines, Fiji and other western Pacific and Indian Ocean islands. *Little tunny:* Atlantic, east coast USA, Florida, Gulf of Mexico, Mexico, Bahamas, Costa Rica, Puerto Rico, Venezuela. *Black skipjack:* Atlantic, western Pacific to Hawaii.

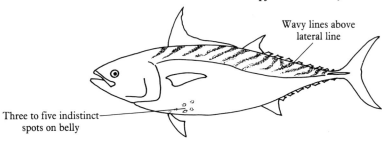

Wavy lines above lateral line

Three to five indistinct spots on belly

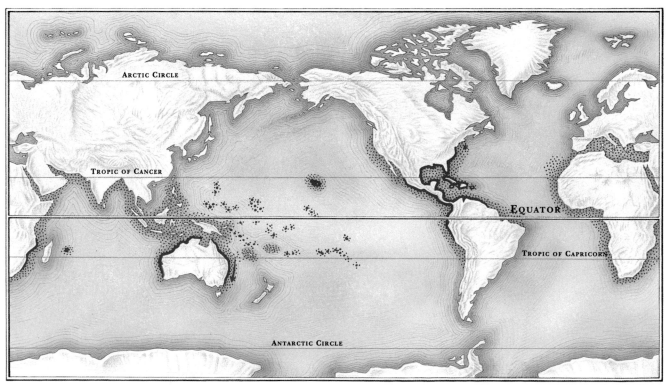

BLUE SHARK

PRIONACE GLAUCA

LINNAEUS 1758

Other common names Blue whaler.

Identifying features Upper body cobalt blue, lower body white. Maximum weight 230 kg (500 lb). Floppy long pectoral fins equal to head length. Large dark eye circled in white with nictitating membrane. Long slim body. No keel at junction of body and tail.

Expected temperature range 10°C–22°C (50°F–72°F).

Typical location Open ocean on and wide of continental shelf, species migrate across the oceans moving with the current. Often found near bait schools and dead mammals.

Fishing methods Drifting with live and dead bait and

chumming. Blue sharks will swim right up to source of oil or flesh chum to take baits thrown or given by hand right at boat. Not generally in demand for food.

Typical fighting characteristics Described as a 'slightly mobile log'. Sluggish fighter that only shows power and real resistance to capture at weights over 90 kg (200 lb). Often ignores hook and line pressure and swims back to source of chum to give opportunity for quick captures on light line. Reluctant to leave boat.

Major sportfishing areas South-east coast Australia, New Zealand, California, Mauritius, north-east coast USA, England, Azores, Canary Islands, Portugal.

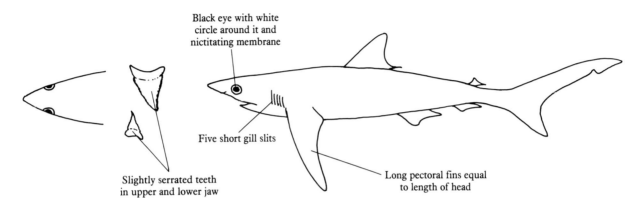

Black eye with white circle around it and nictitating membrane

Five short gill slits

Slightly serrated teeth in upper and lower jaw

Long pectoral fins equal to length of head

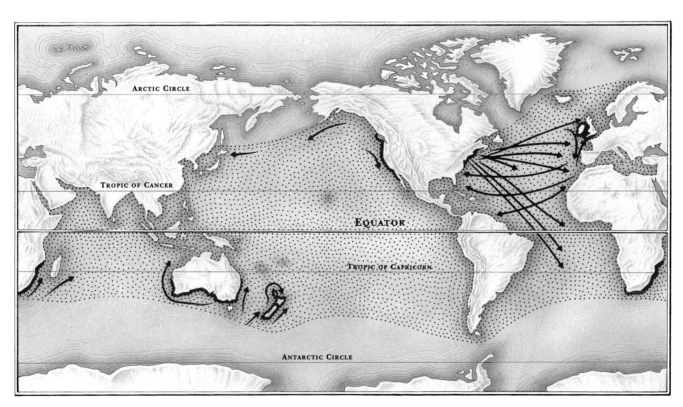

HAMMERHEAD SHARKS

SPHYRNA LEWINI   *S. ZYGAENA*   *S. MOKARRAN*

GRIFFITH & SMITH 1834   LINNAEUS 1758   RUPPELL 1835

Other common names Mallet sharks, great hammerhead, smooth hammerhead, scalloped hammerhead.

Identifying features Upper body bronze and grey, lower body white. Maximum weight 550 kg (1200 lb). Sides of head elongated in wing shape. *S. lewini:* Leading edge of head scalloped in centre. *S. zygaena:* Leading edge of head rounded, not indented. *S. mokarran:* Leading edge of head almost straight, with scoop in centre.

Expected temperature range 18°C–30°C (64°F–86°F).

Typical location Hunting on surface over and beyond continental shelf, sometimes in schools and around schools of bait.

Fishing methods Trolling natural baits intended for billfish. Trolling live bait intended for billfish. Drifting and at anchor—live and dead baits with chum. These sharks will swim right up to the boat chum source to take hand-held or thrown bait. Fly casting in chum trail.

Typical fighting characteristics Despite its ungainly appearance it is a tough opponent, making several long surface midwater turns, though it does not generally fight deep. A worthy opponent on tackle up to 37 kg (80 lb).

Major sportfishing areas East coast USA, Gulf of Mexico, east and west coast of Africa, Mauritius, Australia, New Zealand. In all warm and temperate fisheries.

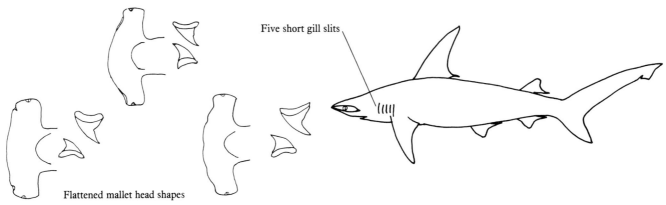

Five short gill slits

Flattened mallet head shapes

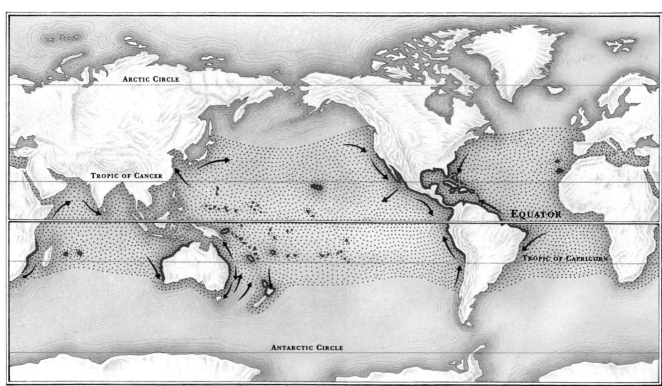

ARCTIC CIRCLE

TROPIC OF CANCER

EQUATOR

TROPIC OF CAPRICORN

ANTARCTIC CIRCLE

MAKO SHARKS

ISURUS OXYRINCHUS *I. PAUCUS*
RAFINESQUE 1810 GUITART MAWDY 1965

Other common names Blue pointer, short-fin mako, long-fin mako, bonito shark, mackerel shark.

Identifying features Upper body cobalt blue, on very big species tending to blue/grey, lower body silvery white. Maximum weight 700 kg (1500 lb). Bullet nose. Long-fin mako has long pectorals and a nose that is less pointed, large dark eyes, no nictitating membrane. Wide single keel at junction of body and tail. Upper and lower lobes of tail almost equal (in other sharks upper lobe of tail much longer than lower). Long gill slits (other sharks have short gill slits).

Expected temperature range 15°C–30°C (59°F–86°F).

Typical location Open ocean near current and temperature lines, around bait schools, over reefs and canyons and submarine peaks.

Fishing methods Trolling with billfish bait. Drifting or at anchor with live or dead baits with chum. Will take baits presented by hand or thrown. Edible quality is good; often sold as swordfish.

Typical fighting characteristics The blue dynamite with the short fuse, at times will jump up to 18 m (30 ft), indulge in fast runs, fight deep and return to attack boat and source of chum. At other times is reluctant, even when hooked, to swim far from source of chum and is inactive, although this changes often once the mako is gaffed. Will attack boats while hooked or swimming free.

Major sportfishing areas North-east coast USA, Florida, Gulf of Mexico, California, Azores, Venezuela, Brazil, Bahamas, Hawaii, occasionally England, Ecuador, Panama, Chile, Peru, Mexico, New Zealand (from where came the name 'mako'), Australia, Mauritius, South Africa.

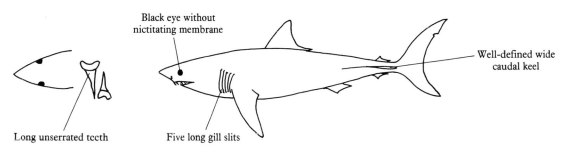

Black eye without nictitating membrane

Well-defined wide caudal keel

Long unserrated teeth

Five long gill slits

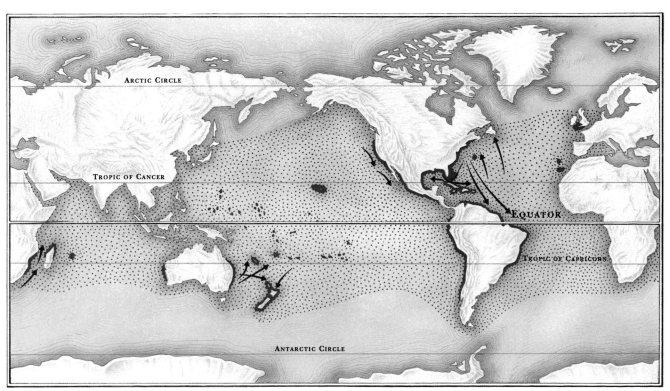

PORBEAGLE SHARKS

LAMNA NASUS
BONNATERRE 1788

L. DITROPUS
HUBBS & FOLLET 1947

Other common names Mackerel shark, salmon shark.

Identifying features Upper body dusky blue, lower body white. Maximum weight 230 kg (500 lb). Conical nose. Large dark eye without nictitating membrane. Upper and lower lobes of tail almost the same length. In most other sharks, upper lobe or tail is much longer than lower. One big and a second small keel at junction of body and tail, white patch at rear of dorsal. Long gill slits (most other sharks have short gill slits). Narrow teeth with short cusps on base.

Expected temperature range 10°C-20°C (50°F-66°F).

Typical location Open ocean following chub mackerel, herring, salmon, squid and bonito. Over and beyond the continental shelf, over canyons, peaks, reefs and banks.

Fishing methods Drifting live and dead baits with chum. Eating quality is fair.

Typical fighting characteristics A dour midwater opponent that does not exhibit the explosive activity of the mako or the initial power of the white shark.

Major sportfishing areas England, north-east coast USA, California, Oregon, New Zealand.

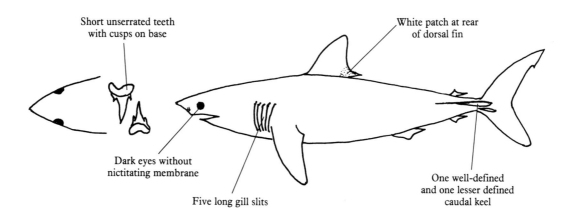

Short unserrated teeth with cusps on base

White patch at rear of dorsal fin

Dark eyes without nictitating membrane

Five long gill slits

One well-defined and one lesser defined caudal keel

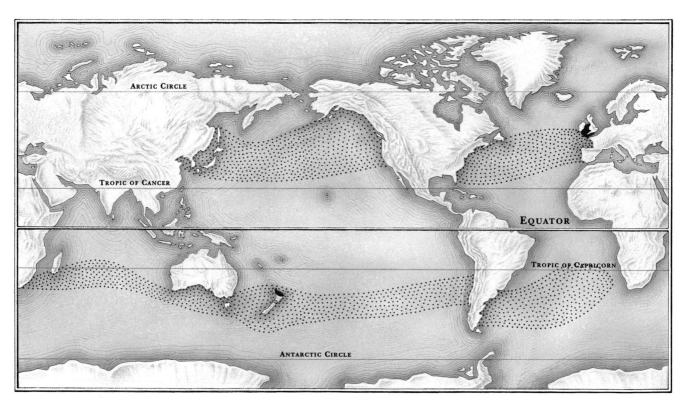

THRESHER SHARKS

ALOPIAS VULPINUS   *A. PROFUNDUS*   *A. SUPERCILIOSUS*   *A. PELAGICUS*

BONNATERRE 1788   NAKAMARU 1935   LOWE 1840   NAKAMARU 1935

Other common names Fox shark, big eye thresher, Atlantic big eye thresher, pelagic thresher.

Identifying features Upper body bluish/greenish/grey, lower body white, often mottled on sides and belly. Maximum size 450 kg (1000 lb). All species have a long upper lobe of tail equal to or longer than length of body. *A. profundus* and *A. superciliosus* have a very large eye, as expected with species that live in deep water. All species have long dagger-shaped pectoral fins.

Expected temperature range 12°C–20°C (54°F–68°F).

Typical location Open ocean on and outside continental shelf, around bait schools of mackerel, menhedden, kahawai, bluefish (tailor).

Fishing methods Trolling baits intended for billfish. Will strike at bait with tail to stun it before taking. Drifting live and dead baits in association with chum. *A. superciliosus* and *A. profundus* are taken usually by drifting.

Typical fighting characteristics Will strike with tail at bait or lure so is often foul hooked in tail. *A. vulpinus* and *A. pelagicus* occasionally jump—a spectacular sight. They are all usually mid and deep water fighters, accidentally taken on tackle of all weights. In California they are targeted on light tackle and in New Zealand, targeted in deep water on heavy tackle.

Major sportfishing areas California, north-east USA, England, Portugal, Spain, Canary Islands, New Zealand, Australia, found in temperate waters worldwide.

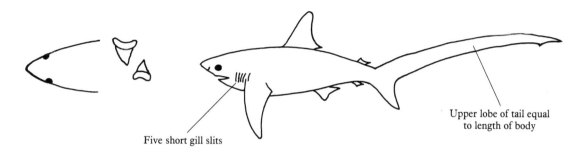

Five short gill slits

Upper lobe of tail equal to length of body

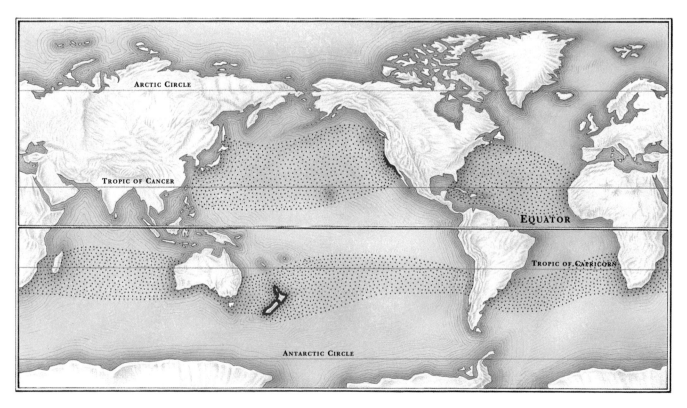

TIGER SHARK

Galeocerdo cuvieri

PERON & LESEUR 1822

Other common names Leopard shark.

Identifying features Upper body striped and mottled in dark grey and light grey, stripes more prominent in juvenile and open water sharks, darker and less obviously striped in inshore waters. Maximum weight 820 kg (1800 lb). Tigerish stripes and mottling, blunt almost square head. Large dark eyes with nictitating membrane. Slight ridge along body at junction of tail and body. Curved cockscomb-shaped teeth.

Expected temperature range 15°C–30°C (59°F–86°F).

Typical location Occasionally in estuaries and bays. More generally in open water on and along continental shelf. Over reefs and along canyons and current lines and temperature change. In tropical waters along and outside the coral reefs. Often with schools of tuna and mackerel.

Fishing methods At anchor drifting with live or dead baits while chumming. Fresh shark liver is excellent as chum, and as an addition to bait. Occasionally they take baits trolled for marlin in tropical waters. Big tigers generally take baits deep. Smaller tigers will feed on or near the surface. Not generally eaten.

Typical fighting characteristics This marine bulldog is a tough midwater fighter that mixes long runs with sounding to midwater. Rolls on leader during fight and at boat. Often comes towards surface to assess what is causing discomfort.

Major sportfishing areas Florida, Carolinas, Hawaii, Australia, New Zealand, South Africa, East Africa, western Africa. Found in all tropical environments.

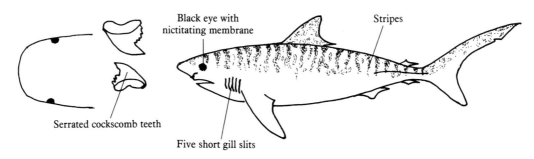

Black eye with nictitating membrane

Stripes

Serrated cockscomb teeth

Five short gill slits

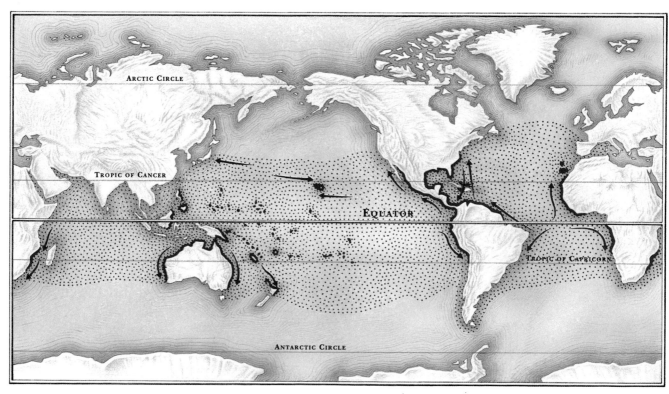

ARCTIC CIRCLE

TROPIC OF CANCER

EQUATOR

TROPIC OF CAPRICORN

ANTARCTIC CIRCLE

WHITE SHARK

CARCHARODON CARCHARIAS
LINNAEUS 1758

Other common names White pointer, white death, great white shark, man eater.

Identifying features Upper body dark to light grey, sometimes dark bronze, lower body white. Pectoral fins usually have black tips. Maximum weight 2275 kg (5000 lb). Bullet head, large black eye, no nictitating membrane. Prominent single keel on body at junction with tail. Long gill slits, big triangular serrated teeth, black patch at junction of pectoral fin and body.

Expected temperature range 10°C–30°C (50°F–84°F).

Typical location In open water and bays around seal and sea lion colonies on islands, moving with migratory whales on their migration with schools of tuna, mullet, kahawai. In open waters over reefs and along continental shelf in current lines.

Fishing methods At anchor or drift with live or dead natural bait while chumming with tuna, menhadden, bunker pilchards and other oily fleshed species. Tuna oil makes excellent slick on surface. The white shark will come up and mouth the boat, the source of the chum, and take bait presented by hand or thrown.

Typical fighting characteristics Occasionally jumps, but usually combines surface runs with midwater fight. Rolls in leader so drag must be minimized to 11 kg (25 lb) and boat maneuvered to keep in front of shark during fight. Will roll in leader at boat.

Major sportfishing areas California, north-east USA, Nova Scotia, southern Australia, South Island of New Zealand, South Africa.

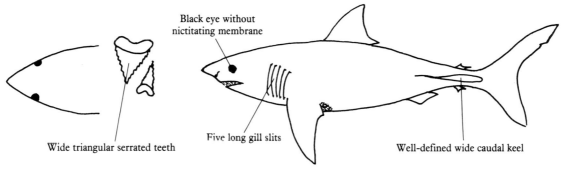

Black eye without nictitating membrane

Wide triangular serrated teeth

Five long gill slits

Well-defined wide caudal keel

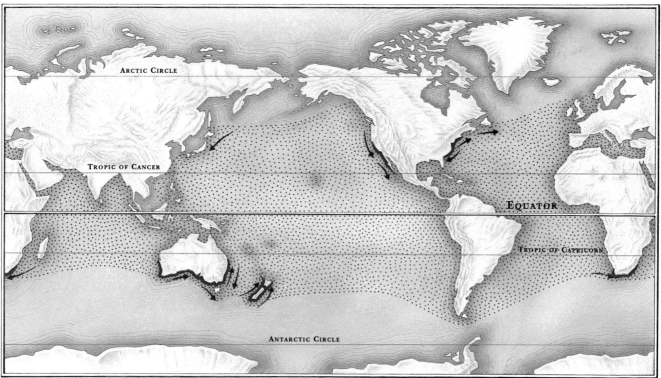

REQUIEM (WHALER) SHARKS

ATLANTIC AND INDO-PACIFIC

CARCHARHINUS ALTIMUS
SPRINGER 1950

C. BRACHYURUS
GUNTHER 1870

C. FALCIFORMIS
MULLER & HENLE 1841

C. OBSCURUS
LESUEUR 1818

C. ALBIMARGINATUS
RUPPELL 1837

C. BREVIPINNA
MULLER & HENLE 1841

C. LONGIMANUS
POEY 1861

C. GALAPAGENSIS
SNODGRASS & HELLER 1905

C. LEUCAS
VALENCIENNES 1839

C. LIMBATUS
MULLER & HENLE 1841

C. PLUMBEUS
NARDO 1827

ATLANTIC

C. PEREZII
POEY 1876

NEGARPRION ACUTIDENS
RUPPELL 1835

INDO-PACIFIC

C. AMBOINENSIS
MULLER & HENLE 1841

C. MELANOPTERUS
QUOY & GAIMARD 1824

C. AMBLYRHYNCHOS
BLEEKER 1856

Common names Big nose shark, copper shark, bronze whaler, silky shark, grey reef shark, grey reef whaler, bull shark, cub shark, Van Rooyens, blackfin shark, blackfin whaler, oceanic whitetip, dusky shark, black whaler, sandbar shark, northern whaler, spinner shark, silvertip shark, silvertip whaler, Caribbean reef shark, lemon shark, pig eye shark, Java shark, blacktip reef shark, blacktip reef whaler, graceful shark.

Identifying features Upper lobe of tail much longer than lower. Eye with nictitating membrane. Apart from *N. acutidens* first dorsal much bigger than second dorsal; in *N. acutidens* the two dorsals are of almost equal size. Teeth slightly serrated in both jaws, wide in upper jaw, narrow in lower. Eye yellowish with small pupil. Head shapes vary with species from blunt to moderately pointed. Black/grey, copper or yellow on back, cream or white below. Maximum size 500 kg (1100 lb).

Expected temperature range 10°C–30°C (52°F–86°F).

Typical location *C. longimanus:* open ocean. *All others:* estuaries and continental shelf, reefs and offshore islands. *C. leucas:* also moves up into estuaries and up rivers into fresh water with fish schools such as mullet.

Fishing methods Live and dead baits on drift or at anchor with chum. Often attracted by fish being played. In tropics occasionally take trolled bait or lures.

Typical fighting characteristics Tough dour fighters that use their powerful pectoral fins to plane down as they circle anti-clockwise. Big species are worthy opponents on heavy tackle. Others are tough, light tackle opponents that fight harder than many of the more charismatic gamefish and sharks.

Major sportfishing areas *Indo-Pacific:* Australia, New Zealand, South Africa, taken even if less welcome in other Indo-Pacific sports fisheries. *Atlantic:* North-east coast USA, Florida, caught but unwelcome at other Atlantic Caribbean sportfishing bases.

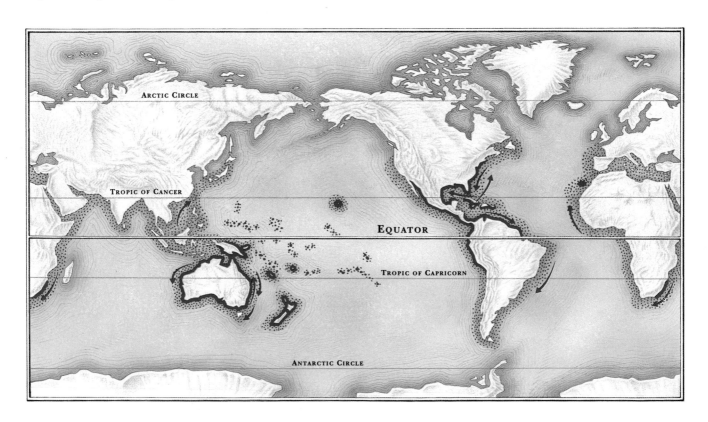

TOPE

Galeorhinus SP.

LINNEAUS 1758

Other common names School shark, sweet William, soupfin shark.

Identifying features No spines on dorsal fins. Pointed translucent nose. Teeth have serrations giving similar appearance to those of small tiger sharks. Upper lobe of tail wide with long wide tip. Body slim, grey to bronze on body, white below. Maximum weight—the British tope (*G. galeus*) which grows to 40 kg (88 lb) is probably the heaviest of the topes in various waters.

Expected temperature range 10°C–22°C (52°F–72°F).

Typical location Open ocean along continental shelf down to 492 m (200 fathoms) and in to coast in 2 m (1 fathom). Over reefs, submarine canyons and along continental shelf.

Usually deep over sea bed in small migratory schools. An important commercial species that has suffered from over-fishing.

Fishing methods At drift or anchor. Chum is beneficial in waters of moderate depth. Baits should be fished near or on sea bed.

Typical fighting characteristics An active light-weight fighter that is regarded by many British Isles anglers as outperforming blue sharks of equivalent weight on light tackle.

Major sportfishing areas British Isles, Norway, France, west coast USA, southern Australia, New Zealand.

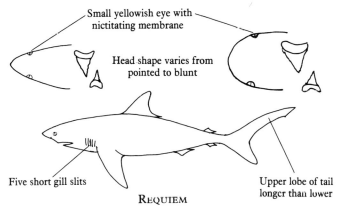

Small yellowish eye with nictitating membrane

Head shape varies from pointed to blunt

Five short gill slits

Upper lobe of tail longer than lower

REQUIEM

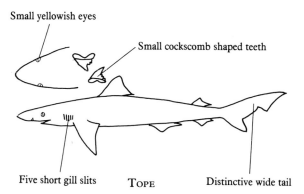

Small yellowish eyes

Small cockscomb shaped teeth

Five short gill slits

TOPE

Distinctive wide tail

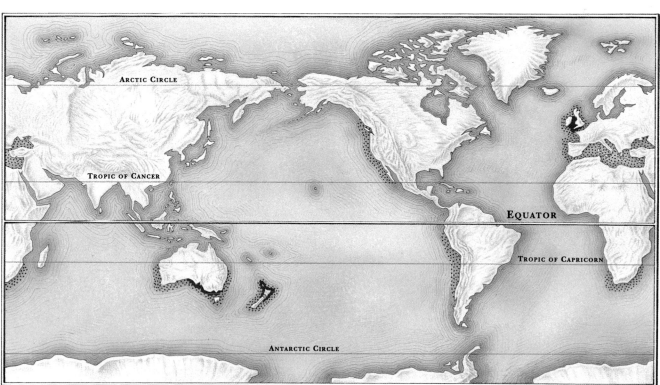

ARCTIC CIRCLE

TROPIC OF CANCER

EQUATOR

TROPIC OF CAPRICORN

ANTARCTIC CIRCLE

TANGUIGUE

SCOMBEROMORUS COMMERSON

LACEPEDE 1800

Other common names Spaniard, narrow-barred Spanish mackerel, snook, kingfish, walu.

Identifying features Upper body dark blue, lower body wavy blue–grey stripes on silver grey (sides and belly). Sides with well defined narrow wavy vertical bars. Maximum weight 68 kg (150 lb).

Expected temperature range 22°C–30°C (72°F–86°F).

Typical location Open ocean over continental shelf, around reefs and islands and along outside reef. Over reefs and holes in the sea bed. Passes and openings between reefs and submarine ridges. Migrate in schools.

Fishing methods Trolling with natural bait—garfish (balao; ballyhoo), mullet, squid, pilchards. Baits sometimes rigged with plastic skirts, squid and feather lures. Slow deep trolling with downrigger or wire line with bait or lures. Drifting or at anchor with live bait in conjunction with chum. Trolling hard and soft plastic lures, knuckleheads, feather lures, spoons, minnows, bibless minnows. Trolling strips with or without plastic skirts or nylon or feather jigs. The biggest fish are loners that have left the school to become a peak predator on a reef or seabed hole. Eating quality is excellent.

Typical fighting characteristics Long surface and near surface runs characterize this fish, which is often compared with wahoo of similar size. The wahoo is faster, but the tanguigue may be more dogged. As with wahoo, tanguigue can often be hooked after chopping baits trolled for billfish if the bait is dropped back in almost free spool then locked up as the drop back becomes tight.

Major sportfishing areas Tropical Australia, Papua New Guinea, Fiji, Philippines, South Africa, East Africa, Kenya, Tanzania, Madagascar, Mozambique.

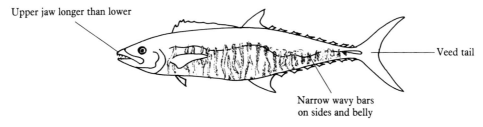

Upper jaw longer than lower

Veed tail

Narrow wavy bars on sides and belly

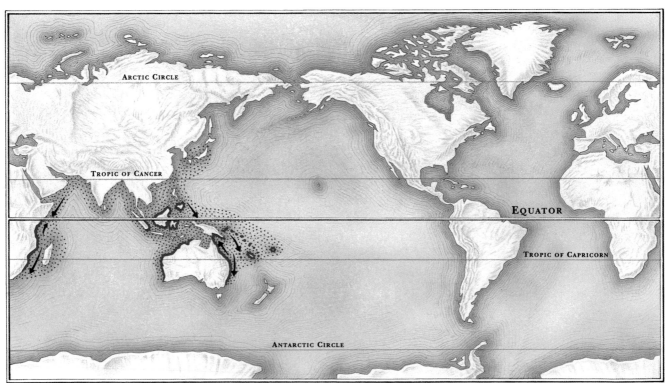

KING MACKEREL

SCOMBEROMORUS CAVALLA

CUVIER 1829

Other common names Kingfish, cavalla.

Identifying features Upper body bluish grey, lower body silver, bright in life. Maximum size 45 kg (100 lb). No bars or spots along body. Fins do not have black or white areas, as do many mackerels.

Expected temperature range 22°C–30°C (72°F–86°F).

Typical location In 18–36 m (10–20 fathoms). Migratory in open ocean, over reefs, wrecks and submarine ridges, around buoys. Working schools of ballyhoo, mullet, chub mackerel, goggle eye. The heaviest fish are usually loners that inhabit a reef or hole in the sea bed without going on with the school. Migrate long distances with schools.

Fishing methods Trolling with natural bait, ballyhoo (balao), mullet, strips, sometimes in conjunction with plastic skirts, squid and feather lures. Slow trolling live and dead baits, with downrigger or wire line. Trolling with lures, spoons, minnows, hard and soft head plastic with or without downrigs. Drifting or at anchor with live baits and chum. Casting with live bait. Eating quality excellent.

Typical fighting characteristics Very fast surface runs with several dives and runs away from boat.

Major sportfishing areas Florida, Virginia, Texas, Louisiana, Carolina, Bahamas, Puerto Rico, Virgin Islands, Venezuela, Brazil, Costa Rica, Cuba.

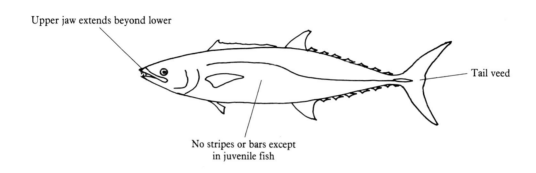

Upper jaw extends beyond lower

Tail veed

No stripes or bars except in juvenile fish

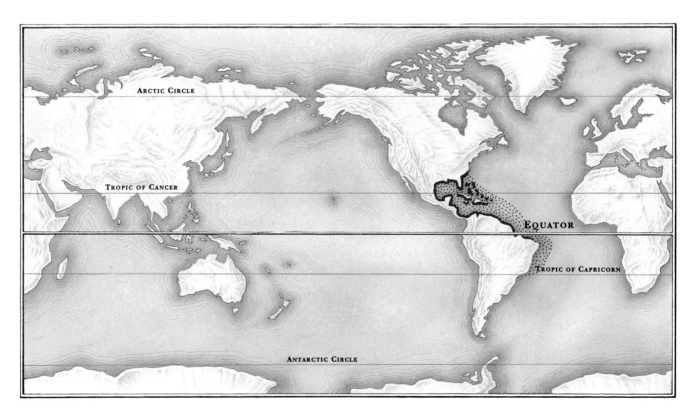

ATLANTIC & CARIBBEAN SPOTTED & SPANISH MACKERELS

CERO
SCOMBEROMORUS REGALIS
BLOCH 1793

ATLANTIC SPANISH MACKEREL
S. MACULATUS
MITCHILL 1815

SERRA SPANISH MACKEREL
S. BRASILIENSIS
COLLETTE, RUSSO & ZAVALLA-CAMIN 1978

WEST AFRICAN SPANISH MACKEREL
S. TRITOR
CUVIER 1831

Other common names *Cero:* sierra; *Atlantic Spanish mackerel:* Spanish mackerel, sierra; *serra Spanish mackerel:* serra; *West African Spanish mackerel:* maquereau.

Identifying features Upper body dark blue-grey, lower body silver. Maximum weight of any species is 10 kg (22 lb) but most are less than half this weight. Marks and spots as key. *Cera:* Long middle body stripe with rows of yellow-orange streaks and small yellow dots. *Atlantic Spanish mackerel:* Two to three rows of round and oval spots. *Serra Spanish mackerel:* Four rows of yellowish orange oval spots. *West African Spanish mackerel:* Three rows of oval spots with thin vertical bars.

Expected temperature range 21°C–30°C (70°F–86°F).

Typical location Offshore on continental shelf, open bays, around islands over reefs, working schools of bait fish.

Fishing methods Trolling small fresh baits, small ballyhoo (garfish), mullet, sardines, pilchards. Trolling strip baits, sometimes in conjunction with plastic squid or feather jigs. Trolling lures, small feathers, small spoons, small jigs, small minnows. Spincasting small metal lures and small live bait, with or without chum. Fly casting. Eating quality is excellent, particularly when fresh.

Typical fighting characteristics Fast surface runs typical of all the mackerel species, ideal on light tackle up to 8 kg (16 lb).

Major sportfishing areas *Sera:* East coast USA, Bermuda, Bahamas, West Indies, Venezuela, Brazil. *Atlantic Spanish mackerel:* East coast USA, Gulf of Mexico, Mexico, Bahamas. *Serra Spanish mackerel:* Mexico, Honduras, Venezuela, Brazil. *West African Spanish mackerel:* Ivory Coast, Senegal, Angola.

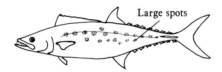

Large spots

ATLANTIC SPANISH MACKEREL

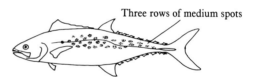

Three rows of medium spots

PACIFIC SIERRA MACKEREL

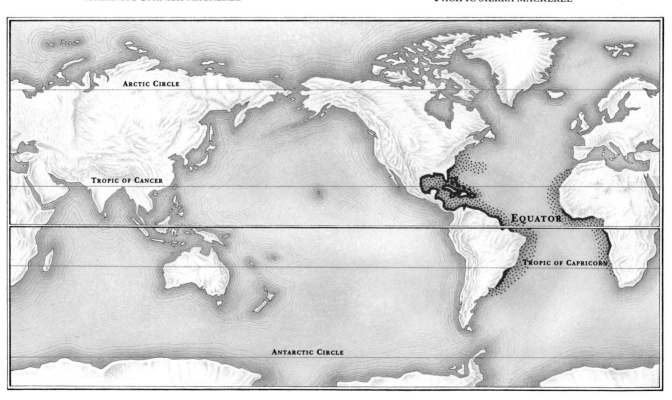

INDO-PACIFIC SPOTTED
& SPANISH MACKERELS

MONTEREY SPANISH MACKEREL
SCOMBEROMORUS CONCOLOR
LOCKINGTON 1879

PACIFIC SIERRA MACKEREL
S. SIERRA
JORDAN & STARKS 1895

QUEENSLAND SCHOOL MACKEREL
S. QUEENSLANDICUS
MUNRO 1943

AUSTRALIAN SPOTTED MACKEREL
S. MUNROI
COLLETTE & RUSSO 1980

JAPANESE SPANISH MACKEREL
S. NIPPONIUS
CUVIER 1831

INDO-PACIFIC KING MACKEREL
S. GUTTATUS
BLOCH & SCHNEIDER 1801

KANADI KINGFISH
S. PLURILINEATUS
FORMANOIR 1966

Other common names *Monterey Spanish mackerel:* sierra, gulf sierra; *Pacific sierra mackerel:* sierra; *Queensland school mackerel:* spotty, spotted mackerel; *Australian spotted mackerel:* spotty, spotted mackerel; *Japanese Spanish mackerel:* spotted mackerel; *Indo-Pacific king mackerel:* spotted spanish mackerel, Indo-Pacific Spanish mackerel; *kanadi kingfish:* snook, spotted mackerel.

Identifying features Upper body dark blue-grey, lower body silver. Maximum weight any species 10 kg (22 lb) but most species are less than half this weight. Marks and spots as key. *Monterey Spanish mackerel:* No spots or bars. *Pacific sierra mackerel:* Four rows of brownish-orange oval spots. *Queensland school mackerel:* Two rows of large blotched spots. *Australian spotted mackerel:* Three to four rows of medium spots. *Japanese Spanish mackerel:* Seven to eight rows of small spots, some spots touching. *Indo-Pacific king mackerel:* Three irregular rows of brownish spots. *Kanadi kingfish:* Black lines and elongated spots.

Expected temperature range 21°C–31°C (70°F–86°F).

Typical location Offshore on continental shelf, open bays, around islands over reefs, working schools of bait fish.

Fishing methods Same as for Atlantic & Caribbean Spotted and Spanish Mackerels, page 40.

Typical fighting characteristics Fast surface runs typical of all the mackerel species. Ideal on light tackle up to 7 kg (16 lb).

Major sportfishing areas *Monterey Spanish mackerel:* Baja, California. *Pacific sierra mackerel:* Baja, California, Mexico. *Queensland school mackerel:* Tropical Australia. *Australian spotted mackerel:* Tropical Australia. *Japanese Spanish mackerel:* Japan, Korea, Okinawa. *Indo-Pacific king mackerel:* Islands of Asia and Japan. *Kanadi kingfish:* Kenya, Madagascar, South Africa.

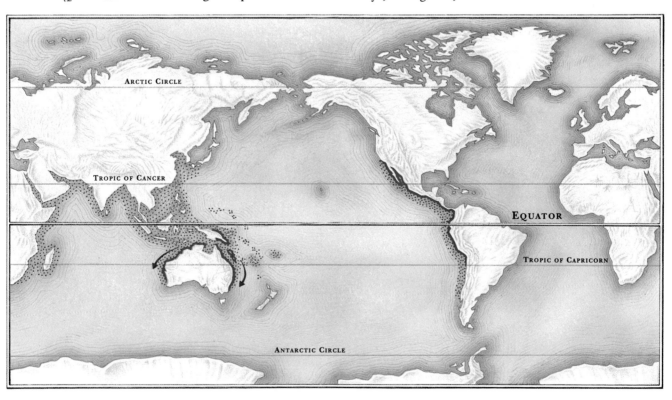

SEERFISH

PAPUAN
SCOMBEROMORUS MULTIRADIATUS
MUNRO 1964

CHINESE
S. SINENSIS
LACEPEDE 1800

STREAKED
CYMBIUM LINEOLATUS
CUVIER 1831

KOREAN
S. KOREANUS
KISHINOUYE 1915

Other common names *Papuan seerfish:* seerfish; *Chinese seerfish:* seerfish; *streaked seerfish:* Queen mackerel, streaker, Spanish mackerel; *Korean seerfish:* Korean mackerel.

Identifying features Similar to Spanish and spotted mackerels. Pectoral fins are wider and more rounded than other mackerels, body deeper than other mackerels, tail more rounded. Upper body is blue-grey, lower body silver. The Chinese seerfish grows to 80 kg (180 lb), while the other species are less than 10 kg (22 lb). *Papuan seerfish:* No blotches or spots on body. *Chinese seerfish:* Large round indistinct spots. *Streaked seerfish:* Sides streaked with narrow dark broken horizontal line. *Korean seerfish:* Prominent lateral line, three to four rows of brownish spots.

Expected temperature range 21°C–28°C (70°F–82°F).

Typical location Along continental shelf of Asia and Papua New Guinea in muddy coastal and major river estuary waters.

Fishing methods Trolling small lures, slow trolling small natural baits. Eating quality good when fresh.

Typical fighting characteristics Active surface runners, similar to other mackerels.

Major sportfishing areas Papuan seerfish: Papua New Guinea. *Chinese seerfish:* Thailand, Japan. *Streaked seerfish:* India, Malaysia. *Korean seerfish:* India, Malaysia, Japan.

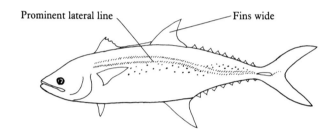

Prominent lateral line — Fins wide

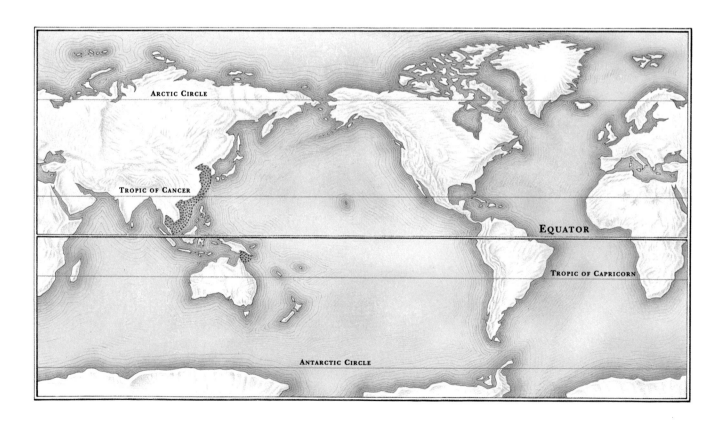

SCALEY MACKEREL

SHARK

GRAMMATORCYNUS BICARINATUS

QUOY & GAIMARD 1824

DOUBLE LINED

G. BILINEATUS

RUPPELL 1836

Other common names *Shark mackerel:* scaley mackerel, large-scale tuna, salmon mackerel; *Double lined mackerel:* scad, scad mackerel.

Identifying features Upper body green, lower body silvery gold. *Shark mackerel:* Small eye, double lateral line with small spots on belly. Maximum weight 13 kg (30 lb). *Double lined mackerel:* Large eye, double lateral line usually no spots on belly. Maximum weight 3 kg (8 lb).

Expected temperature range 25°C–30°C (73°F–86°F).

Typical location *Shark mackerel:* Around islands, reefs and ridges on sea bed over reefs, around flotsam in open ocean

as well as inshore. *Double lined mackerel:* In openings between and outside reefs, over shallow reefs in open ocean.

Fishing methods Trolling small lures, plastic squid, feathers, spoons, minnows. Spin casting small spoons and other small shiny metal lures. Eating quality excellent.

Typical fighting characteristics Several fast surface runs with sounding between runs. A determined fighter, tough and interesting on light tackle.

Major sportfishing areas *Shark mackerel:* Tropical Australia. *Double lined mackerel:* Tropical Australia, Philippines, western Pacific and islands of Asia.

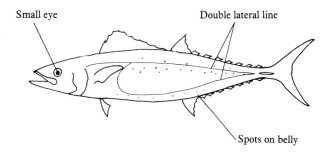

Small eye

Double lateral line

Spots on belly

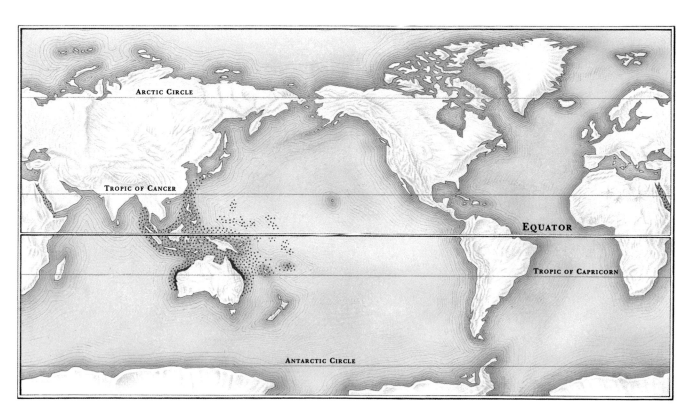

ARCTIC CIRCLE

TROPIC OF CANCER

EQUATOR

TROPIC OF CAPRICORN

ANTARCTIC CIRCLE

CHUB MACKERELS

Scomber australasicus
CUVIER 1831

S. japonicus
HOUTTUYN 1782

S. scombrus
LINNAEUS 1758

Other common names *S. australasicus:* spotted chub mackerel, green mackerel; *S. japonicus:* Pacific mackerel, green mackerel, slimy mackerel; *S. scombrus:* Atlantic mackerel, green mackerel.

Identifying features Upper body dark green with green stripes and undulations, lower body pearly silver. Maximum weight 1 kg (2 lb). Round cigar-shaped body, oblique stripes on back, no keel at junction of body and tail.

Expected temperature range 12°C–28°C (54°F–82°F).

Typical location In schools, in bays, estuaries, around islands and in open water over banks and current upwellings. *S. australasicus:* Australia, New Zealand, Papua New Guinea, Philippines, Japan. *S. japonicus:* Hawaii, west coast USA, west South America, east coast

USA, west coast Africa. *S. scombrus:* East coast USA, Mediterranean, British Isles to Iceland, Baltic Sea.

Fishing methods Bait on ultra-light tackle with bread or fish chum. Little Joe and other multiple feather and skin rigs for bait. Jigging and casting very small lures. Fly casting.

Typical fighting characteristics A fast zippy fighter that is active on line classes up to 8 lb (about 4 kg).

Major sportfishing areas The three species overlap to provide bait and sport in Europe, the Mediterranean, North Africa, north-east coast USA, west coast USA, Baja, California, Venezuela, Argentina, west coast South America, Hawaii, New Zealand, southern Australia, Papua New Guinea to Asia, West and South Africa.

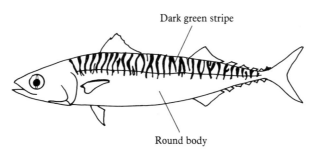

Dark green stripe

Round body

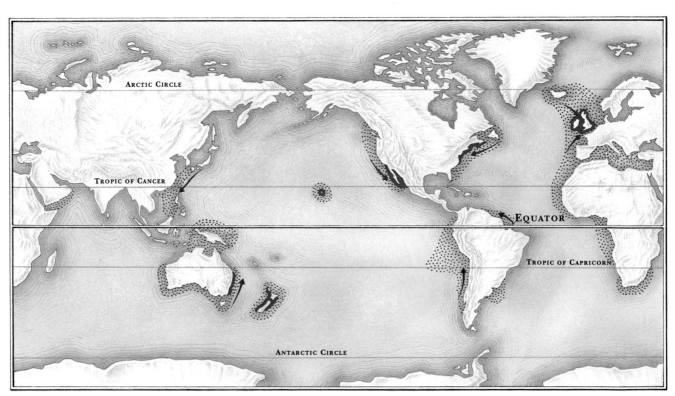

WAHOO

ACANTHOCYBIUM SOLANDRI

CUVIER 1831

Other common names Ono, peto, jack mackerel.

Identifying features Upper body dark blue with wavy stripes. Some stripes in Y-shape, lower body silver. In life can be electric blue and silver. Maximum weight 90 kg (200 lb). Lower jaw projects beyond upper jaw, jaw hinge does not show, upright tail, dorsal fin high, curved and highest at rear. Single lateral line.

Expected temperature range 21°C–30°C (70°F–86°F).

Typical location Open ocean on current lines and temperature changes, around logs and bait schools, over deep reefs and submarine peaks, over holes in sea bed close in to tropical reefs and ledges.

Fishing methods Trolling dead bait in combination with plastic squid, trolling hard and soft plastic lures and big minnows, feather lures, trolling spoons close to reefs, trolling strips often in conjunction with plastic squid, drifting with live bait—chub mackerel, yellowtail, scad, blue runner often with chum. Spin casting live bait. Eating quality excellent.

Typical fighting characteristics In some hot spots these fish are in schools that not only strike at baits or lures but leaders, swivels, double line or where line cuts the surface with spray. Splash and flashy lures are often successful, as are deep running konahead type lures. A super-fast surface run, sometimes followed by shorter runs in mid water. Occasionally jump, particularly when missing bait or lure. Ideal medium tackle species but taken on tackle of all weights as wahoo appear and strike opportunistically when fishing for other species. Wahoo can often be taken after striking and cutting the marlin bait just behind the hook by immediately dropping back slack line then locking up.

Major sportfishing areas Puerto Rico, Virgin Islands, Bahamas, Bermuda, Venezuela, Florida, east coast USA, Gulf of Mexico, Hawaii, Fiji, Guam, Tahiti and other Pacific islands, Okinawa, Marianas, eastern Africa, east and west coast Australia, Mexico, Panama, Ecuador, Costa Rica.

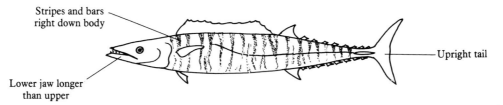

Stripes and bars right down body

Lower jaw longer than upper

Upright tail

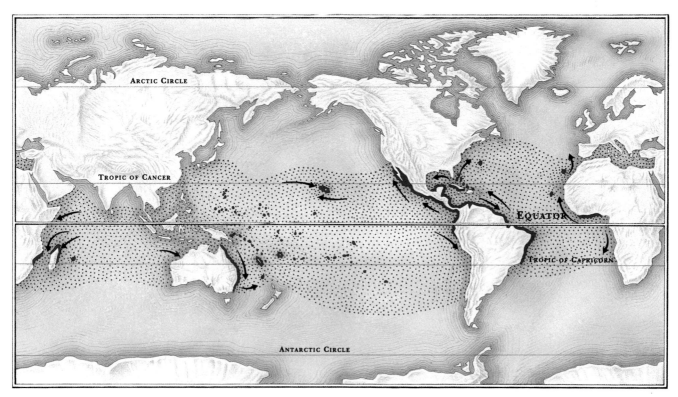

ARCTIC CIRCLE

TROPIC OF CANCER

EQUATOR

TROPIC OF CAPRICORN

ANTARCTIC CIRCLE

MAHI MAHI

CORYPHAENA HIPPURUS   *C. EQUISELIS*
LINNAEUS 1758   LINNAEUS 1758

Other common names: Dolphin fish, dorado (mahi mahi is often preferred to avoid confusion with dolphin).

Identifying features Upper body green or electric blue, or combinations, lower body gold or electric silver. Maximum weight (males are heaviest) up to 45 kg (100 lb).

Expected temperature range 20°C–30°C (68°F–86°F).

Typical location Open ocean around flotsam, logs, weed lines, in warm current. Travel in schools in varying sizes of males and females. Often found at current lines and food upwellings, around FADs.

Fishing methods Trolling dead natural bait—ballyhoo (garfish), mullet, chub mackerel, squid, bonefish. Trolling strip baits often in combination with plastic skirts, or squid or feather jigs. Trolling lures, hard and soft plastic, knuckleheads, minnows, spoons, poppers. Drifting with small live bait, often with chum. Casting small metal lures, minnows and poppers. Fly casting around logs and weed lines. Eating quality excellent, fresh or frozen.

Typical fighting characteristics A surface-running jumping jack that executes perfect sideways and scissor jumps with speed changes of direction. Difficult to gaff and care should be taken when bringing big mahi mahi inboard because of activity and power of tail.

Major sportfishing areas Worldwide in tropical warm-water currents. Gulf of Mexico, particularly in Gulf Stream of Bahamas, the Carolinas, Florida, Puerto Rico, St Thomas, Venezuela, Bermuda, east and west coast Mexico, Panama, Costa Rica, Ecuador, tropical Australia, Papua New Guinea, Hawaii, Fiji, Tahiti, Mauritius and all Pacific and Indian Ocean islands, east and west coast Africa.

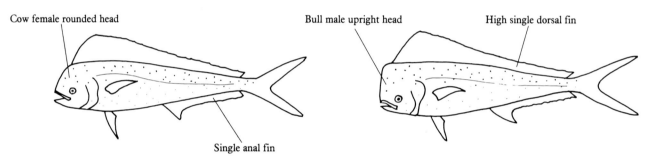

Cow female rounded head

Bull male upright head

High single dorsal fin

Single anal fin

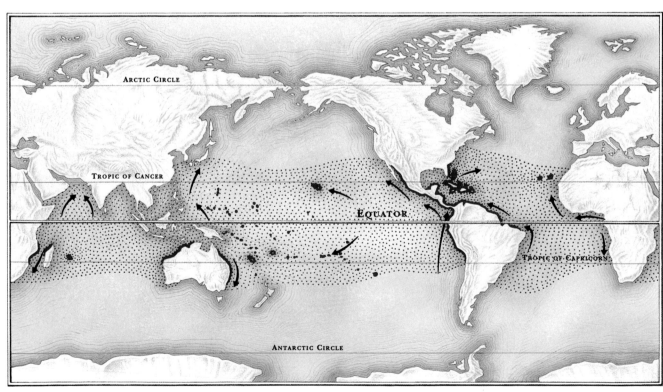

COBIA

RACHYCENTRON CANADUM

LINNAEUS 1766

Other common names Ling, crab eater, cabio, black kingfish, lemonfish.

Identifying features Upper body dark brown with two white long tail streaks, tail wide, lower body lighter brown with belly white. Maximum weight 70 kg (150 lb). Head and body shape similar to remora. Very low, knobbly first dorsal, long second dorsal and anal fins.

Expected temperature range 21°C–26°C (71°F–79°F).

Typical location Around coral and rocky reefs, reef structures and wrecks in open ocean and inshore. Around flotsam, buoys and FADs. Under big feeding rays, sometimes with whale sharks.

Fishing methods Trolling natural baits—ballyhoo (garfish), mullet, strips, sometimes with plastic skirts or feather jigs. Trolling live bait with natural bait—mullet, chub mackerel. Slow trolling deep with downrigger with live or dead baits. Trolling lures, hard and soft plastic lures, spoons, minnows. Casting poppers, minnows. Deep jigging. Drifting or at anchor with live bait—mullet, chub mackerel, crabs, shrimp. At anchor or drift with live or dead baits with chum combined with surface splashing to excite interest. Will follow other hooked cobia, so there is often benefit, as with amberjack, mahi mahi, in tethering first-caught fish. Eating quality excellent, fresh or frozen.

Typical fighting characteristics Very tough opponent at all stages of fight. Determined midwater runs with dives to reef or other obstruction or structure piles to cut line or leader. Difficult to gaff because of spinning. Should be gaffed in upper middle of body.

Major sportfishing areas Florida, North and South Carolina, Virginia, Texas, Louisiana, Mexico, Costa Rica, Venezuela, Bahamas, tropical Australia, Papua New Guinea, Fiji, Pacific and Indian Ocean islands, Okinawa, east coast Africa, Madagascar.

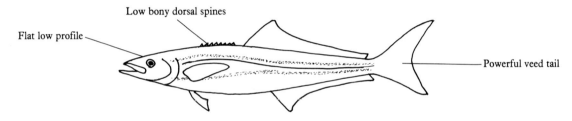

Flat low profile

Low bony dorsal spines

Powerful veed tail

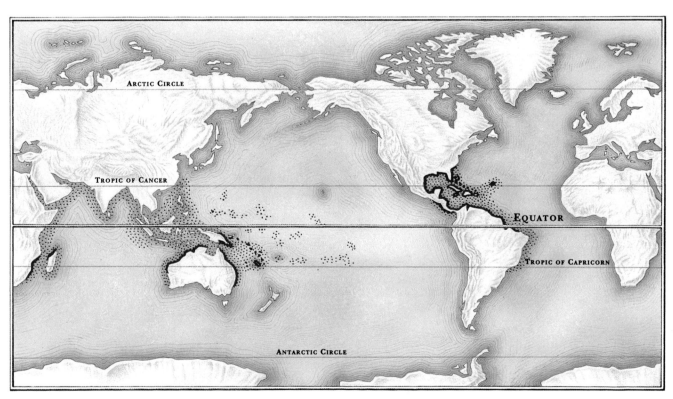

BLUEFISH

POMATOMUS SALTATRIX

LINNAEUS 1758

Other common names Tailor, elf.

Identifying features Upper body greenish blue in life, changing to blue grey after death, lower body silvery. Maximum weight 15 kg (35 lb). Sharp teeth. First dorsal joins to second dorsal. Body is flat, tail powerful and veed. Dark blotch at base of pectoral fin.

Expected temperature range 15°C–25°C (59°F–75°F).

Typical location In bays, estuaries and close inshore on their spawning migration, and following schools of baitfish around rocky headlands and holes and gutters along shore.

Fishing methods Trolling small lures, feather jigs, spoons, minnows. Casting blocktin, squid, sliced metal lures, minnows, spoons, plugs. Casting strips of natural bait fish and squid. Casting live bait, casting lures. Drifting or at anchor casting smaller live baits with chum. Fly casting. The areas where bluefish are feeding can often be smelt as well as seen by surface chopping and bird action. Trolling and casting in this area will often trigger action. Eating quality good when fresh, excellent when smoked.

Typical fighting characteristics Fast surface and midwater runs with occasional jumps. Inshore fishing, use wave action to resist pull from shore. Handle carefully in all sizes because of sharp cutting teeth.

Major sportfishing areas East coast USA into Gulf of Mexico, west and east coast Australia, west and east coast South Africa, Madagascar, Venezuela, Brazil.

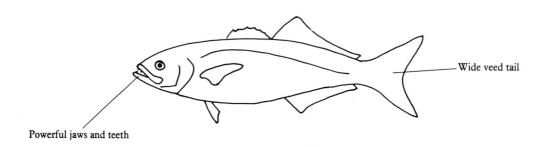

Wide veed tail

Powerful jaws and teeth

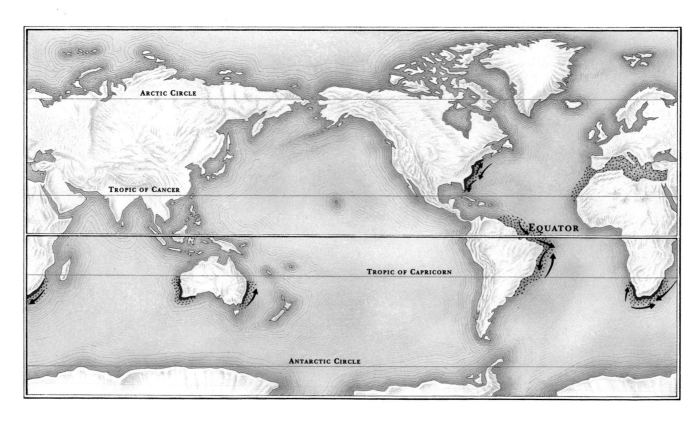

BARRAMUNDI

LATES CALCIFER

BLOCH 1790

Other common names Giant perch, barra, anama, cockup.

Identifying features Upper body greenish grey, often with bronze tints, lower body silver, colors are more brownish on lagoon and river fish. Maximum size 55 kg (120 lb). Head tapered and elongated from shoulder to jaw. Rounded tail. Prominent lateral line. Pink-red eyes. Large scales.

Expected temperature range 25°C–30°C (77°F–86°F).

Typical location Salt water in summer in saltwater creeks and river entrances for spawning. In winter, most have moved up rivers and lagoons, while others still hunt in river and creek entrances and bays.

Fishing methods Fishing oyster rocks, close to snags, tree trunks, rocky areas in creek mouths and holes in streams and lagoons. Slow trolling lures, minnows, spoons. Casting lures, minnows, rattlers, close in and into snags. At anchor with live bait—mullet. The barramundi should be given

time to take the lure before lifting the rod tip. It is often productive to run two lines with trolled lures directly behind one another. Salt water fly casting. Barramundi investigate noise and vibration. Active banging on snags and fishing with rattling lures sometimes triggers action. Best activity in salt water often comes at low tide neaps coinciding with sunrise and sunset at creek and river mouths. Eating quality excellent.

Typical fighting characteristics After hook-up smashes through surface with spectacular mouth-open gill-rattling jumps that lead to surface runs and struggle to reach obstruction and snags. Even if barramundi reach the snag, a patient angler can still catch the fish by waiting until the fish leaves its cover to resume hunting.

Major sportfishing areas Tropical Australia, Papua New Guinea and its islands, Asiatic islands through to continent of Asia.

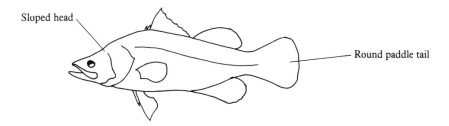

Sloped head

Round paddle tail

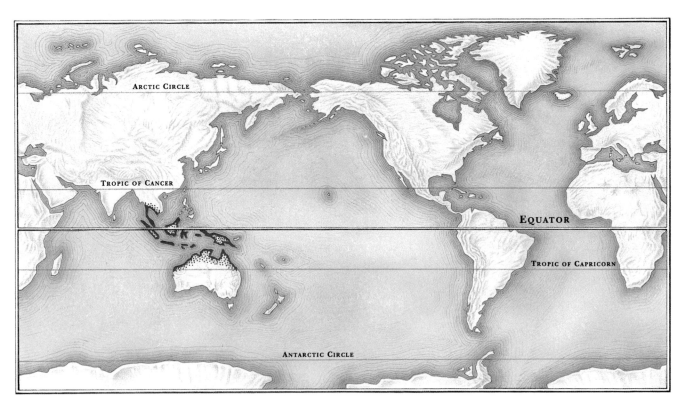

ARCTIC CIRCLE

TROPIC OF CANCER

EQUATOR

TROPIC OF CAPRICORN

ANTARCTIC CIRCLE

AMBERJACK

Seriola dumerili

RISSO 1810

Other common names Great amberjack, samson fish.

Identifying features Upper body olive-brown with darker olive-brown diagonal stripe from mouth to just in front of dorsal, lower body silvery with bronze (amber) stripe along body. Maximum weight 80 kg (180 lb). Insignificant keel at junction of body and tail. No finlets. Single anal fin. Dark colored tail (not yellow as in yellowtail).

Expected temperature range 21°C-30°C (70°F-86°F).

Typical location Open water over reefs and wrecks, around buoys, logs and other flotsam and weed lines.

Fishing methods Trolling with natural baits—ballyhoo (garfish), mullet, yellowtail scad. Slow trolling with live bait. Trolling lures, spoons, feathers, hard or soft plastic plugs. Deep trolling with lures and baits. Casting spoons, minnows, poppers. Deep jigging lead head jigs, candy bars.

Fly casting with chum. They respond to teasing and chum. Tethering of the first caught amberjack will often hold the school and prolong the surface action. Eating quality good.

Typical fighting characteristics A hard, deep fighter with repeated runs and dives. Heads for obstacles to break free. It is often better to try to lead the fish from obstacles and home before fighting hard. A tethered amberjack will often hold the school away from obstacles or give a chance at others in the school. Like yellowtail, they often come to the surface for poppers and noisy lures.

Major sportfishing areas Atlantic and Caribbean: Bermuda, North and South Carolinas, Virginia, Florida, Gulf of Mexico, Cuba, Puerto Rico, Virgin Islands, Venezuela. Indo-Pacific: Hawaii, Fiji, Tahiti and other Pacific islands, tropical Australia, Mauritius and other Indian Ocean islands, eastern Africa, Asia.

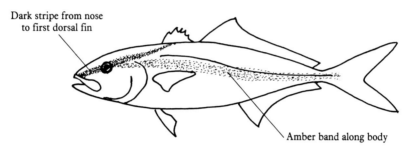

Dark stripe from nose to first dorsal fin

Amber band along body

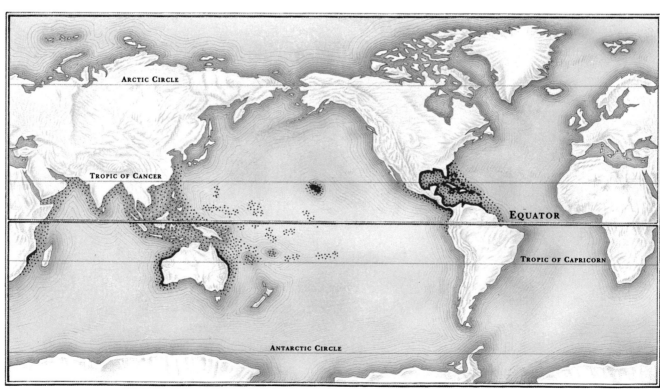

ARCTIC CIRCLE

TROPIC OF CANCER

EQUATOR

TROPIC OF CAPRICORN

ANTARCTIC CIRCLE

PERMIT

TRACHINOTUS FALCATUS

LINNAEUS 1758

Other common names Great pompano, round pompano.

Identifying features Upper body blue, lower body silver. Maximum size 28 kg (60 lb). Oval body with blunt head and humped back, powerful veed tail, no spots on body, first dorsal six short spines.

Expected temperature range 21°C–30°C (70°F–86°F).

Typical location On shallow coral marl and sandy flats and inshore over wrecks and bottom formations. On the flats they move from channels to flats on rising tide.

Fishing methods Fly casting. Spin casting with bait, shrimps or live finney or spider crabs, spin casting small lures. Bottom fishing over wrecks. Eating quality excellent.

Typical fighting characteristics The super challenge of the flats. Repeated fast runs and trick of rubbing mouth on the bottom to free the hook ensures that in shallow water only those kept on a tight line are brought to capture or release. The runs in shallow water encompass every natural obstacle. The hard mouth of permit necessitates multiple strikes (up to ten) to try to set the hook.

Major sportfishing areas Atlantic Florida flats, Bahamas, Honduras and Caribbean Islands to Brazil, Indo-Pacific Australia, Papua New Guinea, Solomons, Pacific and Indian Ocean islands and lagoons, East Africa, Asia.

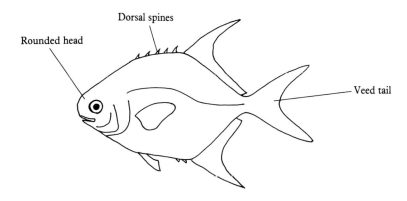

Rounded head   Dorsal spines   Veed tail

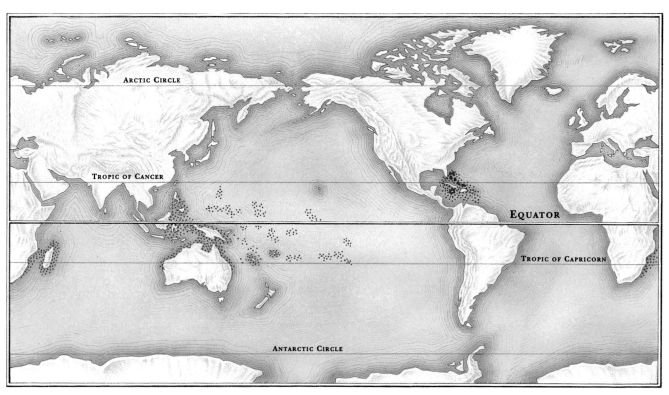

THE FUN FISH

BARRACUDA

Sphyraena barracuda
WALBAUM 1792

Other common names Giant pike, great barracuda.

Identifying features Upper body blue-grey, lower body silver with scattered dark blotches. Maximum weight 45 kg (100 lb). Pointed head with underslung jaw that is no longer than upper jaw. Flat razor-sharp teeth with longest teeth just under nose. Body long and elongated, wide veed tail. No keel on body.

Expected temperature range 21°C–30°C (70°F–86°F).

Typical location Juveniles in lagoons and shallow flats. Adult loners around reefs and openings and passes in and between reefs, along submarine ridges and over isolated peaks. Big barracuda will often become the peak predator at a reef area or hole in the sea bed.

Fishing methods Trolling natural baits—ballyhoo (balao; garfish), mullet, trolling strip baits with or without plastic skirts or feather jigs, lures—spoons, minnows, feather jigs. Deep trolling with lures and baits. Drifting or at anchor with chum. Casting with lures (shiny metal, poppers, minnows, and fluorescent green or pink surgical tube lures) and bait. Saltwater fly casting. Popular as an eating fish in some areas, not eaten in others partly because of concern for ciguatera.

Typical fighting characteristics High-flying jumper on light tackle, particularly in shallow water. Fast surface run then shorter runs before coming to boat. Razor teeth require careful handling in capture and release.

Major sportfishing areas Florida, Bahamas, Puerto Rico, West Indies, Mexico, Fiji, Tahiti, Hawaii and all Pacific islands, tropical Australia, Papua New Guinea, eastern Africa, western Africa, Mauritius, Seychelles and Indian Ocean islands.

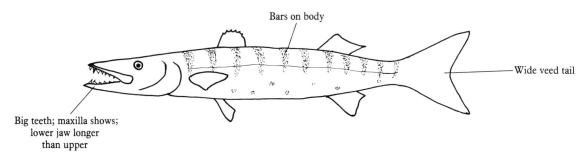

Bars on body

Wide veed tail

Big teeth; maxilla shows; lower jaw longer than upper

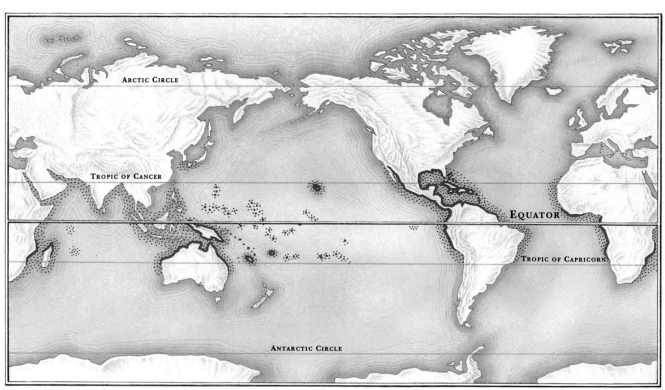

S N O O K

Centropomus undecimalis
BLOCH 1792

Other common names Robalo.

Identifying features Upper body olive-green, sometimes with bronze overtones (black line along body and tail), lower body silver. Maximum weight 30 kg (65 lb). Long protruding lower jaw. Heavy black line from gill cover to vee of tail. Spined dorsal fins of almost equal size.

Expected temperature range 19°C–30°C (66°F–86°F).

Typical location In salt to fresh tropical waters around mangroves, snags, bridges and other structures that give cover. In Central America in surf and river mouths, in fresh, brackish and salt water.

Fishing methods Casting lures, minnow plugs, poppers, propeller plugs, bucktail and nylon jigs, spoons. Drifting or at anchor with live bait—mullet, shrimp, crabs, pinfish. Fly fishing, particularly in holes on the sea grass flats. From bridges and structures when cast into and across current. Most fishing is casting in close to snags and other likely places and in holes or down current of oyster and rock bars. Productive fishing tides vary with locality. Eating quality is excellent.

Typical fighting characteristics Spectacular gill-rattling jumps immediately after hook-up. Will try to reach safety in snags, mangroves, oyster and rock bars and other cover.

Major sportfishing areas Atlantic Caribbean, Florida, Costa Rica, Honduras, Venezuela, Brazil, Pacific Mexico, Costa Rica, Ecuador, Peru.

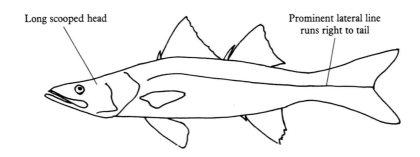

Long scooped head

Prominent lateral line runs right to tail

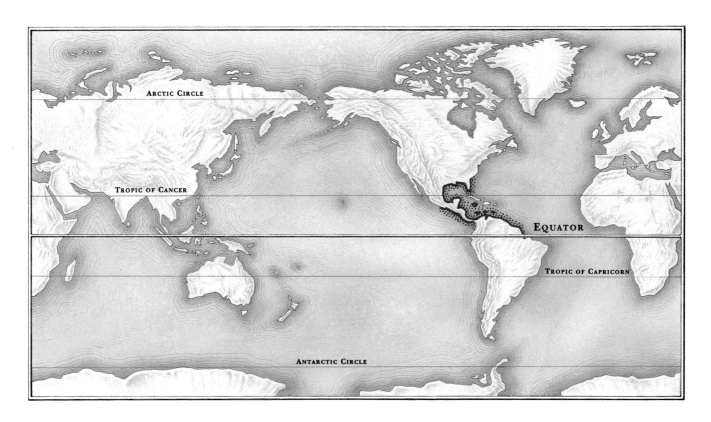

ARCTIC CIRCLE

TROPIC OF CANCER

EQUATOR

TROPIC OF CAPRICORN

ANTARCTIC CIRCLE

ROOSTERFISH

NEMATISTIUS PECTORALIS

GILL 1862

Other common names Pezgallo, papagallo.

Identifying features Upper body greenish black, sweeping black stripes across head and body, lower body gold and white. Maximum weight 56 kg (125 lb). Seven long ribbon-like elongations on first dorsal fin, body shape similar to amberjack.

Expected temperature range 21°C–30°C (70°F–86°F).

Typical location Just outside and in surf over sandy bottom with bait fish congregation. Often in shallow water 1 m (3 ft).

Fishing methods Slow trolling small bait fish—mullet, jacks, chub mackerel in 2–5 m (6–15 ft) water. Trolling lures—minnows, feathers, small plastic lures. Casting lures—minnows, spoons, poppers. Drifting with live bait from boat—mullet, chub mackerel, small jacks. Casting live and natural bait from shore. Fly casting after teasing with plug.

Typical fighting characteristics Fast runs to deeper water, fight deep as possible. Occasionally jump. Small fish run to shore shallows.

Major sportfishing areas Eastern Pacific from Baja California, Mexico to Chile and Galapagos, Ecuador, Costa Rica.

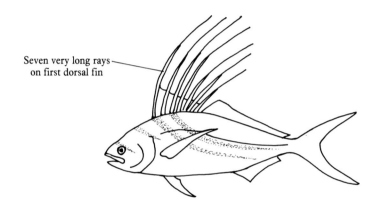

Seven very long rays on first dorsal fin

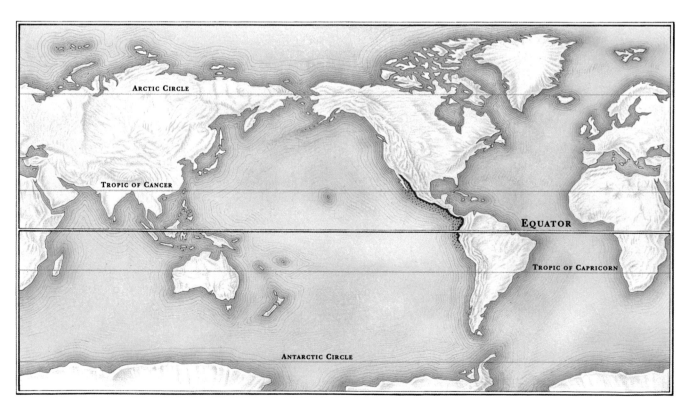

BONEFISH

ALBULA SPP.

VULPES LINNAEUS 1758

Other common names Banana fish, o'io.

Identifying features Upper body blue-grey silver, lower body and sides brilliant silver. Maximum weight up to 10 kg (22 lb). Underslung jaw, single dorsal fin, cylindrical body.

Expected temperature range 22°C–30°C (72°F–86°F).

Typical location Shallow coral sand flats and lagoons, deep water on reef dropoffs.

Fishing methods Fly casting, spin casting small lures, casting bait—shrimp, conch and crab. Bottom fishing outside reefs and shoreline.

Typical fighting characteristics Once hooked, gives fast zipping runs before being brought to capture or release.

Major sportfishing areas Atlantic: Florida, Bermuda, Bahamas and other West Indian islands, Belize, Mexico, Venezuela, Brazil. Indo-Pacific: Mexico, Costa Rica, Panama, Hawaii, Tahiti, Christmas Island and other Pacific islands, Mauritius and other Indian Ocean islands, Madagascar and eastern Africa.

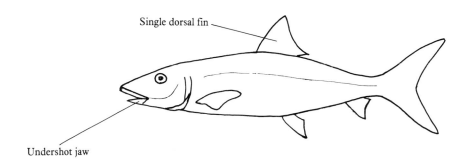

Single dorsal fin

Undershot jaw

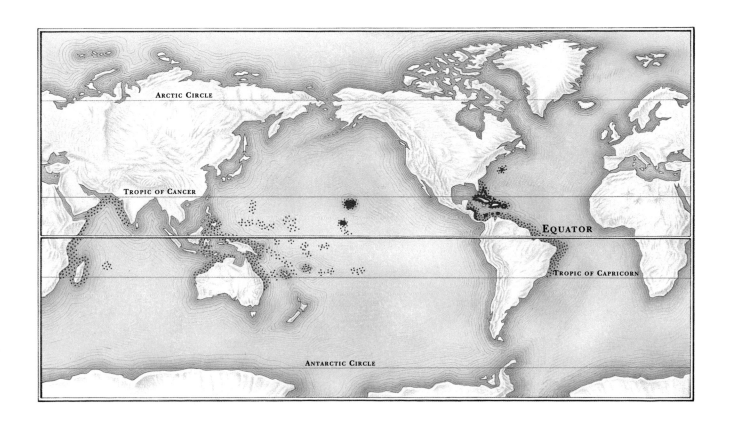

ARCTIC CIRCLE

TROPIC OF CANCER

EQUATOR

TROPIC OF CAPRICORN

ANTARCTIC CIRCLE

THE FUN FISH

QUEENFISH

SCOMBEROIDES COMMERSONNIANUS   *S. LYSAN*
LACAPEDE 1802   FORSKAL 1775

Other common names *S. commersonnianus:* largemouth queenfish; *S. lysan:* double spotted queenfish; *Both:* leatherskin, dart, skinny, lai.

Identifying features Upper body blue-green, lower body silver with golden tints. Flat silvery body, bluish green on back, shiny silver belly, large dark spots along body, blunt head, prominent lateral line, strong forked tail. Eating quality is fair, maximum weight 16 kg (35 lb).
S. commersonnianus has a single row of round spots above the lateral line. The usual number is between five and eight. *S. lysan* has a double row of spots, one row above and one row below the lateral line with five–eight spots in each row.

Expected temperature range 21°C–30°C (68°F–86°F).

Typical location Mouths of estuaries, around offshore mainland islands, rocks and inshore reefs. They feed actively at top or bottom of tide with most activity at low tide. Smaller related species hunt bait school over and along outside reefs. In Africa reported to move with whale sharks.

Fishing methods Trolling spoons, minnows, small plastic trolling lures and poppers. Casting spoons, minnows and poppers. When in feeding pattern can be taken on saltwater fly after teasing with hookless poppers.

Typical fighting characteristics A fast active spectacular jumping acrobat. Gives a performance that rivals the other great flat sides species, mahi mahi.

Major sportfishing areas Thailand, Philippines, Papua New Guinea, Hawaii, Indonesia, northern Australia, eastern Africa.

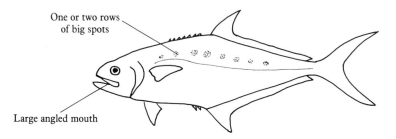

One or two rows of big spots

Large angled mouth

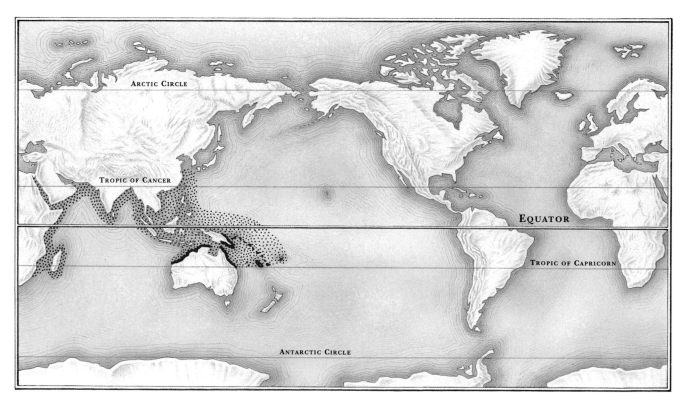

ARCTIC CIRCLE

TROPIC OF CANCER

EQUATOR

TROPIC OF CAPRICORN

ANTARCTIC CIRCLE

CLASSIFICATION

TARPON

ATLANTIC   INDO-PACIFIC

MEGALOPS ATLANTICUS   *M. CYPRINOIDES*

VALENCIENNES 1846   BROUSSONET 1782

Other common names Silver king, sabalo, ox-eye tarpon.

Identifying features Upper body greenish blue sometimes with golden tints, lower body silver. Maximum weight *M. atlanticus* 135 kg (300 lb), *M. cyprinoides* 13.5 kg (30 lb). Herring shape. Big silver scales. Single dorsal with long whip-like ray at base. Lower jaw slanted up and reaches beyond upper jaw.

Expected temperature range 19°C–30°C (66°F–86°F).

Typical location Taking air rolling on surface in channels, cuts, along shallow banks. In mangrove creeks and rivers. In brackish and salt water.

Fishing methods Fly casting. Spinning with lures. Trolling with plugs, spoons, feather jigs and natural baits. Drifting or at anchor with live or dead baits of mullet, crabs, shrimps, pintfish and other local species, particularly at night and early morning. The mouth is hard and the tarpon is often difficult to hook. Angler must wait until the tarpon's mouth is closed before striking.

Typical fighting characteristics One of the greatest piscatorial jumpers. The spectacular jumps are interspersed with surface and deep runs within the limitations of their habitat. A stubborn fighter even in shallow water. A big tarpon may resist for hours.

Major sportfishing areas East and west coast Florida, Bahamas, Mexico, Panama, Belize, Costa Rica, west Venezuela, west coast Africa, Gabon, Indo-Pacific, Australia, Papua New Guinea, Asia, East Africa.

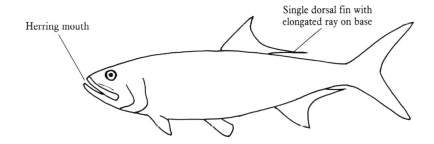

Herring mouth

Single dorsal fin with elongated ray on base

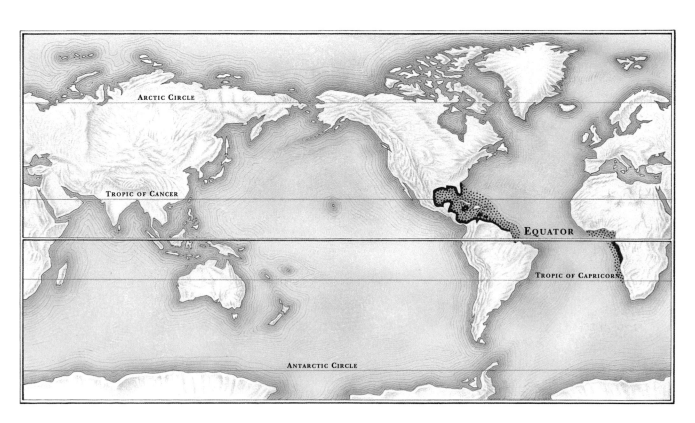

ARCTIC CIRCLE

TROPIC OF CANCER

EQUATOR

TROPIC OF CAPRICORN

ANTARCTIC CIRCLE

GARRICK

LICHIA AMIA
LINNAEUS 1758

Other common names Leerfish.

Identifying features Upper body blue–grey or brown, lower body silvery white. Maximum weight 36 kg (80 lb). Flat-sided body with prominent sinuous lateral line. Spiny non-membrane first dorsal. No spots or blotches on body.

Expected temperature range 15°C–25°C (59°F–77°F).

Typical location Inshore around rocks and beach along surf. Rounding up to feed on mullet and sardines, bluefish.

Fishing methods Drifting with live bait, mullet, sardines, pilchards. Casting lures, spoons, sliced metal, minnows. Eating quality fair.

Typical fighting characteristics This is a fast-running species that uses its body shape in the water to put pressure on line.

Major sportfishing areas South Africa, east, south and west coasts.

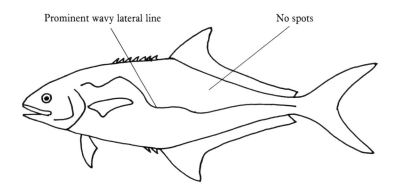

Prominent wavy lateral line   No spots

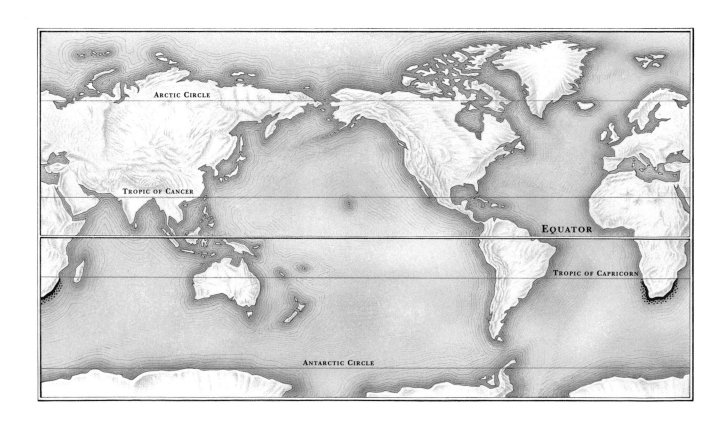

THREADFIN SALMON

POLYNEMUS SHERIDANI
MACLEAY

Other common names King salmon, king threadfin.

Identifying features Upper body yellow–grey, lower body silver, pectoral fins yellow–orange. Maximum weight 45 kg (100 lb). Five long filaments originating at throat. Head rounded with underslung jaw. Prominent lateral line. Powerful forked tail.

Expected temperature range 21°C–30°C (68°F–86°F).

Typical location In shallow water and muddy creek and river mouths. Often seen in schools at ebb slack tide alongside steep creek banks and mangrove snags. Seeks food with its filament fins.

Fishing methods Trolling lures, minnows, plugs, particularly at low neap tides. Casting lures, minnows, plugs at dawn. Drifting or at anchor with live bait—mullet, shrimp, crab. Often taps the bait or lure either with filaments or head before taking it in its mouth. Hook-up comes from lifting the rod tip after the second 'tap'. Fly casting. Eating quality excellent.

Typical fighting characteristics Combines fast running in all directions with spectacular jumping. An exciting fighter that never gives up and uses all available water across the surface and as deep as possible in its environment. Uses snags and mangroves to its benefit to break off. This is a great, challenging fish.

Major sportfishing areas Tropical Australia, Papua New Guinea, Asiatic islands. Other smaller threadfin species occur in Hawaii and many Pacific and Indian Ocean islands. Another great threadfin occurs on the Asiatic mainland.

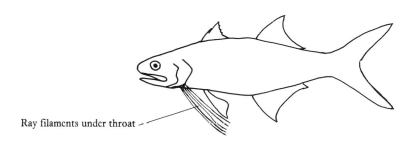

Ray filaments under throat

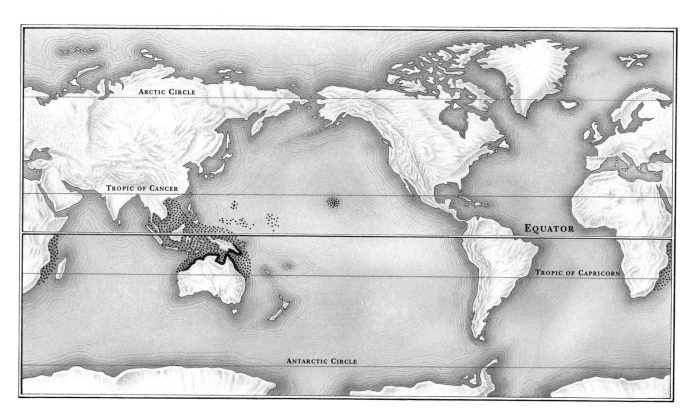

S A L M O N

SALMO SALAR   *ONCHORHYNCHUS TSHAWYTSCHA*   *O. KETA*   *O. KISUTCH*   *O. GORBUSCHA*   *O. NERKA*

LINNAEUS 1758   WALBAUM 1792   WALBAUM 1792   WALBAUM 1792   WALBAUM 1772   WALBAUM 1792

Other common names *S. salar:* Atlantic salmon (major species); *O. tshawytscha:* king salmon, chinook salmon (major species); *O. keta:* chum salmon; *O. kisutch:* coho salmon (major species); *O. gorbuscha:* pink salmon; *O. nerka:* sockeye salmon.

Identifying features Upper body bronze with red or black spots (darker at spawning time), lower body silver. Small fleshy second dorsal (adipose) fin, trout-shaped body (though spots on body do not generally have circles around them as do trout). Jaws in males hooked (kype), particularly at approach of spawning. Maximum weight Atlantic salmon 49 kg (110 kg), king salmon 60 kg (130 lb), chum salmon and coho salmon 16 kg (35 lb), pink salmon and sockeye salmon 7 kg (15 lb).

Expected temperature range 0°C–20°C (32°F–68°F).

Typical location Open ocean near shoreline, estuaries and river mouths. In rivers, anodromous species, that is, migrates and returns for spawning. Under birds or surface-feeding bait, or proven trolling areas, tide rips. *Atlantic salmon:* Northern Atlantic, Canada, Iceland, British Isles, Norway. *King salmon, coho salmon and pink salmon:* Northern Japan to California. *Chum salmon:* Sea of Japan to California. *Sockeye salmon:* Japan to California.

Fishing methods Fly casting, trolling with two hooked baits, whole or cut herring, candlefish, anchovies, sardines. Casting with trolling lures, with spoons and plastic squid and shiny flashing plugs and minnows. Casting with bait (salmon eggs). Trolling with flies or flies and spinner combined. Eating quality superb.

Typical fighting characteristics Tough active fighter with classic jumps. A highly sought prize on all tackle, as well as traditional fly. A most important angling challenge.

Major sportfishing areas Atlantic Canada, Greenland, Maine, Ireland, British Isles, Norway, Sweden, Pacific Alaska, Canada, Taiwan, Japan, Russia, Oregon, northern California.

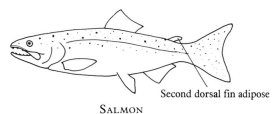

Second dorsal fin adipose

SALMON

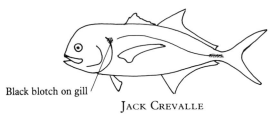

Black blotch on gill

JACK CREVALLE

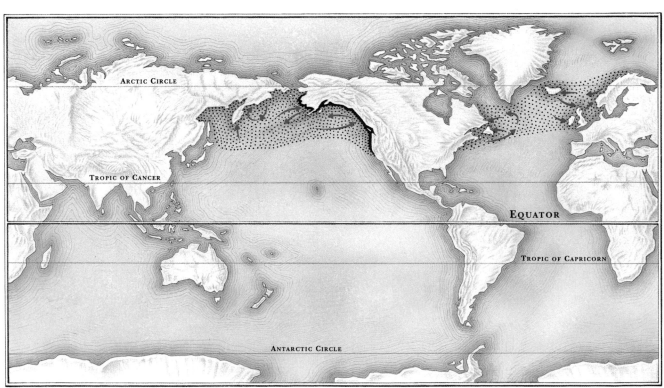

ARCTIC CIRCLE

TROPIC OF CANCER

EQUATOR

TROPIC OF CAPRICORN

ANTARCTIC CIRCLE

ATLANTIC CARIBBEAN JACKS AND TREVALLIES

CARANX HIPPOS   *C. LATUS*   *ALECTIS CILIARIS*
LINNAEUS 1766   AGASSIZ 1829   BLOCH 1788

Other common names *C. hippos:* jack crevalle; *C. latus:* horse-eye jack; *Alectis ciliaris:* African pompano, threadfin trevally.

Identifying features *Jack crevalle:* Upper body blue–grey, lower body silver. Black spot on base of pectoral fin. Black spot on operculum. Small scaled area on otherwise scaleless area on body in front of ventral fins. Juveniles striped with black. Maximum size 30 kg (70 lb). *Horse-eye jack:* Upper body blue–grey, lower body silver. Area in front of pelvic fins covered with scales. Maximum size 14 kg (30 lb). *African pompano:* Upper body green–blue, lower body silver. Four to six thread fins (long in juveniles, short in adults) on front rays of second dorsal and anal fins. Maximum size 28 kg (60 lb).

Expected temperature range 21°C–30°C (70°F–86°F).

Typical location Around reefs and rocky islands, over ridges and in passes and openings between reefs. Around peaks on outside of outer reefs. In channels and lagoons. These species range from shore lines to outermost reefs. *Jack crevalle:* Western Atlantic, Novia Scotia to Uruguay, West Indies. *Horse-eye jack:* New Jersey to Brazil, Bermuda, Bahamas, West Indies. *African pompano:* World-wide occasionally with allied species in tropical oceans.

Fishing methods Trolling dead natural bait: ballyhoo, mullet, squid with or without plastic skirts. Trolling live bait—any fish, including mullet, chub mackerel, yellowtail scad. Trolling lures, spoons, hard and soft plastic plugs, minnows, poppers, plastic squid, feather jigs. At drift or anchor—deep jigging, lead jigs, candy bars, metal jigs. Casting lures from rocky shoreline and surf—minnows, poppers, spoons (lures should be retrieved fast). Casting lures from boats drifting or at anchor—minnows, poppers, flashy metal lures. Fly casting with chumming. Jack crevalle and horse-eye jack have dark flesh and are not popular eating. African pompano is good to eat.

Typical fighting characteristics One of the toughest deep fighters that never gives up. The fish often beats anglers by heading for obstructions to cause breakoff.

Major sportfishing areas *Jack crevalle:* Western Atlantic coast USA, Florida, Gulf of Mexico, West Indies. *Horse-eye jack:* Right through Atlantic and Caribbean from USA to Brazil, Bermuda, Bahamas, West Indies. *African pompano:* Worldwide, Florida, Bahamas, West Indies, Tahiti, Fiji, tropical Australia, Papua New Guinea, Philippines, Kenya, Mauritius, Madagascar.

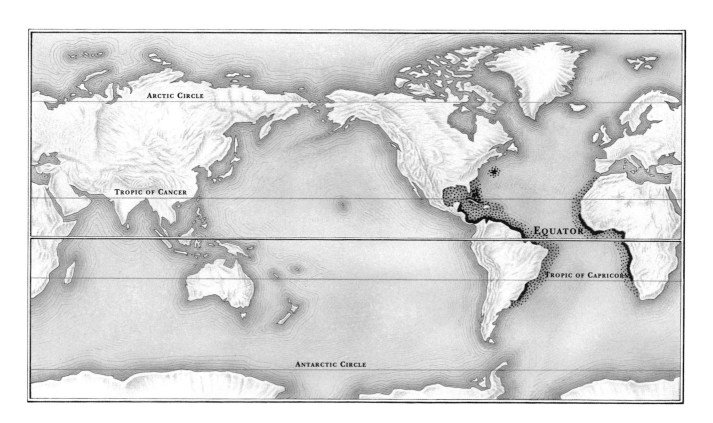

INDO-PACIFIC JACKS & TREVALLIES

CARANX IGNOBILIS   *C. SEXACIATUS*   *C. MELAMPYGUS*
FORSKAL 1775   QUOY & GUIMARD 1824   CURVIER & VALENCIENNES 1833

Other common names *C. ignobilis:* giant trevally, ulua, turrum; *C. sexaciatus:* big eye trevally, ulua, turrum; *C. melampygus:* bluefin trevally, ulua, turrum.

Identifying features *Giant trevally:* Upper body dark grey to olive-green, lower body silver. Oval patch of scales in middle of otherwise scaleless area in front of ventral fins. Blunt head. No spot on gill cover or at base of pectoral fin. Maximum size 80 kg (180 lb). *Big eye trevally:* Upper body dusky grey-greenish blue, lower body silver. Spot on operculum. Maximum size 9 kg (20 lb). *Bluefin trevally:* Upper body turquoise-blue with blue or black spots and electric blue fins and tail, lower body silver. Sloping head, second dorsal and anal long. Maximum size 50 kg (110 lb).

Expected temperature range 21°C–30°C (70°F–86°F).

Typical location Around reefs and rocky islands, over ridges and in passes and openings between reefs. Around peaks on outside of outer reefs. In channels and lagoons. These species range from shorelines to outermost reefs.

Fishing methods Trolling dead natural bait—ballyhoo, mullet, squid with or without plastic skirts. Trolling live bait—any fish including mullet, chub mackerel, yellowtail scad. Trolling lures, spoons, hard and soft plastic plugs, minnows, poppers, plastic squid, feather jigs. At drift or anchor: deep jigging, lead jigs, candy bars, metal jigs. Casting lures from rocky shoreline and surf: minnows, poppers, spoons (lures should be retrieved fast). Casting lures from boats drifting or at anchor—minnows, poppers, flashy metal lures. Fly casting with chumming. Giant and bluefin trevally are good eating; big eye trevally is fair eating.

Typical fighting characteristics One of the toughest deep fighters. The fish often head for obstructions to cause breakoff.

Major sportfishing areas *Giant trevally:* Indo-Pacific islands and continents from Hawaii and Marquesas through to East Africa, Kenya, Australia, Papua New Guinea. *Big eye trevally:* From Pacific coast of America to eastern coast of Africa, Kenya, particularly Hawaii, Philippines, Tahiti, Fiji, Papua New Guinea, Malaysia, Australia. *Bluefin trevally:* From Pacific coast of America to east coast of Africa, Philippines, Fiji, Tahiti, Australia, Mauritius, Indonesia, East Africa, Kenya.

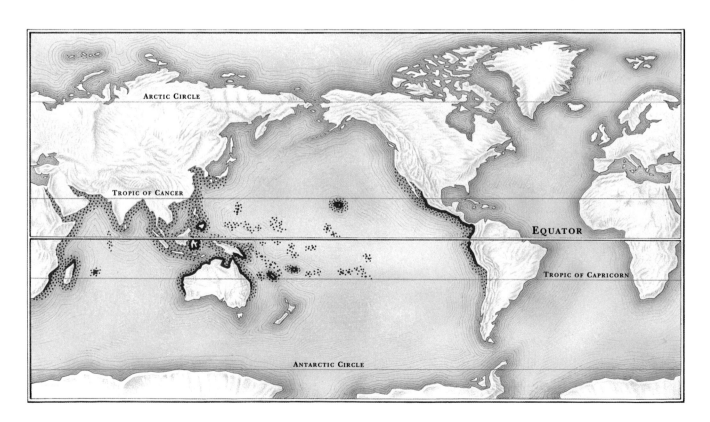

YELLOWTAIL

SERIOLA LALANDEI DORSALIS
GILL 1863

S. LALANDEI LALANDEI
CUVIER & VALENCIENNES 1833

S. LALANDEI AUEROVITTATA
SCHLEGEL 1844

Other common names *S. lalandei dorsalis:* California yellowtail; *S. lalandei lalandei:* southern yellowtail, cape yellowtail; *S. lalandei auerovittata:* asiatic yellowtail.

Identifying features Upper body blue-green (green in big fish), lower body yellowish white, tail and fins yellow. No finlets, single anal fin. Yellow tail and yellowish fins. Yellow stripe along the elongated body, low keel at junction of body and tail. Maximum weight 70 kg (150 lb).

Expected temperature range 18°C–24°C (64°F–75°F).

Typical location Close to shore and rocky islands. Sometimes over sand as they follow bait schools. Usually over rocks, reefs, peaks and plateaux. Under kelp paddys (California) and other flotsam.

Fishing methods Trolling dead natural bait—chub mackerel, kahawai, yellowtail scad, sardines, anchovy. Slow trolling, drifting or at anchor with live bait—chub mackerel, kahawai, yellowtail scad, sardines. Deep trolling with lures or baits deep or on deep trollers. Drifting or at anchor—deep jigging lead head jigs, candy bars, minnows, poppers when near surface. Trolling lures, spoons, feathers, hard or plastic head plugs. Fly casting with chum. Chum is effective for yellowtail. A hooked yellowtail brought to boat and tethered will often attract and hold others in a school. Eating quality good for all species.

Typical fighting characteristics A hard, deep fighter with several runs and dives. A tougher opponent than some of the other more attractive species. Big fish particularly will escape by diving for sea bed obstructions or kelp. It is often beneficial to allow bait to be swallowed and fish led by boat drifting or motoring slowly away from obstacles before striking hard and fighting with hard drag.

Major sportfishing areas *California yellowtail:* California, Mexico. *Southern yellowtail:* New Zealand, Australia, Lord Howe Island. *Cape yellowtail:* South Africa. *Asiatic yellowtail:* Asia, particularly Japan. Species follows bait schools from Atlantic to Indian Oceans in South Africa.

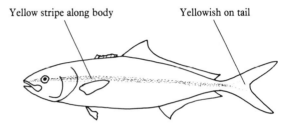

Yellow stripe along body   Yellowish on tail

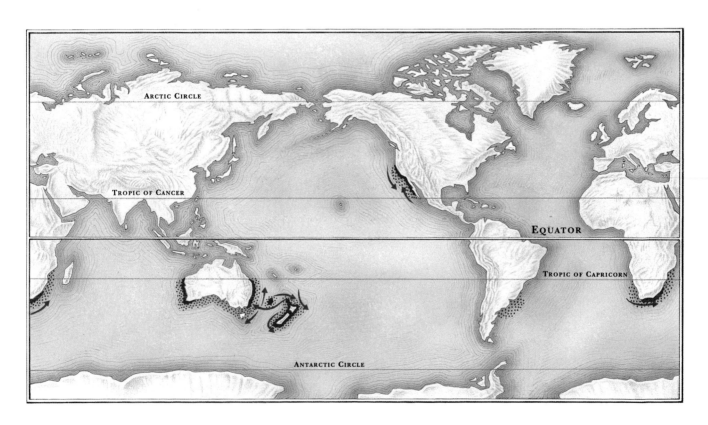

WHERE TO FIND THE FISH

BILLFISH

IDENTIFICATION: GENERAL

There is no more surefire way to get varying opinions from fishermen than by asking the simple question: 'What is it?' Differences of opinion, even by scientists, continue even in this modern era of communication and information. This is particularly true as fishermen move further offshore and discover new fisheries.

There has been long-standing controversy on the number of species of billfish in the world's oceans. Scientists have disagreed with fishermen and taxidermists about some species, including the presence of blue marlin in Indo-Pacific waters. In the 1960s scientists everywhere finally agreed that the Atlantic offers two species of marlin—blue marlin and white marlin—whereas the Indo-Pacific produces three—blue, black and striped. To these add Atlantic and Indo-Pacific sailfish, broadbill swordfish and short-nose spearfish of the Pacific and Indian Oceans, and the long-nose spearfish of the Atlantic, plus the spearfish in the Mediterranean, and identification can provide a continuing basis for fiery debate.

The argument can be further spiced by discussing variations between juvenile and adult, midget and

A *black marlin almost ready for wiring. Photo: Peter Goadby.*

monster, plus variations in build and outline. Color is not a big help in identification except in adding further controversy as the color of all billfish varies between live and dead fish, between wet and dry, between lit up and the dark bronze, between tropical and temperate, all evident at various times.

It is incredible to reflect that English-speaking scientists recognized the existence of blue marlin in the Pacific and Indian Oceans as recently as 1954. Even when scientific papers were published, some, particularly in areas far from where these super fish live and terrorize the bait fish, tuna and squid schools, disputed classification and identification.

It was scientifically neat to have white and blue marlin in the Atlantic, and striped and black marlin in the Indo-Pacific, but nature is not always neat, and added one species, so there are three, not two, in the Indo-Pacific Oceans.

Additional confusion was created by experienced fishermen and the taxidermists who recognized species. These practical people had unique opportunities to work with all the giant fish in life and action, opportunities not often available to scientists. The Pacific fishermen's name 'silver marlin' perfectly described the vibrant colors of black marlin in the hot tropical currents. These marlin

The action and the luminous colors of this hooked Atlantic blue marlin at St Thomas, Virgin Islands, show why it is so keenly sought by sportfishermen. Photo: Darrell Jones.

in the vibrant warm-water colors were not recognized as the same fish in their slate, drab, colder-water coloration.

Billfish sometimes show bronze tones in varying degrees. They sometimes show neon colors and sometimes very little color, adding further to the difficulty of identification. Even the color of the stripes varies. Sometimes stripes show on billfish that are usually non-striped. These stripes, so evident on some billfish in life, may disappear by the time the fish is weighed, so anglers wonder whether their eyes are deceiving them and scientists then question the angler's color observations.

Awareness of these problems makes it easy to understand the queries of practical and practising fishermen. The arguments go on, and there is the chance of further confusion, particularly in the Atlantic, where some of the great Indo-Pacific Ocean wanderers ignore the neat borders envisaged for them. On the ocean there are no borders and Japanese longline fishermen, the masters of the high seas, have even recorded black marlin from Cuban waters.

Standard scientific measurements assist scientists with their identification keys to separate species. These can include length or characteristics of fins and proportions that may vary as the fish gets bigger and heavier.

It is now generally accepted by scientists that in the Indian and Pacific Oceans there are six billfish species. They are:

- Broadbill swordfish (*Xiphias gladius*) Linnaeus 1758
- Sailfish (*Istiophorus platypterus*) Shaw & Nodder 1792
- Short-nose spearfish (*Tetrapturus angustirostris*) Tanaka 1915
- Three marlin: blue (*Makaira mazara*) Jordan & Snyder 1901; black (*Makaira indica*) Cuvier 1832; striped (*Tetrapterus audax*) Phillipi 1887

In the Atlantic and Caribbean the species are:

- Blue marlin (*Makaira nigricans*) Lacapede 1802
- White marlin (*Tetrapturus albidus*) Poey 1860
- Sailfish (*Istiophorus albicans*) Latreille 1804
- Long-nose spearfish (*Tetrapturus pfleugeri*) Robins & de Sylva 1963
- Mediterranean spearfish (*Tetrapturus belone*) Rafinesque 1810

It is important to realize the variations in body shape and proportions that come with age and condition. Photographs of fish on a weigh station or even on the deck with some fins depressed do not give a real impression of body thickness, or that billfish (other than broadbill and to a lesser extent blue marlin) are oval, not round, in body shape. Sailfish are even more flat-sided and so weigh less, much less than the weight indicated by looking at them side on. Sailfish have appreciable girth only in full adult fish. When photographing, pull all fins so they show, taking care that the hands do no show in the photographs.

While it is fairly easy to identify the broadbill swordfish, the sailfish and the spearfish, it is much harder to correctly identify the marlins, particularly as juvenile and full adults. Black marlin, for instance, can normally be identified by their immovable pectoral fins, but this does not apply to black marlin of less than around 55 kg (110 lb).

At this weight or less it is often possible to move the pectoral fins alongside the body, although they will still not lie flat, as will the pectorals of white, blue and striped marlin. For this reason observing the shape of the pectorals is just as important as their folding characteristics, as sometimes *rigor mortis* can create a false impression. Black marlin pectorals are aerofoil and sickle-shaped, whereas other marlin have pectorals that are flat, more evenly tapered and less sickle. Fully adult striped marlin heavier than 140 kg (300 lb), resemble blue marlin in body shape and proportions, thus adding to confusion.

The dorsal and anal fins of all marlin, sailfish and spearfish fold down into streamlining grooves. Broadbill swordfish in excess of 24 kg (50 lb) have immovable fins. At less than this weight they may be movable to some degree.

The shape of tails assists in identification. Sailfish tails are veed, blue and black marlin symmetrically sickle, striped marlin straight-edged and angled at the tips. Familiarity with the shape and weight of bills and the mandible (lower jaw) also helps in correct identification, which is much better than simply hoping the naming is correct for record claims.

MARLIN

The great fisherman, author Zane Grey, wrote millions of words that stirred the imagination and brought scenes of land and sea to vivid life. But for fishermen, three words of his never fail to start the adrenalin, to relive the action. Those words are: 'There he is!'

For Zane Grey, as for most fishermen, the words to excite full drama should be 'there *she* is'. Zane Grey was always after the biggest and heaviest of the fishes, and in marlin they are the females.

Those three words mean much to every marlin fisherman; they help put marlin on the angling peak and keep them there. They bring back in memory the following wavery, shadowy, brown shape that suddenly lights up, dons vibrant colors as it viciously slashes at bait or lure or fades away into the blue depths without

a strike. They bring back memories of sickle tails riding the ocean swells or cruising slowly on top with the tail and sometimes an erect dorsal fin slicing the surface ahead of the tail to give a guide to the size and species of the fish.

There are memories of crash strikes, where in a blur of action, a bait or lure disappears in a huge hole in the water, so the skilled eagle eyes of experienced fishermen do not have a chance to register even a millisecond of the bait or lure-taking action. There is only time to shout 'STRIKE' so the anglers can go to the rod. Those words, 'there he is' also describe an empty ocean and sky with boat hooked up, backing up or running a fish, a fish deep and unseen, then suddenly a bill, a head, shoulders, and the whole fish is clear of water and

A small Great Barrier Reef black marlin turns a kawa kawa bait to swallow it head first. Photo: Mike Kenyon.

A KEY TO BILLFISH IDENTIFICATION

THE FOLLOWING KEYS HELP EVEN WHEN THE FISH IS BRIEFLY ALONGSIDE THE BOAT FOR TAG AND RELEASE. THE SHAPE OF THE DORSAL AND THE LENGTH AND DIAMETER OF THE BILL ARE HELPFUL CHARACTERISTICS FOR TAGGING IDENTIFICATION. IT IS OF COURSE MUCH BETTER TO RELEASE THE BILLFISH EVEN WHEN NOT SURE OF ITS IDENTIFICATION, RATHER THAN TO GAFF AND KILL IT JUST TO FIND OUT WHAT IT IS.

WHAT TO LOOK FOR:

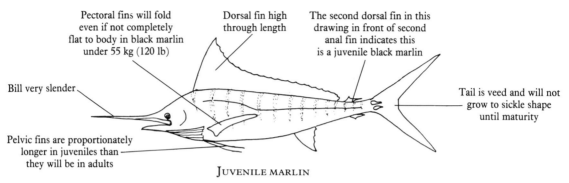

Pectoral fins will fold even if not completely flat to body in black marlin under 55 kg (120 lb)

Dorsal fin high through length

The second dorsal fin in this drawing in front of second anal fin indicates this is a juvenile black marlin

Bill very slender

Tail is veed and will not grow to sickle shape until maturity

Pelvic fins are proportionately longer in juveniles than they will be in adults

JUVENILE MARLIN

Broadbill
(WORLDWIDE, ATLANTIC AND INDO-PACIFIC)

Long, flat oval jaw; in adults fins immovable; first dorsal high, same shape as upper lobe of tail; body compressed into flat keel at junction of body and tail.

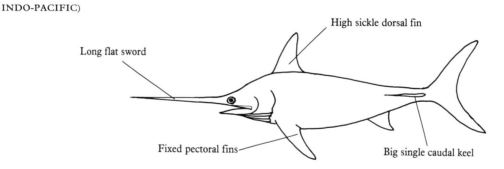

High sickle dorsal fin

Long flat sword

Fixed pectoral fins

Big single caudal keel

Sailfish
(ATLANTIC, INDO-PACIFIC)

Slender round bill; straight mandible (lower jaw); very high dorsal (almost length of body); dorsal highest in middle; tail slightly veed; pectoral fins very long, lateral line clearly visible.

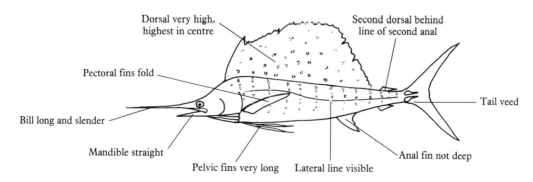

Dorsal very high, highest in centre

Second dorsal behind line of second anal

Pectoral fins fold

Tail veed

Bill long and slender

Mandible straight

Pelvic fins very long

Lateral line visible

Anal fin not deep

Black marlin
(INDO-PACIFIC)

Heavy round bill; down-curved heavy mandible (lower jaw); low rounded dorsal less than half body depth; pectoral fins curved and aerofoil in section—fixed (immovable) in black marlin more than 55 kg (120 lb); second dorsal *in front* of start of second anal fin; anal fin depth about equal to height of dorsal; tail semicircular; single lateral line visible in most weights, particularly juveniles and jumbo size marlin.

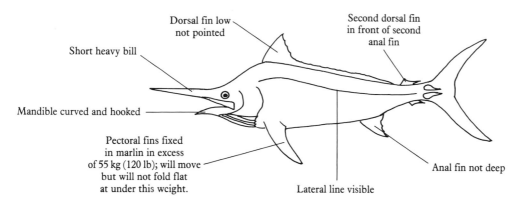

Dorsal fin low not pointed

Second dorsal fin in front of second anal fin

Short heavy bill

Mandible curved and hooked

Pectoral fins fixed in marlin in excess of 55 kg (120 lb); will move but will not fold flat at under this weight.

Anal fin not deep

Lateral line visible

Striped marlin
(INDO-PACIFIC)

Slender round bill; long straight mandible (lower jaw); high dorsal—first three high rays almost equal height; dorsal about equal to body depth—not so obvious when larger than 120 kg (264 lb); pectoral fins tapered and flat; second dorsal behind start of second anal fin (anal fin deep); tail slightly veed, cut away at tips of both lobes of tail; flesh above eye shows eye when skin is removed; single lateral line clearly visible.

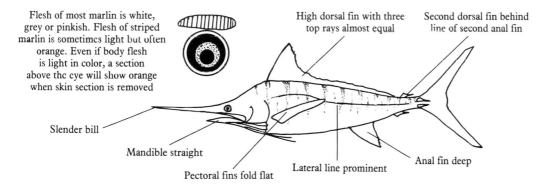

Flesh of most marlin is white, grey or pinkish. Flesh of striped marlin is sometimes light but often orange. Even if body flesh is light in color, a section above the eye will show orange when skin section is removed

High dorsal fin with three top rays almost equal

Second dorsal fin behind line of second anal fin

Slender bill

Mandible straight

Pectoral fins fold flat

Lateral line prominent

Anal fin deep

White marlin
(ATLANTIC)

Slender round bill; straight mandible (lower jaw); dorsal high and rounded—tapers to rear from 9th ray onwards; anus close to anal fin—less than half depth of anal fin; second dorsal slightly backward of start of second anal; lateral line visible.

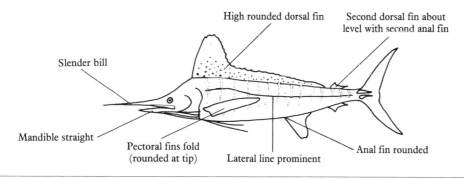

High rounded dorsal fin

Second dorsal fin about level with second anal fin

Slender bill

Mandible straight

Pectoral fins fold (rounded at tip)

Lateral line prominent

Anal fin rounded

A Key to Billfish Identification

Continued

Blue marlin
(ATLANTIC,
INDO-PACIFIC)

Moderately heavy round bill; slightly curved mandible (lower jaw); medium high dorsal; pointed dorsal about three-quarters of body depth; pectoral fins tapered and flat; second dorsal behind line of start of second anal fin; anal fin medium depth; tail strongly semicircular; lateral line not visible in adults. Atlantic blue marlin has as many as three or more chain links. Pacific blue marlin has single chain link and partially single lateral line.

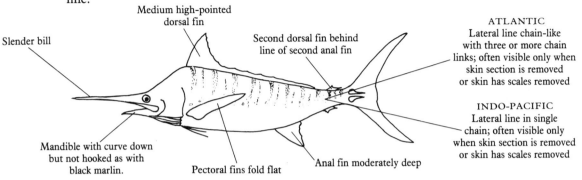

Short-nose
spearfish
(INDO-PACIFIC)

Very short round bill—not much longer than straight mandible (lower jaw); dorsal long and high, highest at front, rounded at tail; short pectoral; anus separated from anal fin by approximately length of depth of anal fin; tail veed.

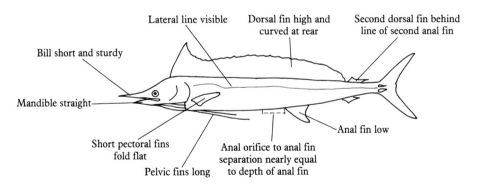

Long-nose
spearfish
(ATLANTIC)

Slender round bill; straight mandible (lower jaw); from 15th ray dorsal long and high, rounded at rear, highest at front; short back to tail; rounded pectoral; tail veed.

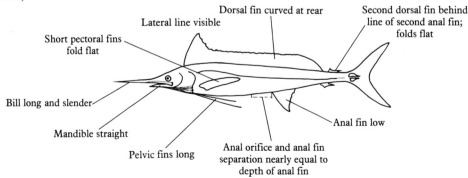

The camera catches the instant that marlin, such as this Kona striped marlin, leave the hole in the water. Photo: James Watt.

part of the sky. The involuntarily shouted words describe when the fish has turned blue water into opal froth and white spray, with the fish jumping, tail walking and changing direction. The fish so much part of the sea becomes part of the sky.

'There he is' can be the skipper's words for a marlin sighted down in the clear water and for the leader to be taken as the fish comes closer to the boat for capture or tag and release.

No fish creates more excitement than marlin; no other fish has gained more respect, is instinctively thought of for tag and release and is more important to the economy of recreational fishing ports, fishing destinations and sportfishing generally.

In the Atlantic the feisty white marlin—the jumping jack—and the superfast, supertough, in all sizes from midget to monster Atlantic blue marlin are the two species that have created industries of boat building, bait catching, tackle manufacturing, magazine publishing, accommodation, travel, taxidermy, photography and fishing clothing right through to fishermen's polarizing glasses.

In the Pacific and Indian Oceans, three marlin species create and support those industries. The Pacific blue marlin, the black marlin and the striped marlin are all top fish. As in the Atlantic, the widespread ocean-wandering blues are exciting fish in all sizes, from lightweight aggressive, needle-billed speedsters to the perfectly proportioned, maximum-size female giants. These are the heaviest and biggest of all the marlins recorded commercially. They seem to be even bigger and heavier than their Atlantic relatives.

The striped marlin, the Indo-Pacific cousin of the Atlantic white marlin, is the smallest and lightest of the three Pacific species, growing to a maximum of around 250 kg (550 lb). If the striped marlin is the Grand National competitor of the marlins and the blue marlin the champion Cup and Derby winners, the third Pacific marlin, the black, is the angry rhinoceros of the ocean. It is found in rocky coastline waters right along the cliffs and headlands as well as in the expected marlin waters, the deep water. Some black marlin become local fish and stay in an area even when the water cools lower than the usual temperature minimum for this species.

Marlin are shown by tag and release to migrate or wander over long distances and many of the Pacific black marlin have been proven by tag and release and subsequent recaptures to have called Australia home. Microscopic larval black marlin have been taken in Bongo nets and other plankton trawls outside the Outer Reefs near Lizard Island. They substantiate reports of black marlin sighted spawning in the Great Barrier Reef area of the Coral Sea.

It seems logical that after a year or two in those waters the black marlin begin their migrations. Marlin tagged in the Cairns–Lizard Island fishery have been recovered from a 180-degree radius of their breeding area, south along Australia's east coast and to New Zealand, north and east around Papua New Guinea and east at least as far as Kiribas, south of Hawaii. Small black marlin tagged off New South Wales have been recovered almost back at the latitude in which most of the tagging of the adults has been carried out. In the Great Barrier Reef fishery, more than 90 per cent of the marlin hooked are released to continue their life cycle and give a worthwhile number of tags and releases for indicative data on migration and growth.

Tagging in the Atlantic and eastern Pacific and at Kona in Hawaii also shows that all the marlin species wander and migrate and appear to have regular schedules to return. Many of the recaptures are a year or annual cycle near the point of capture and tag and release.

The Tuna Club at Avalon, Santa Catalina was founded after Dr C. F. Holder landed a 92-kg (183-lb) bluefin tuna in June 1898. The emphasis at the Tuna Club changed from tuna to marlin as the great schools of surface feeding tuna gradually disappeared and anglers tasted the excitement and challenge of fishing for marlin worldwide. Ernest Llewellyn caught the first marlin, a striped, on rod and reel in 1903. This first fish of 63 kg (125 lb) opened up a new world of sportfishing that spread to warm waters in most parts of our globe.

Australia was the scene of the first black marlin capture on rod and reel when Dr Mark Lidwell successfully landed a small black marlin of around 40 kg (80 lb) at Seal Rocks near Port Stephens in 1910. The skeleton of this 190-cm (6 ft 3.5-in) marlin is in the Australian Museum. Marlin have formed the basis of the exciting sportfishing industry in all oceans wherever the warm clean ocean waters and other natural environ-

mental factors and access combine to bring man and great fish together. The continuing refinement of fishing tackle is in itself recognition of the stamina, speed and tenacity of marlin; they are indeed VIFs (Very Important Fish).

Marlin, particularly Indo-Pacific black and striped marlin, are taken in water as shallow as 9.2 metres (5 fathoms) close inshore as well as their expected wide offshore environment of 55 metres (30 fathoms) and out over the ocean's depths.

It seems hard to believe that black and striped marlin up to 90 kg (200 lb) have been taken by anglers with live bait from rocky headlands. The combination of shape of headlands, deep water close in, and the warm water of the tropical ocean currents pushed by current and wind right inshore has opened up a whole new challenge for land-based gamefishing. In this fishing there is no chance of rocks 'backing-up' to assist line recovery.

The marlin's usual environments are reefs, peaks and canyons in water depths deeper than 55 metres (30 fathoms) out to the 180-metre (about 100-fathom) dropoff from the continental shelf and other deeper edges and dropoffs. These are the bottom features that are most productive and are home for the bait schools, attracted by the food plankton in the upwellings. The combination of the bottom features combined with temperature differences, warm current edges, warm current eddies and upwellings are the marlin 'hot spots'.

WHERE TO FIND THEM

Billfish hunt right into the coastline, as proven by rod and reel captures of black marlin, striped marlin and sailfish onshore from the rocky headlands in Australia and South Africa. Success in boat fishing usually comes in offshore water of 55 metres (30 fathoms) or deeper. In most areas other than Cairns, where the big blacks feed and congregate along the outside reefs, the heaviest marlin are generally caught over ridges in depths of 55

metres (30 fathoms) or more with 180 metres (100 fathoms) an important depth for striped, black and blue marlin along the continental shelf and its canyons.

Marlin fisheries are associated with some of the most beautiful islands and land areas in the world. Hawaii, Puerto Rico, Australia's Great Barrier Reef, the Bahamas, Virgin Islands, New Zealand, Florida and Mexico would be popular tourist destinations even without their great

An airborne black marlin clears the Coral Sea. Photo: Paul Murray.

marlin fisheries. These and other less photogenic marlin fishing areas owe much to the attractions of these great fish.

All marlin species can be fished with a variety of methods. Some methods are more productive than others and vary in the various hot spots.

Because of their preferred temperature ranges, the best marlin fishing occurs during the warm months. There are, however, some year-round, twelve-month fisheries sustained by warm currents and water temperatures.

The marlin lunar timetable varies from fishery to fishery. It is interesting to assess the best fishing periods not only by season or month, but by moon phase. Captain Laurie Woodbridge, the dean of the Cairns–Lizard Island charter fleet, while stressing the importance of the word 'generally' in regard to moon phases, says for Cairns Great Barrier Reef waters, 'Four days after the full moon you will see more black marlin than any other day in the month. Yes, right in the middle of the waning moon, there they are . . . Even though you get this flurry of action on the wane, it is generally (there's that word again) believed that the first quarter to the full and last quarter to the new are good fishing periods offshore.' Laurie Woodbridge stresses the importance of keeping records and studying the tide and moon when the big fish and numbers of fish are there. The keeping of a diary and study will show that fish tend to fall into a definite pattern through the year, and over the years in each area. In writing about marlin fishing off Cuba, Ernest Hemingway said, 'Marlin seem to feed best after the first quarter through to the full moon, to drop off during the last

The head wagging of this black marlin puts tremendous strain on the line. Photo: Sean Wallace.

quarter. They usually drop off in their feeding for a day or so when the moon is full.' Great Atlantic captains would have known and expected optimum results at certain moon phases and times in various areas. The peak times were known for their home waters by the great New Zealand captains Francis Arlidge, Jim Whitelaw, Pat Edmonds, Snooks Fuller, as do captains all round the world who fish successfully wherever they go. This

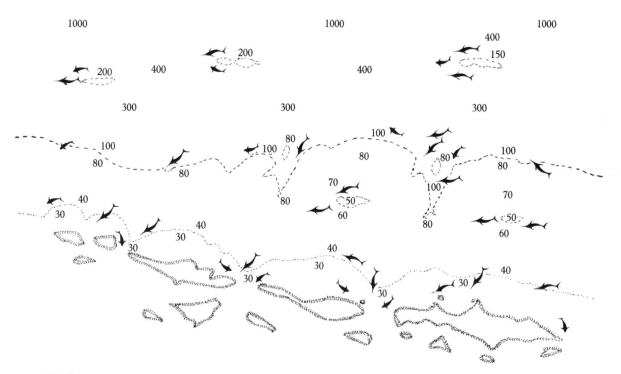

Where the big fish should be, outside the reefs.

A *Hawaiian marlin shows characteristics of both blue and black marlins. Photo: Captain Sadu Frehm.*

no doubt is one of the reasons why it is said, and generally seems true, that 10 per cent of the fishermen catch 90 per cent of the fish.

Despite the expected peaks of activity, much of the best, most pleasant and productive fishing takes place in non-peak times and at those associated with lower wind speeds. It often seems to blow harder at the time of spring tides, particularly those of the full moon.

In Hawaii and many other parts of the world it is believed that the best time to fish for marlin is in the week of the dark of the moon, particularly on days when there are at least two tide changes and preferably three in the fishing day. This theory is based on the logic that marlin will feed actively during the day if restricted by darkness in their night hunt. Graph reproductions of the data kept by the Hawaiian International Billfish Association shows the high incidence of strikes, even in the deepest of water, coinciding with the top or bottom of the tidal change.

There are of course, other natural factors that account for marlin activity and successful fishing.

The water temperatures that warrant trolling fall in a known range for billfish, tuna and other pelagics (that

is, 15°C–30°C; 59°F–86°F). It is a waste of time, fuel and money, fishing when water temperatures are below the minimum acceptable to the billfish, but out on the ocean there is only one rule—there is no such thing as 'one way' or 'always', and great fish have been found and taken when they should not have been there. These are fish that have apparently diverted from their normal wandering pattern to become local residents.

Best results come with trolling over known reefs, canyons and crevasses and along the 180-metre (100-fathom) or deeper shelf dropoffs. Even in depths of 360 metres (2000 or 3000 fathoms) most action and success comes at the top and bottom of the tide changes. Other factors influencing where to troll are the presence of bait schools, current lines, temperature edges, current upwellings, weed and flotsam lines, sea kelp clumps, logs, man-made FADS and any natural havens for bait fish. Like other marine animals, marlin kill and eat fish in great quantities, so the appearance and position of bait schools is important.

Logically much successful fishing is done in proximity to the presence of the bait schools. Skipjack tuna, yellowfin tuna, small bluefin and other tunas, mullet, garfish (ballyhoo), mackerels of all types and sizes from kingfish and tanguigue to the small striped, common mackerel of the world's oceans, pilchards and other small fish species are the dominant bait sources. In New Zealand, kahawai and trevally in their countless numbers and schools are the natural prey for the hungry marlin. It is logical to use live or dead baits of the same species on which marlin are feeding. Constant watchfulness of sea and sky for activity will show the presence of bait schools. Schools of squid are not always obvious unless recorded on depth sounders and sonar, yet they are an important factor in the presence and time frame for marlin. One of the advantages in running a depth sounder or fathometer when trolling is the location of deep-swimming bait species, and in fact, many baits are shown and indicate a prime fishing area even though nothing is showing on the surface to give this indication.

When operated by experienced crew, color sounders will indicate the type as well as the depth of bait schools. The giant pelagic billfishes not only feed on the bait fish usually found near the surface, but on reef-dwelling demersal species on the ocean bottom. Small sharks, broadbill swordfish and small marlin are all grist to the mill of this speedy peak predator in which the bill is a club, as well as a spear used in gaining food. Many marlin use their bill to stun their prey and then swallow it headfirst. Occasionally fish, particularly small tuna, clearly show having been speared when they are taken from the throat and stomach of caught marlin.

In some fisheries the time of day can be important in the strike rate, for instance off the Great Barrier Reef most action seems to come after 2.30 in the afternoon, although many mornings are also productive. In most areas it seems that strikes and action will come at any time through the day depending on factors other than time of day.

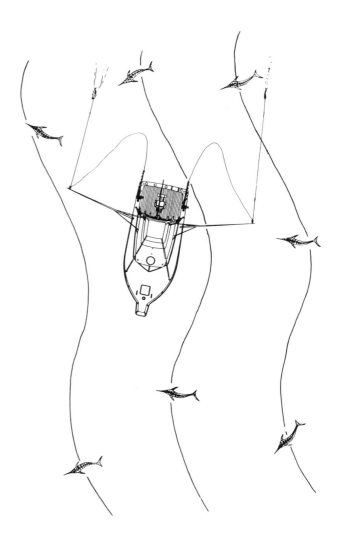

Marlin usually swim down swell so boats logically troll along the swells.

The dream of the thousands of anglers who fish Kona, Hawaii, each year—a 181 kg (400 lb) blue marlin showing its colors. Photo: John Jordan.

It is now widely accepted that the productive times and areas to fish natural baits are when and where the great gamefish are in concentration for various natural reasons. Of course lures will also produce billfish and tuna in these concentrations or pack conditions.

Conversely, it is widely accepted that lure fishing often produces when the billfish are scattered and travelling in very deep water or feeding well below the surface. Experienced, dedicated and successful bait skippers and crews will change to artificials in areas and at times when their experience and judgment indicate that it will be most productive.

SUCCESSFUL METHODS OF FISHING FOR MARLIN FROM BOATS

Marlin are caught from boats by the following methods:

- Trolling with dead natural baits
- Trolling with live natural baits
- Drifting with live or dead baits
- Fishing at anchor with live or dead baits
- Trolling with lures
- Casting live or dead baits.

How to troll with dead natural baits: The traditional world method for taking marlin since Ernest Llewellyn's 1903 first marlin capture was by trolling with dead natural baits—lures are the method of the 1990s. These are rigged in such a way that they skip or swim naturally. That first striped marlin and many marlin caught around the world fell to the attraction of flying fish. In Florida the skilled skippers and crews learned how to rig baits from mullet and their local ballyhoo (garfish). Their skill was introduced to potential marlin areas with baits rigged additionally on bonefish, small tuna and mackerel species. In New Zealand, kahawai were the number one bait. In Australia prior to the evolution of the Great Barrier Reef marlin fishery, bonito, yellowtail kingfish, mullet and garfish (ballyhoo) were the logical baits. Skipjack, bonito and small-toothed mackerel were the chosen baits in South American waters. In the prolific fisheries of Cabo San Lucas flying fish are a number one bait choice. The successful marlin areas of Venezuela and Costa Rica are fished with the full range of baits, from small mullet to skipjack and the local toothed mackerels.

The Atlantic coast of the USA has a big population of eels, so it was logical that much of the success in the active and prolific marlin fisheries of Atlantic City, Cape Hatteras and other major ports came from eel baits. Eels were also reproduced in plastic or soft rubber so anglers could troll eel baits even if natural eels were unavailable.

In all the marlin fisheries around the world, local pelagic fish of various sizes from 500 g (about 1 lb) in the green chub mackerels, along with sardines, scad, and goggle eyes, yellowtail scad that school so prolifically, through to the big baits such as skipjack and other small tuna species up to about 3 kg (7 lb), are regarded as ideal skipping baits and filleted strip baits. The development of the Cairns-Lizard Island black marlin fishery was part of the world trend towards the trolling of big (up to at least 10 kg or 22 lb) natural baits as a skipping or splashing bait. This was a natural development not only because of the availability of fish of this size and the action when rigged for trolling, but because of the size of the marlin being sought.

Giant blue marlin are taken on natural baits as well as lures in many hot spots. In the Atlantic, the east coast of the USA, Walkers Cay, Puerto Rico, the Virgin Islands, the Ivory Coast of Africa and the Azores produce fish from all methods. This is also the case in the Indian Ocean grounds of Mauritius and Western Australia and in the Pacific Ocean locations of Australia's east coast, New Zealand, to Micronesia and Polynesian islands, Hawaii, and Mexico where fishing methods are mixed,

T*he jumping jack white marlin shows why marlin gamefishing is so exciting. Photo: Gil Keech.*

particularly between lures and live baits. The general world trend for marlin is with trolled lures or slow trolled live bait.

The number of lines trolled with baits varies between heavy and light tackle. With medium and heavy tackle it is usual to troll only two baits, generally from outriggers. On lighter lines, four or even more small natural baits may be trolled in conjunction with a teaser. These small baits are often rigged with plastic squid, plastic skirted jigs, lure skirts or feather lures over the head of the bait. Strip baits cut from tunas, mahi mahi (dolphin fish), mackerels and wahoo are also popular and successful rigs, particularly for small billfish, again when rigged with plastic squid, hexheads or feather lures.

Moldcraft and other plastic squid and soft head pushers are ideal in hookless teaser daisy chains. Top skippers such as Hooker's Skip Smith and Peter Wright who seek light tackle billfish records around the world for their anglers may not troll natural baits or hooked lures until a marlin raises and follows the trolled teasers. The rigged and ready bait or lure on the chosen tackle category is then trolled in position alongside the teaser that has raised the fish so the hooked offering will be struck and give a chance for a hook-up. The teasers may be brought in as soon as the baits are in position so the fish's interest will be directed only at the bait.

The rigged baits trolled on heavy tackle for big fish are generally a tuna or mackerel-type fish rigged as a skipping bait with hook on top or just in front of the head, on the left outrigger, plus a much smaller swimming bait of some kind of mackerel or mullet on the right outrigger. The swimming bait is trolled further behind the boat than the skipping bait.

The action and depth at which swimming baits are trolled is often improved by rigging a ball or oval sinker on the leader loop under the head. Skipping baits are towed about 30 m (90 ft), and swimming baits about 40 m (120 ft) behind the boat, depending to some degree on size and sea conditions. Baits should be rigged so they do not spin, not only because of the unnatural appearance, but because of the extensive damage that can be done to lines. See also Points for Successful Bait Trolling, page 226.

The hook-up: Florida captain Bill Hatch provided the key to deliberate and successful angling for billfish. Through keen observation and understanding of their feeding action, this great captain realized that billfish generally hit their prey to stun it, and then pick it up to swallow head first. Examination of stomach contents and observation of feeding habits to this day support his original deductions. Captain Hatch instructed his anglers to give 'drop back', that is, to allow the line to run freely from the spool with only enough drag to prevent an overrun for at least a count of ten. At this time, if a pause indicated that the marlin or other billfish had taken the bait to swallow it head first, the angler would increase his drag and immediately strike and, hopefully, hook the fish. With this knowledge his anglers were able to catch previously rarely or accidentally hooked billfish. Bill Hatch's drop back technique is now used with slight variations in bait trolling right around the world. Recognition of the need and benefit of the drop back also assisted in live bait and dead bait fishing on the drift, slow trolling or at anchor.

In the Cairns–Lizard Island fishery, as in some others, when fishing only two lines, depending on wind conditions, line is allowed to trail along the surface of the water to act as an automatic drop back. Some skippers gun the boat to help anglers hook up immediately this bag of line becomes taut and line is running from the reel. Others prefer the angler to judge when to strike with the advice of captain and crew. They wait until the fish is running definitely with the bait and thus give more time before hook-up. Both methods are effective, but the latter is generally more beneficial, particularly if the marlin are not feeding voraciously and may be striking at the bait to kill for some reason other than the dictates of hunger.

Angling history credits Captains Bill Hatch and Charlie Thompson of Florida with the development and refinements of the drop back. It is not known who commenced the evolution of teasing and the fast cranking back of a bait if a hook-up does not occur on a strike.

Despite the printed references to benefits of teasing, some skippers and anglers in many parts of the world still prefer the ultra-cautious technique of long drop back with virtually no drag. It was felt there was benefit in even pulling line by hand from the reel into the water without drag so the marlin could take and swallow its stunned prey naturally. The marlin was not struck by the angler with or without the boat going ahead until minutes had passed, minutes that seemed like hours. After a pause the fish was pulling line freely from the reel and the marlin was struck. This was an exciting, although nerve-wracking, method of drop back or hook-up.

The current thinking is to rig for a quick hook-up.

Then, if the marlin drops the bait or just hits but does not take it, teasing by winding the bait quickly back towards the boat will change a placid fish swimming away to an excited predator chasing, slashing and taking its 'stunned' food. Both Kip Farrington and Ernest Hemingway refer to this teasing in their writings, yet it was not often practised until recent years. There is no doubt that the teasing technique is almost as important for success as the drop back. Some of the great marlin captures have been made after a marlin has taken or at least struck at the bait and swum away as often as three times. The key to the marlin returning to the bait is the quick retrieval of line on to the reel or the angler pulling by hand to give the bait, or what is left of it, the appearance of escaping.

The savage return of a marlin to bait remnants or only a part of the bait head, or to an otherwise bare hook for a second, third or fourth strike is difficult to explain if natural baits truly look natural to the fish. The similar violent and related strikes that are made at soft and hard plastic lures indicate that marlin and tuna may hunt and feed in response to vibrations received along the lateral line, and in response to what they seem to be hunting by sight or by vibration, rather than by their sense of smell.

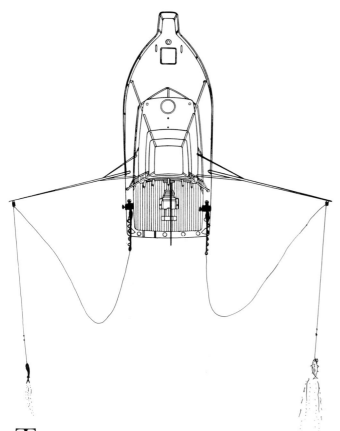

The automatic drop back that often assists billfish hook-up rate when only two baits are trolled.

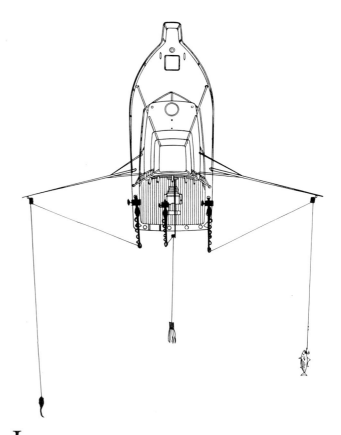

In some bait trolling, particularly in high winds, the automatic drop back is not practical. Some anglers and crew prefer minimum drop back on water and in the air with the angler giving and timing the drop back.

Action of Fish

- Attracted to the baits by boat, baits and chum or vibration of other hooked fish
- Surveys baits as prospective meal

- Hits bait to kill, or grabs bait

- Takes bait in mouth, swims off slowly

- Swallows bait during 'pause'
- Swims on faster than before

- Jumps, runs very fast or panics in an effort to be rid of the hook
- Struggles against hooking, line drag and forward way of the boat
- Jumps or runs fast and sounds after hooking

Action of Fisherman

- Reel alarm click ratchet is 'on'. Set drag lightly. Watch baits for movement or quick 'hits'
- Be ready to work baits gently and to replace with fresh or live baits if necessary
- Exercise care to prevent overrun and at the same time be alert to feed line to fish that are very shy (as marlin may be in temperate waters). Sometimes it is necessary to gently retrieve line to keep contact with the fish and its movements
- Bring in other outfits. If anchored, crew quietly drop dan buoy on anchor line so that the boat can be maneuvered
- Keep all weight off the line

- The angler should strike after a short time, say a count of five
- Three or four sharp lifts of the rod with the boat going fast ahead should be enough to set the hook firmly
- Strike immediately, with the boat going ahead

- Ease drag a little so rod can be placed in chair gimbal

- The boat can be backed up and when the fish slows down the boat can be maneuvered to recover line

The Hooker crew are ready to take the wire on this hyperactive black marlin. Photo: Jacquie Acheson.

This 147 kg (325 lb) blue marlin at St Thomas, Virgin Islands, dogs along the Pescador as the crew take the leader for angler Ralph Christiansen Jnr. Photo: Captain Bill Harrison.

How to troll with live baits: This method is successful, particularly when the baits are trolled around the bait schools from which they were caught, or with pre-caught baits from the boat bait tank. Live baits are also effective where there is an upwelling and where the sea bed configuration of reef, ridge or canyon gives a locality worthy of time spent in slow trolling. Baits are pulled about 30–40 m (90–130 ft) behind the boat.

Boat speed for live bait fishing is the slowest of all

trolling methods, with a top speed of around 4 knots. Skipjack tuna are the most popular and successful of live baits around the world, although the little tuna and kawa kawa (mackerel tuna) are also prime species. In New Zealand, because the kahawai and trevally are the usual bait school species, success comes from trolling these species, particularly kahawai.

In California, Mexico, Australia and many other areas, chub mackerel, scad and goggle eyes are ideal live baits and can be cast to tailing and finning marlin. The benefits of these small live baits are their suitability for smaller size and weight hooks which suit lighter leaders and smaller marlin.

Many anglers and skippers prefer that the line trolling the live bait be held by the angler who is to take the strike. This has the benefit that the angler can actually feel and advise of any panic of the bait, and even the most gentle tap from a billfish when it stuns the bait and takes it. The angler should be able to tell the skipper exactly how bait and quarry are interacting.

Others prefer to fish with the line with the live bait held lightly in an outrigger clip halfway up the outrigger. This enables the angler to be in the shade, cool and presumably alert. It ensures the skipper the benefit of a drop back with only a light hold on the line, whereas an inexperienced or buck fever angler may hold the line too hard, strike too soon or pull the bait away from the fish. As with dead bait fishing, marlin should be given time to turn the bait and swallow it head first before striking to set the hook. The strike drag should be set at between 25 per cent and 33.3 per cent of the line class breaking strain. During trolling, whether held by hand or in the outrigger clip, the drag should be set at just enough to prevent an overrun from a crash strike.

Dead baits or even a lure or two trolled right on the surface can add to the effectiveness of trolling live bait, even at the slow speed of live baiting. I first became aware of this when fishing with Sir William (Alf) Stevenson at Cairns. We had taken a yellowfin about 10 kgs (20 lbs) and quickly rigged it. A deck hose kept it alive and oxygenated until we reached the deep water, then it went over for what we believed must be a sure strike for Alf.

Nothing happened so Alf said, 'It's our last day, put out a skip bait for yourself as well!' So out went an ox eye herring—small tarpon bait on my 60-kg (130-lb) outfit. A few minutes later, even though the big live bait restricted possible trolling speed and the dead bait was flopping in what was to us an unnatural manner at that speed, we had truly unforgettable action. Two big black marlin came up behind the bait. They ignored the panicky live yellowfin bait as they zeroed in on the skipping bait. The smaller marlin struck and took that flopping bait. That marlin weighed 517 kg (1137 lb) to be only the seventh marlin more than 454.5 kg (1000 lb) taken in Australia. Some captains, such as Bobby Brown, Bart Miller and Geoff Ferguson, are consistently successful with live baits.

How to drift with live or dead baits: Success from drifting or at anchor generally comes when the techniques are used over or along ledges or reefs, around bait schools and in other areas where marlin logically should be. One advantage of this is that other fishing can be carried out at the same time as the lines are out for marlin. Fishing can be carried out on the bottom for snappers and other species, with bait or jigs plus fishing for tunas, amberjack and yellowtail kingfish. In Florida, Tommy Gifford and other innovative skippers combined all of this with running a live bait for marlin and sailfish from a fishing kite. With the right wind conditions, this method can be very effective and the kite bait can be used to tease

Charles Perry removing hooks from a white marlin before releasing it at Oregon Inlet, North Carolina. Photo: Charlie Hayden.

an interested billfish into action. It is important when fishing with a float while at anchor or drifting that the float used be rigged lightly so that it will break away immediately on the strike and not spook the marlin. For this reason only enough drag should be applied through the reel to prevent an overrun in the event of a fast strike.

If mako sharks are expected in the fishing area, the light float line should be two or three feet in length (70 cm–1 m) to minimize chance of cutoffs from makos that attack the balloon or other float.

The hook-up technique is similar to that in slow trolling with live bait, with the additional factor that if at anchor, it is imperative to slip the anchor line. Successful anglers use a long drop back time to allow any fish that has taken the bait plenty of time without drag before striking. They let the line run freely from the reel until there is a pause, then allow a count of at least five before striking the fish. This is hard on anglers' nerves, but critical in the hook-up. If the taut line starts heading to the surface, indicating a fish ready to jump before the angler has struck, the fish has felt something is wrong and is racing to the surface to rid itself of the bait fish. If this happens, there is still a good chance of a hook-up by immediately striking hard and often until the fish is hooked or jumps and throws the bait or runs away from the boat. Depending on conditions and number of outfits that can be used, drifting baits should be from 10 m (30 ft) on the surface to down around 100 m (300 ft).

Many marlin hooked while fishing at anchor or drift are hooked either on big dead baits on heavy leaders rigged for sharks or on small live baits rigged on mono-

filament leaders for tuna. These contrasting leaders add to the challenge, and to the crew's need for expertise.

While fishing at anchor the dan buoy float on the anchor line must be ready to slip overboard so the boat can be maneuvered and the marlin played clear of this obstruction.

Marlin are taken commercially drifting at night, though this technique is rarely practised recreationally. The difference in success rate is naturally related to the number of baited hooks that can be fished.

How to cast live or dead baits for marlin: The innovative sport fishermen of California realized that when striped marlin were swimming slowly on the surface or appearing to sun themselves, they would not always react to trolled dead baits or lures, no matter how skillfully these were rigged or presented. Days of probable frustration were turned into days to remember by the casting of live mackerel, sardines or other live bait to striped marlin and broadbill visibly swimming along the surface. This technique naturally spread to Mexico's Cabo San Lucas and is now an important part of the success of their year-round fishing. It has led to the development of new types of rods and reels that are more suitable for casting these lightweight baits than conventional trolling rods. When trolling tackle was used for casting, the line could be coiled on deck or in a bucket or other smooth container, and the live bait leader thrown by hand in front of the surface-swimming marlin. Some boats now have live bait tanks forward as well as in the cockpit.

Once the marlin takes the bait, the fish is struck quickly because the small size of the cast baits enables the marlin to swallow it at the time of the strike. If bigger

*S*mall black marlin are tough light tackle opponents at Port Stephens, New South Wales. Photo: Peter Goadby.

baits are used, the longer pause and longer drop back are further factors in a successful hook-up.

The technique of trolling while searching for billfish on which to cast live baits is exciting but the real excitement comes when tailing fish are seen. The angler then goes to the bow, or in some cases casts from the cockpit, endeavouring to place the live bait in a position where it will be taken by the marlin. Co-operation and communication between angler and crew are important.

Sometimes the cruising marlin are near bait schools and crew or other anglers can fish for fresh live baits on the spot with Little Joe or other small feather and skin multiple-bait catching rigs. These will provide fresh and lively baits of the size and species that the marlin may be ready to feed upon. The skipper from the bridge logically has the best visibility and should clearly direct angler and crew to the position of the marlin the boat is working. The bow of the boat is 12 o'clock and the transom 6 o'clock.

Captain James Bass of the beautiful Bertram *Blowout* showed the benefit of this communication between skipper and angler as we tried several swimmers before a marlin grabbed the lively mackerel cast to it.

The rods evolved for live bait casting have lighter, more flexible tips than trolling rods, although much the same butt power. The reels take advantage of space-age materials to be lighter in weight in the spool and overall to improve casting ability with the light baits. This flexibility at the tip not only facilitated casting, but reduced the overall length of the rod because of this quick bend during the fight.

The presentation of the bait is usually best done from the bow although chances often come at other positions around the boat. If hooked from the bow, it is fought from there until the angler can walk to the cockpit. In small boats the marlin may be played from the bow. In ideal circumstances the marlin is cast to in the 4 to 8 o'clock positions with the angler already in the cockpit.

Southern California and Baja provide the ideal surface conditions for live bait casting. The sight of marlin cruising on the surface is worth the day at sea. The hook-up and fight followed by tag and release is an extra bonus. One day out from Palmilla on Baja around the edge of the fabulous Gordo Bank we counted 40 tailing striped marlin, a memorable sight to anglers from the western Pacific but routine in this eastern Pacific fabulous fishbowl.

Marlin fishing—on the drift or at anchor: Marlin fishing is now often equated with surface or near-surface trolling. The obvious results of commercial longliners, artisinal fishermen of past and present and sport fishermen in many areas are often ignored. Statistics show that many of the world's biggest marlin, as well as the vast majority of marlin taken, are on the drift commercially.

The take by the commercial longliners and the flaglines (short longlines) puts tremendous pressure on the stocks and survival of billfish and tuna. This pressure reflects not only the efficiency but real potential of drifting or fishing at anchor where the billfish are or should be.

Fishing in these modes always had a special attraction for pioneer sporting fishermen. Each area they visited had established artisinal fishing where the natives of the countries went out to sea in canoes or small boats and returned with marlin and tuna that dominated the fragile craft. In his expeditions to many parts of the world, Michael Lerner spent hours and days fishing with the drifting method and baits at depths fished by the local fishermen.

Of course the longliners and flagliners have an advantage that cannot be matched recreationally in the sheer number of hooks and baits. Japanese fishing papers and international investigation have shown that marlin are target species for longliners as well as being the oft-quoted 'incidental' catch when tuna fishing.

Recent research with electronic tags has highlighted the importance of 73 m (40 fathoms) in the cruising and hunting life of marlin. They spend much of their time at this depth so it is logical to drift with baits down deep or to fish at anchor with baits deep.

In the great New Zealand striped marlin fishery, the boats would often stop for lunch while the skipper 'boiled the billy'. This time was not wasted as baits were fished down deep in what was often the quiet part of the day. At Mayor Island, a great part of the fishing day was spent in drifting because of the possibility of big thresher sharks. Not surprisingly many of the marlin hooked were not the expected striped, but the heavier occasional blue or black marlin.

One of the great benefits of this non-trolling fishery is that it gives anglers every opportunity for a smorgasbord of species in all weights. Giant tuna, mid size tuna, plus all the sharks and the oceanic gamefish are potential opponents. If sharks are unwelcome opponents, the use of monofilament leaders gives every chance of cutoffs. Unfortunately, monofilament is also easily cut by wahoo, which would be welcome strangers.

Fishing from drifting or anchor boats also gives the added benefit of fishermen being able to fish for other species, whether on sea beds or surface, to add to activity and sound and vibration attraction.

Every oceanic species is potentially available with this method. Chances of action can be improved dramatically by use of chum (berley). The cubing of fillets and small fish adds to the effectiveness of fishing by this method.

One of the exciting features of this non-trolling method is that it can be sight fishing. As chum works its attractant magic, fish of all species and size are lured to its source—the boat. The ocean around the boat can become a living fishbowl. Sometimes free-swimming hunting marlin cruise into sight before they attack the live, dead or strip baits. Sometimes sharks of all species, with attendant pilot fish and remora, provide silent, frightening sights at boatside. Sometimes tuna cruise majestically or zip and flash through the chum. Some-times strikes come from baits set at favored depths, the fish peeling line from the spool slowly or at fantastic speeds before the fish is sighted.

Marlin fishing in non-trolling modes gives the added spice of finding unknown species as well as unknown size. There is no sure way of predetermining what will attract the offered bait.

Despite the speed they exhibit after being hooked and the savagery they show when slashing at trolled baits or lures, marlin generally take the bait slowly and cautiously. Anglers must be alert to movements of floats, of line coming slack or moving out a few feet. Marlin often hunt up-current, so a slack line or float moving against the current indicates action. Anglers must be watching the baits and floats, looking for fish, alert for unusual indicators. Vigilance and alertness are hard to maintain, with sometimes the only visible action the regular distribution of chum and a few apparently disinterested birds.

The caution of marlin dictates that reel brakes, ratchets and clicks should be just enough to prevent an overrun in case of a speed strike. Anglers must be alert to switch click or ratchet off and ease the drag and pull line by hand from the reel to the fish. Often the angler will feed line without weight on the fish at all. Often line will need to be recovered back on to the spool to minimize the chance of the marlin swimming across loose line in the water, until the swallowing pause and faster swimoff indicate that it is time to try to set the hook. Of course if the fish speeds up and heads for the surface, the angler should strike hard and quickly to try to ensure hook-up before the fish can throw the hook by jumping. Marlin hooked at drift or anchor are fought as if hooked in trolling.

Marlin and big sharks usually take baits slowly and cautiously, in contrast to the power they exhibit later.

A *junior size black marlin performs surface acrobatics at Cape Moreton. Photo: Mike Kenyon.*

*B*aja striped marlin give every opportunity for action. Photo: Al Tetzlaff.

Tuna take baits at speeds that vary from medium to superfast, depending whether they hook themselves while taking the bait. Small sharks swim off with the bait at high speed as if anxious that some other critter may steal the chosen food. It is important that floats break away as soon as the marlin takes the bait. The float line should be around 60 cm (2 ft) long to minimize the chance of cutoff by a mako.

Once a bait is taken, all the other lines in the water are brought inboard while the angler concentrates on his strike and hook-up. The fighting technique is the same as for marlin hooked while trolling. The marlin has the advantage that it may be heading down into the depths at time of being hooked. Marlin often fight deep and sometimes do not zip back to the surface. More often marlin hooked by all methods will head for the surface and reach for the sky. Sometimes the size and species of the opponent are not known until right at boatside for gaffing or tag and release. Whether kept or released they are an angler's dreamfish.

POINTS TO REMEMBER FOR SUCCESS WITH MARLIN ON DRIFT OR ANCHOR

- Set drag and ratchet just hard enough to prevent an overrun.
- Put floats on light breaking lines.
- Anglers and crew should be alert to fish and bird activity and line or float movement.
- The fish that has taken the bait unseen can be of any size and species.
- Care must be taken to prevent overrun before hook-up.
- Immediately the cockpit is clear, gaffs, gloves, wire cutters and tag pole must be ready for use.
- Remember that even though marlin are sought as the opponent, the hook-up could have been on marlin, sharks or tuna, so it is important to be ready with a range of gaffs and tail ropes—just in case.
- In the event of double strike, double hook-up on separate fish, try to assess which fish is smaller (more likely to be taken quickly), or which fish is hooked on heavier tackle.

- Fight this fish hard from the chair or standing up, then go for the other fish.
- Anglers should be awake and alert to minimize chance of marlin taking more than one bait, as a fish that is hooked or entangled on more than one line is not eligible for a record according to the published IGFA rules.
- It is beneficial if the skipper checks regularly with binoculars from bridge or tower, checking for fin, surface activity and bird activity.
- If depth and circumstances allow, jig or fish with other tackle to catch other fish. Remember the vibration of smaller live fish being caught will attract other fish.
- Spincasting to schooling fish such as small tuna in the chum trail will add to activity and attraction.
- Check with sounder that drift is maintaining wanted depth and whether big fish are between the boat and sea bed.
- A sea anchor may be useful to improve angle and rate of drift.

Anchor fishing naturally has many links with drift fishing.

- Again it is important to fish where the fish should be. The boat should be positioned on reefs and peaks so the baits are along the edges of canyons and dropoffs of the reefs.
- Have the anchor line rigged and ready with a dan buoy so that the anchor line can be dropped immediately there is a run or strike from a marlin. The boat can be maneuvered or the current used so boat and fish and line are clear of this obstruction.

Live bait slow trolling has similar facets to fishing on the drift.

How to fight marlin: If the fish hooked is jumping or running towards the boat, the skipper guns his motors to move the boat away from the fish and help keep tight

Mike Lerner congratulates a happy Ernest Hemingway on his Bimini blue marlin. Photo: IGFA—Lerner Expedition.

line. This action minimizes the chances of the fish charging into the boat and minimizes the possibility of it jumping with mouth open towards the boat and throwing the hook. If the fish is running away from the boat, peeling line at frightening speed from the spool, the boat is backed up as fast as fish and boat ability dictate.

Once the marlin has settled down, many skippers and anglers prefer to change from backing up with the leader coming over the body and tail to running the fish so it is resisting with head and muscles the pull of the line and reel drag. Skippers will maneuver the boat not only to keep the marlin working against the drag and the boat, but to change the direction and depth in which the fish is heading. Most hooked marlin run towards the deep water or in some cases, particularly on rough days, towards the direction they were already travelling.

Constant pressure with no letup or slack will see changes in the fish's swimming pattern and direction, and when tired they sometimes circle in the manner of tuna. Even though angler, skipper and boat all contribute to the minimizing of belly in the line from an apparently straight-running fish, a belly of some size will occur and sometimes give the effect of the fish having come free before the line again comes tight. Some successful anglers in Panama developed a technique of deliberately creating a line belly to assist in tiring the fish, but more generally and particularly with light tackle on fast fish, the loop or belly is kept as narrow as possible.

When fishing light tackle, it is usual to prevent breakage by dropping the rod tip when the fish is jumping.

To minimize the chance of breakoff on medium and light tackle and with giant fish, it is imperative, particularly with lines of little stretch, to back the drag off (in some cases right back to free spool) when a jumping fish quickly changes direction. The fish may be travelling on the surface at speed in excess of 48 km/h (30 mph), and the weight of the belly of line will quickly cause a breakoff.

It is difficult to realize that line running through the water under tension can be considered as similar to running around a solid rather than through clear liquid. One of the most thrilling sights in marlin fishing, other than that of a jumping fish, is when a fast-running fish and the boat are in such a position that a column of spray jets from the surface from the line.

The constant and alert watching of baits and lures is an important factor in successful marlin fishing. There are many times when the action of a skipper or crew—teasing, or presenting a fresh bait or a live bait—will change a follower to a taker. Vigilance is what turns 'nothing' days into 'something' days.

Whether fishing baits or lures, the fighting technique is much the same. Once the strike occurs and the angler has the rod, other lines are brought in as part of clearing the cockpit for fighting space. It is most important to make sure the baits and lures are put right into the cabin

The tag pole is ready although the leader is again out of reach as the chair is pulled around by the jumping black marlin. Photo: Greg Edwards.

or right forward in the cockpit. This is to prevent any chance of leaders going overboard or out the scuppers. If this happens hooks can be pulled into crew's legs or feet and leaders can tangle around the propeller.

If a chair is used, a harness would be on the chair, ready for the angler or crew to attach the harness clips to the reel even as the cockpit is being cleared either before or after the fish is hooked. With the marlin hooked and jumping or running, the skipper backs up to minimize line loss or to help in recovery while gaffs, ropes, gloves, tag poles and wire cutters are made ready. Outrigger halyards are often taken from deck level to the flying bridge just in case, as black marlin or white marlin usually do a boatside jumping exhibition. So crew mobility, speed and balance are imperative in the cockpit.

Taking the leader on marlin: Many marlin are lost right at the boatside before they can be gaffed or tagged and released. A great strain and responsibility rest with the crew members taking the leader or handling gaffs or tag poles.

The leader man must be ready with marlin, particularly black marlin, and mako sharks, for the fish to jump. If a big fish jumps away from the boat, he must release the wire to prevent dislocated joints, going overboard, or breaking the leader. It is for this reason the angler winds the swivel to the rod tip, eases the drag and puts the ratchet or clock on and is ready with his left hand to prevent overrun and backlash.

Once the angler has the swivel to the rod tip or the leader in reach of the crew, the leader man takes hold and without jerking or bullocking, pulls the leader so the marlin is within reach of the gaff or tag pole.

On light tackle where the monofilament leader and double are often joined by an improved Albright or Uniknot so the leader can be wound on to the reel, it is the angler who brings the fish boatside into gaff or tagging range. With this rig, the leader is usually in two pieces with the swivel or snap swivel joining the sections. The first section of 24-kg or 36-kg (53-lb or 79-lb) monofilament has 45 cm (18 in) of heavier monofilament or light piano wire or stainless single strand wire attached to a snap swivel. Once a fish is tagged, the crew takes a wrap of the monofilament and cuts or breaks the leader wire.

How to gaff marlin: Many of the early fishing writers stressed the logic of gaffing marlin near the tail region so that the fish's propeller could be lifted clear of the water. Most skippers and crews now prefer, if a fish is leading, to gaff it in or just behind the dorsal fin, and as deep down the body as the gaff allows, where flesh and muscle minimize the possibility of gaff tearout.

If the marlin is not leading when the leader is taken, and is still heading away from the boat which is backing up, some skilled crew men reach out and place the gaff hook under the body immediately above the anal fin in muscle and bone ray area, the only non-ripping area for a gaff on the underside of the fish. Once gaffed, a tail rope is necessary in many cases to complete the catch. The marlin should be subdued with a billy or club to terminate the struggle. If size or transom door allows, the marlin can be slid inboard and fishing may continue.

In onshore marlin fishing and on long-range boats, gaffing is done with long flexible gaffs to hold and lift the fish clear of the water and on to the fishing platform. Naturally two or three gaffs are required to lift the fish.

Marlin fishing is regarded as the pinnacle of saltwater sportfishing. Anglers, skippers and crew thrill to the challenge of the crashing blind strikes with the fish clearing the surface like a jet at full throttle. A big fish clear in the air where a split second before there was nothing but unblemished sea and sky is unforgettable. There are strikes that give humans more time to see, to think and react: a following shadow is tipped by a dorsal fin above the surface, a bulge of water is pierced by a bill and sometimes a wide-open mouth. At other times the strike to kill the lure comes only after teasing a following fish with drop back and fast recovery. Sometimes the billfish, after raising every watcher's blood pressure and heart rate, drops down in the depths and disappears.

All marlin have the ability to peel line from the reel at blistering speed and to make the reel click scream above the rumble of the diesels, causing an instant surge of adrenalin for the fishermen.

The power, size and speed of marlin as well as giant tuna has forced the continuing change and improvements in fishing tackle. They are special fish in all sizes and weights from juvenile to massive adult.

All marlin create in fishermen an intense feeling of excitement, respect and admiration. No other fish mean as much to so many fishermen.

MARLIN FISHING ON TROLLED LURES

There is no dispute that marlin can be and are caught on live or dead baits, and always will be, but bait is not the only or necessarily the best way to attract action in all fishing areas. Data and experience show that there are times and areas where fishing is most productive from use of baits, and that there are times and areas when trolled lures are not only the most productive, but the best and sometimes virtually the only chance of success.

The boat speed at which lure fishing is practised ensures that the lures and hooks are presented in front of the greatest possible number of fish. The inherent problems of availability of bait fish and skill and time in rigging and trolling speed can also inhibit fishing time and thus results from fishing with baits. In lure fishing, lures can be bought from a store or lure maker already rigged—ready to go fishing, ready for action, and ready for quick change or replacement.

It sometimes takes years of effort in new and developing sport fisheries to pinpoint the exact times and places for fish action, so the trolling of lures to cover maximum territory and thus find the hot spots is most logical.

Once the data or times and places are known, the natural baits may be the more productive, correct choice, but having been successfully established on artificials, most fisheries continue to fish and develop with this method.

Take a rigged lure, add water of the correct temperature over a likely sea bed configuration and stand by for marlin action. Lure fishing is instant fishing.

The comment is sometimes made (by fishermen who do not practice or are not successful at lure fishing) that the great ocean gamefish do not in nature feed on plastic. They point out that fish and squid are found in fish stomachs, plastic is not. Despite this thought, the facts are that marlin and tuna of all sizes do strike hard and often at hard and soft plastic or metal-headed and colorfully skirted trolling lures.

A Baja striped marlin shows why the species has its reputation for aerial acrobatics. Photo: Peter Goadby.

GAFFING TECHNIQUES

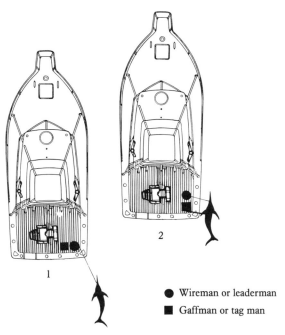

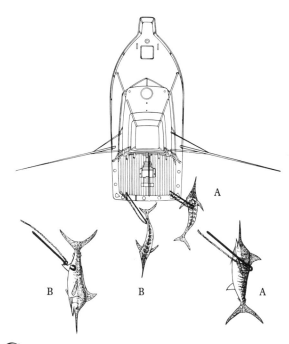

● Wireman or leaderman

■ Gaffman or tag man

Gaffing is logically done on the port side of the boat so crew are working right-handed. The leader man takes the leader with gaff man behind him, then as fish is pulled into gaffing range, moves forward so gaff man can reach fish at shoulder. The same procedure applies in tag and release except that after tagging fish, the tag man cuts the leader behind leader man or removes hooks if possible so leader man can release wire while he is ready and balanced.

Gaff billfish for minimum chance of tearing in the shoulder (A) or the anal fin (B) bone structure, not in tail area or stomach section.

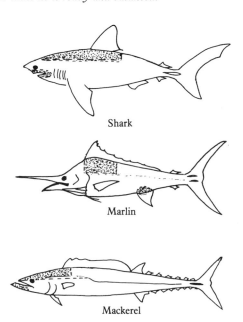

Shark

Marlin

Mackerel

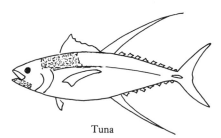

Tuna

The effective and best holding gaffing areas. If fish activity and mouth opening allows it then a gaff in the lower jaw is effective. Fish to be released should not be gaffed other than a release gaff in the lower jaw. Gamefish taken for eating should be gaffed where meat damage is minimised in the head or lower jaw. Gaffs should be placed in areas of strength and deep muscle tissue. Gaffing in the tail area causes activity and tail threshing and should be avoided.

The argument that the great saltwater gamefish do not eat plastic could apply equally to trout and salmon which do not eat feathers, plastic or metal, yet are usually taken on these materials in sport, or to the speedy toothy mackerels and wahoo which do not eat metal, but are taken for commercial as well as recreational use on metal spoons, wood, plastic and feathers.

Every day in fresh and salt water the visible evidence can be seen that the world's great and classic gamefish, despite their highly developed sight, do strike hard and often at a variety of lures. Sometimes marlin just strike with bill at the head of the lure or on the leader ahead of the lure.

To change this pattern of strikes with zero hook-ups, zero fish at boat, some reduce the strike drag in trolling mode to just enough to prevent an overrun. This light initial drag gives the marlin the chance to turn the lure and get it where the hooks can take hold, instead of being pulled away from the striking fish. Trolling smaller lures often gives a more effective hook-up rate. Big lures certainly attract fish of all sizes, but many of the big lure strikes are not followed by hook-up.

Another way to overcome the problem of shy marlin is to use an extra outrigger out from the bridge or tower down the centre line of the boat. Ideally a roller type outrigger release is best for this shotgun rig. The lure from this centre outrigger is trolled well back on wave nine or ten specifically for shy and following marlin and for another chance at strike from a marlin that has struck and not hooked on one of the lures trolled closer to the boat. Unsuccessful trolling consumes time and money so use of proven lure designs is most logical. There are many top makers.

The how-to to success with lures has variations evolved in various areas, but generally the Hawaiian techniques and patterns remain the basics for success on offshore trolling lures anywhere. These basics of lure trolling are:

- Troll where the fish should be, because not even the best lures in a perfectly trolled pattern can produce action where the fish aren't. Knowledge of where the fish should be comes with experience and research. Keep a diary or log.

- Troll in a pattern of lures that suits the boat. Trial and experience will show what works best for each boat in lure shape and trolling pattern. Variations come from the size and shape of the boat, its action in the sea, its wave wake, the angle of vee in the hull, and even the boat propellers and power.

- Troll colors of lures known to be successful. These should resemble the coloration of local bait fish or squid populations, and take into account the light conditions of the day. Put out a proven selection of color combinations of light and dark.

- Troll shapes to suit the water surface. A few designs

A *striped marlin takes to the air off Baja California. Photo: Peter Goadby*

work well and produce in all seas, but most are designed to be most successful in either rough or smooth water.

- Troll each proven lure at the distance and on the wake wave that suits the lure. Work out which lures work best from outriggers, from the centre rigger, on flat lines or when pulled down even closer to the water with line releases of some kind.

- Troll a pattern of lures in which all lures work at their best at the same speed. Some lures that work well at higher speeds (12–15 knots) do not work well at 8–10 knots or normal lure speed, and should be trolled only in high-speed pattern.

- Troll the number of lures that commonsense, crew and angler experience, speed, sea conditions, outriggers and rod holders indicate as practical. Most skippers troll four lures, some five or more with a shotgun lure far out. When travelling at higher speeds in excess of 15 knots, it is usual to troll only two or three high-speed lures, usually those with bullet heads.

- Troll a proven wave pattern. If four lures are run, these are often placed on waves four, five, six, and seven, or waves four, six, eight and nine or ten. If five are trolled, they may be on waves three, four, five, seven and eight, or even starting close in on two, or any combination back to wave nine or ten or even further. Some skippers troll a fifth lure in the centre well back at the tenth wave wake, the shotgun lure, instead of short. They troll other lures, outrigger and flat line, inside that long lure. The lure positions are often described as long outrigger, short outrigger, long flat and short flat.

- Troll from outrigger with stinger or tag lines or direct from outrigger halyard with outrigger clip. Troll short or close in, on flat lines from rod tip or pull lower down towards water surface with an outrigger clip.

MARLIN LURES

LISTED BELOW ARE PROVEN AND REGULARLY SUCCESSFUL LURE AND SKIRT COLOR COMBINATIONS.

Head colors

1. Transparent light blue with mirror, shell, reflective tape or stainless steel insert.

2. Transparent green or clear with green and yellow top or bottom strip with mirror, stainless steel or reflective tape insert.

3. Black or clear with black insert with pearl or reflective tape strips, or pepper and salt (black with crushed abalone, pearl or paua shell) or purple reflective insert.

4. White or clear or clear blue or green tint with white, pearl or abalone, stainless steel, paua shell or silver reflective insert.

5. White, clear, or clear tint, blue, green with silver, blue or green inserts with holes.

Skirt colors

1. Light or dark blue outer skirt over dark green and gold or lime green. Pink or white over silver inner skirt.

2. Green with gold outer skirt and green with yellow, lime-green or silver inner skirt.

3. Black and silver outer skirt over green, pink, orange, lime-green or purple inner skirt. Black and silver outer skirt over purple and silver, red and silver inner skirt or black over pink.

4. Light blue outer skirt or other light color over pink, yellow, white or silver inner skirt.

5. Any light color combinations.

OTHER LURES THAT ARE ALWAYS WORTH HAVING READY, RIGGED FOR CHANGE TO SUIT THE DAY OR AID FISHING ACTION, ARE:

6. Clear with stainless steel, mirror or tape insert with blue strip on top or bottom of lure.

7. Clear with white, silver, stainless steel, light green or pink reflective tape insert.

6. Light blue, white or silver outer skirt over light green or pink inner skirt.

7. Red over yellow, blue over white, green over yellow or gold, blue over silver, blue over pink, blue over green.

A selection of lures suitable for marlin lure trolling. (Left to right) Murray Bros, Joe Yee, Winfred Ho, C&H, R&S, Doornob, Pakula, Top Gun, Hypalon, Moldcraft.

Some lure riggers add either one or two strips from lure skirt material in gold or hot pink or yellow colors to the skirt combinations. Some fishermen prefer the tough, fairly stiff skirt materials such as Moldcraft or Newell. Some combine stiff and soft skirt materials, while some still prefer the original red or black rubber-and-upholstery fabric that was popular before the ready availability of soft plastic squid and skirts. In the Indo-Pacific, preference is towards the soft-squid Japanese and Sevenstrand type skirts. In the Atlantic preference seems to be for the tougher, less stretchy, thicker skirt materials.

The importance of lures in the offshore fishing scene is demonstrated not only by the successful and growing lure captures, but by the number of already successful offshore fishermen who head back to Hawaii and fish the Kona Hawaiian Billfish Tournament and the Hawaiian International Billfish Tournament for more reason than just competition.

Apart from the pleasure of fishing in these prestigious tournaments, one of the prime reasons is to learn and relearn, to update on successful saltwater, deepwater lure fishing. Hawaii is the university of successful lure trolling for billfish and big tuna. It was developed there and the Hawaiian technique is now the fastest growing and successful method of fishing for marlin right around the world. Lure fishing is the ideal way to explore fishing grounds and define areas for potentially viable bases.

So running well-proven designs and color combinations is most productive. Lures from successful makers—Joe Yee, Gary Eoff, Marlin Magic, Sadu, Rose, Lock Nut and Ho of Hawaii, Top Gun and Pakula of Australia, Murray Bros, R&S, C&H, Sevenstrand, Doornob, Schneider and Braid of the USA and Africa's Striker—are consistent fish takers in hard plastic, as are Frank Johnston's Moldcraft Lures of USA. In soft plastic

there are successful lure makers in most other fishing countries—Mexico, Papua New Guinea, Japan, Tahiti, Guam and New Zealand. It is sensible to check before the day's fishing with the skippers and crews on charter or private boats, to work out a lure pattern to give potential for results.

The dark colored skirt combinations—brown and pink, black and purple, dark green–light green–black over red, green and pink—can be used effectively with either dark or light colored heads, but are generally combined with dark heads. Lure fishermen in many countries believe it is logical and beneficial to have one or two dark-colored or dark-colored-skirted lures in the trolling pattern. Their theory is that the dark lure head and skirt are easily seen from below, with lure and bubbles silhouetted against the light of the surface. Most feel it is very important also to have at least one clear lure head that flashes and shines from its inserts of pearl or tape, mirrors or stainless. Some successful lure fishermen include a metal or weighted plastic jet head or Doornob shape in their trolling pattern. These two lure designs are for faster trolling, and are particularly effective when trolled at 12–16 knots. Most kona head designs, whether scooped or pusher (non-scooped) or straight runners, work best at 8–10 knots. Knucklehead lures work well at slower speeds—as slow as bait trolling speeds (4–7 knots).

Some fishermen experience the problem of skirt material, particularly the softer squid type skirts, tangling around the hook. This problem can be prevented by cutting the skirts so they are shorter than the barb position on the hook. Some fishermen prefer their lure skirts to be cut dead even and square, others cut the material so it is tapered.

Many of the most successful color combinations are

Cozumel white marlin are ideal light tackle adversaries. Photo: Gil Keech.

old faithfuls, designed with the colors of mahi mahi (dolphin fish), mackerel, tuna, saury, flying fish or other local natural food fish colors. Some successful combinations of reds and yellows do not seem to relate to nature's colors at all, but work because they may excite or annoy the big fish. Modern scientific papers report that even though fish cannot see colors in the same way as humans, they can distinguish them. This could be why some head and skirt color combinations regularly produce and are proven most effective.

Despite the regular success of fish and squid type look-alike colors, there seems little doubt lures may bring a high strike and hook-up rate, not by their natural appearance to marlin or tuna, but by vibration, flash, sound, action and bubbles that trigger annoyance or curiosity.

The peak predators of the ocean, the billfish, tunas, mackerels and mahi mahi, have large, well-developed and effective eyes, so it is conjectured that even the best-rigged natural baits may not fool the fish. Some theorize that despite the natural smell, color and action of these fish baits, many of the strikes are triggered by some of the same factors as with lures.

The size of modern lures in a successful pattern usually ranges from a maximum of around 100 mm (4 inches) head length and 250 mm (10 inches) skirt length with a trend towards smaller lures around 200 mm (9 inches). The long monster heads of years ago that produced many strikes but gave a low proportion of hook-ups and fish at the boat have declined in popularity and use. Every year in Hawaii, as in other fishing and even non-fishing areas, new shapes and color combinations are designed, tried and adopted or discarded. Perhaps even more than the fish they seek, lure fishermen are prey for new lures. They are convinced that this is *the* one, this is the special producer. Trolling with light (below 10 kg; 20 lb) tackle limits the maximum size of the lure and hooks that can be trolled sensibly and productively.

OTHER DEVELOPMENTS IN MARLIN LURE TROLLING

Experienced fishermen often say, 'This is the only way to' or 'That is a waste of time that never works'. Every time it seems there is a tried and proven only way or a clearly defined example of 'don't do this, it won't work', someone comes along and tries and proves something different, something that is diametrically opposed but works successfully.

It seems only a few years ago that many fishermen believed there were no benefits in trolling one or more dead baits in conjunction with live baits. Similarly, there was an expressed belief that there were no benefits, in fact it was counter-productive to troll one or more lures while trolling live or dead baits at bait-trolling speed. Yet now it is known there are benefits in trolling one or more lures in conjunction with live bait, at live bait speeds of 3–4 knots or slower, instead of their usual lure trolling speed of 8–10 knots. Marlin sometimes take the dead bait in preference to the live bait or take a lure awkwardly acting at slow speed instead of the live or dead bait trolled enticingly at bait speed.

The traditional proven trolling method with lures, particularly for billfish, is to set strike drags hard (¼ to ⅓ of line class) and to gun the boat immediately to help set the hooks. Now there is a recent method contrary to this previous advice. This technique, perhaps logical for Moldcraft and other soft-head lures, works also with hard-head lures on the conventional clear polyester or other hard plastic lures. This radical technique is to troll at normal lure trolling speed, but instead of setting the hand strike drag and heavy rubber band or outrigger release hard, some fishermen now troll with a weak setting on the outriggers, and strike drag just enough to prevent overrun. This method is in line with the accepted natural bait drop-back philosophy to give the billfish every opportunity to turn the lure to swallow it head first.

The logic of this method, which is used on both hard-head and soft-head lures, is obvious when considered with the hook-up success on small kona heads and other trolling lures on light 4 kg (8 lb), 6 kg (12 lb), 8 kg (16 lb) and 10 kg (20 lb) line classes. The success of lures on light tackle in hot spots as far apart as the Caribbean, Costa Rica and Australia is proven, so consideration of the light hold, light drag technique is worthwhile. Those who advocate and practice this light technique use it with both hard heads and soft heads, despite the often expressed belief that marlin will not return to strike at a hard head if the hook-up was missed on the initial strike. We know that sometimes marlin will strike a lure repeatedly before hooking up and that they can sometimes be triggered into returning to strike and kill after an unsuccessful hook-up. The teasing of the marlin and quick line recovery often turns a missed hook-up into a return strike, hook-up and marlin at the boat. The teasing technique has proven as successful with lures as with baits. Some who use the light drag techniques run the line to a lightly set outrigger clip which holds it, as in bait fishing, and then troll a loop of line down to the water surfaces for an automatic drop back to give the marlin every chance to turn the lure head first.

Sometimes the line is held lightly or through an outrigger release and tension held by the brake of the

Two striped marlin tailing at Palmilla, Mexico. Photo: Peter Goadby

reel. In essence the technique is related to bait rather than to conventional trolling technique with hard or soft-head lures. This technique requires concentration, readiness to be right there immediately a strike occurs or there are billfish behind the lure. This is as in bait fishing, and is a basic imperative for success in all trolling, though often not sufficiently taken into account in offshore trolling.

This technique enhances the sign on the boat of skilled Panamanian Captain Louis Schmidt, an expert

with baits: 'The price of a marlin is eternal vigilance'.

Most of the hot lure designs and sizes can be trolled on all line classes down to 15 kg (30 lb). The lines under the 15-kg (30-lb) class, which are ideal for smaller billfish, the school billfish and other similar pelagics, are successfully fished with smaller lures and sharp hooks. The hook sizes trolled in lures have reduced over the years. This is a result not only of experience, but of a general reduction in the length and diameter of lure heads. See also Points for Successful Lure Trolling, page 227.

LAND-BASED MARLIN FISHING

Most fishermen associate their thoughts of gamefish, particularly for billfish and tuna, with fishing from boats. Boat handling, backing up, running the fish are all essential skills necessary for taking big fish from boats. But in some parts of the world billfish and tuna species up to 90 kg (200 lb) are sought and taken from immovable fishing platforms, the rocks. In this fishing there is no benefit from yelling, 'Back up, back up'. The only movement or change of angle comes when the fisherman changes position and that has natural limitations.

Traditionally, many species of gamefish have been taken by shorefishing methods or from jetties, bridges and other structures, as well as from boats. The quest for and successful capture of black and striped marlin, sailfish, and yellowfin and bluefin tuna from the rocks is, however, a more recent development.

These species now join tarpon, bonefish, snook, barramundi, salmon and many of the shark species as the summit of shore-bound angling.

Land-based gamefishing is practised in countries where environmental conditions combine to bring the

fish in range of the shorebound fisherman instead of the fisherman travelling long distances to sea looking for fish. The necessary environment is where accessible rocky headland formations are washed by an ocean current. The current must be of a temperature to carry the cherished gamefish, the rocks should drop off quickly in the ocean to a depth of at least 10 m (30 ft) and preferably deeper right along the rock formation. Best results are associated with the wind and current generally in the same direction to generate plankton-rich eddies and upwellings to provide the base for the life cycle and species associated with wide offshore. A few sections of the coastline in Australia, South Africa, Hawaii and New Zealand all have the natural features that have led to their establishment of successful land-based gamefishing. Many other countries have formations and currents and conditions that should be productive for those who want to fish offshore species without going offshore to rock and roll. The rock formations at the tip of Baja, California are just one such area.

Rods used for land-based gamefishing are usually

around 2.5 m (8.5 ft). They are light and flexible in the tip section and powerful in mid and butt sections. The light, flexible tip assists in casting of live baits and is sensitive to the activity of the live bait when a big predator is in the vicinity. The power butt and mid section give the angler stick to meet the power of the big fish. They also give lift to help offset the weight and action of the fish when it is in proximity to rocks or gaffs. Special gaffs have been evolved to make gaffing and lifting up the rocks possible. For extreme heights, some of the gaffs are designed to slide down the line and leader with heavy cord attached. Others have long flexible handles to reach from rock fishing positions to the fish.

Although pioneering rock captures were made with star drag reels, the ready availability and reasonable price of lever drag reels of aluminum and other lightweight materials has encouraged fishermen to change to the most modern designs, in various brands. Both narrow and wide spool reels designed for 24-kg (50-lb) line are popular. Line used is generally 15 kg (30 lb) and 24 kg (50 lb). Surprisingly, many ocean gamefish hooked on the live baits do not head out to sea. Much of their swimming and jumping parallels the rocks in deeper water. Skilled pumping, hard effort and of course a slice of Lady Luck brings the fish to within gaffing range. Then comes the long arduous climb with assistance from other anglers to bring the capture back to the top of the headland, to the waiting vehicle to take the land-based gamefish prize to be weighed.

The southern section of the coastline in New South Wales, particularly inside Jervis Bay at the northern headland, is the locale for captures that defy the conventional fishing imagination. Black and striped marlin and yellowfin in excess of 90 kg (200 lb) have been landed to join the growing list of rock-caught species.

Western Australia added the concept of balloons blowing with the wind offshore to get their live baits out from cliffs. They added sailfish to the list of gamefish caught from the rocks as well as tanguigue (narrow-barred mackerel), cobia and other usually offshore species.

In Australia thoughts of the challenge of really big fish from the rocks were triggered by the success of high-speed lure fishing from the headlands and cliff platforms. The change from the frantic activity of high speed spinning, with its stress on reel gears, to drifting live baits in those waters where the current ran along the rocky headlands was a natural fishing evolution.

This fishing revolution appealed to those who climbed cliffs and didn't fish boats for various reasons. These rock gamefishermen caught and carried their small live bait fish, and kept a few alive in a children's portable swimming pool. They are often fishermen who camp overnight on rock ledges so they will have precedence at the favored fishing location. They are often young, always enthusiasts.

Giant trevally of various species, the deep fighting hoodlums called ulua in Hawaii, are tough opponents anywhere. They grow in excess of 70 kg (150 lb), and

for more than sixty years have been a magnet for shorebound fishermen of Hawaii at night as well as during the day.

Despite the loss of habitat and ecological changes that have caused a decrease in activity at the once-productive Bamboo Ridge on Oahu, there are still many active, but often difficult-of-access and secret shorefishing areas in the Hawaiian islands. At Hawaii's South Point, ulua, tuna and even marlin can be seen working around the cliffs. The rock platform Bamboo Ridge was so called because of the collection of bamboo and later heavy fiberglass fishing rods that stood on it each night while baits soaked and the rock fishermen waited patiently. Small bells attached to the rods give warning for the angler that something is working one of the baits on the rods he has in position. Many of the world record ulua come from Hawaii's rocky fishing spots. As in Australia, the fishermen are usually equipped with several rods. Some are 3.6 m (12 ft) in length and a combination of bamboo and fiberglass. Much of the productive time is at night, a time of added danger needing even more skill to land the fish. The rods arc held upright in tubes drilled into the lava and rocks and often equipped with safety lines.

Giant trevally of three species, ulua, amberjack (kahala), and occasionally yellowfin tuna, are the quarry for Hawaii's rock fishermen.

The fascination of these fish has attracted fishermen from the different population migrations to the islands

The Nikon records the blue water ballet or the 'dance of the striped marlin' at Palmilla, Baja California. Photos: Peter Goadby.

with much of the now-successful interest coming from Hawaiian fishermen of Japanese descent. The Hawaiian cliff formations mean that much of the best fishing is often 6 m (20 ft) or higher above the sea with water depths that drop away sharply to 30–45 m (100–150 ft) as the islands rise precipitously from the ocean depths. They fish with tapered pyramid sinkers of up to 300 g (10 oz) with soft wire bent in a hook shape cast into the wide base.

These wires straighten when the angler strikes or wishes to cast again for better position, or if a fish takes the bait. Once the line and sinker anchor is in the chosen position, the baited hook and leader with clip swivel or split ring is slid down the line until stopped near the sea bed by a swivel over which it cannot pass. Other fresh baits can be slid down the line when the fisherman believes his bait of eel or live bait may have been chomped up by small fish or crabs.

Despite the Hawaiian rock angler's awareness that the ulua, the biggest of their family, and the amberjack will readily respond to chumming, this is not generally done as it also attracts unwelcome sharks and eels.

While the rock fishermen were the first to be successful back in the 1930s and possibly earlier with giant ulua in excess of 45 kg (100 lb), the first angler

A black marlin jumps and the long-handled rock gaff is ready. Photo: Simon Cassetari.

known to successfully land tuna from the rocks in excess of this weight was in South Africa. Southern bluefin tuna weighing between 14 and 24 kg (30 and 50 lb) were taken spinning from the rocks and ledges of Rooikrantz at Cape Point in Cape Province in 1945 and from the South Pier at Durban in 1939. Then in 1948, angler Karl Weigel landed a big tuna of another species, a yellowfin of 37 kg (82 lb). Yellowfin of 52 kg (114 lb) and 69 kg (150 lb) were landed prior to 1955, with others of these weights during that year.

Angler Jack Wheeler in 1956 caught a yellowfin of 72 kg (156 lb) after a two-hour fight. This angler in 1957 while fishing from a boat off Mussel Bay had caught a 330-kg (720-lb) black marlin after a fifteen-hour fight to give him two great fish within 13 months.

Sharks (big white sharks and other species) have long been caught from the rocks at Hermanus, Kalk Bay, South Africa. At Hermanus, W. Selkirk and other anglers successfully landed big sharks with the aid of a float. The float was an 18-litre (4-gallon) paraffin can, sealed and pumped with air to resist crushing from water pressure. When fished from Nottingham reels on 3.6 m (12 ft)-long bamboo rods with perseverance and skill, the rock anglers landed white sharks up to and over 360 kg (800 lb). The big can floats restricted the ability of the big sharks to sound and roll, but the achievements of the anglers with their simple reels that did not have a brake system are still incredible. The linen line on these reels was 15 and 24-thread 24–37 kg (50–80 lb) test.

Shark are also taken from rocks and shore in many other countries. Big sharks, including the 60-kg (130-lb) and all tackle world record tiger shark of 810 kg (1788 lb) were taken from a jetty in Cherry Grove, South Carolina by Walter Maxwell. From shore and jetties, big tarpon are taken in Florida, while roosterfish are taken from shore in Baja California, Mexico, Peru, Ecuador and Chile. The development of billfishing from headlands has opened a new dimension for sportfishing.

It is ironic that boat anglers who have searched far offshore and returned unsuccessful to port may be greeted with news that the fish they sought were caught that day by anglers who didn't leave shore for their fishing.

SAILFISH

Sailfish hold a unique place in the hearts and minds of fishermen. These are the fish whose beauty and color live on in countless homes, offices, clubs and restaurants as one of the ocean's great fish move into man's environment. They are the peacock of the sea with glorious colors and graceful winged bird shape.

They are a blend of marine savagery and efficiency in the way they hunt. The beauty and mystery of these acrobatic jumpers—whose muscles can propel the slender needle nose body at a calculated 113 km/h (68 mph)— makes them the light tackle fisherman's dream fish.

Sailfish have been the subject of thousands of magazine articles, of chapters in fish books and of a classic book, *The Sailfish, Swashbuckler of the Open Seas* by Jim Bob Tinsley. Fishermen seeking sailfish have the privilege of seeing nature and evolution in action. They can see first hand an answer to the standing question: Why do they have the sail? What is its use?

How to Increase Safety when Fishing from Rocks

Don't fish alone

Don't turn your back on the sea

Don't go down to the water to retrieve terminal tackle

Do watch your chosen fishing location for fifteen minutes to make sure it is safe

Do be aware of change and velocity of waves triggered by tide change or changes in wave height

Do wear safe footwear with non-slip soles

Do plan on how to return to safety in case you fall into the sea

Do tell others where you are going to fish and when you expect to return

Do have a line and float ready for emergency use

Do gaff fish from high above the wave level in safety

Don't ever risk life in quest for fish. There are always other days

Do, above all, keep cool

A *black marlin, jumping inside Jervis Bay, New South Wales, hooked from the rocks. Photo: Greg Finney.*

*S*ailfish above and below the surface have a natural attraction for the artist as well as the fisherman. Bill Goadby Lawrence has used watercolors to perpetuate the warmth of the ocean current and the active, beautiful fish. Photo: Peter Goadby.

Those who have been under way or drifted near these fish as they hunt and ball up their prey can see the answer. That apparently flimsy, supposed balance-destroying sail when upright, turns the slender-bodied sailfish into a silhouette of a monster fish, increasing the visible body depth by a factor of five in combination with the long-rayed pelvic fins.

Sailfish are an intriguing, challenging and at times annoying light tackle opponent in the world's tropical waters. The dorsal fin sail adds mystique and uniqueness as well as beauty to this fish. This spectacular jumper offers everything sought in offshore fishing on light tackle, everything offered by its bigger billfish relatives. Sailfish add interest to any tournament or fishing even when other, bigger billfish are the hoped-for opponents. To their beauty, whether they are to be taken or tagged and released, can be added the visual benefit of looking bigger and heavier than they are. Sailfish work in schools and respond to every fishing method, yet at times are particularly frustrating and difficult to hook.

Part of the excitement with sails is that they are often sighted, worked and teased. At other times, blind striking at live or dead trolled baits is the only indication of their presence. Schools of these ideal light tackle opponents are pinpointed not only by the traditional bird and bait association, but by free jumping fish or one of the ocean's most striking and intriguing sights: sailfish cruising with sail up and set clear of the surface.

Free-jumping sailfish in association with balled bait in calm clear water give fishermen the opportunity to see these fish hunting co-operatively. Fishermen become humans privileged to witness natural activity and feeding in nature's fishbowl, the hunters and the hunted, part of nature's fabric.

The apparently random free-jumping sailfish are part of an organized ruthless, co-operative feeding pattern. The jumpers, like most ocean-feeding predators, work anti-clockwise. This surface jumping with sail down and often landing flat helps ball up the bait fish into tight masses. Ballyhoo, garfish, small ocean toadfish, goggle eye and yellowtail scad are bait species preyed on by sailfish.

The surface indicators of the free jumping sails are repeated into the depths by other sails, again circling anti-clockwise, with sails fully extended and long pelvic fins fully down so the fish looks like a massive and beautiful butterfly. Sailfish generally do not rush into and monster the bait ball they have patiently created. Instead they gently take their prey from the outside of the column of bait in their circling.

WHERE TO FIND THEM

Sailfish are expected in tropical waters, although they do sometimes appear far from expected locations after riding the warm current. In the Caribbean and some other locales, tag and release has shown that they migrate over long distances from Florida to at least Venezuela.

In Australia, the sailfish schools (as supported by tag and release results) are local populations. These locals do not move long distances north and south. The recognized populations and their hot spots may be separated by as little as 160 km (100 miles). Sailfish range from coastal waters that not only may be green rather than the azure blue of the warm currents, but distinctly brownish, discolored by heavy inflow of fresh water from major river systems.

They are often found over sandy as well as reefy sea beds in association with the bait schools which may be down deep. Echo sounder and sonar show the position of the small fish schools, which could be goggle eye, yellowtail, the wavy striped greenback chub mackerel or sea toads (puffer fish) and ballyhoo (balao or garfish).

Thinking skippers often catch live bait from schools of the bait species at sea. They use them immediately and productively for deep slow trolling or drifting or for casting them near the bait schools.

At certain times sailfish are also found around coral reefs and sand cays with reefs, as well as the passes, channels and outside edge of the outer reefs where warm currents are close inshore.

FISHING FOR SAILFISH

The hook-up of sailfish on the troll was a challenge that, once solved, opened the door to successful trolling for all billfish species. Captain Bill Hatch of Miami is credited with the concept and the introduction of the drop back in trolling for sailfish. One of his crew was the equally legendary Tommy Gifford. The development of outriggers by Captain Tommy Gifford helped not only the improved action and position of trolled baits, but the effectiveness of drop back. Fishing for sailfish also influenced the technique of rigging and development of trolled baits, both whole fish and strips. Subsequently live bait fishing evolved, with kites introduced to the east coast by Harlan Major, to be followed by live bait fishing around the bait schools at Stuart and Palm Beach, Florida.

Live bait fishing for sailfish evolved in two ways, with bait fish taken from inshore and with those caught offshore where the sailfish were feeding. Those taken offshore were captured by cast nets, a technique used off Stuart and Palm Beach.

Light tackle is synonymous with sailfish right around the world.

This tropical aerial acrobat is taken on all forms of tackle. They can be cast to, fished from anchor or drift, and trolled with live baits, dead baits and lures. The

A Pacific sailfish, with glowing colors, lifts itself clear of the water in Costa Rica. Photo: Darrell Jones.

A Pacific sailfish flies clear at top speed. Photo: Darrell Jones.

sight of the slender bill and distinctive sail is thrilling, whether deliberately fished for or an incidental strike and hook-up. Sailfish are exciting fish.

They are ideal antagonists for beginners in offshore fishing. On balanced tackle their spectacular activity creates interest, plus a desire to continue and fish for bigger billfish. Memories come easily with sailfish, even in combination with the modern trend to tag and release. Even if the angler's first or other billfish is tagged and released or just released, he or she can still have a trophy of the day's fishing, and superb fish, by simply giving the approximate weight and dimensions of the fish to a taxidermist. In these days of fiberglass as well as skin mounts, the taxidermist can supply a mount of the actual sailfish in glowing living colors.

Pacific sailfish are bigger, heavier and even more colorful than their Atlantic cousins. Sailfish were identified in Picos' *Naturalis Braziliae*, published in Holland in 1648. The Indo-Pacific sails were recorded by Bernard and Valentjin, and a stuffed sailfish from the Indian Ocean was taken to London, where it remains in the British Museum. The biggest in the Atlantic appear to be off central Africa. There was a belief that some of the big sailfish in this area may be Indo-Pacific sailfish that have straggled around the Cape of Good Hope and into the Atlantic, along with the occasional black marlin, striped marlin and southern bluefin from the Indian Ocean taken in longline captures in the Atlantic.

Sailfish are usually trolled for with live or dead natural baits. Like other billfish species, they are often most active when the wind chops the surface and the billfish can ride down the swells. Polarizing sunglasses give angler and crew the opportunity to see the strike. Often birds and surface activity with balled-up bait indicates the likely presence of sailfish. Sometimes the bait and sails are down deep, revealed by echo sounder or sonar; sometimes the slender tail slicing down the swell shows the presence of the fish. Sometimes there is no indication of the fish until suddenly one or more slender,

wavery shapes move up to the baits, a slender bill slashes down on the head of the bait, and the line comes clear of the outrigger clip and runs slowly from the spool. Often the pause of sailfish turning and swallowing the bait is almost undetectable.

Some fishermen believe a count of five to ten from the time of the fish hitting the bait to angler striking will provide a hook-up, whether the strike is on flat line or outrigger line; others play it by ear and strike when they feel the sailfish has swallowed it. The modern trend of running a small feather or plastic jig or plastic skirt over the head of the natural bait aids the strike and hook-up rate, as it adds excitement and toughness to the bait and gives more chance by teasing after the initial strike.

Ballyhoo (garfish), small mullet, flying fish, chub (green) mackerel, goggle eye, yellowtail scad and strip baits are the most successful trolled natural baits, although other small fish species used for live bait such as goggle eye, yellowtail scad and green chub mackerels are also productive as dead baits. Sailfish also take small konaheads, knuckleheads and other plastic head and skirted lures, as well as wooden and plastic minnow type lures. They sometimes unexpectedly take big konaheads trolled for marlin and tuna to add welcome variety to any day's fishing. Live baits are sometimes trolled, but more often fished drifting and casting into and around the schools of balled-up bait. In Florida particularly, at Stuart and Palm Beach, ballyhoo (garfish) are sometimes taken by cast nets in the balled-up bait schools to be used on the spot. Live baits of various kinds, particularly goggle eye and mackerel, are taken out from shore for each day's fishing in live bait tanks that are now important and necessary equipment on boats seeking sailfish.

In eastern Australia and some other successful fishing areas, live baits are cast on heavy spinning rods into the bait schools worked by the feeding sailfish.

The spinning rods are used to deliver the small live baits to strategic positions right in front of the circling predators, along and into the bait schools to swim and

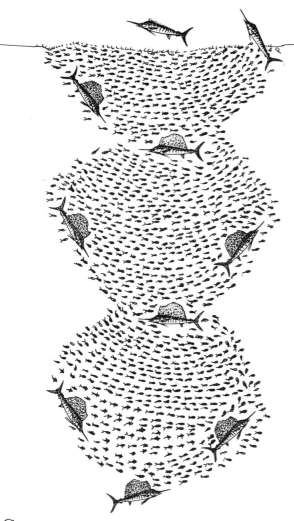

Sailfish ball the bait school. One will work the surface by jumping anti-clockwise in a tight circle with sail and fins folded. Others in the school will circle below the surface at various levels with dorsal fins and pelvic fins fully extended to look as big as possible to assist in rounding up the bait.

The ideal light tackle opponent—Atlantic sailfish at Cozumel, Mexico. Photo: Gil Keech.

drift with the baits. Other live baits may be cast by hand on slack line from trolling rods to supplement those cast on spinning rods.

Even if the live baits are not taken while the bait and sailfish are active on the surface, they may be taken down deeper if the drift with deep swimming baits is allowed to continue. Use of the echo sounder and sonar will confirm the presence of live bait under the boat, even when it is not showing on the surface. Fresh live baits can often be caught from these same schools to give anglers every chance. Sometimes, however, even when bait is visible, best results come with trolled baits. Every day may be different.

Fishing kites are used off the Florida Keys, particularly off the dropoff of the reefs outside Islamorada, Marathon and Key West, to produce sailfish strikes when other methods are not successful.

Fishing with live or dead baits from a kite,

An Atlantic sailfish takes to the air at Cozumel, Mexico. Photo: Gil Keech.

A *large Costa Rican sailfish changes into top gear above the surface. Photo: Darrell Jones.*

A *Costa Rican sailfish 'lit up' before release. Photo: Darrell Jones.*

*C*osta Rican sailfish combine barrel rolls and a balancing act with more conventional tactics. Photo: Darrell Jones.

A Pacific sailfish at Costa Rica about to be tagged and released. Photo: Darrell Jones.

particularly with baits of blue runners or other live bait gives great results with sailfish and marlin, while fishing for other species at other depths along the reefs or sea bed features with other methods.

There is sometimes agreement between the devotees of the various fishing methods for sailfish. Live baits drifting and casting have allowed a much wider section of fishermen to enjoy and experience the thrill of fishing for sailfish. There is, however, something very special about angling for these 'swashbucklers of the sea' in the classical manner—trolling carefully prepared and rigged natural or strip baits.

Occasionally, particularly in calm weather, sailfish, either singly or in small schools of three or more, will cruise on the surface with sails raised.

This is a thrilling and treasured sight and gives an excellent chance of a strike. These are often bigger fish than those found in the usual school and conditions. While the slender sailfish epitomizes the symmetry, beauty and colors of the billfish, it can also exhibit the smashing savagery and dedication to feed and killing that is also synonymous with billfish. The smashing power and kill are multiplied dramatically with size in the other billfish.

Teasers run in conjunction with a trolled bait pattern continue to be popular. Some crews run one or two strings of bubble-creating splashing lures such as pushers with or without jet holes, others prefer a daisy chain or coathanger spread of Moldcraft or similar soft plastic squid. Plastic teasers and natural teasers, particularly the Panama strip, run without hooks are successful in raising sailfish as well as other billfish to the boat, where fly fishermen can cast their saltwater flies. Fishing rules stress that the way must be off the boat. Teased sails will chase the Panama strips or other teasers maneuvered by the crew or other anglers to maintain billfish interest.

At 40 kg (88 lb) the body thickness and depth of the sailfish increase markedly. From this weight upwards they increase in power and toughness while still retaining their active, acrobatic performance. Despite the dramatic increase in power of big sailfish, they are always popular anglers' goals at any weight on any light tackle class.

Sailfishing is often done with leaders combining monofilament and light single-strand wire jointed with a snap swivel. The monofilament may be 24 kg (50 lb) or 37 kg (80 lb). The wire is light so that after tagging for release the mate takes and holds his wraps of the leader to break the light wire. If the fish is quiet, he may take the bill to retrieve the hook, as well as to hold the sailfish as the forward way of the boat quickly aids re-oxygenation.

Light tackle leaders around 2.9–3 m (8–9 ft) are very practical because they are long enough to clear the average-sized fish. Gaffing or tagging can then be done by one other person without the necessity of the leader being taken in hand and the fish being lost through the added pressure.

SPEARFISH

Spearfish are the least known of the world's billfish. The two species of most importance to anglers are the long-billed spearfish of the Atlantic and the short-billed spearfish in the Indo-Pacific Oceans. There is another relatively short-billed spearfish, the Mediterranean spearfish: unfortunately, none of these spearfish grow to the weights of the other billfish. However, despite their small size, they strike at lures intended for bigger billfish. Angler interest in the 'Spear Chucker', as it is familiarly called in Hawaii, is spasmodic. The vivid coloration, eating quality, and only occasional catch sparks real interest in them when caught.

They are an incidental catch in many warm-water trolling sport fisheries. It is a pity that there are not specific fishery areas and methods for them, so these smallest of billfish could be sought on tackle balanced to their weight. Spearfish give a good account of themselves when fought on light tackle, with splashing jumps and a long run.

The short-billed spearfish is difficult to confuse with any of the other Indo-Pacific billfish. The only possibility would be confusion with a broken-billed juvenile striped marlin. However, a quick check of distance between the anal opening and the anal fin is a distinguishing feature; in spearfish they are widely separated whereas in the other billfish they are close together.

Big long-billed spearfish of the Atlantic can be confused with white marlin. In the long-billed spearfish the second dorsal is closer to the tail than the second anal, the reverse of the positions on the white marlin, and the dorsal is curved at the rear instead of tapering straight. Once the fish is out of water into the cockpit, a clear difference can be measured. In the long-billed spearfish the anal opening is nearly the depth of the anal

Artist–scientist Guy Harvey brings alive the billfish of the world. This print was originally created for the Billfish Foundation. Photo: Peter Goadby.

Glowing, neon blue Pacific spearfish regularly take lures trolled for bigger billfish at Kona, Hawaii. Photo: Jacquie Acheson.

This baby short-nose spearfish, which has a long bill at this age, does not bear much resemblance to the adult it will become. Photo: courtesy Dr David Grobecker, PORF.

fin, whereas in white marlin it is closer than halfway.

Hawaii consistently produces more short-nosed spearfish than any other known area. Despite the relatively small size of the Atlantic and Pacific spearfish, relatively few fishermen have taken or tagged these fish to complete a full hand of world billfish brought to boat.

It would be interesting to know whether any boat has, in the Pacific, the Atlantic or the Caribbean, ever brought in or tagged all the billfish available in those oceans in any one day. In fact, few boats would have caught all available billfish in their watery world in a season. It is ironic that the smallest species, which seem to be a link between the mackerels and billfish, are the least prolific in anglers' catches.

BROADBILL

The red silk kite fluttered above the surface, incongruous and seemingly out of place against the remoteness of sea and sky. The kite height and direction were regulated by a great fisherman, Captain Geo. Farnsworth, as he used it to bring a bait enticingly into position in front of the fish swimming with dorsal and tail clear of the surface.

Captain Farnsworth's angler was hopeful of success, because of the successful teamwork developed with his captain. No one had yet caught one of these fish on rod and reel. The kite they used had successfully presented baits that hooked and caught bluefin tuna while other skippers and anglers wondered how they did it and went fishless. Now they were baiting the broad-sworded gladiator of the sea from that fragile red silk kite.

The rest of that day made angling history. William Boschen, who is credited with the design and concept of the world's first star drag reel, called by maker Vom Hofe the B'Ocean, landed that broadbill, and so became doubly enshrined as a first prize winner. The year was 1913.

Broadbill are still regarded as saltwater angling's greatest prize, even though their capture is a little easier and more widespread through the development of night-time drift fishing. Boschen fought his 162-kg (358-lb) first broadbill, without benefit of harness or chair, from a small single motor launch.

Broadbill have always been regarded as the ultimate angling challenge. Because of their characteristic cruising on the surface in a few areas of ocean (apparently to re-oxygenate), fishermen can see them, but then the difficulties start. Broadbill are exasperating to bait, to hook and to fight, as well as to find.

Swordfish have been recorded in Greek and Roman writings. The scientific name *Xipnias gladius* comes from both Greek and Latin, both meaning 'sword'. In 350 B.C., Aristotle called them 'broadbill'.

They are tough opponents, combining some of the best and most difficult characteristics exhibited by marlin, tuna and sharks. To these characteristics of difficulty must be added the special factors of soft mouth, soft skin and tissue. These difficulties negate modern technique and powerful tackle, so that even when a bait is taken and a hook-up effected, there is still the problem of pulled hooks, a problem exacerbated by power of angler and tackle. These difficulties remain, whether broadbill are fished in the classic hunting method of sight fishing, which requires perhaps the greatest dedication and single-mindedness of any sportfishing, or by the more recent night-time drifting live baits which is, as well as the long-established dead bait presentations, sometimes successful.

One of the highlights of my fishing has been the opportunity to fish for and bait broadbill in California using the classic method of seeking, spotting and presenting the bait in daylight. Florida's successful development of night fishing by drifting the canyons and

Gaffs are ready on the coverboard as Captain Doug Osborn watches intently while Michael Lerner fights a Chilean broadbill. Photo: IGFA—Lerner Expedition.

other likely broadbill hot spots, pioneered by the Webb brothers, produces broadbill for those prepared to fish in often difficult and uncomfortable conditions. The greatest chance of success with these fighters in Australia, New Zealand, Hawaii, Venezuela and other areas where broadbill do not commonly cruise on the surface is in night-time drifting. Each method requires skill, preparation, hard work, vigilance and concentration. Each gives fishermen a chance to tangle with the greatest gamefish. It is unfortunate for anglers that there are relatively few known areas in the world where broadbill can be consistently visually fished on the surface. Chile, the locality for many broadbill records over the years, is still producing great fish taken by the classic method of searching, sighting and presenting baits.

Ted Naftzger, who has taken more broadbill by sight fishing than any other angler in world angling history and has proved a master on all tackle classes for all marlin and giant tunas, rates broadbill as the ultimate challenge. Ted, an incredibly accurate judge of just how much pressure to apply to the limit of the line breaking strain combined with uncanny understanding of what the fish is doing, could have weighed many more and bigger broadbill than he has by fishing with the benefits of IGFA rules. Instead as a past president of the Tuna Club of Avalon he fishes Tuna Club rules. When fishing in California, Ted fishes to the Tuna Club tackle regulations, even though he knows the shorter leader of 4.5 m (15 ft) increases the difficulty of capture. IFGA rules allow a maximum leader of 9 m (30 ft) and 12 m (40 ft) combined in double and leader. Anglers should always fish to IGFA rules in case of a potential world record catch.

Broadbill range from tropical to cool waters worldwide. The few known places where they regularly cruise on the surface include California, Baja, north-east USA, and of course Chile, Peru and Ecuador.

Swordfish are usually deep water fish expected in 110 m (60 fathoms) and deeper, although they have been sighted feeding on school fish right alongside beach and rocky headlands. Study of Japanese longline data and commercial catches should give the times and places.

Best results usually come fishing canyons along the 185-m (100-fathom) dropoff, and the edges of deep water banks and features on the sea bed. Success in night fishing is often associated with areas known as productive longline grounds.

Sight fishing with dead and/or live natural baits:

Daylight fishing for broadbill means hunting for fish, with all on board looking for the distinctive sickle fins. Eyes scan and search ceaselessly from tower, from bridge and deck level. Binoculars are a great help for long-range identification, just as they are with tailing marlin. Birds and bait action and water color changes—just in case broadbill are associated with these indicators—are more readily observed. One of the frustrations proving the dedication and single-mindedness of broadbill fishermen is that they deliberately bypass and ignore tailing marlin that would surely take a bait or lure and bring some action in the day. They know that if they are distracted and spend time in accepting the chance for marlin action instead of searching for broadbill, they may miss their chance at their objective.

Singlemindedness was clearly brought home when fishing with Kay and Dick Mulholland on their Uniflite, *Lady Kay* from Ventura, California. It was decided and quite clear than even though we were all dedicated marlin

The fabric that dreams are made of, a big Chilean broadbill. Photo: IGFA—Lerner Expedition.

fishermen at other times, marlin and tuna would be ignored if found. We were looking and fishing for broadbill. None of us regretted the decision to spend these days in the quest for broadbill.

Preparation for broadbill starts with meticulous checking of tackle to be used. The reel brake should be super-smooth. On heavy tackle—37 kg (80 lb) and 60 kg (130 lb)—the brake must be set to give no more than 10-kg (22-lb). On lighter tackle one-quarter to one-third of line class should be set. The reason for the 10-kg (22-lb) maximum is to minimize the chance of pulled hooks.

Baits of two or three kinds must be rigged on the monofilament leaders with razor-sharp hooks. Squid are the No. 1 bait, the others being pelagic fish common in the area to be fished. Barracuda, skipjack tuna, and mackerel may be successful if the squid are not taken after four or five presentations to the slowly moving fish.

At this stage of growth broadbill swordfish do not yet resemble the majestic adult into which they will grow. Photo: Bob Fewell, courtesy Dr David Grobecker, PORF.

Rigged and spare squid should be packed in plastic bags so they do not come into contact with ice or fresh water that will discolor the baits so they do not present naturally.

Once at sea, keen eyes, binoculars, plus the choice of likely areas and experience, will give an angler the best chance to bait a broadbill.

Most broadbill fishermen prefer to bait a fish while it is swimming straight at a constant cruising speed rather than a fish changing direction and speed and circling. Once the fish is sighted the boat speed is dropped until steerage is just maintained. The engine revolution should not be further varied until the fish has taken or slashed at the bait. All noises, including voices and vibration, must be minimized until hook-up time.

Many fishermen try to run the bait about 70 m (80 yards) behind the boat. They have another 35 to 40 m (40–50 yards) of slack line on the water ready as drop back from rod tip to where the line is held. Many are reluctant to use outriggers and outrigger clips. This is done by some successful broadbill crews with the line held from the flying bridge.

Many skippers try to keep the boat up-sun of the fish while presenting the bait so they and the angler can see as clearly as possible what the fish is doing. Although some skippers and anglers believe it does not upset the fish, most will try to avoid putting boat wake across the cruising fish as they position the bait.

The bait should be passed slowly in front of the swordfish about 0.6 metres (2 feet) under the surface. It should pass within 6 m (20 ft) of the big fish. Many skippers do not want the bait to break the surface. Sometimes after several passes at this depth, the bait may be given more line so it runs deeper if the swordfish swims further under the surface, even if lost from sight. It may pick up a sinking bait where it was last seen.

In his books, Kip Farrington stressed that the line should not be retrieved while near a cruising broadbill, even for a short distance to gain better positioning.

When a bait is taken or struck by the sword, the motors should be pulled out of gear ready for the angler's or skipper's decision to strike to set the hook or hooks. Broadbill baits are often rigged with two hooks to give a better chance of a solid hook-up.

The action of broadbill taking a bait may vary between a gentle tap and a violent, savage slash. The angler's strike should if possible be after the pause that comes with big fish swallowing the bait. The pause that follows the swallow and swim-on may be longer than experienced with marlin and sharks. A slow count of five after the resumption of swimming should be sufficient. Sometimes after taking the bait the broadbill will immediately rush towards the surface. In this case the angler should strike immediately. At other times, whether line is taken in a series of jerks or smoothly without apparent pause, 60 m (70 yards) of line out from the reel should provide every chance. Anglers above all should be patient, should be thinking, trying to feel exactly what the fish is doing, to keep in touch with the fish before committing to the strike.

At all times during the fight, the effect of reel brake with decreasing spool diameter and bag and drag of line in the water must be considered. If there is a bag or long length of line out, the angler must ease the reel brake to minimize the pull on the hooks and maximize the chances of the hooks staying in place. Once line is recovered and the line is shortened and leads straight to the broadbill, the brake can be increased, back to its previous level.

It is important to keep working the fish, to give no respite. Backing up, running the fish and planing the

A *Tutakaka New Zealand broadbill shows why, it is known as the 'Broad Sworded Gladiator of the Sea'. Photo: G. E. Angus.*

Captain Bill Hatch and angler, Mrs Helen Lerner, help the Chilean crew use the gin pole to boat Mrs Lerner's broadbill. Photo: IGFA—Lerner Expedition.

fish should all be directed at bringing fish and boat close together. The circling maneuver that so often works on marlin, sharks and other fish may be counter-productive with broadbill, because it could increase line drag and the ratio of pulled hooks.

Sight fishing with cast live baits: Anglers in California and Mexico often cast a live bait on lighter tackle from the bow of the boat to the surface-cruising fish. Some boats have a pulpit and an additional live bait tank forward, so anglers can readily fish live bait for striped marlin and broadbill. Experienced fishermen like to have

two casting anglers and tackle ready to cast the live bait to broadbill in these circumstances. The first mackerel in the water will often race back to the boat for protection of the hull as it is chased by the broadbill. A second bait presented to the broadbill, as it tries to monster the first bait but can't reach it because of the boat hull, will sometimes be readily taken.

The problem with broadbill once they are found, baited and hooked, is not only in their fighting characteristics, whether deep or on the surface, but in the frustrating proportion of pulled hooks.

In his 1883 *History of Swordfish* published in

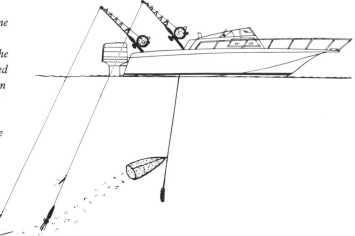

Hawaiian fishermen continue to use traditional Ika Shibi stone fishing to lower chum to the expected broadbill and tuna depth. Small pieces of chum are wrapped in an open-ended cloth bag (the Havna bag). The stone or lead sinker-weighted chum line is rolled around the bag of chum. The rolled chum line is held by the chum drop line while it is lowered to the desired depth. When the drop line is jerked sharply the rolls of chum line come free, the bag opens and the chum scatters and sinks to start its attraction. The procedure is carried out at regular 20 minute intervals until nearby baits are taken.

Washington DC by the Government Printer, George Brown Goode referred to the number and size of the swordfish off Chile and Peru. Despite modern fishing pressure these waters are again providing record captures.

There is no doubt that one of the most magnificent fish ever taken is Lou Marron's 60-kg (130-lb) class broadbill of 536.5 kg (1182 lb). The superb cast of this fish in the clubhouse of the Rod and Reel Club of Miami ensures that it is never forgotten, as well as visually providing a challenge for someone to catch a bigger swordfish. Swordfish created awareness and excitement centuries before their quest by rod and reel anglers. They were known and recognized many centuries before marlin, sailfish and spearfish were identified. They were taken by drifting at night, by the Mediterranean traps and by those who fished with harpoons centuries before the modern slaughter by longlines and drift nets.

Dr C. F. Holder, who triggered the establishment of gamefish clubs and rules and ethics, was a fisherman whose interest in big fish preceded as well as continued during his sportfishing. Long before he caught his milestone tuna at Avalon, Santa Catalina, California, he was interested enough in broadbill to take a trip on a harpoon sloop from Woods Hole to search out beyond Block Island. That trip was successful with three broadbill. One of the harpooned broadbill was 3 m (9.5 feet) long. Holder wrote, 'Though I have frequently caught sharks that measured 13 feet [4 m] I never saw one that equalled the strength of this formidable creature.' Appropriately, it was William Boschen, a member of the Tuna Club Dr Holder founded, who captured the first broadbill with rod and reel.

Drifting at night with live or dead baits: In many waters broadbill do not surface cruise in daylight to give anglers a chance to see and bait them. There are chances, often with better odds, fishing out wide and deep at night. While heading out early in the morning to fish, the Webb

brothers of Miami realized that commercial fishermen, many of whom had learned the techniques in their original home, Cuba, were heading back to port with broadbill captures. The Webbs applied this night-drifting technique to sportfishing in the areas where broadbill should be. They added the benefits of cyalume light sticks to their fishing, with the result that a successful sport fishery was created. Unfortunately the value of the fish caught triggered a commercial fishery that after a few short successful seasons caused a frightening decline in stock from longline overfishing right along the US Atlantic coast. Now in other parts of the world the stocks have been drastically reduced, not only by longlining, but by the cursed driftnet fishing.

Night sportfishing for any species is quite different from fishing in daylight. Every difficulty is magnified. The horizon is not defined, the sounds and effects of wind and waves are magnified, the danger of ship rundown is dramatically increased. Suddenly the difficulties of holding position over the bottom and regulating depths of bait, present but relatively small in daylight, are magnified. A continuous watch for ships and other boats is necessary. The night-time performance of sharks, particularly high-flying makos, adds to the challenge and danger at boatside.

One of the benefits of this night-time fishing experience, apart from the chance of swordfish, is that of simply being part of another, different world. The fishing lights in and over the surface attract and show sea creatures not often seen in daylight. Squid and small fish have moved right into the top water levels. Squid can often be caught to provide fresh live baits and replace those eaten by other squid or fish. Out and below the lights, the environment is truly 'eat or be eaten'. Various shark species, particularly makos, blues and threshers, oil fish, opah (moonfish), or one of the big tunas, plus any other deep water species that come towards the surface with the food chain that rises in the evening and sinks back to the depths as the morning approaches, provide action. Night fishing broadbill crews may experience the thrill of makos, the blue dynamite with their short fuses flying out of the darkness of sky to jump as high or higher than the flying bridge. Razor curved teeth, black eye and blue and silvery white body show dramatically in the lights at eye level with the skipper. The use of monofilament leader minimizes the shark catch and time of involvement, but as so often happens, particularly when unwanted, the sharks don't cut off and fight right to the boat.

Broadbill at night, as in daytime fishing, strike in varying ways. There may be a smashing blockbuster that tears line from reel and shakes the rod in its rod holder, chair or cover board while the line disappears at blinding speed, or a gentle, almost imperceptible take. Sometimes squid or fish will be belted and slashed while the line slowly rolls from the spool. There is then the swallowing pause and faster follow on to give the angler the chance to strike. Night-time broadbill often race towards the surface to jump or run once they or the angler have effected a hook-up.

The cold blue or green glowing light stick provides a possible big fish attractant when affixed to the leader or concealed in the bait. On the leader, they are important markers for positioning visually the leader and fish to assist boat maneuvering in darkness.

Some night-time broadbill fishermen prefer to fish in the dark of the moon, working on the belief that the fish will come even closer to the surface; others prefer the time of full moon. The amount of moonlight in any night is taken into account with current and sea conditions, in determining the depth of the baits. It is difficult to fish with more than three lines so baits should be positioned and sometimes weighted to cover the productive depths.

Sea anchors can be used to help control the rate of drift and to make the boat action more comfortable. Sometimes natural conditions dictate to drift with only two lines. Depths of bait vary from 10 m (32 ft)–90 m (300 ft). Lead weights on light breakaway thread can be used to help keep the bait at the chosen depth. Plastic bottles, styrene foam blocks and balloons can be used as floats, again with lightweight breakaway threads. The light breakaway threads are a must so the bait will be free, not resisting pull or swallowing by the fish. Heavy resistance alerts the fish, which then usually does not proceed with taking the bait. Downriggers with the release set very light are also sometimes used to hold the bait down deep.

There are differing opinions as to when to strike for hook-up, as hook pulling is always foremost in fishermen's minds. Some set the reel drag at the maximum strike they will be using (10 kg or 22 lb) on heavy tackle, particularly when using curved point hook models such as those used commercially on handlines and some longlines, particularly in Hawaii. Others keep the brake

light, as they would for sharks or marlin in drift fishing; they are prepared to let the fish take the bait and move away with it slowly, then wait for the pause to swallow and to swim away again before the angler strikes to set the hook. If the broadbill races towards the surface before being struck by the angler, it should be struck immediately, as the fish is either hooked or aware of an object to be rid of by jumping and throwing clear.

Taking the leader: Another crisis point with broadbill, as with so many other fish, is when the leader is in reach and in hand. It should be agreed by angler, skipper and crew alike whether the leader man is to pull as hard as the leader will allow or to handle it carefully at about the same pressure exerted by the angler during the fight. Both the maximum muscle and kid glove technique have their strong advocates, with results to prove their contentions. My personal preference is in between—to be careful not to provoke a quiet fish, but to use as much power as the leader will take on an active fish to give a shot with gaff or tag when the leader is in hand. Either way can be wrong, particularly with broadbill, so agreement on the plan for handling the leader is imperative for good teamwork.

Where to gaff: Because of the soft flesh of broadbill, the gaff or gaffs must be placed to ensure maximum bite over the body. Just behind the dorsal fin into the shoulder is usually best. A tail rope will secure the catch until a meat hook can be slipped through the lower jaw so the prize fish can be brought on board.

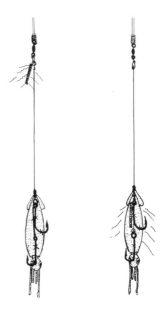

Cyalume lights are effective for broadbill in green as well as blue or other colours. The cyalume light stick is helpful when attached to the top of the leader as it shows the position of the bait, attracts fish and, during the fight, shows the position of the leader. The cyalume light stick can be inserted inside the rigged squid as shown in the diagram on the right.

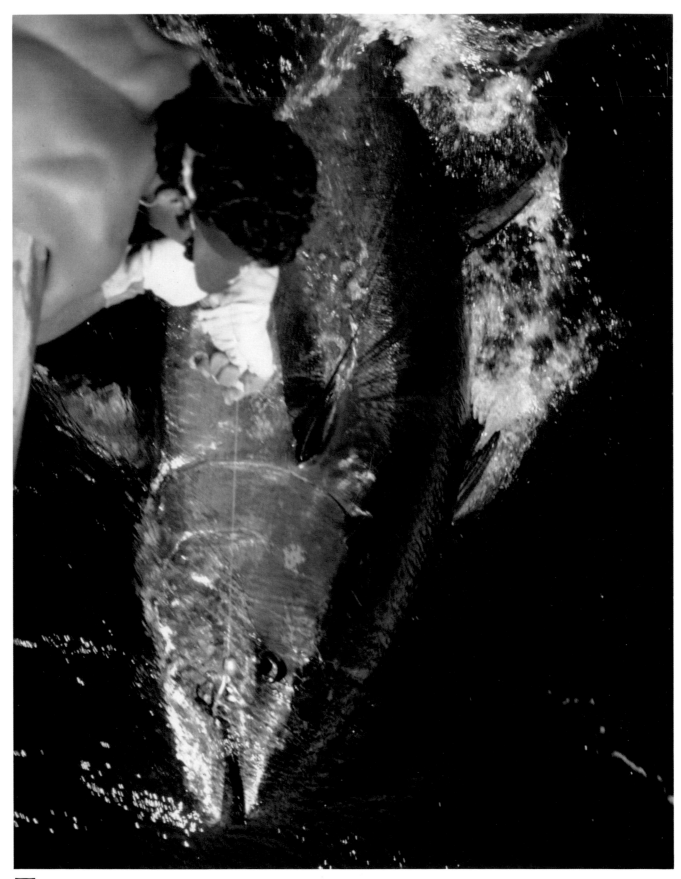

The immense bulk of the bluefin dwarfs the wireman. It is easy to see why giant bluefin were called horse mackerel by US commercial fishermen. Photo: Paul Murray.

T U N A

Tuna are major gamefish species, spread through the world's oceans. They range from the giant northern bluefin that could weigh in excess of 730 kg (1600 lb) down to the ubiquitous striped tuna that provide pleasure, action, food and bait in all oceans. All tuna, irrespective of size, are fast, tough, deep fighters. They are sought by anglers for their fighting abilities first and their food qualities second.

The world record species are the following: little tunny (*Euthynnus alletteratus*, Rafinesque, 1810), black skipjack (*Euthynnus affinis*, Kishinouye, 1920), albacore (*Thunnus alalunga*, Bonnaterre, 1788), kawa kawa—mackerel tuna (*Euthynnus affinis*, Cantor, 1850), Pacific big eye (*Thunnus obesus*, Lowe, 1839), southern bluefin tuna (*Thunnus maccoyii*, Castelnau, 1872), northern bluefin tuna, giant bluefin tuna and bluefin tuna (*Thunnus thynnus*, Linnaeus, 1758), dog tooth tuna (*Gymnosarda unicolor*, Rüpple, 1838), long tail tuna, also called northern bluefin tuna or Oriental bonito (*Thunnus tonggol*, Bleeker, 1851), blackfin tuna (*Thunnus atlanticus*, Lesson, 1830), skipjack tuna or striped tuna (*Euthynnus pelamis*, Linnaeus, 1758), and last but certainly not least the yellowfin tuna (*Thunnus albacares*, Bonnaterre, 1788). IGFA world records are also granted for the bonito (*Sarda orientalis*, Temminck & Schlegel, 1844 and *Sarda australis*, Macleay, 1880), *Sarda chiliensis*, Cuvier, 1831 and *Sarda sarda*, Bloch, 1793.

There are several small tunas closely related to the bonito which are mainly of interest as bait species. These include the leaping bonito, the frigate tuna and the bullet tuna. There are two other tunas which, although relatively common in cold southern Pacific waters, because of their food source and environment are only occasionally taken by recreational fishermen. They are the butterfly tuna and the slender tuna.

Most tuna are worldwide species. The skipjack is regarded as the most widespread pelagic fish. The biggest of these very important fish is the northern bluefin tuna or giant bluefin; the smallest of the major sport tunas is often the skipjack or the three *euthynnus* species also used so successfully as live or dead bait. These species and those of the sizes in between are important on the world's fishing calendar offshore and some are also important in bays and estuaries.

Northern bluefin, yellowfin, albacore and to a lesser extent the deep-swimming big eye have been and are a backbone of the recreational fisheries in many ports in many countries. Southern bluefin tuna became a prime reason for active gamefishing in southern Australian and southern New Zealand waters. Longtail tuna with their confusing Australian local name of northern bluefin (not to be confused with the giant bluefin) are an important and key species in the development of sportfishing in many tropical western Pacific and Indian Ocean localities.

The magical colorful, powerful yellowfin also win many trophies and many point scores in hotly competitive clubs, as well as providing much of the year's seasonal backbone for the offshore recreational industry in many tropical ports. Giant yellowfin mainly challenge the anglers on southern Californian long-range boats that travel from San Diego to the islands south and west of Mexico and Baja, California. The IGFA heavy tackle records come from these voyages when live bait activity and these giants that appear out of the darkness are part of a unique big boat stand-up fishing challenge.

Albacore, the ocean wanderers, are consistently important at California and many other areas where the water temperature, current and close proximity of the continental shelf dropoff bring this top eating and top fighting light tackle tuna into importance.

The Indo-Pacific reef-dwelling dog tooth tuna would be a constant attraction to visiting anglers were it not for their rarity. They seem to be quickly fished out under regular pressure. Unlike the other oceanic tunas, the dog tooth, whose habit is marauding around the living coral of the outer reefs and reef openings, are apparently not present in big schools. It is also a great pity that this determined, deep-fighting tuna with its characteristic jerking tail beat is not more prolific. It is a species of great challenge for its fighting ability as well as its uncommonness and the quality of its white flesh.

It is also a great pity that in the development of many of the world's offshore recreational fisheries there are not yet defined hot spots for surface fishing the big eye, although the Canary Islands approach that trolling potential. These barrel-bodied challengers grow to in excess of 180 kg (400 lb) and are great fighters, whether taken on trolled konaheads on the surface or on live or dead natural baits down deep. Big eye are consistently taken by longline fishermen in most tropical and temperate waters. It is possible, now that recreational fishermen are working longer hours with more tide changes and wider offshore, places to fish for big eye will be found. It is likely that the north-east USA method used by Tred Barta and other Atlantic fishermen and anglers of trolling a big pattern of konaheads over the wider offshore canyons and peaks will finally provide big eye action. The action-packed challenge with multiple strikes off the north-east coast of USA along the shelf and way out beyond the 100-fathom drop may spread to other countries. The main factors in big eye action are the right locality and fast trolling of konaheads in

From this beginning, tuna have become the reason, the platform, for sport fishermen around the world. Their fighting characteristics, the range of species in size, and the range of environment give opportunity for sport as well as food, from every type and weight of tackle. Some of the smaller species fight so hard that very often fishermen say, 'Just as well they don't grow bigger or we could never land them.'

Dr Holder's record bluefin weight was surpassed by fellow Tuna Club members and then by Atlantic fishermen. The record was held by Mitchell Henry in English waters before returning to the US and Canadian waters. The quest for bigger fish was in full cry around the world. Giant bluefin tuna were found in the Atlantic, from the warm waters of the Bahamas to the cold green waters of the northern USA and Canada. The giant tuna, particularly in the Bahamas, forced improvements and refinements in rods, reels, lines and all tackle, in boats and their equipment and in boat handling and technique. All around the world the perfectly aerodynamically shaped tuna, propelled by their powerful symmetrical tails, wander in schools, harrying the bait fish and squid. Tuna of various species are found wherever there is deep salt water. Apart from the northern bluefin tuna, the giant that migrates from cold through tropical waters, most tuna are found in temperate and tropical waters in water temperatures between 13°C and 26°C (55°F to 79°F).

Tuna are able to keep their body temperature higher than the water in which they are swimming. Scientists such as Hawaii's Richard Brill are studying this phenomenon. Dr Brill and Dr Kim Holland have also added to knowledge of tuna and marlin habits by productive studies, often in difficult conditions, by following the electronically tagged fish.

Whether there is a Pacific and an Atlantic species of giant bluefin or one world species, there is no doubt that these ocean-crossing fish are valuable and highly sought sporting fish in all sizes, wherever they are.

The glowing colors, elongated fins and power of the yellowfin generally make this species no. 2 in the tuna hierarchy. It would be good if those strikes meant a billfish, but if not, there is still satisfaction at the chance of a yellowfin. Big eye tuna and southern bluefin in weight and size ranging between yellowfin and giant northern bluefin may be bigger, but their power and tough fighting means that they are sought by heavy tackle fishermen trolling lures, as well as lighter line classes with live bait. Another incentive for those who take the opportunity to fish for yellowfin tuna is that there is the opportunity for multiple strikes and catches from the school. A single strike on lures can sometimes be turned into multiple action by quick use of chum and live bait or cast lures.

The skipjack, with its pyjama-striped body, is regarded by scientists as the most widespread of all fish. As with other tuna, skipjack have a variety of names: oceanic bonito, striped tuna, bonito. As always the variety of names causes confusion. Two prominent and active members of a Californian club were fishing in New Zealand where they read of Australian anglers taking striped tuna. Striped tuna? They'd never caught those. Here was a new species for them.

They extended their trip to Sydney, Australia to seek 'striped tuna', and chartered a boat. Their wishes were quickly fulfilled as the boat found a school and their lures were quickly taken. After a typical jerky never-give-up fight the tuna were gaffed and lifted aboard, and the anglers realized they had learned in an expensive way that this was the same fish prolific in the waters of Hawaii, Fiji, New Zealand—the familiar skipjack. The day's fishing was made more memorable when one of the 'striped tuna' was rigged and put back as a live bait. This was in turn taken by an unsighted fish that quickly revealed itself as a 100-kg (220-lb) black marlin, a species they had not previously caught. So the visit for striped tuna finally paid off as a black marlin quest.

Atlantic anglers are lucky that in addition to the big tuna species and the smaller species similar to those in the Pacific and Indian Oceans, they have their ocean medium-size fireball, the blackfin tuna, in the western Atlantic and Caribbean.

Tuna in their various species and sizes cover all salt-water environments from bays and estuaries across the plain and reefs of the continental shelf. The continental shelf dropoffs provide maximum yellowfin and big eye congregations.

There seems no doubt that while some of the tunas wander or migrate over long distances, others are local stocks. Sometimes a day's catch at oceanic crossroads such as Hawaii will show apparent variations in shape and proportions of body.

Tuna fishing success from rocky headlands that jut into the warm currents on Australian and South African coasts remind boat anglers of just how close tuna come to shore. Yellowfin up to 70 kg (150 lb) have been taken with live bait on rod and reel from the rocks. Kawa kawa, long-tail tuna and bonito, as well as black and striped marlin, are also taken in these localities. Currents and their back eddies sometimes come into and inside entrances to bays to combine in a shorebound hot spot that can rival boat catches.

The tunas sometimes move in shoals of two or three species of yellowfin, longtail, skipjack, big eye, kawa kawa and northern and southern bluefin to give additional challenge.

The northern bluefin is the heaviest and biggest of the tunas and deserves its name, giant bluefin tuna. It grows to at least five times the expected maximum size of southern bluefin, which generally does not grow in excess of 160 kg (350 lb).

Big eye tuna, particularly in the northern Atlantic over the canyons and dropoffs along the north-east coastal states of the USA, will at times and tide conditions strike savagely in multiple strikes on fast trolled lures. At other

TROLLING TACTICS

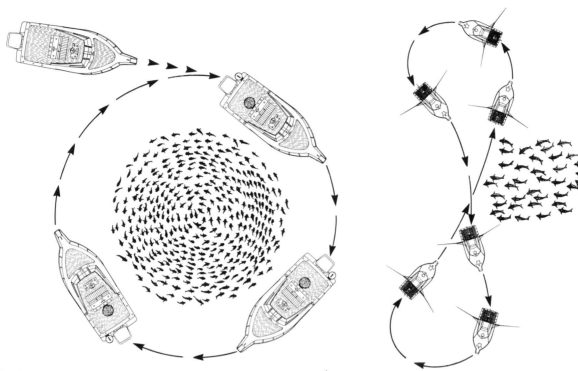

The safe way for several boats to troll a bait patch and for additional boats to enter the trolling sequence.

A practical all-round pattern for one boat to work a school for best presentation and minimum frightening of fish.

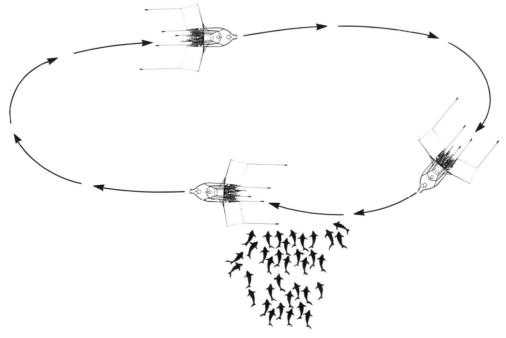

A safe and productive pattern for more than one boat to work a school.

times this species is taken by drifting live baits deep. Whether hooked on a lure on the surface or deep on drifted baits, big eye gives really tough, deep circling fights that test the skill, strength and technique of any angler and crew.

Northern bluefin are found where bait fish and squid provide food concentrations. When bluefin were prolific some incredible fishing took place alongside trawlers and herring seiners. For anglers the fighting of giant bluefin around nets, lobster trap floats and other obstacles gives added challenge. Accounts and memories of pioneers who battled bluefin in man-powered dories generated interest overall in tuna and fishing. Members of the pre-war USA Tuna Cup teams such as Bill Goadby Lawrence had all enjoyed a baptism of tuna battles around major natural obstacles from dories as well as converted commercial lobster boats. The super quarterhorses of the ocean, the fully equipped gamefishing cruisers, were still well in the future.

Once a tuna is hooked it is logical to try to bring it to boat for gaffing or tag and release as quickly as possible, particularly in waters where sharks can be a problem. Sharks are habitual predators on tuna of all sizes, as tuna, unlike the billfish and other sharks, do not have weapons to retaliate. Tuna use their blinding acceleration and speed to escape. Part of the speed and acceleration comes from the heat exchangers that keep the tuna's blood a few degrees higher than the temperature of the surrounding ocean.

The heat exchangers of the two giant bluefin species that migrate on regular routes from tropical to cold temperate waters are more developed than in any other tunas.

The dog-toothed tuna of the Indo-Pacific reef area is most unusual in several ways. One is, as its name implies, that it has prominent peg-shaped teeth; another is that it does not have any scales, whereas most have some scales even if only on their shoulder area. Another dog-tooth characteristic is that its chosen habitat is close in, right along the outer edge of outside reefs and in the openings of these reefs. The flesh of the dog-toothed tuna is as white as that of the albacore, in contrast to the red flesh of other tunas and bonito.

All tunas are sought intensively commercially. They are valuable catches taken by all methods—purse seining, longlining, drift netting, pole and bait, drop line, or rod and reel. The peak prices are given in the Japanese market for fresh chilled high-fat tuna such as bluefin, southern bluefin, big eye and yellowfin. At times, depending on the market demand, supply and fat content of the fish, the Japanese market price could be as high as A$40 per kg. Purse seine and other net-caught fish generally do not meet the top sashimi requirements. Tuna are important food species everywhere. From pre-Christian times, the Mediterranean coasts were the sites for giant traps that jutted from shore and took the giant bluefin on their annual migrations into and along this almost-

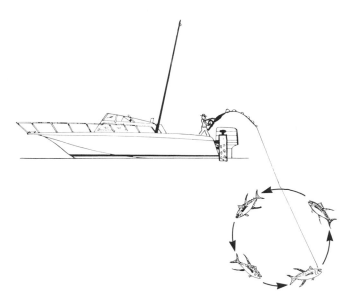

A typical circling line win and loss of a circling tuna. It is important to feel and to maintain line pressure, lift and recovery while the fish circles upwards.

landlocked sea. These traps were finally dismantled in the 1980s as the stocks of bluefin dwindled after remaining constant for more than 2000 years. Modern fishing take by longline and purse seine of the northern bluefin is protected by quota and scientific monitoring.

Commercial fishing pressure has necessitated closed seasons, quotas and scientific monitoring of the population because of the possibility of extinction. Quotas on southern bluefin have also been agreed on by the fishing management authorities of Japan, New Zealand and Australia. Concern for stocks of albacore as well as the kill of other animals and wastage also caused international concern that led to banning of high-seas drift nets.

One of the most impressive sights in nature was the once-relentless passage of schools of giant bluefin tuna through the clear green water along the yellow sand bottom of the Bahamas banks. Bimini and Cat Cay were synonymous with giant tuna. These island jewels were the gathering place for the fishermen who came to participate in the epitome of angling competition between man and great fish. The flying start to the tournaments was impressive. Boat speed, as the boats turned water into spray and froth, was important, not just for the spectacular start but in searching, finding and working the schools. Competitors hoped for windy days that generated surface chop synonymous with great fishing in the Bahamas.

Success with giant bluefin within or outside the tournaments forced change, thought and evolution in skippers, crew, anglers, rods, reels, boats and fishing technique that spread to all offshore fishing. The charisma and challenge of the fish and fishing lifted fishing for giant tuna to a pinnacle of sophistication not often achieved elsewhere. Some of the world's top anglers rated the 'stop them or pop them' success ingredient of giant tuna fishing as an even greater challenge than that of huge billfish. The philosophy for many was: marlin are good, giant bluefin are great. Many of our improvements of boats and tackle reflect the importance of the giant bluefin of the Bahamas. The power of the giant tuna forced the creation of Bimini twist and Bimini roll for knots, tuna towers and tuna doors, gin poles and A-frames on boats, meat hooks as gaffs, heavy tackle roller guides, bent butts, seat harness, reels with super drags and dependability as well as gear changing to lift and control the powerful fish. Changes in rod pumping with awareness of benefits of short pumping plus recovery of only a few centimetres of line, of not letting the fish rest and re-oxygenate, were all necessitated by giant tuna.

The captains and crews from nearby Florida, as well as further north, brought their boats across the Florida Straits to join anglers in the thought, preparation and perspiration necessary to meet the challenges. Initially, it seemed that the only way to beat the giant tuna and the blue marlin in the Bahamas and offset the shark problem was to move to heavier and heavier tackle. Thirty-nine thread was the theoretical equivalent of today's 60 kg (130 lb) tackle. This was deemed not heavy enough, and anglers tried 54 and even 72 thread. Line strength was not the answer to these fish, who would still often get over the edge of the bank and into the depths, where time and sharks worked against the fishermen. The solution was in technique, in skill and teamwork from skipper, crew and angler. Many of the great skippers had previously been great crew, bait riggers, leader men, fish spotters. They understood the problems and worked to solve them. Somehow it seems that Tommy Gifford and his crew were at the edge of

development. In those great tournaments, the Merritts, Walter Voss, the Staros brothers, Red Stuart, Charley Hayden and Mutt Coble and other top skippers and crews were there to give their anglers every chance.

Bill Carpenter and Elwood Harry were two of the great tuna competition anglers, at one with all aspects of the fight. It was appropriate that these two top anglers not only dominated many Bahamas tournament wins, but led in tag and release programs, with tuna they released recovered after long distance trans-Atlantic crossings. Both subsequently became presidents of IGFA, leaders in rules, ethics and conservation for the world's fish.

Knowledge gained on bluefin of all sizes spread to the fishing of all big tuna. Fighting with high drag settings and maneuvering the boat to cut across the fish to keep minimum line in the water are inherent in success with all tuna. These are fish that do not expend energy in flashing jumps and surface acrobatics. Short pumps that do not let up on the fish, so line is spooled back on the reel as fast as the fish allows, are mandatory. Tuna fishing has given an insight into the circling, swimming action of fish against pressure exerted by angler, boat and line.

The smaller tuna species and juveniles of the giant tuna exhibit many similar characteristics with their own variations in their fight. It is fair to say that, apart from any tuna accidentally choked with a big live bait, there are no easy tuna. Most are tough: the best chances come from the occasional tuna that fight on the surface instead of circling deep. The fast run into the depths can cause some tail-wrapped fish. If tuna are brought to boat tail wrapped, it is important (if they are to be taken, not tagged or released) that the leader is not taken. The fish should be brought by the angler into range of fixed head gaffs. These gaffs can lift the tuna tail clear of the water. If the leader were to be taken and subsequently come clear of the tail, there is every possibility of a broken leader or damaged hands as the suddenly freely swimming fish propels itself back towards the deep.

NORTHERN BLUEFIN TUNA— GIANT BLUEFIN

No two scenes are more typical of one fish species and yet more different than these with giant bluefin tuna in the Atlantic: in one, the translucent green water over gold sandbanks, plus warmth and brilliant sun, is dominant; in the other the sea is dark green and sombre, the sky often grey or foggy, the sun giving light rather than warmth, and the cool, moisture-laden air penetrating even warm wet-weather clothing.

Although giant bluefin occur in the north Atlantic and Pacific Oceans, the Mediterranean and Adriatic Seas, they are remembered most in the north and central Atlantic and Caribbean fisheries. Yet they should not be forgotten as the original object of recreational fishing and rules in the Pacific at Santa Catalina.

This ocean-crossing species comes close inshore, within reach of anglers, particularly in the Atlantic off

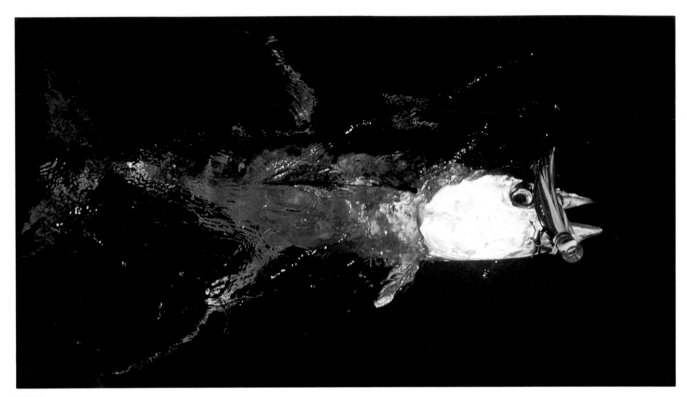

Whether hooked on trolled lures, or live or dead bait, yellowfin are rightly regarded as one of the superfish. Photo: Tim Simpson.

the north-east coast of USA and Canada's Maritime Provinces where they enter water 18 metres (ten fathoms) or shallower. In the clear green water of the Caribbean in early summer they are the epitome of tropical fishing. Later in summer and into autumn, in their long-established migration and quest for food, they move into the rich green of the cool Atlantic. Newfoundland, with the frozen blue of its drifting icebergs, where schools of herring and mackerel are massacred by the steadily weight-increasing hungry-feeding bluefin, has been the scene of incredible tag and release fishing.

The sight of giant bluefin close behind the boat is one of the most thrilling in fishing. The giant shield shape glows with a golden sheen, while the dark blue back and silvery white belly become a background for the golden bronze overtones. The torpedo head and barrel body are propelled by the strong upright tail in a ceaseless quest for food. Juvenile bluefin around 27 kg (60 lb) as well as schools of younger and lighter fish around 13 kg (30 lb) were once prolific in the Atlantic and Pacific. Head boats, big day charter boats bristling with rods and loaded with fifty or sixty anglers, were once popular, as they regularly provided action and catches. These fish brought pleasure and food to thousands of anglers on these boats. Those days are gone, but they could return if management measures were firmly taken with quotas that regulate catch, whether by the purse seiners, by longliners or other methods, including recreational catch. The frightening decline of this species in the 1960s through purse seining

of juveniles should always be kept in mind. Commercial bluefin fishing took such quantities of some year classes of bluefin that extinction is still possible for this great fish.

The highlighting of the endangering of bluefin stock appropriately came from the recreational tag and release programs of Frank Mather of Woods Hole Institute. His data highlighted the plight of the species by the high and quickly growing number of tag returns. Without tagging and release the problem might not have been flagged in time and there would have been further reduction to even more critical levels in breeding population.

In the Bahamas the giants are usually baited after sighting. Skilled skipper and crew constantly utilize the visibility from the tuna tower and flying bridge. They scan the surface continuously, working from horizon to close into boat. They search for the dark shadows against the golden sand, for humps of pushing fish, all indications of giant tuna. Further north in the colder water bluefin also responded to fishing with chum at anchor or drift as well as trolling. On some of the popular and successful tuna fishing hot spots such as the Mud Hole or Rosie's Ledge, it would seem impossible, from the sheer number of boats and anchor lines, that any hooked tuna could be brought to boat. Despite this congestion and obstacle course, successful bluefin action occurs. Live and dead baits are successfully used with chumming. It is incredible to see the boils and pushes that lift and disturb the surface of the water, the knife tails slicing the surface, as tuna move closer and pick up the oily menhaden (or bunker) or mackerel used in the chum. Anglers and boat galvanize into action when a bait is inhaled, the reel screams and the fight is on. The dropping of anchor and dan buoy allows the boat to be maneuvered behind the anchored boats into open fighting water.

Herring and Atlantic mackerel, which are present in massive schools, are chosen baits for the single or daisy chain bait rigs.

Giant bluefin are taken drifting as well as trolling in the Canadian Maritime Provinces. Herring fishing produces natural chum with fish fallout. Live mackerel and other suitable live bait can often be caught in the prime drifting area. This is where the thousand-pound-plus giants are taken. Giant fat tuna perhaps as old as seventeen years, feeding ceaselessly, packing on the weight, are in prime condition in these waters. Nova Scotia, Prince Edward Island and New Brunswick have all provided great fishing, with the majority of the heavy tackle records coming from Prince Edward Island or Nova Scotia.

Bluefin tuna appropriately are the species for which the world's first international tournaments were fished. US pioneering angling author Kip Farrington organized the International Tuna Cup with the Sharp Cup Match at the unbelievable rip at Wedgeport, Nova Scotia. Later, as the bluefin population moved and decreased, this tournament was moved to nearby Cape St Marys, Nova Scotia.

The Wedgeport fishery provided the classic sight of boats trolling without going forward against the power of the rip. Motors propelled the boat forward but the current negated the power of the motors. Boats with hook-ups would quickly drop back in the choppy water as the tuna and current took the boats close to Bald and Tuskett Islands and other obstacles. Conditions provided a unique environment for competition, big fish, the current in the rip, and the even standard of the converted lobster boats skippered and crewed by skillful, good-natured, co-operative fishermen. No one who competed will ever forget the fog and sunshine of the green Atlantic, the midday chowder, the action that came from trolling and drifting, the first look down at the sturdy colorful boat far below at low tide at Cape St Marys, the mixture of accents and friendliness that is Nova Scotia. Somehow visiting anglers became part of the living past as well as the present. It is indeed a tragedy that the tuna population has not been sufficient to keep this unique international tournament on an annual basis. Those of us who had the opportunity to represent our countries and compete for the Sharp Cup in the International Tuna Cup Match were fortunate indeed, whether the match was at Wedgeport or at Cape St Marys.

Pioneer heavy tackle anglers Michael Lerner and Ernest Hemingway were masters of angler aggression, fighting with maximum drag, dominating the fish techniques on heavy tackle. Within a few short years,

*C*aptain Paul Murray *of* Cookie *captured this series that shows the power and determination of a feeding giant bluefin chasing a 3.5 kg (8 lb) bluefish. Photos: Paul Murray.*

Charlie Hayden steadies the chair as IGFA president and master tuna fisherman, Elwood Harry, fights a giant bluefin off Newfoundland. Photo: Gil Keech.

under the tutelage of master captain, boat handler and innovator Tommy Gifford, lady and light tackle anglers were also taking these great fish.

Bluefin fishing in the Bahamas is one of the pinnacles of the sport of offshore fishing. The fish are spotted visually, and the boat is maneuvered to cross in front of the school, then slowed down as the mate puts one of his carefully prepared mackerel and mullet baits overboard. Tommy Gifford and some other skippers combined the bait with a big white feather lure and pork rind strips over the head of the bait. The idea of this addition was to aid the skippers' ability to see the hooked fish as he maneuvers to aid his anglers and keep the tuna from deep water. Once the bait is in place in front of the school, the angler waits, tense, ready, hoping that the bait will be taken by one of the lead tuna before it can be mutilated by the razor gang, particularly barracuda. Once a tuna strikes and hooks up, the angler fights with maximum drag as the captain maneuvers the boat to keep the tuna from the dropoff where it could sound deeper and deeper to be vulnerable to the sharks. In the peak action at Cat Cay and Bimini, the top bluefin anglers such as Elwood Harry and Bill Carpenter would show their endurance, as well as technique and understanding with the captain and crew, as they fought several fish a day in head-to-head confrontation.

The technique of trying to dominate the fish, to fight with hard drag without letup, is used at all the world bluefin hot spots, even where there is a minimum shark problem and the fights may be far from the deep water dropoffs. The sight of one or more bluefin striking at the baits, particularly the herring or mackerel trolled in a daisy chain of six or seven unhooked fish trolled on the same leader with the hooked last bait, is unforgettable. In the Atlantic, the distinctive smell of tuna cruising or feeding upwind is also used to give fishermen clues on where to troll or drift, as it is in some waters with broadbill.

Light tackle anglers on boats of all sizes also enjoyed the northward migrations of the smaller battling bluefin. The head boats with their parties of many anglers would be alive with wagging rods as the anglers hooked up and the excited fishermen followed their running and circling fish to avoid tangles and breakoffs while the birds attracted by chum and fish action added to the noise and activity. These scenes of action of vast schools of bluefin in any size are now generally only memories.

Strike and fighting drag for bluefin should be high with strike drag at one-quarter to one-third. This drag is often increased as the fish slows down.

The northern bluefin tuna are also found in the north and central Pacific and occasionally off California. Some small schools of various sizes and odd fish also wander south to mix with southern bluefin schools causing angler confusion as to the identity of their catch. Externally the difference between the bluefin, northern and southern, is in the coloration of the keels alongside the tuna's tail. On northern bluefin the keels are black, and on southern bluefin they are yellow. Northern bluefin are truly the giant of the tunas. They grow to 770 kg (1700 lb), whereas southern bluefin in the Indian and Pacific Oceans grow to a maximum of 180 kg (400 lb). This means that bluefin in excess of 180-kg weight are in all probability northern bluefin.

Bluefin and other tuna should be gaffed in the shoulder close to the head with a fixed head gaff, then held and pulled in hard against the boat hull until another gaff or meat hook is positioned. Anglers should recognize and use the upside circling of the tuna, by applying short pumps and trying to hold the double line onto the reel spool.

Piano wire is usually used for bluefin leaders. Wire gauges from 8 to 12 are popular. Light leaders produce more action and strikes than heavier leader material.

The way it used to be—a school of giant bluefin tuna between 182 and 363 kg (400 and 800 lb) swim across the Bahamas Bank. Photo: Charlie Hayden.

SOUTHERN BLUEFIN TUNA

The magnetism of big tuna for the world's top anglers was shown in 1960 when George Thomas III forged a living link between northern and southern bluefin.

George Thomas, a past President of the Tuna Club at Avalon, Santa Catalina, had already experienced the best that bluefin in the waters of Southern California and Nova Scotia could provide. He won the tuna buttons for various weights and classes available at his home club, and took a world record on 24 thread (37 kg or 80 lb test) while practising with Tommy Gifford for the International Tuna Cup Match at Wedgeport. Geo. exceeded 10/1 with bluefin on 24-thread category and fished in a winning USA team. When he heard of big southern bluefin off Tasmania, he came and tried his skill. He had success with many fish including an Australian record.

Southern bluefin in Australian and New Zealand waters are usually taken by trolling lures such as feathers, feather and plastic squid combinations, knuckleheads and konaheads; small and medium lures generate action and hook-ups even in big southern bluefin tuna. Small lures are ideal for school size fish. The most productive areas are around and over features rising in the sea bed and along temperature variations and upwellings.

Trolling and fishing at anchor or on the drift with natural baits is not a practical alternative in much of the prolific southern Australian and New Zealand waters because of the prevalence of barracouta in great schools which are as damaging to baits as the barracuda in tropical waters. The range of southern bluefin extends from South Africa to southern Australia and New Zealand.

The stock of southern bluefin is under similar danger and fishing pressure to that experienced by the northern bluefin tuna. Southern bluefin tuna world records are jointly held and set off Australian and New Zealand coasts. In the areas where southern bluefin are expected, there is always the possibility of the unforeseen, a hook-up from the northern bluefin, a giant even bigger and heavier than the expected fish, the southern bluefin.

Strike and fighting drag should be set at one-quarter to one-third by experienced fishermen. Southern bluefin will sometimes fight with fast runs and circles on the surface.

Flexible multi-strand wire is often used for southern bluefin because of the barracouta presence in numbers. If it were not for these fanged hordes, monofilament leaders would be productive.

The quest for southern bluefin parallels the challenge and mystique of the closely related northern giant bluefin, with which they have so much in common in fighting power and methods.

A bluefin ready for release is swum on the wire to aid its resuscitation: Photo: Paul Murray.

*C*harlie Hayden starts his wraps to wire a bluefin in Notre Dame Bay, Newfoundland. Photo: Gil Keech.

ALBACORE

Albacore do not grow to the size and weight of the heavyweight members of the tuna family. Despite this, these ocean-wandering species are attractive for fishermen who are prepared to fish far offshore seeking the plump longfin. The sporting characteristic of albacore is one reason for their popularity with anglers, whether on party boats with their dozens of eager fishermen, or on the specialized gamefishing cruisers. The other is that they are prolific in their schools and great to eat—the chicken of the sea.

In California the importance of albacore is acknowledged with light-tackle tournaments specifically for albacore and the recognition of the first of each year by the various active southern Californian clubs.

In areas such as southern California, where head and party boats search actively and skillfully for the longfins, thousands of fishermen have the chance to try their skill, their patience and to make dreams come true. Crew are ready with live bait to scoop out as chum as soon as one of the trolling rods bends and the scream of the reel tells that wandering albacore have been found.

Sometimes the albacore caught trolling are the total bag for the trip, at other times the combination of hooked fish, chum, live baits, and cast lures triggers action that continues for a long period with multiple hook-ups. Action such as this is a time for self-control, a cool head, calm consideration for others and analysis of what is happening and what needs to be done.

Suddenly the frenzied activity is over, the sound and visible action is gone, as the dark blue and silver fish are gathered and marked for each successful fisherman, while the vivid blue body stripe fades. For the fishermen, there are memories of the action, the challenge of the chase, the adrenalin impact of fighting the fish and thought of future enjoyment of their catch. Some will swap their fish for already canned albacore or keep them for preparation at home later in a variety of ways, with memories of a day at sea, of friends and fish action.

This species responds to shiny metal heads with skirts of feathers or plastic in a variety of color combinations. Red and orange, blue and white, green and yellow, pink and white are as effective in other waters as they are off California. In the Atlantic, the red and black combination is also regularly trolled.

Combination methods and techniques are used successfully in the quest for the longfins, trolling with lures until fish are found and then teased with chum and live bait. The value of studying water temperatures, of working the offshore banks and other wide features on the sea bed far from shore, have benefited other fisheries. The techniques of stand-up fishing with various tackle, of casting with live baits, of success from multiple hook-ups and fights with mobile fishermen following the fish around the boat, has influenced fishing for other species. Another lesson learned is to troll lures and colors in a pattern that has been successful before on that boat.

In many fishing areas albacore fishing tends to be much more accidental. These are deep water ocean wanderers that are sometimes present, sometimes not. Some of the heaviest and record size albacore are taken where they are not regularly caught in the big schools evident in other areas.

As is the case with the other pelagic species, recreational fishing has suffered from intense commercial fishing methods which in many instances constitutes overfishing of stock. In many cases recreational anglers pick up the trend of serious stock depletion long before it shows in widespread commercial fishing returns. The massive take of albacore by the insidious high seas drift netters are yet another indication of overfishing, particularly in the North and South Pacific. Albacore stock is so seriously depleted that scientists and some rational fisheries managers are concerned for future survival.

Anglers seeking albacore are fortunate that they will take a variety of small lures trolled fast. Some of these lures, such as hexheads and similar combinations of metal and plastic, are the same or have evolved from commercial albacore trolling lures that can be successfully trolled fast while the boat travels to cover the miles until fish are found.

As with other tuna, there is no need for long leaders or those of the maximum length allowed in line classes under IGFA rules. The ideal length is dictated by the

Wherever they occur, the long-finned albacore are welcomed as light tackle sport fish as well as for their superior eating qualities. Photo: Peter Goadby.

height of rod tip from the surface of the water. This length allows the leader to be taken if necessary, but also facilitates gaffing of the fish without the leader being taken.

Albacore should be fought on lighter tackle, up to 15 kg (30 lb), with the reel brake set at one-third line breaking strain.

YELLOWFIN TUNA

From tropical to temperate waters, these beautiful and powerful fish give added excitement to the word 'tuna'. Yellowfin tuna are a tropical species that, luckily for anglers, are also prolific in many temperate waters. These are great fish, highly regarded in all sizes and in all localities where they are fished. Captures made from Californian long-range boats off Mexico, particularly during the hours of darkness, dominate the heavy tackle and all tackle captures. These giant yellowfin look even bigger and more colorful at night than they really are. The darkness of sky and sea is illuminated into a patch of light, brighter than day, with a looming backdrop of rocky island reaching back into the sky.

Wherever they are found, yellowfin respond to live as well as whole and strips of dead fish as baits and chum. Best results come to anglers who work hard with their bait and do not simply put out a live bait or strips and doze off hoping for a strike. Live baits and strips should be thrown into the chum trail regularly, often in conjunction with chunks. Live baits should be active. If not taken in reasonable time or if swimming sluggishly, the live bait should be replaced. It is incredible how

often a live or other bait is taken as it sinks after being thrown out, particularly if this coincides with a few chunks. Big yellowfin in the chum swimming confidently, feeding, dominant in their environment, are an incredible sight. In clear water hunting, feeding yellowfin truly deserve their Hawaiian name *Ahi* (fire) just as they do when hooked and hurtling towards the bottom.

Many types of chum are effective. The chum bucket on the transom is an important plus in fishing on Australia's east coast. Small pieces of chum going without break into the current are part of the success pattern. Another part is use of oily flesh fish such as tuna, mullet or mackerel; in the Atlantic, bunker menhaden and pilchards are ideal.

The necessary amount of chum varies with conditions. In some cases the scraping up and use of two or three skipjack in a day's fishing or a few cans of sardines with holes pierced in the can will be sufficient. On other days, big quantities, even two or three hundred pounds of fish, may be needed.

One key factor in tuna chumming particularly, and to a lesser extent for sharks and marlin, is the use of

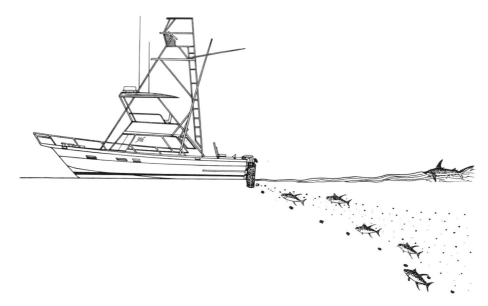

The benefits of chum are an oil pattern on surface; sinking chum in mid water; and chunks that can be seen and sink deeper.

chunks of fish in the chum trail. Chunks about 5 cm square (2–3 in) are ideal. Cutlets of green chub mackerel, scad or other small school bait species, or cubes cut from fillets of bigger fish including the tuna species, are ideal. Yellowfin and other tuna use their big, well-developed eyes in their quest for food. The chunks used in chum are big enough to see, but not big enough or in such quantity to meet all the food needs of a hunting tuna. It is interesting to examine the stomach contents of caught tuna and see just how many of the chunks the tuna has gulped. Chunks also sink quickly and deeper to where the tuna might be, and help raise them. Quantities of bread and other floating light-colored foods are also worthwhile additions to the tuna chum pattern.

Yellowfin fishing is often at its most productive at the time of the full moon. Overcast sky and cloud and choppy water also add to surface activity by giving cover to the fish in a way not possible with light and clear sky and calm surface water.

The reel drag when yellowfin tuna fishing with live or dead baits or strips at anchor or drift should be set just hard enough to prevent an overrun from a big, fast-running fish. The hook is set after a count of around five. There is usually only time for the brake to be turned to STRIKE, the rod tip lifted and reel handle turned once of twice before the hooked tuna streaks off, out and down. Yellowfin sometimes stop and almost immediately after the first short run turn back towards the boat. This gives the angler a chance to quickly recover line, and occasionally, by quick, short pumps, bring the fish to boat before it again runs out and down in a characteristic run.

Some anglers and crews set the brake at strike in an effort to try to hook the fish as soon as it grabs a bait. The instant strike/hook-up technique is also sometimes used for bluefin at drift or anchor. Experience has shown that an overrun-preventing brake with ratchet on, plus the count of five technique, is generally most effective. It is always worthwhile to have chunks ready to throw to tuna sighted in the chum, but which are not yet feeding. Leader diameter is important as yellowfin have excellent sight. The leader should be thin and of minimum visibility. On light tackle, 10-kg (20-lb), leaders could be as light as 15 kg (30 lb). On 15 kg (30 lb), leaders could be 24 kg (50 lb) when the fish are shy. If they are taking the baits freely, heavier leaders can be used. Sometimes to get strikes it is necessary to eliminate the leader altogether and put the hook straight on the single-line leader material. It is always handy to have several leaders of different weights already rigged, just in case. Black swivel and snaps appear to be less visible. Hooks are often sanded or painted to reduce shine and visibility.

One of the challenges in fishing for yellowfin is that more than one fish can be fought at a time. Multiple fights with several anglers hooked up at the same time are possible, with cool heads, experience and recognition that tuna usually circle in the same direction. Yellowfin circle anti-clockwise, so experience and backing off on reel brakes, carefully watching when lines are close to each other, or crossing over, is essential. Lifting one rod with drag eased over the other, also with drag eased, usually means safe landing of both fish. Yellowfin are ideal fish for standup fighting on all line classes with the circling fish fought and walked by the angler right around the drifting or anchored boat.

Big yellowfin hooked on the troll also come with multiple strikes. It is more difficult to handle multiple strikes on heavy trolling tackle than on lighter line classes, but despite this it is often done, with one fish (hopefully the smallest) being fought first from the chair while the other anglers do the best they can and play their fish as hard as they can until the fighting chair is available.

If possible, yellowfin and other tuna should be gaffed before their backs break the surface. Ideally they should be gaffed behind the head and deep in the shoulder with fixed gaffs, although small-size fliers are also used.

Yellowfin take medium and small-size konahead and

bullet head lures trolled in patterns for marlin, sometimes with multiple strikes. They strike freely at metal jet heads and other medium metal-headed lures trolled faster than the plastic konahead lures. In some areas, particularly in Hawaii and eastern Pacific, yellowfin are associated with dolphins, and skippers troll in front of the mixed schools as they do in front of schools of tuna, aware that the biggest are usually at the head of the school.

Yellowfin should be struck and fought at one-quarter to one-third of line class. Anglers should combine short pumps with the yellowfin habit of circling upwards and then down. Recognition, timing and use of this circling can aid reasonable time in captures of yellowfin even on light line classes. Commercial fishermen believe that the full moon is the most productive time for yellowfin.

Live bait fishing is generally most effective, with lightweight leaders. The leader strength is often only one or two line classes heavier than the line used. The light leader and small live bait hook size work against bullocking and wrapping live bait leaders. It is therefore logical to use either leaders that can be wound on to the reel or short 2.5–3 m (8–9 ft) leaders so the tuna can be brought into gaffing range by the angler without the need for anyone to handle the leader. The length is governed by the height of the boat from the water.

Yellowfin should be gaffed in the shoulder or head with a fixed gaff and pulled in against the side of the boat. A flexible-handled fixed gaff, with a short rope coming from the handle as an added safety measure, is most effective.

BIG EYE TUNA

Big eye are not taken on the troll in many areas as regularly as other tuna species. Traditionally a few of the tough, deep-bodied fighters were taken with drifting baits deep off Chile, Peru, or Ecuador. They are occasionally taken off southern California, and confuse anglers expecting yellowfin or bluefin. In the eastern Atlantic, where they were thought of as short-finned yellowfin, they are taken trolling and drifting deep, as in north-east USA and the Azores and Canary Islands. They are a wide ocean-ranging species, now recognized in their own right. They are successfully fished particularly off north-east USA out over deep canyons and peaks. The ideal combination of early morning, bottom configuration and lure pattern trolled fast results in multiple strikes and incredible and outstanding fishing far offshore.

Big eye offer the best characteristics of bluefin and yellowfin fishing combined with the added ingredient of being less prolific and with more mystery for sport-fishermen than the better-known big tuna. Their deep barrel-like bodies are full of power. It is indeed a pity that big eye are not more accessible in more areas.

The aggressive successful exciting technique used by Tred Barta and other north-east USA captains would give a most worthwhile addition to offshore fishing action in other fisheries. Big eye are taken extensively by Japanese and other commercial longliners in the Exclusive Economic Zones (EEZ) and in the nearby high seas areas of many countries. These catch statistics from the deep longlines give a clear indication that big eye are there to be taken if a productive method for sport-fishing is developed and proved in such widespread areas. Further study building on the success pattern of north-east USA would be desirable in other areas where sea conditions make this possible.

There seems little difference between the fighting ability of the four big tunas—northern bluefin, big eye,

Ralph Clock and a Baja big eye tuna on a long range trip from San Diego. Photo: courtesy Ralph Clock.

yellowfin and southern bluefin—although their performance varies with condition, water temperature, depth of water and baiting methods. There is no doubt that big eye clearly deserve their high rating in the heavyweight classes. Big eye are something of a deep water mystery fish, seen as juveniles and adults but not often seen by sportfishermen in middle sizes. Though not very common, big eye are rightly rated very highly by anglers.

These tuna, when hooked drifting with deep baits, are particularly tough fighters. At least when hooked lure trolling, the angler and skipper have a chance to try to control the hooked tuna once the other lines and lures are inboard or being recovered.

Reel drag and other fighting characteristics are similar to those used for bluefin and yellowfin tuna on similar tackle.

KAWA KAWA (MACKEREL TUNA), LITTLE TUNNY AND BLACK SKIPJACK

These three tuna with their backs patterned in oblique, wavy lines are junior torpedoes that between them cover the world seas close to land.

Kawa kawa (*Euthynnus affinis*) are found from eastern Africa to Hawaii and Tahiti and the Marquesas; little tunny (*Euthynnus alleteratis*) are found in the eastern and western Atlantic, Caribbean and Mediterranean; and black skipjack (*Euthynnus lineatus*) are found in the eastern tropical Pacific, and occasionally as far west as Hawaii, where the kawa kawa is the common member of the family.

These three tuna provide light tackle sport close to land masses around the world and are highly regarded as sporting and bait species. They are tough and active, power-packed, never-give-up, fast-running fighters.

Skipjack and black fin are the tunas that cause anglers to be pleased they don't grow to the jumbo size of the big four, as some doubt whether their skill and tackle would cope. They grow to a maximum of 18 kg (40 lb) but are usually much lighter.

These tuna often take small cast and trolled lures. Small baits such as pilchards, with and without chum, are also effective. At other times, perhaps when feeding on very small fish or small planktonic creatures, they ignore all offerings, much to the frustration of the anglers hopefully casting or trolling.

Sometimes after ignoring all offerings, some of the school will suddenly 'turn on' and take everything trolled or cast before reverting to their previous non-activity. They are great fighters on light tackle when already feeding or attracted by chum.

The action and take is often best at top or bottom of the tide slack water.

These hardy red-flesh tunas are popular, highly sought bait fish, whether for use alive or dead or used in strip or cut baits. They are ideal for chum and cut as chunks. The red flesh and shiny silver skin are often irresistible to bigger tuna species as chum and strips.

The eyesight of these species, as with other tuna, is particularly discerning, and minimum strength leader

F*rom underwater it is easy to see the power and symmetry of the Indo-Pacific longtail tuna. Photo: Tim Simpson.*

and line diameter give greater chance of hook-ups. There is always a strong probability of multiple hook-ups when trolling, as one strike triggers others in the school. A lure cast to the vicinity of a strike will often trigger another strike in a chain reaction. If there is one disappointing characteristic of these three species, it is that their edibility does not equal their fighting and bait standards.

These species come into bays and estuaries and will take lures cast and retrieved at high speeds from rocky headlands. They are ideal opponents on line classes of light and ultra light up to 10 kg.

Strike and fishing drag should be one-quarter of line class when trolling to minimize chances of the hook ripping free.

Bait casting tackle fished from outboard-powered dinghies is ideal for these tough fighters. This combination offers similar challenge and experience to that of the big tunas on heavy tackle.

Spinning tackle and saltwater fly tackle fights are also real challenges close inshore that bring the best of tuna fishing to many who have no opportunity to fish far offshore for big fish.

LONGTAIL TUNA

Longtail tuna are a tropical Indo-Pacific species that are great sporting fighters. This inshore species grows to a maximum weight of 44 kg (90 lb), but most grow to 23 kg (50 lb). However, the 14 kg (30 lb) fish are the most common.

This tuna combines the attributes and characteristics of the mackerels and the tuna. The longtail are fast as well as tough and unrelenting fighters. Like other tunas and tarpon, longtail can be particularly frustrating as they show on the surface, chopping into schools of bait and splashing and leaping as they feed.

This tuna responds to baits such as small pilchards, hardyheads and anchovies when presented with chum at anchor or drift. They also give great action on trash fish and squid from trawlers, particularly when trawlers clear their nets. They take baits and lures freely when coaxed into feeding patterns, but at most times are particularly frustrating when they can be seen splashing and rolling, but resist taking lures and baits, no matter how skillfully presented.

The best chance of action in trolling comes with the small lures, feathers, Christmas trees, spoons or natural baits such as ballyhoo and small mullet trolled where there are known to be holes or other features on the sea bed at top or bottom tide slack water. Once hooked, they should be fought with hard drag, but care must be taken to avoid breakoffs. Even experienced light tackle tuna fishermen are caught unprepared for their power and speed. Anglers who have proved their tackle and technique on yellowfin and bluefin have to rethink their drag settings and pressure when pitted against longtail. Fly fishermen are amazed at the speed, power and doggedness of this species.

Strike and fighting drag should be at one-quarter of line class with the angler ready to ease as line reduces with long, fast runs on the surface or deep.

Longtail resemble kawa kawa and the two other wavy-backed junior torpedoes in build with big shoulders cutting away to minimum diameter at the junction with tail. They move similarly into shallow waters of estuaries and bays and in these usually calm waters are ideal fish to teach anglers not only how to handle rod and reel, but how to work to get the fish to strike, despite their reluctance to take bait or lure. Longtail are taken offshore in waters frequented by yellowfin and juvenile southern bluefin when these species are working within 7 km (5 miles) of islands or coast.

Trolling and standup tackle are used in boat fishing. Spinning tackle is ideal for presentation of lures of light weights as well as poppers. Longtail give saltwater fly fishermen a tough, challenging workout that tests anglers and tackle to the limit.

DOG-TOOTH TUNA

When a bait or lure trolled for marlin close to tropical reef disappears, many species below the surface could have been responsible. The strike may be a marlin, a yellowfin, a giant trevally or one of the razor gang. If the fight continues without jumps down deep, particularly when close to reef edge, the hook-up may be an unusual tuna—a tuna with big teeth, white flesh and no scales— the dog-tooth tuna. These fish head down towards the reefy ridge, reef edge, or opening fringed with cruel coral that could mean line cutoffs.

It is a great pity that this sharp-toothed living coral reef marauder, dog-tooth tuna, is found only in the tropics of the Indo-Pacific region from Tahiti to the east coast of Africa. It is a species that more anglers should have

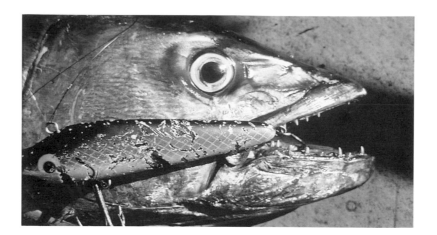

Mangled lures and monstered baits are characteristic marks of the reef-dwelling dog tooth tuna. Photo: Tim Simpson.

the opportunity to encounter and try to beat in their tough natural environment.

Dog-tooth combine the deep fighting characteristics of the reef-dwelling trevallies, the speed of the mackerels and the doggedness of the tuna family with a distinctive jerking tail beat. Like the trevallies and jacks, they dive for the cutting-off cover of coral heads before using their speed, power and circling tactics. Even 30-kg (66-lb) dog-tooth tuna put on a tough fight on heavy 60-kg (130-lb) class curved butt tackle ready with strike drag set for giant black marlin.

Dog-tooth are usually taken with trolled lures and trolled baits right along the live coral of outside reefs and passes. They also respond to deep jigging but usually beat the lighter tackle used in standup jigging with breakoffs and cutoffs being much more common than captures. Unfortunately, dog-tooth are not really common even in their chosen locations, and reduce with fishing pressure, becoming noticeably less common as fishing increases. Tagging and releasing of dog-tooth tuna shows that they remain in the same area and appear to be in small populations.

This is one species that is not fished for with chum. The rough bandit country preferred by dog-tooth is home for numerous fast-moving, aggressive requiem (whaler) sharks and pugnacious tiger sharks.

Dog-tooth take deep swimming lures such as minnows and spoons, high speed minnows as well as konaheads, knuckleheads and feather lures. The natural baits taken include those rigged as marlin baits as well as garfish (ballyhoo) and mullet for smaller gamefish.

Deep trolling off reef edges and passes with both lures and baits is often productive.

Strike and fighting drags should be between one-quarter to one-third of line breaking strain to exert maximum pressure on the tuna to bring it to gaff or tagging range before it can be chopped or mutilated by sharks.

SKIPJACK TUNA

The surface of the ocean is churned white as chunky bodies fly and clear the surface in low jumps. This scene is repeated in more localities around the world by skipjack tuna than by any other species. Skipjack are more than an important commercial, bait and chum species; they are an important light tackle sporting fish.

Most of these barrel-bodied striped power packs are taken at around 3–5 kg (8–12 lb), but they grow larger than 18 kg (40 lb) in Hawaii and some other places. Big skipjack give a good account of themselves even on heavy tackle.

On light tackle, skipjack can give anglers a long tough fight, and in the usual school weights live fully up to their reputation of tough scrappers with pace and quick, zipping changes of direction.

It is interesting to watch the angler's facial expression when the small tuna is brought to boatside and then, before gaffing or netting, powers off yet again down and away in a manner befitting bigger and heavier fish.

Skipjack cannot be bulldozed to the boat, partly because of their fighting characteristics, but also because hooks easily rip free. It is for this reason that when sought purely for chum, the trolling lures of small feathers, plastic squid or combinations of plastic feathers or metallic sheet Christmas trees are rigged with double hooks rather than single.

These tuna are ideal opponents on all light-tackle classes and by all methods—fly casting, casting, spinning, trolling with small lures, and at drift or at anchor.

The skipjack tuna is found in all depths of water,

from cliffside to high seas. They move in schools of their own kind or with immature yellowfin, bluefin or albacore.

They can be held around a fishing boat within fly or lure casting range by chumming. Small light colors or shiny metal lures are preferred, but at times skipjack will take lures of all sizes and colors, even those trolled for marlin.

In addition to their popularity for sport, bait and chum, skipjack are popular catches by recreational fishermen because of their edible quality, particularly for sashimi. Such is their effectiveness as live bait that some Australian, Hawaiian and Panamanian captains will spend what could be valuable fishing time seeking skipjack for live bait for a billfish—something that must be repeated in nature thousands of times each day.

When trolling for the tuna, lures should be pulled in front of the school to maximize results and minimize the chances of the school sounding. At times, particularly if the schools are worked regularly, it is necessary to troll only the small lures intended for skipjack as leaving big lures out for marlin may spook the flighty school. It is often necessary to troll just two or three small feathers, plastic squid or nylon jigs well back, 50 metres (160 ft) or more behind the boat. As with other tuna that may or may not have the feathered markers of sea birds over the feeding fish, crew and anglers should keep careful watch on the fish and birds as they can disappear from sight surprisingly quickly.

Sometimes skipjack strike at one or all of the lures where there was absolutely no visual indication of any activity.

It is often worthwhile leaving a firmly hooked or tethered tuna in the water behind the boat while running other small lures beside it. This sometimes works with skipjack, as it does with dolphin fish, amberjack and yellowtail.

Strike and fighting drag should be kept light to minimize hook ripouts. A landing net is helpful in lifting captured skipjack from the water. If they have to be gaffed, the gaff should be placed high in the shoulders to minimize shock and damage.

BONITO

Most fishermen usually have to travel long distances offshore to tangle with tuna species. Longtail and little tunny are exceptions; so too are the slender, silver, striped-bodied bonito.

Bonito's chosen habitat is close in to rocky headlands and inshore islands. They are popular for bait as well as for the sport they provide on light line classes. These are fish that can be fished near major centres of population. This allows anglers to enjoy brief dawn, early morning or evening sport without cutting into a hard daily working schedule.

Bonito are ideal antagonists on ultra-light and light tackle, in all categories from fly to trolling. Bonito, before intense fishing pressure and inshore ocean pollution, were available in big schools that actively competed for and struck at small feather, plastic and metal lures.

The power and toughness of bonito in resisting capture is shown on all tackle and fishing methods, even where there is no forward motion of a boat to peel line from the reel. They can be taken by casting and retrieving metal lures at high speed from headlands, as well as from boats in close to rocky shores. Bonito are ideal opponents for fishermen starting their involvement in sportfishing, particularly for those starting to fish with casting tackle, or for those learning with lighter tackle.

In trolling it is important to notice not only the location of the strikes and hook-ups but the angle at which the boat was travelling. Bonito will often strike with the boat travelling in one particular direction, and not in others.

In some ways it is a pity that the bonito are such effective baits as this in some way instinctively detracts from their well-deserved reputation as gamefish in their own right.

They should be fought with light brake, except on very light tackle because of the incidence of pulled hooks.

TUNA FROM THE ROCKS

Tuna are truly tough opponents wherever they are found. In Hawaii, South Africa and Australia, sea and shore conditions combine to give shore fishermen a chance to do battle with these tough, deep fighters. The Australian and South African developments proving that big tuna could be taken from the rocks were a natural progression from bait fishing, spinning and high-speed spinning from rock platforms at the base of cliffs that are washed by the warm ocean currents and eddies.

In Hawaii the capture of tuna followed from the successful quest for ulua (giant trevally). The first of the big tuna were taken by spinning and high speed

A KEY TO TUNA IDENTIFICATION

THE FOLLOWING KEYS HELP EVEN WHEN THE FISH IS BRIEFLY ALONGSIDE THE BOAT FOR TAG AND RELEASE. IT IS OF COURSE MUCH BETTER TO RELEASE THE TUNA EVEN WHEN NOT SURE OF ITS IDENTIFICATION, RATHER THAN TO GAFF AND KILL IT JUST TO FIND OUT WHAT IT IS.

WHAT TO LOOK FOR:

Northern bluefin, giant bluefin (ATLANTIC, INDO-PACIFIC)

Pectoral fins less than 80 per cent length of head; length of pectoral fin doesn't reach line between first and second dorsal; caudal keels dark; finlets yellow with black edges, second dorsal and anal fins short; second dorsal higher than first; very deep round body.

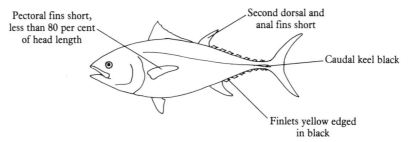

Pectoral fins short, less than 80 per cent of head length

Second dorsal and anal fins short

Caudal keel black

Finlets yellow edged in black

Southern bluefin (INDO-PACIFIC)

Pectoral fins less than 80 per cent of head length; pectoral fin does not reach line between first and second dorsal; second dorsal higher than first dorsal; caudal keels yellow; finlets yellow with black edges; second dorsal and anal fins short; very deep round body.

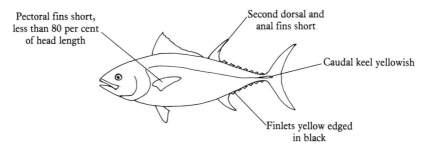

Pectoral fins short, less than 80 per cent of head length

Second dorsal and anal fins short

Caudal keel yellowish

Finlets yellow edged in black

Longtail tuna (INDO-PACIFIC)

Pectoral fins longer than in giant (northern) and southern bluefin, but do not reach between line of first and second dorsal fin; caudal keel darker; finlets yellow with grey margins; second dorsal and anal fins short; long slender body; long upper and lower lobes of tail.

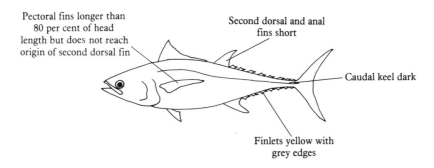

Pectoral fins longer than 80 per cent of head length but does not reach origin of second dorsal fin

Second dorsal and anal fins short

Caudal keel dark

Finlets yellow with grey edges

B*lackfin tuna*
(ATLANTIC)

Pectoral fins moderately long (reach line of second dorsal); first dorsal higher than second dorsal; caudal keels dark; finlets dusky with trace of yellow; second dorsal and anal fins short; deep round body.

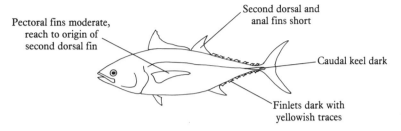

Pectoral fins moderate, reach to origin of second dorsal fin

Second dorsal and anal fins short

Caudal keel dark

Finlets dark with yellowish traces

A*lbacore*
(ATLANTIC, INDO-PACIFIC)

Pectoral longer than line of first dorsal and anal; second dorsal lower than first dorsal; finlets and caudal keels dark; white edges at rear of tail.

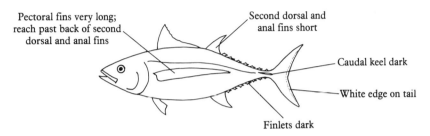

Pectoral fins very long; reach past back of second dorsal and anal fins

Second dorsal and anal fins short

Caudal keel dark

White edge on tail

Finlets dark

B*ig eye*
(ATLANTIC, INDO-PACIFIC)

Pectoral fin long (more than 80 per cent of length of head); pectorals back to line of second dorsal and are very long in juveniles, but absence of white edge as in albacores on rear of tail and yellow finlets instead of dark as in albacore still distinguish juvenile big eye from albacore of same size. First dorsal higher than second dorsal; second dorsal and anal short; very big eye; very deep round body.

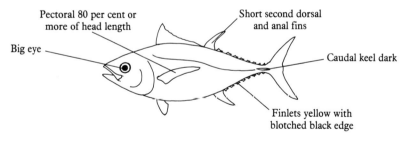

Pectoral 80 per cent or more of head length

Short second dorsal and anal fins

Big eye

Caudal keel dark

Finlets yellow with blotched black edge

Y*ellowfin*
(ATLANTIC, INDO-PACIFIC)

Pectoral fin long (reaches back past line of second dorsal). In adults second dorsal and anal very long, in juveniles dorsal and anal short. Yellow stripe along body including caudal keels; finlets yellow with black edge; body moderately deep.

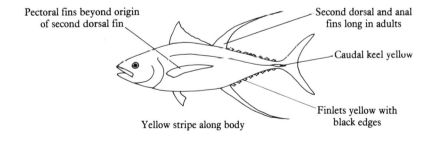

Pectoral fins beyond origin of second dorsal fin

Second dorsal and anal fins long in adults

Caudal keel yellow

Yellow stripe along body

Finlets yellow with black edges

A KEY TO TUNA IDENTIFICATION
CONTINUED

Dog-tooth tuna
(INDO-PACIFIC)

Pectorals short; no scales on body; prominent lateral line; prominent round teeth; second dorsal and anal fin short; finlets greyish; big eye; moderately slender body.

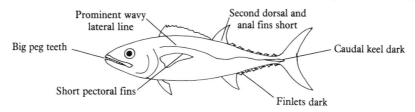

Prominent wavy lateral line
Second dorsal and anal fins short
Big peg teeth
Caudal keel dark
Short pectoral fins
Finlets dark

Skipjack tuna
(ATLANTIC, INDO-PACIFIC)

Pectoral fins short; second dorsal and anal fin short; finlets short; four to six prominent stripes along lower part of body; no stripes on back.

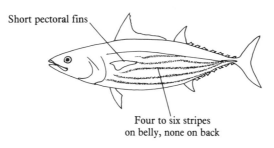

Short pectoral fins

Four to six stripes on belly, none on back

Kawa kawa,
little tunny,
black skipjack

Pectoral fins short; up to five indistinct dark blotches on body below pectoral fins; finlets dark; caudal keel dark; wavy stripes and bars on top of body.

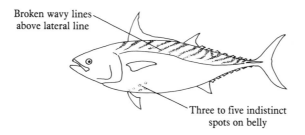

Broken wavy lines above lateral line

Three to five indistinct spots on belly

Bonito
(WORLDWIDE)

(Australian, eastern Pacific, Striped and Atlantic.) All four species that make up bonitos worldwide are similar with slender body, short pectoral fins, finlets and caudal keels dark, almost horizontal stripes along top of body in some species. On Australian and New Zealand bonito the stripes extend onto the belly.

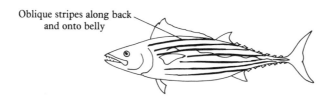

Oblique stripes along back and onto belly

Slender build

spinning for bonitos, smaller inshore tuna species and yellowtail. It is easy to visualize the exhilaration that followed those first captures. Southern bluefin tuna, yellowfin tuna, longtail tuna, kawa kawa and skipjack have all shown that they can be taken by shore fishermen from rock platforms by high-speed spinning or live bait.

The first marlin, a black taken from the rocks in Australia by Tony Axiak, was also taken by high-speed spinning in 1973. Then others and big yellowfin tuna were taken with live bait.

Live bait fishing is the most successful onshore technique for big tuna, just as it is offshore on boats. Occasionally, as would be expected, the hooked tuna head at top speed irresistibly out from shore, but more often the reels hold enough line to cope with the runs. Lever drag or aluminum reels with their attendant reduction in overall weight are ideal. Before the development and availability of these reels, the shore anglers used 6/0 star-drag reels. The subsequent availability of aluminum spools and increase in gear ratio helped shore anglers until aluminum lever drag reels with their smooth increased braking area became readily available.

The formation and short length of the productive rock platforms restrict the mobility and options of the angler. Success comes to those who recognize what the fish is doing, when to apply pressure, when to lead and tire it so it can be led to gaff.

The scene at the rocks when someone hooks up with a big marlin or tuna is surely one of the most unusual in any fishing. The blue of the sea, the white tops of the breaking waves contrast with eroded brown rocks, the brown colors of shore and greens of sparse headland vegetation is broken by pockets of color. Personal tents or sleeping bags and a child's plastic swimming pool show that the anglers put in long hours waiting for the fish. The swimming pool holds a few chub mackerel or yellowtail scad, yakkas, goggle eyes in water aerated by battery-operated aerators. These important bait fish are either caught in the early morning at the platform or transported down the cliffs from other bait-catching areas.

The angler is encouraged with advice from the other anglers, even though much of it is impossible to follow, as the fish has its own objectives. Then when it is close inshore, they assist the angler with gaffs and ropes to lift it on the rocks. The journey back up the cliffs to motor vehicles that will take the capture to scales to add another page in the chapter of rock gamefishing is often as difficult as the fight, but this is not a lone battle. It requires the strength and ingenuity of two or three, as big fish are notoriously difficult to carry up cliffs.

Fishing for gamefish from the rocks, jetties and piers is firmly established, with some of its devotees resisting invitations to fish from boats for the same species. Somehow these fish take gamefishing back to its start— man against fish with the odds in favor of the fish.

POINTS TO REMEMBER FOR SUCCESS WITH TUNA

- Sharp hooks.
- Use light leaders and small short-shank hooks. Tuna have excellent vision for heavy tackle.
- Strike and fighting drag one-quarter to one-third, can be increased if fish and conditions allow.
- Increase pressure when fish is on the upside of its circle as it swims.
- Chum in a combination of fine particles and chunks.
- Multiple strikes can be handled as tuna usually circle anti-clockwise, as do most fish.
- Fight the tuna hard without rest.
- Quick short pumps combined with recognition of the upside of the circle will assist the catch.
- Gaff with fixed head gaffs, and hold fish in against the boat.
- Standing up and walking while fishing allows more than one fish to be played.
- Because of the attraction for sharks, caught tuna should be brought on board, not left hanging over the side.

- Quick use of chum when a tuna is hooked trolling will often attract the school to the boat chum line for day-long activity.
- Troll or cast in front of, not through, the tuna school.
- Single hooks often attract more strikes than two hooks, as rigged for billfish trolling.
- Watch for tuna splashing and working on the surface.
- Tuna in Hawaii and the Eastern Pacific are often associated with dolphin or porpoise activity, with tuna and dolphin mixed in a school.
- Feeding bluefin leave a distinctive odor in the water. Fishermen use this to find tuna.
- Giant bluefin in flat surface waters hump the surface of the water over their backs. These pushers show the presence of the school.
- Try to prevent the tuna fighting straight down on the rod tip. A fish played at an angle of 60° or less can be more easily led and lifted.
- In shallow water the boat should be maneuvered outside the fish to keep the fish heading into shoals.

White sharks travel long distances in the open ocean as well as being dominant hunters around seal colonies. Photo: Ron and Valerie Taylor.

SHARKS

The water shimmers and moves, apparently empty, a marine desert. Suddenly, there is a wavy shape down deep, indistinct, small and seemingly insignificant. Sometimes the first indicator is a slender fin that breaks the surface, sometimes two fins—the dorsal and tail betraying the presence of the marauder.

For some fishermen, these sightings mean the start of the action. For others they're a recipe for disaster. Sometimes there is satisfaction in seeing a fish disappear into the razor-edged jaws of a shark, but for many fishermen, the opening of the jaws is synonymous with loss, good fish chopped and mutilated. For those interested, it is important to try to identify the species of the rough-skinned bandit, but for others, who cares? It's just another rotten shark.

The swimming action, as well as the water-covered silhouette, gives experienced fishermen some indication as to the species. Sometimes, whether down deep or at the surface, the body size itself is simply heart-stopping, and the silence generates more excitement. A first thought is that surely a mass that size should only be propelled by a noisy motor! Sharks of all sizes are silent. The only sounds are manmade, and nature's killing sounds heard when the shark rips and tears into its prey with head and jaws snapping.

Most sharks including tiger sharks, blue sharks and other carcharhinids—the requiem (whaler sharks) and hammerheads—swim with a flexible, sinuous action through the whole body. With hammerheads, the quick action looks like exaggerated wriggling. White and mako sharks swim more rigidly; they seem to hold position with their fins while propelling themselves through the water with short, stiff tailstrokes. The power of those tails shows not only in the spectacular jumps, but in the wake from their propulsion equipment. Threshers demonstrate the flexibility inherent in their apparently rigid body construction by whipping the tip of their tail in front of their head to stun fish, which they then take as food.

Color in the water is often not much help in identifying the various shark species. The blue of makos and blue sharks often looks brown below the surface, and most of the others appear yellowish while submerged, only showing the variations in body color at gaffing or tagging when their backs are out of the water.

A yellowish form shadowing a trolling bait is often a shark of some species, particularly a hammerhead. The wriggling, swinging head action of the hammerhead gives a pointer as to whether that shadow is wanted or unwanted. Hammerheads and makos commonly take trolled baits, but all sharks will do so occasionally.

It's unfortunate that the most positive identification of sharks comes only when they are out of the water. If lifted into the cockpit, a live shark reacts violently to examination. On the weighing gantry at the dock, they can be more safely measured and their distinctive dental armory examined. The teeth of most species aid positive identification. Identification problems come often with the twelve/fourteen requiem (carcharhinid) species other than the distinctive tiger and blue sharks. The teeth of these other carcharhinids show only slight variations, visible only to trained shark identifiers. Even then, examination of drawings, keys and photographs may be necessary for final opinion.

It seems that in creating this contrary requiem shark family, nature has conspired to cause problems for humans. Sharks are common everywhere, and most are hard-fighting, worthy opponents. In Australia, the fishing record-keepers lump all requiem carcharhinids except tigers and blue sharks in one species group in recognition of their common fighting ability, as well as the difficulty of their identification, even when onshore.

Sport fishermen seek dangerous sharks, not only in Australia and New Zealand, but also in California, northeast USA and England. In many countries there are shark fishing clubs whose members specifically seek the rough-skinned, razor-toothed predators in preference to other sporting fish, or where other species are out of range.

It is important, both for scientific record-keeping and for other reasons, to correctly identify any sharks that are weighed or tagged. Some requiem sharks, particularly tigers, lemon, oceanic white tip and blue sharks have readily distinguished features. Once close to the boat, ready for gaffing or tagging, or even when swimming free in the chum trail, they are relatively easy to identify because of these features of shape and coloration. The main problems lie with identification of the other carcharhinids.

Tiger and blue sharks, two contrasting species, have large black eyes, similar to those of white sharks, makos, porbeagles and threshers. Nature and evolution have given them these large dark eyes, sometimes described by fishermen and photographers as 'black pits of hell'. Most other shark species have small yellowish or greyish eyes with vertical cat's eye pupils. These small eyes are efficient in all light conditions, whether dull or bright, but are surely less effective than the bigger, dark eyes of the ocean-roaming predators. The dark-eyed tigers and blue sharks have a third eyelid, a white nictitating membrane that slides across the eye when the shark is close to its prey and attacking, or when it's excited and working up to the attack.

A *tiger shark gulps a chunk from a marlin. Photo: Sean Wallace.*

White sharks, makos and porbeagles do not have nictitating membranes but are able to roll their eyes back when attacking, so that the white of the back of the eye shows instead of the outside dark eye color. This sometimes causes species confusion, particularly following attacks or warning passes at divers, who noticed that the dark of the eye suddenly became white as the shark became aggressive.

Sharks of most usual interest to anglers are worldwide species, the roamers of deep water, plus some of the big requiem carcharhinids, such as *Carcharhinus leucas* and others. They maraud in inshore waters and even move right into freshwater rivers and lakes. Most sharks have a timetable of appearances dependent on the currents, water temperature, the presence of bait in the food chain, spawning and mating.

The heaviest potentially record-breaking sharks are white sharks (*Carcharodon carcharhias*, Linnaeus, 1758). White sharks, along with their other bullet-nosed relatives, the blue dynamite makos (*Isurus oxyrinchus/ glancus*, Rafinesque, 1810) and the less pugnacious and unspectacular porbeagle (*Lamna nasus*, Bonnaterre, 1788) all have the ability to maintain body and blood temperature at as much as 8°C (16°F) above the water temperature to give great muscle power and acceleration.

The bulldog of the sea, the tiger shark (*Galeoderdo cuvieri*, Lesseur, 1822) is also massive. Some carcharhinids, particularly *Carcharhinus falciformis* (Peron & Lesever, 1822), *C. galapagensis* (Snodgrass & Henle, 1905), *C. obscurus* (Leseur, 1818), *C. brachyurus* (Gunther, 1870), *C. leucas* (Valenciennes, 1839), *C. amboinensis* (Muller & Henle, 1841), *C. albimarginatus* (Ruppell, 1837), *C. perezii* (Poey, 1876) are fairly heavy, while others, such as *C. limbatus* (Muller & Henle, 1841), *C.*

melanopterus (Quoy & Gaimard, 1824), *C. longimanus* (Poey, 1861), *C. plumbeus* (Nardo, 1827), *C. brevipinna* (Muller & Henle, 1841) and the Atlantic lemon shark (*Negaprion acutidens*, Ruppell, 1835), are all great opponents for lighter tackle.

The blue shark (*Prionace glauca*, Linnaeus, 1758), with its dark blue body and large dark eyes, is another that offers light tackle action in the warm to temperate waters of the world. The blue of the blue shark is similar to that of the mako, but blue sharks lack the powerful tapered caudal keel at the tail, and the upper lobe of the tail is much longer than the lower one. The other blue-hued sharks, makos and porbeagles, have tail lobes almost equal in length. It is, however, the long floppy pectorals of the blue shark, fins that are equal in length to the length of the shark's head, that aid identification.

The tope (*Galeorhynus galeus*, Linnaeus, 1758) is a school-type shark with a slender body and a broad upper lobe to its tail. It is not dangerous to man, but gives light tackle sport and pleasure in temperate waters.

Hammerheads are easy to identify by family, although species identification between the three giants of this family needs more care (*Sphyrna lewini*, Griffith & Smith, 1834, *S. mokarran*, Ruppell, 1835, *S. zygaena*, Linnaeus, 1758). Equally easy to recognize are threshers (*Alopias superciliosus*, Lowe, 1840), *A. pelagicus*, Nakamura, 1935, *A. vulpinus*, Bonnaterre, 1788) which have an upper lobe to the tail equal to the body length.

Shark fishermen all agree that despite their often unsavory reputation, sharks are tough and dangerous opponents, worthy of the technique, time and effort that goes into their capture or tagging.

Sharks are generally reviled in written and spoken word around the world. The word 'shark' conjures ugly images to both fishermen and non-fishermen. Fishermen, whether commercial or recreational, have the sickening experience of seeing potentially great captures wasted, mutilated and useless. To commercial fishermen shark attack is synonymous with loss of income, damaged gear and perhaps a chance of financial ruin. To recreational fishermen sharks can cause the waste of a potential record of a good capture, and to all fishermen they add danger, whether swimming free, hooked, jumping, and particularly when attacking fish at the wire at boatside. Of course to swimmers, surfers and divers and survivors of sinkings or crashes, sharks add a gruesome risk of mutilation and death.

Despite all this, sharks are great adversaries for sports fishermen, a worthy quarry sought in many parts of the world, often the only really big fish in some areas. The days are long gone when those recreational fishermen who deliberately sought sharks were considered as seeking second-rate fish. Many species of sharks are tough, dogged fighters, usually swimming deep and constantly circling against the power of the boat and angler. Some sharks can be outfought and outmaneuvered by experienced anglers with the help of skillfully handled boats, but this applies to many fish across the spectrum of species.

Sharks are important in the fisheries of many countries. Australia, Great Britain, New Zealand and the east coast of the USA hold most of the IGFA world records for the shark species.

Makos, white sharks, hammerheads, tigers, blue sharks, tope, threshers and porbeagles are fished worldwide to gain record recognition. Sportfishing for sharks has a unique dimension; they can be sought in most aquatic environments, even in some tropical areas in the almost-fresh water of lakes and rivers. Their habitat ranges from the deepest oceans, through the shallower water, to headlands and beaches and into the estuaries and rivers. Freshwater lakes such as Lake Nicaragua with subterranean access to the sea are inhabited by large, dangerous requiem sharks. Shark fishing has provided a base for other sport fisheries in some areas. The knowledge gained while people are out fishing for sharks often establishes what other fish species are available, and at what times. Shark fishing is generally less costly than fishing for some of the other higher-profile or highly publicized fish species. One reason for this is that fuel usage is less in shark fishing than in fishing for species that respond primarily to trolling. Sharks can also be caught without the use of boats at all, and heavy sharks of most species have been caught from shore and jetties. The whaling station and sea wall at Durban provided a unique combination for land-based shark fishing and giant white sharks up to and over a reported 454 kg (1000 lb) were caught there. This was a thrilling and muscle-testing fishery as the anglers tried their strength and skill along the sea wall, fishing with simple long rods and Nottingham reels. Shore-based shark fishing has always been popular in Australia, Florida and other places where beaches, headlands and jetties provide fishing platforms for the sharks in the natural environment. The world record tiger shark on all tackle and 60 kg (130 lb) class was landed from the Cherry Grove, South Carolina jetty by Walter Maxwell breaking a record which had until

At the Shark Angling Club of Great Britain, the weight of this English mako is shown to interested watchers. Photo: Crossberg.

then traditionally been held in the warm water areas of Australia. This was a mighty tiger catch under any circumstances and truly doubly worthwhile for a land-based angler.

Hammerheads and requiem sharks (whalers) of various species are generally taken from onshore locations. Lemon sharks and the grey nurse, sand tigers or ragged tooth are other species that can be caught from the shore.

Shark captures by shore and jetty fishermen and generally inshore are taken on every type of tackle including fly, bait-casters, spinning and boat tackle, from the lightest right through to the 60 kg (130 lb) class.

SUCCESSFUL METHODS

Chum or ground bait is a key ingredient in the mix of successful offshore shark fishing. Care must always be taken in the use of chum close to shore and in other locations where people may be in the water. Common-sense must be combined with the awareness of where the chum will end up and where the sharks could be attracted. Chumming is most effective if both surface and sinking material are used. Tuna and other oily fish are ideal for surface slick and sinking chum. Tuna oil is effective in a drip or mixed with other chum.

Fish of all kinds, particularly those that are high in oil, are ideal for the sinking chum. Fillets of big fish such as tuna can be processed through a chum can, berley bucket or mincer so that there is a continuous line of fine particles. Best results are gained by adding chunks about two to three inches square of fish or slices of smaller species such as slimy mackerel, which also aid the chum pattern. These chunks not only provide a visual chum line as they sink and shine in the water, but are big enough to induce the big fish into feeding so that they respond more positively to the baits drifted away from or alongside the boat. Pilchards, sardines, anchovies, herrings and mackerel are ideal chum stock, as they are silvery as well as rich in blood and oil. In the interests of safety, commonsense and consideration for others, it is imperative to analyse where the chum will run and its effects, so dangerous sharks will not be attracted to areas where they could come into contact with or proximity to people, whether swimming, diving or indulging in other aquatic activities. The IGFA wisely does not grant records to sharks or fish caught with the use of mammal chum or baits. Anglers have now found that fish and tuna oil are very effective as is the vibration from fish being played by anglers.

There is considerable danger to anglers and crew at all times when shark fishing. Most shark species are dangerous and can inflict damage at both ends of their bodies. The head, with its chomping razor-sharp teeth, and the flaying tail covered in rough sandpaper-like skin, combined with the strength, activity and bulk of sharks, make them difficult and dangerous to handle from boat or shore. Sharks of many species swim right up to the boats originating the chum trail, and confidently approach boats catching other species of fish. This habit, although it assists the shark angler, is responsible for some of the damage and destruction caused by sharks against humans and their boats.

Some of the most potentially productive shark fishing can be done during the hours of darkness. Sharks naturally take advantage of the cover of darkness to move inshore and towards the surface from deep warm water. They become increasingly confident and dangerous at these times. Whilst fishing at night is productive, it is even more dangerous than in daylight, and great care must be exercised even by experienced fishermen.

In shark fishing it is possible to take advantage of natural chumming activities created by schools of feeding fish, and by trawlers clearing the trash fish and other marine life from their nets. As with tuna fishing, when fishing in natural chum, best results come by using the bait species or predator species that are the object of local feeding activity, or trash fish from the nets, as bait or chum. Predatory species, including sharks, once in their feeding pattern more readily take the fish on which they are already feeding.

Successful shark anglers vary their technique depending on the speed and activity of the shark. They can be burnt out against a hard drag, yet there is no doubt that some species fight more actively and resist capture more doggedly against a hard drag and a jerky pumping line retrieval than they do against a smooth, less violent line-recovery action and less drag. This partly accounts for the numbers and weight of sharks taken on light tackle, particularly in the 10 kg (20 lb) and 15 kg (33 lb) categories.

Sharks are generally hooked from stationary boats, although makos and hammerheads regularly take trolled baits, as do tigers, threshers and the requiem sharks, though less often. In warm tropical waters the requiem shark species are most active and will take trolled lures as well as baits. Fishing from anchor or on the drift is the usual method for deliberate attempts to catch sharks. In fishing from anchor, a dan buoy should be attached to the anchor line so the boat can be easily driven or drifted free of the potential line-tangling and line-breaking anchor line. On heavy tackle with a hard drag, it is possible that a fast-running synthetic fishing line can burn through the anchor line on contact and cause the loss of the anchor, as well as weakening the fishing line. The dan buoy should be attached to the anchor line in such a way that it can be quickly slipped clear of the boat and should have flotation sufficient to support the anchor line in the run of the current. Once the hooked shark is caught or lost, the boat can return to the dan

Mako sharks combine beauty, color and menace. Photo: Mark Deeney.

A 70 kg (150 lb) requiem shark is used as an attractant for the massive, predatory white shark. The size of the big marauder can be judged by the comparison of the white shark's mouth and the partially swallowed shark between its jaws. This is one shark that did not swallow its prey head first. The chum pot on the transom of Yackatoon also played its part in attracting and holding the shark with chum. Photo: Mark Deeney.

buoy, the anchor line can be retrieved, and chumming and ideally the fishing action may recommence at the same place with a minimum break in the effectiveness of the chum line. Sometimes a shark, or sharks, is waiting on return to the original position.

Some crews attach containers of chum or oil to the anchor line or dan buoy to maintain the unbroken chum trail, but experience has shown that this can lead to cutoffs between anchor and dan buoy by sharks attracted to the chum.

Skill, strength and timing are required by the crew when taking the leader. The wire retrieval must be positive and smooth, not jerky. The wire man must be aware of what the shark is trying to do and know when to wrap with his gloved hands, when to lead and when to hold on and apply maximum pressure. Several different kinds of wire are successfully used in shark fishing leaders in both stainless steel and carbon steel configurations. The non-rusting benefits of stainless steel may be offset by the fact that some shark species, particularly great whites and makos, can cut some stainless wires. Carbon steel cable types, which are tougher, more durable and generally resistant to cutting, are popular. Nylon coated wire is popular in all weights right up to heavy wire with thick coating that gives a diameter similar to that of a lead pencil. The nylon-covered wires made for fishing and the even heavier types made for clothes lines or control cable are very popular in some of the established shark fishing areas. No doubt the success of the nylon-covered wire will spread to other parts of the world as awareness of the benefits becomes more obvious in record taking. Those who choose to use the big diameter and apparently clearly visible nylon-covered heavy wire are convinced that sharks are more likely to freely take baits on this type of leader, even in the heavy 273-kg (600-lb) and 363-kg (800-lb) test wires than with thinner uncoated wire. The nylon covering appears to also minimize the rolling characteristic of some shark species. Single-strand wires such as piano wire or prestraightened galvanized wire in big diameter (.040 and .045) are also used, but cable is generally chosen by those readily seeking big sharks. However, sharks are fished on all tackle categories, depending on the expected weights of the sharks usually found.

Most crews make their leaders close to the maximum length allowed under the IGFA rules to give added insurance against damage by rolling, even though this shortens the allowable length in double line (where longer is handy). The leader man may increase the pressure and pull or lead the shark to gaffing range. Many potential records are lost by the rolling of the sharks at any time during the fight as well as close to the boat. The wire-wrapped sharks have their tails and abrasive skin in contact with the fragile line.

Swivels, with or without snaps, must be the strongest available; so too must the hooks in their chosen sizes. In the past, shark hooks were usually 16/0, 18/0 and 20/0, sizes that are still first choice for the real monsters. Modern thinking and technique with smaller baits has seen a move towards smaller hooks. Most crews use single hooks instead of the double-hooked shark rigs of the past. They believe there is less chance of hooks being straightened or twisted out of shape when only one is used. In two-hook rigs, with the hooks separated by the

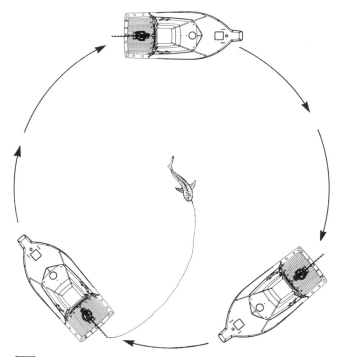

The proven Port Stephens method of shark fishing for big sharks with the boat circling constantly. This works for other fish as well as sharks.

High flying makos leave unforgettable memories of jumping and aggression. Photo: Greg Parea.

Makos in any size are active jumpers flying high, then turning and heading back to the water head first. Photo: Peter Goadby.

maximum length of leader allowed in the rules, there is a greater chance that both hooks will become embedded in the shark, often one in the jaw and the other outside where the twisting, swimming and rolling action of the shark works against both hooks. The use of the two-hook rig does not seem to noticeably improve the hook-up rate.

Floats are commonly used to regulate the depth at which the bait is held. In shallow water the acceptance of baits is increased by a bait about a metre (three feet) above the sea bed. This depth is particularly effective for tigers and requiem (bull and whaler) sharks. In fishing in depths of 8–30 m (25–90 ft), best results come with one bait floated 1–2 m (3–6 ft) from the bottom, and another at 10 m (30 ft) from the surface. If more than two baits can be positioned without tangling, another bait can be drifted about three metres (ten feet) from the surface. Other baits are held in the water depths between sea bed and surface. Crews logically should have at least one other bait rigged and ready to give to sharks that swim right up to the boat. If sharks are seen in the chum line or around the boat, but are not confident enough to swim up to the side of the boat where a bait can be fed, it is often productive to drift one out about three metres (ten feet) from the surface. When fishing in deep water, bait depths are usually 50 m (150 ft) from the surface, one about 30 m (90 ft) from the surface, one about 10 m (30 ft) from the surface, and one at 4 m (12 ft). If more outfits and baits are fished, they can be placed so they are in depths in between these.

Use of different-sized plastic bottles or foam allows the baits to drift in a variety of positions. In fast current, breakaway lead sinkers or weights can be attached to the leader to hold the bait at its planned depth.

Some of the baits should logically be in the chum trail, and for that reason lines fished further from the boat have their baits deeper and the shallower baits are held closer to the boat. Tangling is minimized if the furthest-out baits are placed in position first, and those closest to the boat are placed in the water and positioned once the others are set. Experience has also shown that a bait in combination with sinkers, deep troller or other weight, fished straight down from the transom, is productive for the sharks cruising deep and not yet rising to the chum.

Mako sharks have many habits that annoy and cause problems for the fishermen. One of these habits is to chop with their long razor-sharp teeth at balloons, bottles or floats used to suspend the baits. It is annoying to wind the line in, retrieve the float, and find that the carefully rigged bait, leader, double line and swivel have been cut cleanly without the tell-tale ratchet or clicker indicating that a shark was in the vicinity. To minimize this loss, many anglers use 60–90 cm (2–3 ft) of light thread between the float and the fishing line. In shark drift fishing, as with drift fishing for marlin, broadbill and tuna, if floats are used they should be held with light thread that will break free immediately the bait is taken. Use of a heavier thread which is hard to break will warn the fish of an unnatural condition as it pulls against the float and will often cause the fish to drop the bait before it can be turned and swallowed.

Despite their reputation for voracity and savagery, sharks are usually fairly deliberate in their feeding and swallowing, except when in a feeding frenzy. For this reason, drags and clickers and ratchets should exert just enough pressure on the line to prevent an overrun in the event of a fast strike. Once the line commences to run from the reel, the angler should pick up the rod and be ready to prevent an overrun in the event of sudden surge or acceleration. Patience is the key to success and the angler should not start striking to set the hook until the shark has paused and turned the bait and swallowed it. A slow count of five to seven after the pause generally assures a satisfactory hook-up. Striking before the pause to swallow pulls the bait clear of the shark's mouth where it has been held prior to swallowing. Sharks that have taken baits and gulped them down right alongside the boat can be struck more quickly, but it is important to remember that more missed hook-ups result from impatience and striking too soon than from any other reason. If it is the plan of the day for each shark to be fought one at a time, then the other lines should be retrieved as soon as the first bait is taken, the dan buoy dropped and the boat used to maximum benefit in the fight. Some crews prefer to fight their sharks from dead boats and walk their hooked fish around the boat. They plan to hook others and play two or three at one time on light tackle. Size of the hooked shark usually dictates this decision. Multiple catches are more practical for light tackle fishing than heavy. When the wire is taken by the crew, great care must be taken to drop the recovered wire back over the side as it is retrieved to minimize the possibility of wire tangling around someone or something and the crew being dragged overboard.

Gaffing sharks is another activity in which the natural build and body characteristics increase crew difficulty. Rolling, thrashing and tough skins all combine to maximize degree of difficulty and minimize results. For this reason, gaffs should be razor-sharp as well as of maximum strength. Shark gaffs are generally of carbon steel rather than the stainless type. It is also beneficial to have a metre or so (three or four feet) of heavy cable between gaff rope and the gaff for protection from the shark's choppers. Once the gaff hook is placed in position in the shark, whether in its mouth or anywhere along the body, it should be held in with maximum human strength as well as having been tied off before gaffing is attempted. The ease with which sharks roll out of and throw gaffs, even if these have prominent barbs, is quite incredible. Several gaffs should be in position and ready for use. A large strong meathook is very useful in controlling the shark by placing in the jaw. The rolling habits and strength of the shark make it imperative that care and coolness are utilized by the crew when wiring and gaffing even though instinctively it is a time of maximum activity, maximum adrenalin, of shouting and excitement. The crews that keep their cool and yet exhibit maximum strength and utilize their experience are most successful.

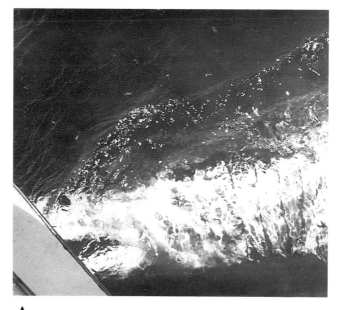

A *big hunting mako is a fearsome sight up close. It dominates the fisherman and the boat. Photo: Terry Healey.*

White sharks in their feeding pattern are rated as the most dangerous of all sharks because of their size and power. Photo: Ron and Valerie Taylor.

If the captured shark is not wanted, it can be tagged and released to add to scientific knowledge, or can be sacrificed as chum to increase the effectiveness of chum in attracting and exciting other sharks that may be bigger than the first taken. Fresh shark liver is ideal chum and sharks often respond to the fresh blood and entrails.

Makos—the blue dynamite—are regarded as interesting, worthy opponents, the peak of the shark species, even by fishermen who hate sharks. Of all sharks they are closest to the true gamefish. Makos take trolled baits and lures and are capable of spectacular jumping that rivals the aerial acrobatics of any other fish, including the billfish champions. Ernest Hemingway, who once held the Atlantic record for makos, described them as one of the few fish that will retaliate and strike at the boat and its human adversaries. Makos sometimes attack boats even if these craft are not engaged in shark fishing. There are many cases of their attacking and jumping into boats during the fight and at boatside. There are recorded instances where a mako has broken free and then after a short respite returned to the attack on the boat.

Makos must be treated with caution, common sense and respect at all times. Fishing history has many instances where humans have been damaged by makos, often after they had been considered as played out or actually caught. A mako thrashing and capable of causing damage with both head and tail is a fearsome sight in a cockpit, whether it gets there by jumping or by rolling inboard on the gaff rope. There have been instances where some hours after gaffing, the powerful blue bodies and long curved razor-sharp teeth have combined to strike violently at their antagonists on the boat or even while being weighed. Sometimes after being hooked and breaking free of line and leader or the hook coming free,

the previously hooked mako has returned to bite viciously at propellers, rudders or chum cans, or have taken other baits.

The dominant eyes of the mako are big and black, the feature also of the closely related white sharks and porbeagles. These three species are unique in the world of sharks in that the temperature of their blood is warmer than that of the water in which they live. The blood at above water temperature and their torpedo-shaped, superbly designed body with its strong muscle structure, gives them explosive power for speed and jumping.

Makos can be fought on a hard drag a third of the line class but if fought with this weight of break, the angler must be ready to drop the rod tip in the direction of the shark if it starts jumping and ease it off when it runs fast and changes direction, as sharks often do. These sharks sometimes swim to the boat after being hooked instead of swimming away or sounding. Angler and crew are then faced with the decision of whether to take the shark quickly, taking advantage of its confidence or aggression in swimming to the boat, or whether to try to play it out. The thought that a shark can become very aggressive and attack the boat is at the back of fishermen's minds at all times. The decision when to try to take it or bring it to boatside for release often has to be made in a split second; whether taken quickly or slowly, this can result in either the loss of the shark or hurt to the crew.

The white shark, called by Zane Grey 'the White Death', is the best known and most feared of all the predatory sharks. It is equipped with a frightening array of teeth which, when combined with its power, sheer size and occasional aggression, gives understanding of its reputation. This species is the heaviest and biggest of the man-eating sharks, and commonly grows to 454 kg (1000 lb), even to three times that weight. The tiger is the second biggest and heaviest of the dangerous shark species with only occasional specimens exceeding the magic four figures. Makos, hammerheads and threshers also exceed that 1000-lb weight. The requiem, the whaler or bull sharks also grow to heavy weights, but only rarely are they seen in excess of 1000 lb.

The white shark is by nature and evolution a hunter and killer of mammals as well as fish. It preys on seals and dolphins and harasses whales, particularly if the giant cetaceans are sickly or incapacitated. White sharks of all sizes, including monsters over 1000 kg (2200 lb), occasionally show fishermen that like its cousin, the blue-bodied mako, it too can clear the water. A jumping white shark is a fearsome sight, and although rarely seen, is not to be forgotten. A big white shark is always an awe-inspiring sight as it glides around the boat with its stiff yet graceful swimming action. Human watchers quickly become conscious of those big jet black eyes. Jim Cowell, a great angler and record holder on this species in South Australia, aptly raised the question of who is the hunter and who is the hunted. Because of white sharks' natural propensity to hunt and eat seals of various sizes, this species strikes shock and instant fear and awareness into fishermen. This shark lifts its fearsome head clear of the water alongside the boat. It is at this time, and because of the habit of confidently coming right to the boatside to take chum, that the shark can be given a baited hook by hand. White sharks, with the closely related mako, are responsible for many attacks on boats.

In fighting the angler, many white sharks tend to position themselves near the surface or in mid water. They often run fast, stripping line from the reel accompanied by the noise of the screeching ratchet. Because of the speed and power exerted in their running, they sometimes burn themselves out quite quickly. A high proportion of white sharks are lost because they roll and tangle in the leader if this is felt along their body.

There are two ways to minimize the rolling and line-cutting problem. One is to use minimal drag setting, and even on heavy tackle to use no more than 11 kg or at the most 15 kg (25–30 lb). The boat technique to minimize the effect of rolling is to maneuver the boat after hook-up so that the boat, angler and line are ahead or slightly ahead and out to one side of the swimming shark. White sharks roll in a flash, often before an angler can ease the drag; sometimes even as they take the bait the wire is felt. The leader becomes tangled around the body and the caudal keels and the line is rubbed on the rough skin or tail. White sharks are basically temperate water species and give sporting fishermen in the cooler climates

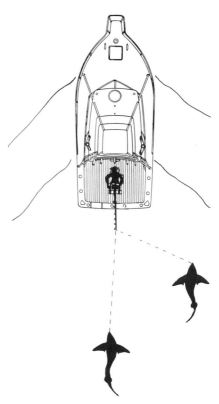

The loss of big white sharks through their habit of rolling and tangling in the leader can be minimised and usually prevented by maneuvering the boat so the head of the shark is toward the boat. Backing up so the tail of the shark is towards the boat and the leader along the body triggers rolling and loss.

Hammerhead sharks sometimes congregate in schools below the surface even though they cruise singly on the surface. Photo: Ron and Valerie Taylor.

A Key to Shark Identification

THE FOLLOWING KEYS HELP EVEN WHEN THE FISH IS BRIEFLY ALONGSIDE THE BOAT FOR TAG AND RELEASE. IT IS OF COURSE MUCH BETTER TO RELEASE THE SHARK EVEN WHEN NOT SURE OF ITS IDENTIFICATION, RATHER THAN TO GAFF AND KILL IT JUST TO FIND OUT WHAT IT IS.

WHAT TO LOOK FOR:

Hammerheads   Elongated flattened wing-like head.

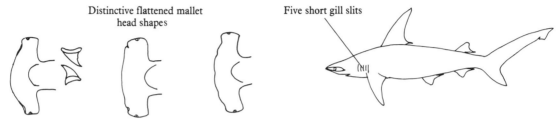

Distinctive flattened mallet head shapes

Five short gill slits

Threshers   Upper lobe of tail equal to length of body.

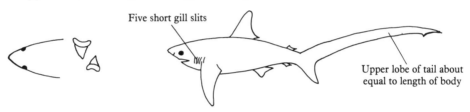

Five short gill slits

Upper lobe of tail about equal to length of body

White shark   Bullet head; large dark eye; long gill slits; tail with almost equal lobes; keel at junction of body and tail; dark blotch behind pectoral; no nictitating membrane; triangular serrated teeth in upper jaw, narrower serrated teeth in lower jaw.

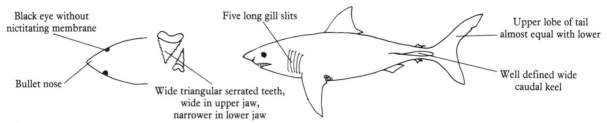

Black eye without nictitating membrane

Bullet nose

Five long gill slits

Wide triangular serrated teeth, wide in upper jaw, narrower in lower jaw

Upper lobe of tail almost equal with lower

Well defined wide caudal keel

Mako   Bullet head; large dark eye without nictitating membrane; tail with almost equal lobes; keel at junction of body and tail; blue color; narrow slightly curved teeth on both jaws.

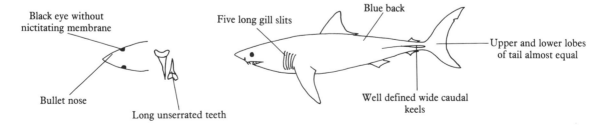

Black eye without nictitating membrane

Bullet nose

Five long gill slits

Long unserrated teeth

Blue back

Well defined wide caudal keels

Upper and lower lobes of tail almost equal

P_orbeagle_ Bullet head; large dark eye without nictitating membrane; long gill slits; tail with almost equal lobes; two keels (one prominent and a smaller keel at junction of body and tail); white patch at lower rear of dorsal.

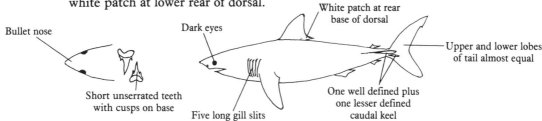

T_iger_ Wide almost square head; large dark eye with nictitating membrane; short gill slits; cockscomb-shaped serrated teeth in both jaws; slight keel at junction of body and tail; blotched stripes on upper body; upper lobe of tail much longer than lower.

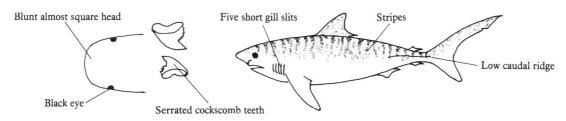

B_lue shark_ Pointed but not bullet-shaped head; large dark eye with nictitating membrane; short gill slits; slightly curved serrated teeth in upper jaw, narrower and serrated in lower jaw; no keel at junction of body and tail; upper lobe of tail much longer than lower; long pectoral fins equal to length of head; upper body blue.

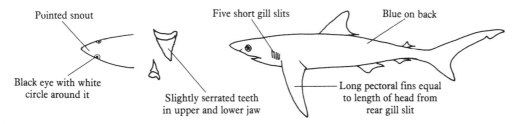

C_archarhinids_
(REQUIEM
(WHALER) SHARKS) Head shapes vary with species from blunt to moderately pointed; all have small yellowish eye with elongated pupil and nictitating membrane; short gill slits; upper lobe of tail much longer than lower; no keel at junction of body and tail; color of upper body varies with environment from dark grey through bronze and yellow to light grey color.

This family could be called the 'Except Sharks' because every characteristic of the various species has exceptions, for example, lemon sharks have two equal-sized dorsals while all other carcharhinids have a large first dorsal and small second dorsal.

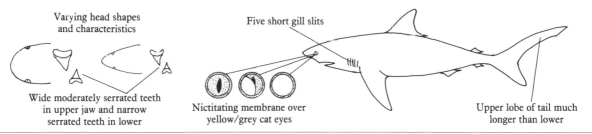

White sharks are just one of the species that can be successfully baited right at boatside. Photo: Bob Millar.

particularly appropriate as these are the shark families that are responsible for attacks and fatalities in all water from fresh to ocean depths.

The habitat of many of these sharks is associated with land rather than open ocean environs, so they are regularly in contact and conflict with humans. Scientifically the group includes tigers and blue sharks, although records and recognition for these two species are given separately from the others.

Over any length, in their range of weights, many members of this family are tough, determined fighters. They run hard and fight deep, to provide a fight that exceeds many of the more glamorously recognized species. Perhaps because of the commonness, difficulty in positive identification and deserved reputation as human attackers, they do not have the aura and charisma accorded makos, white sharks and tigers. Despite this, they are more-than-worthy opponents, particularly in deep water where they use the resistance and characteristics of the big strong pectoral fins to resist lift, and circle deeper.

These sharks offer a combination of the difficult characteristics of other sharks without the incredible rocket launch to the sky of the makos. These are great fighters that provide sport and action in many countries, particularly in tropical to temperate waters. Like most sharks other than whites, they should be fought hard, as usually they give minimal rolling problems. They should be fought to restrict their desire to stubbornly

strip baits held or floated near the surface sometimes get a strike when even live baits are ignored. They are unpredictable hunters that will follow and try to attack carefully rigged trolling marlin baits to be an unwanted nuisance, yet will be frustrating non-takers when wanted by anglers.

Care should be taken to minimize noise, shouting and pointing at circling hammerheads, as they are often shy, cautious, ready to run from possible danger.

The range of size of hammerheads provides challenges on all line categories. They can be fought on hard drags between one-quarter to one-third line breaking strain.

These species have a small mouth for their length, so use of small-sized hooks is warranted. Use of small-diameter lighter breaking strain leaders can also be effective, as hammerheads do not warrant nor necessitate heavy cable monster leaders and hooks.

The multiple species of the requiem (whaler) shark family as a group includes some of the toughest fighters, pound for pound or in any length.

The common names of these sharks reflect some of their characteristics—bull, dusky, lemon, copper, black, silky, bronze, white tip, silver tip, black tip, and whaler are descriptive. Somehow the word requiem is

A huge white shark, estimated at over 2272 kg (5000 lb), returns to take more chum and eventually a second leader and bait after breaking line on the first fight. The shark also won the second fight to continue its ocean dominance. Photo: Bob Millar.

circle deep, particularly in the current. Straight down is the angle of maximum disadvantage for the angler, so circling with the boat or planing with the boat is needed to break the losing pattern.

Like many shark fights, continuous backing-up is not the solution to the problem of bringing fish to boat; circling and planing are effective tactics. These sharks can be fought according to the approach of bluefin tuna fishermen fighting to stop giant bluefin going over the drop into the deep: 'Stop them or pop them'!

The tope is an important light tackle opponent in temperate waters. This school shark is excellent to eat as well as providing sport. Small baits, light leaders and light tackle balance with this species.

POINTS TO REMEMBER FOR SUCCESS WITH SHARKS

- Sharp hooks.
- Drift or anchor in areas and water where fish should be—near reefs, near 185-m (100-fathom) line and current lines or other known shark habitats.
- Keep alert for any visible near-surface fish or bait schools.
- Drift near trawlers or commercial boats which are putting 'rubbish' fish back overboard. Use their trash fish for bait.
- Keep alert for panic vibrations from live baits when predators appear, or movement of floats.
- Check live baits to make sure they are working, alive and active.
- Replace tired live baits regularly.
- Fish with baits and lines in a pattern of depth, with some in the chum trail.
- Set reel with a light drag, just enough to hold bait and prevent overrun.
- Move line in or out to spread wear, so rub is not all in one place.
- Balloons or floats should be tied with lines light enough to break on a strike. Use about 60 cm (2 ft) of thread in case of mako or other attack on float.

- Chum regularly to maintain unbroken trail. Use chum that covers a range of water.
- Baits must be regularly checked for damage.
- Some lines may need weights or sinkers to get baits to a wished-for level.
- Check drags often so that they are not set too hard.
- Use click as warning and overrun preventer.
- Throw over live unhooked and discarded bait fish occasionally.
- Make sure lines have not tangled.
- Chunk some fish for sinking chum.
- Cover all water levels with live or dead baits.
- A dan buoy (float) should be attached to the anchor line so it can be slipped if a hooked fish has to be chased.
- If fish are sighted but not striking baits, try decreasing hook and leader size.
- If shifting boat position, keep chum trail unbroken as much as possible.
- Keep pressure on the shark, don't rest. Plane or circle with the boat to lift shark to more favorable position. Don't fight with fish straight down.
- Gaff in mouth or body, not near tail.

SHARK FISHING —
SHORE, ROCKS, JETTIES AND ESTUARIES

Most people associate shark fishing and shark captures with fishing from boats. This is a wrong assumption as in many locations around the world shorebound fishermen deliberately seek the toothy predators. One of the great plus factors for those who fish for sharks is that they are expected wherever there is access to salt water. Some species of requiem (carcharhinid) shark can even be caught far from where they are expected in waters that are fresh, not salt or even brackish.

Sharks fight as actively and doggedly and are often more difficult to land from onshore or jetties than they would be from boats. Sharks in shallow water use currents, tides and wave action to resist capture. One of the thrilling dangerous facets of shark fishing in shallow water is the close contact of gaffing and landing the fish. The heaviest land-based shark of personal involvement was a well-conditioned tiger of 275 kg (600 lb) that took a bait thrown by hand from outside our camp. We were seeking barramundi and threadfin salmon on ultra-light tackle, but sure enough one of the party of anglers could not resist what would happen to a big bait around sunset. The sand was churned by digging, straining feet up and down the beach as the unknown crittur put maximum strain on the 24 kg (50 lb) outfit. Then against the red

*O*ffshore fishermen in the waters of Great Britain also catch thresher sharks as well as the more usual blues and porbeagles. Photo: British Shark Angler's Club.

of the setting sun a distinctive dorsal cut the surface and suddenly things became deadly serious. Finally the tiger was in shallow water, touching as the waves left its body. We had no gaff, so the only way was to grab that flailing tail and gradually get that grey mottled body up to where a tail rope could be used. The rough tail sandpapered skin from our hands and we were thrown about like ninepines before it was beyond escape. It was an incredible shark, hooked just 20 metres from the shore of the estuary camp. That was the only big shark we took, but virtually every bait was taken by a shark of some size, mainly of the many requiem 'carcharhinid' sharks.

One of the problems to be overcome in onshore shark fishing, whether from rocks, beach or surf, is to get the bait to the desired depth and position of the hunting and killing ground of the predators. An offshore breeze is a real help, aiding the use of balloon floats to drift the bait. If type of tackle and wind and sea conditions are not suitable for casting, it is often possible to get the bait out by casting by hand, as if fishing with a handline.

The leader length is as critical in onshore shark fishing as it is from boats because of the shark's rough skins, teeth and rolling. There is conflict in practical fishing from shore between the need for maximum length leader allowed under the IGFA rules, water depth, casting and simply getting the bait to the desired position. One way to assist in this problem is to use a two-piece leader that slides. These leaders can be held to half length for drifting and casting, then moved out to full length by the pressure and weight of hooking the shark. The sliding leader is made by using two swivels, one attached to each length of wire, one end with the hook, the other with the swivel. The leader can be restrained at its short length by breakaway thread and the shark fought with full length.

Hooked sharks usually run parallel to shore, fighting to stay in deep-water channels and gutters. There is not much the shorebound angler can do if a big shark heads resolutely straight out to sea into the wide blue yonder as line disappears from reel, the bare metal of an empty spool fast approaching, except to say, 'Oh, dash it! This lovely animal has taken all my line. Well done!' or something similar.

The shark's swimming action can sometimes be changed by jerking the rod as it again strikes the fish and then being easy on the brake combined with smooth pumping. As in boat fishing, the most critical time of the fight is when the shark is played into shallow water near shore or close in to the rocks. This is the time when skilled positive assistance is imperative. It is a time for care and patience as well as fast positive action. The angler and helper must use the action of waves and water as

*Z*ane Grey's last big fish, a great white shark in South Australia. Photo: IGFA.

much as possible. They must also remember that hook and leader may not be as heavy and strong as those used in boat fishing.

The same philosophy in fighting the shark, in finalizing the capture, applies in fishing from jetties or bridges. Here there are two alternatives—one is to try to lead the shark into shallow water or to gaff and tail rope from high up. IGFA rules allow the use of gaffs longer than the 2.4 m (8 ft) overall from high structures. Jetties and bridges facilitate the current and tide presentation of baits to get them where sharks should be as they project into deeper water as well as attracting food fish for the predators.

Chum is of course beneficial in attracting sharks to the baits and fishing area. It is important also to remember that the vibration of other hooked fish attracts sharks.

*A*long with most other pelagic gamefish, Belize (Central American) wahoo are attracted to red and yellow, and red and orange lures. Photo: Darrell Jones.

THE FUN FISH

WAHOO

Anglers and crews seeking marlin or giant tuna often speak the word 'wahoo' with dislike and annoyance. To those seeking action and food on lighter tackle, however, the cry of 'wahoo' is one of excitement, joy and objective achieved.

Anglers inexperienced in blue water fishing for billfish must wonder what has happened when with a flash of light, and without the hooks being touched, the action of a bait or lure changes; the line is then retrieved to the cockpit with mutterings of 'wahoo' and derogatory remarks about the culprit's parentage.

At other times wahoo are most welcome fish. This fish has a special charisma not just because of its racehorse build and its razor teeth, but because of its sizzling surface run, particularly in the first run, which is one of the fastest of all gamefish. This fish has all the characteristics to excite fishermen, whether they rate wahoo as good guy or bad guy, villain or hero.

Even the names, both common and scientific, are interesting. The crew on James Cook's *Endeavour*, north of Tahiti, caught the first of these speedsters to be recorded in the Western world and scientifically named. The fish carries the Latin adaptation of Solander, commemorating Daniel Solander, the great Swedish scientist on this ship. The name 'wahoo' logically dates from the early whalers and missionary settlers seeing and utilizing the fine edible species in the Hawaiian Islands; then and now, Oahu, which they pronounced and sometimes spelt 'wahoo', was an important base. The Hawaiians had long recognized the quality of wahoo with their name *Ono* meaning 'good'.

Wahoo have been glowingly written up by early blue water fishing authors Zane Grey and Kip Farrington as well as by current writers. It is the sheer blistering speed of wahoo that lives in the memories of those privileged to see the column of spray jetting from the surface as the line slices the water and disappears from the reel spool. This initial run is sometimes repeated two or three times. One of the special excitement factors of fishing for wahoo, particularly with konahead and knucklehead lures, is the chance of multiple strikes and hook-ups along reef edges or suddenly from out of the blue in the deep water of the current. The quick dropping of a newspaper sheet or a plastic bottle (to be retrieved later) will provide a floating marker for relocating the position of a striking fish in the current.

Wahoo are school fish, so in addition to multiple strikes there is always the probability of cutoffs at swivel, or where the line pierces the water. When fishing where schools of wahoo are expected, it is beneficial to use single line down to the leader instead of the end. Nylon-covered wire can be joined to the single line so a flexible 49-strand leader with the lure can in turn be attached to a snap or snap leader.

Fiji, Tahiti, and Bermuda are beautiful islands associated with great wahoo. The first Tahitian International Tournament was held at Bora Bora, surely one of the most picturesque islands in the world. It seemed logical that a great canyon in the dominating peaks would continue in the sea bed and be home to big fish. As we trolled into the logical area that day, we changed our rigs to minimize cutoffs and landed eight wahoo, the

*F*ew anglers experience the pleasure of jumping wahoo. Here, one jumps horizontally instead of the more common sky-reaching vertical jump. Photo: Darrell Jones.

M*ahi mahi respond to a wide range of lures and baits. Photo: Tim Simpson.*

biggest 54 kg (118 lb) and the smallest 35 kg (77 lb).

Success around coral reefs with this species comes when trolling the passes and openings and where there are holes or ridges in the sea bed. Ridges that rise offshore from the depths of the outside reefs are always productive; so too are offshore peaks and canyons where the water temperature shows the possible environment for these toothy tropical species (21°C–30°C; 70°F–86°F).

One of the amazing sights in offshore fishing is when a calm sea and clear water allow a clear view of the super-fast razor gang as they cruise in a trail of chum. In these circumstances action comes from a combination of light wire leader and live bait.

Despite the razor teeth many wahoo are taken on marlin-intended konahead lures rigged on heavy monofilament. The possibility of wahoo cutoffs is one of the reasons why wire is used as the leader material on the second hook.

These fish do much damage by scarring and chipping the hard plastic lure heads and by cutting and slashing like a razor the soft plastic skirts or soft plastic heads. Instant (60 second) glue will sometimes enable repairs to be done to soft plastic skirts, but often the slashing attack damages the skirt irreparably so it is suitable only for contrasting stripes on other lure skirt combinations.

Wahoo don't often jump but when they do they soar like a javelin into the air and return to their natural environment, cleaving the surface with hardly a splash. As with the other big mackerel specials, early morning or late afternoon is the most productive time to fish for wahoo. They will, however, strike at any time during the day, particularly if they are in a competitive feeding cycle rather than the more usual lone strike.

Natural baits of all kinds, particularly whole swimming baits, are also appealing to wahoo, that strike even on bait rigged with two hooks for the razor gang bait manglers. It is truly amazing the way that, despite the speed at which they take maximum flesh, they just miss the hooks in a split second, often without knocking the bait from even lightly set outrigger clips.

Action lures such as konaheads, knuckleheads, minnows and flashing lures such as spoons are consistently attractive to wahoo. The tooth power of the fish leave their distinctive spaced and straight cut of the teeth that are the wahoo trademark on other than metal lures. Strip baits rigged from ballyhoo (garfish), mullet, scad and baits intended for marlin are natural baits that bring action from wahoo.

These speedsters are great on light tackle of all types and in all categories. They are often compared with their more inshore relatives, tanguigue in the Indo-Pacific and kingfish in the Atlantic, but somehow the Hawaiian name *Ono* is the most descriptive.

MAHI MAHI—DOLPHIN FISH

Different gamefish are popular and exciting for different reasons. These may be color, fighting ability, availability, acrobatics, eating quality without unpleasant association in any way, and just plain excitement. They are combined in one fish called in many areas mahi mahi, its Hawaiian Polynesian name.

Unlike wahoo, its ocean current companion, mahi mahi were known and recorded by long-ago mariners. Perhaps the name 'Dolphin', confusing it with the marine mammal dolphin, came from its habit of swimming around the bows of sailing ships, particularly when the ships were becalmed in the Doldrums. They swim around all flotsam as it drifts along the warm water current.

Mahi mahi are now known as fast-growing fish that can increase by 14 kg (30 lb) in a year, making them a likely species for aquaculture. There are two species— *Coryphaena equiselis* is smaller and less prolific than *C. hippurus*.

In the eyes and minds of offshore recreational fishermen, mahi mahi will never be considered food for hungry people. They will be remembered as glowing chameleons, acrobatic jumpers, marauders that prey on the crustacea and fish that travel and shelter with drifting objects.

Because of their known habit of schooling and working around flotsam, they are sought by charter and private boats working warm water. Weed and current lines are prolific producers. Sometimes crews drop floating mats or other material on the way out and work these before picking them up on the way back to port, to add to their chances of capture.

Mahi mahi, a golden headed sideways-scissors jumper, are the species that have given fishermen the idea of tethering one of the caught fish back behind the boat to help hold the interest of other fish in the school. They are unusual fish in that the male is bigger and heavier than the female. Spawning can take place right through the year.

Mahi mahi are traditionally an integral part of the tourist charter fishing industry. They are the fish that show the character, excitement, action and food potential present for those who fish offshore. Until they have seen them, visitors just cannot visualize the color changes from glowing green and gold with electric blue spots to light blue and vivid silver. Some color phases even briefly show black on back and upper body. These rapid color changes alone would make this a talked-about fish, but so do the scissor jumps, one after the other, that characterize the fight of these piscatorial jumping jacks.

Mahi mahi do not come inshore in shallow water with the current, as do marlin and yellowfin. They take whole and strip natural baits and lures. Sometimes the strikes come in apparently open water without flotsam, but most action comes in front of, alongside or behind flotsam; usually the larger the obstacle, the more productive the fishing. The time that the floating objects have been in the ocean is also important—sometimes a small article that has been in the ocean for a long time will have more fish in attendance than newer and bigger flotsam.

The angled head of the mahi mahi male is differently shaped from the curved head of the female of the species.

KINGFISH

Florida is synonymous with the development of light tackle sportfishing. Methods developed in the warm waters and reefs of that state have spread around the world. One of the fish that made this possible is the kingfish. This inshore mackerel is a top fish, not only for its fighting qualities, but for its edibility. Many are taken by deep trolling, as well as trolling at the surface. They are taken by deep jigging on lures as well as whole natural and strip baits. The edibility of kingfish is part of the reason for the serious decline in population and fish action for recreational fishing.

Their schooling, migrating and habitat have made them susceptible to gill nets. They are also ideal for tourist fishermen, fast with multiple runs and determined dives, attractive yet marauding gamefish with razor teeth. Tourists obviously appreciate them (not least for their

edible qualities) and are prepared to charter regularly in order to have a chance at kingfish. This is one of the saltwater gamefish around the world's fisheries that is obviously worth more as a recreational fish than as a purely commercial catch.

There is a particular feeling about early morning and evening trolling for saltwater gamefish. This is evident in trolling for kingfish—waiting in the early quiet for one of the deep baits and spoons to be taken. Rods bend and are on the strike, and line is pulled from the reel. Some kingfish fall to lures or baits trolled deep on wire lines. Even though catches made on this line are not eligible for IGFA and other recreational fishing organizations, the wire line strike may trigger similar action on lines or baits on deep trollers or surface lures.

These savage strikers also respond to fishing at anchor

or on the drift with chum, while lures are cast or jigged or live baits such as blue runners, goggle eye or small reef fish are presented. The presence of kingfish is sometimes shown by shearing scissor bites on reef and other fish being brought to surface. The predator can be identified by its sharp straight bite. Barracuda tend to strip and leave ragged edges, and sharks leave curved bites.

With or without chum, kingfish are also productive over reef dropoffs or obstructions on the bottom. The biggest kingfish have often changed from marauding and wandering with the school to loners, the dominant predators in a limited area.

Kingfish should be fought with a hard drag to be brought to boat as quickly as possible to minimize the chances of mutilation by shark bite.

Kingfish, with their response to many methods of fishing, can be fished most enjoyably on all tackle and line classes at the lighter end of the spectrum. Light leader material and dark-colored swivels and snaps will aid success in fishing for these razor-toothed speedsters.

TANGUIGUE— NARROW-BARRED MACKEREL

These are found in the Indo-Pacific and are called kingfish in some areas. They are almost identical to the Atlantic kingfish except that the body has wavy stripes as well marked as those on freshly caught wahoo. Indo-Pacific tanguigue grow bigger and heavier than their close Atlantic relatives. They have the same basic characteristics, although the migrating schools may be more numerous and may travel longer distances.

Ron Jenyns with two record size tanguigue off Brisbane. *Photo:* Courier Mail.

One of the great marine sights anywhere in the world takes place annually off Townsville's Rib and Bramble reefs. These narrow tiger-striped fish hang in the early or later afternoon glowing light, living silvery giant raindrops suspended in a moment of time as they go through their ritual of ensuring the continuation of their species.

Wahoo sometimes rise arrow straight from below into the sunlight as they strike trolled bait or lure. Similar heart-stopping and unbelievable jumps come from tanguigue and Atlantic kingfish before they are hooked. The sudden presence of an elongated silver bar of light, quivering as it turns to slip back into the water with hardly a ripple, is a sight that once seen is never forgotten. Fishermen watch in hope of repeat performances. Sometimes the tanguigue execute a short series of jumps after being hooked, but usually streak out and down in the first of a series of runs that test drag and fishermen.

These fish should be fought on a hard drag, not only to bring them to boat but to minimize the possibility of shark mutilation, which is a problem in both recreational and commercial fishing for tanguigue. Commercial fishermen often troll slowly with weighted, all-wire lines with double hooked garfish (ballyhoo), or small mullet or spoons.

Recreationally they are taken with a range of lures. If spoons other than high-speed designs are fished, the trolling speed is slow, dictated by the spoon. Other lures that work at this speed are minnows and feather lures and feather-squid combinations. Konaheads in a variety of sizes are effective at higher speeds.

Wooden and plastic minnows, especially the high speed bibless designs, are freely taken, particularly when trolled in dinghies and small boats close to the reef edge dropoffs and reef openings.

Lure fishing for these manglers is a form of masochism indulged by anglers who carefully buy and rig beautifully colored and finished lures knowing that the marks of success mean that they will simply be brutalized and mangled by teeth and jaw power.

Tanguigue are an important commercial as well as recreational species with commercial fishermen often adapting recreational techniques and lures to improve their success. The silvery sheen of the skin and body shape makes smaller specimens ideal marlin-trolling baits despite their soft flesh. For giant black marlin they have been used up to and in excess of 14 kg (30 lb). Thus they have triple value as a light tackle sportfish, for their edibility, and as bait for other species.

Chumming with small live fish or dead chum with chunks is effective, particularly with live baits fished over ridges and peaks rising from deep water outside shallow reefs. With all fishing methods, most action comes at the top or bottom of the tide and at early morning and later afternoon fishing. Tanguigue are taken by all fishing methods with the boat stationary or trolling.

The fishing challenge of Lizard Island and the Great Barrier Reef is immediately associated with giant black marlin. Bait is always welcome, so some crews and anglers head out in dinghies as soon as light allows to try for scaly mackerel, kawa kawa or whatever in the time before breakfast. With Billy Fairbairn guiding our dinghy, I landed tanguigue bigger than 14 kg (30 lb), the heaviest being 22 kg (48 lb); a superb fishing challenge on the bait-casting outfits and 6-kg line we trolled.

The first few runs of these fish are as exciting as any fish anywhere. Like their close Atlantic relative the kingfish, tanguigue are one of the base species for a successful light tackle sportfishing centre. It is unfortunate that because these mackerel prey on reef fish, they are sometimes the cause of poisoning in humans and household pets from ciguatera, the natural poison passed through the food chain as reef fish feed on poisonous algae and in turn become food for bigger fish, even some that are usually open water migratory species.

Andy holds up the boss of the 'Razor Gang', a big tanguigue. Photo: Greg Edwards.

SPOTTED AND SMALL SPANISH MACKERELS

Wherever they occur around the coastlines and reefs, small mackerel species are top light tackle sport, bait and food fish. In many areas they are taken when the anglers are seeking and hoping for their big relatives, tanguigue and kingfish. In addition to those taken in conjunction with other species, all these mackerel are sought as sporting fish in their own right.

These small mackerel are sought with smaller lures than their heavyweight relatives. Small knuckleheads, konaheads and spoons, both low- and high-speed, feathers, plastic squid and feather squid combinations, and at times saltwater flies are all successful when trolled as well as cast using the methods for which they are designed.

As baits, all these mackerel within their size range can be rigged either to skip or to swim. The reaction of chase and kill by marlin, big tuna and sharks and their own bigger relatives of the razor gang show the merciless pressure and harrying to which smaller species, even gamefish species, are constantly subjected by bigger predator species. The cutting teeth of these small mackerels make it sensible for the teeth to be scraped free of the jaws before they are rigged as baits.

BARRACUDA

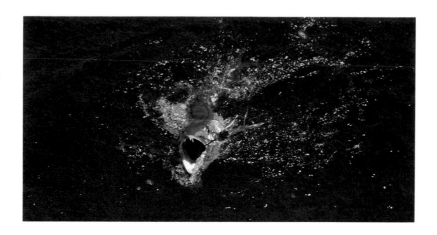

The toothy equipment of this Bahamas barracuda shows why they are the scourge of lures and baits offshore. Photo: Peter Goadby.

These snaggle-toothed marauders range from the clear shallow waters of the coral marl flats to the deep water outside tropical reefs. They prowl menacingly around reef edges in the reef openings as well as over the ridges and other natural and unnatural underwater formations.

The sight of a hooked barracuda, a wriggling bar of blotched silver in the clear green water over golden sand and darker patches, is one of light tackle fishing's unforgettable sights as are their spectacular slashing jumps.

In Florida and Caribbean waters, surgical rubber tubes rigged with one or two hooks are most successful lures cast over the flats. Even though barracuda are school fish, up to 7 kg (15 lb), as they grow bigger, towards their maximum size, they become loners, the dominant predator on some reef, peak or opening.

'Cuda everywhere have an unpleasant reputation, partly because of their sinister appearance, partly because of the possibility of attack on humans, partly also because of their annoying habit of mutilating other hooked fish regarded as more edible and exciting gamefish. Barracuda look sneaky and, with their dental equipment and the possibility of human attack, they are often treated on suspicion that if they *look* mean and dangerous, they *are* mean and dangerous. They must always be handled carefully while being boated or released.

Many legends support the belief that barracuda live for many years and stay in the same locality. One interesting story comes from the Hawaiian island of Maui, where the Hawaiians in some villages released the barracuda they caught and threw a few *opelu* (chub mackerel) into the water as food for the barracuda. Gradually as the fish apparently became conditioned to associating the outrigger canoes, nets and *opelu* schools and therefore the Hawaiians with food, they rounded up the *opelu* schools under the canoes ready with net. The net was then lifted and some *opelu* were thrown to the fish that made the *opelu* take possible.

Barracuda are ideal light tackle opponents, taken on fly, bait-casting, spinning and trolling tackle. Chumming is effective in concentrating a number of fish in an area and inciting action. Fluorescent green or pink is often effective on lure coloration just as it is in the 37-cm (15-in) lengths of surgical rubber. White, silver and other shiny colors are generally effective, but so too are combinations with orange and red, yellow and lime green. Small spoons are often effective, whether trolled or cast so the action is right on the surface, or weighted or trolled on downrigger to take it deep. Small konaheads, knuckleheads and minnows are all effective. As with other gamefish, results in the deliberate fishing for barracuda can be improved by keeping a hooked fish in the water while others are sought by casting or jigging. These fish are important in tropical sport fisheries all around the world and are sought with great enthusiasm for their fast surface run and occasional flashing jump.

Florida and Caribbean barracuda are great sport on shallow flats as well as over offshore reefs and wrecks. Photo: IGFA.

COBIA

For some sportfishermen, cobia are a source of natural interest, mystique and burning ambition to catch them. There is no doubt that these fish are different, challenging, deserving in every way of their high reputation and regard. They are seasonal in most waters and are labelled by anglers not only as top opponents, but 'smart' fish that are different in their fight, cunning in their use of line-breaking natural and manmade obstructions, difficult to catch, but great game species with high edible qualities.

One of their distinctive features is the difficulty they create in safe gaffing. They not only resemble sharks, with which they are often confused as they cruise through the water, but have the habit of some shark species of rolling and spinning on the gaff. For this reason they are best gaffed in the centre of the back under their dorsal fin. Like sharks, they are associated with remora, the suckerfish that hitch rides to their food sources on big marine animals, particularly sharks, marlin and turtles. In Florida and some other areas, cobia are closely associated with the shark's relatives, the rays. Cobia swim around big rays and benefit by picking up food disturbed from the sand by the rays digging along the sea bed seeking food.

This species has several common names that tell more of their story. They are called crabeaters because they seek and eat crabs, and black kingfish because of their dark-brown coloration and their association with yellow-tail kingfish in Australia.

Fishermen who have been fortunate enough to watch cobia eyeing the baits and lures will never forget the experience. One or more of the brown flat-headed shapes will often follow and watch without striking. On outside reefs and bomboras where the swells lift into surf and the water changes from blue to opal, fishing at the cobia hot spots is challenging as well as thrilling. The confident brown shapes come from the protection of the reef to follow like marine sheepdogs, coming up to the baits and lures, watchful yet curious, ready to feed but not striking. Suddenly one or more baits or lures will be taken and the fight is on. The hooked fish will head for their rocky home accompanied by the others in the school. If the initial problem is overcome by the angler and skipper and the fish can be led to obstacle-free waters, there is a battle royal that continues until the fish are within gaffing range, followed by the expected gaffing problems.

Sometimes the fish is initially struck with a light drag in the hope it can lead away from cutting-off obstacles. Hopefully once clear of the reef, drag can be increased and the fish worked harder.

Cobia, particularly big fish in excess of 23 kg (50 lb) exhibit apparent cunning as well as power in their fighting. They often respond to chum and live bait around the obstacle such as platforms and light beacons that give the benefit of protection and a source of food, particularly crabs. Fights won by the fish will never be forgotten, as they show many of the characteristics and challenge of the fish.

We were fishing in Moreton Bay where permanent lights on platforms delineate the shipping channel. Each of the platforms at certain months is home for a school of cobia. Knowing they were there, even getting them to strike, was one thing; the problem was to land them around the rusty pylons with their razor-sharp oysters and barnacles.

Despite chum and fresh and live bait, it was never easy to get the cobia to strike. Commercial fishermen would fish with 37-kg (80-lb) tackle and fight with a very hard drag to try to literally pull the fish from the obstacles. Sport fishermen tried light tackle and hoped for the cunning technique of letting the fish take the bait, then with the boat drifting away or very lightly

Cobia are challenging fighters whether hooked over wrecks, reefs or in the vicinity of feeding rays. Photo: Scott Mitchell.

*A*valon *skipper,*
Peter Bristow, fished
Point Lookout, South
Queensland, for his
world record 45 kg
(100 lb) cobia on 15 kg
(30 lb) test. Photo:
courtesy Peter
Bristow.

under power, leading the big brown bruiser away from the structure. The first stages were carried out successfully, the chum raised the cobia, the live bait was irresistible, current carried us 100 m (310 ft) from the pylon where we found the fish. The cobia was comfortably swimming with the bait until 150 m (465 ft) clear, the angler set the drag, struck, and the fight was on, with the boat between the fish and the pylon where it had taken the bait. Sure enough the plan seemed to work, with the fish running away from that pylon. Then we realized too late what it was doing. It went like a torpedo for another pylon a quarter of a mile (400 metres) away, then the line was limp, cut and broken—another win to cobia, zero to the fisherman.

Cobia take trolled natural baits such as garfish (ballyhoo) and mullet, live baits of all kinds and the full range of lures trolled and at drift or anchor. Chum of small fish or fresh from a trawler is often effective. Most action usually comes at the top or bottom tide slack water. In Florida, the Gulf Coast and the Carolinas, cobia are taken in association with feeding rays. They are also taken by deep jigging. Wrecks are also home to cobia. Florida and Bimini captains are particularly skilled at coaxing the brown bombers to the surface above the natural and manmade obstructions so their anglers can take them or try to take them on a variety of tackle.

In addition to the challenging experience of fishing for cobia, there is the further experience of their quality as an edible fish. The flesh is top-quality, whether fresh or after freezing.

THE JACKS AND TREVALLIES

Wherever they occur and in whatever size, pound for pound, kilogram for kilogram, no group of fish resist capture on rod and reel better than the deep flat-sided *carangidae*, variously called jacks, trevallies and local names right around the tropics. Most of these fish do not move far from the rocks and reefs that give them protection and are home to the fish and crustacea that are their food. They swim closely in their schools, ever ready to smash into schools of anchovies or herrings at early morning and late afternoon on top and bottom of the tides.

Irrespective of size, coloration, and species, these are tough, deep plugging fighters that don't give up. They use their powerful deep body and veed tail to go down to where an obstruction will rub the line so the fish can escape. The odds are with these fish in their chosen environment.

Jacks and trevallies are tough opponents for dinghy as well as shore and big boat fishermen. Photo: Alex Julius.

Charlie Hayden shows his big African pompano taken within sight of the Florida high rises. Photo: courtesy Charlie Hayden.

Some jacks and trevallies show glowing colors. Photo: Tim Simpson.

AMBERJACK

Amberjack are a tropical warm water species with habits, fighting characteristics and attributes similar to those of their cool and temperate water relatives, the Pacific yellowtails. The amberjacks are equally tough to fight, equally cunning in the use of obstacles and obstructions, equally important as light and medium tackle opponents. Saltwater anglers know that if they can handle amberjack on light tackle they can handle all species of equal weight. Amberjack are one of the staple saltwater challenges that use every trick used by other species that do not waste energy and oxygen jumping.

Anglers who have experience with big yellowtail and big amberjack disagree about which is the tougher opponent. Some enthusiasts believe they could outpull or outdog even yellowfin tuna. Whether this is correct is open to conjecture, but they certainly are great and difficult opponents, particularly if obstacles are in range. Both are particularly difficult to land after hooking while trolling. Both can be coaxed to the surface away from their obstacle-equipped homes by being chummed and teased with splashing plugs or poppers or the vibration of dead fish dunked and splashed to give sound and vibration of feeding activity. Both species follow hooked mates from the school to the surface and so give the opportunity for continuing action.

They are an important species right around the world's tropical waters, whether deliberately planned for and targeted or welcome unexpected catches from trolling. A big amberjack will outfight other species of equivalent weight. In Bermuda and Florida, guides have pinpointed the most likely amberjack hot spots. The St George's Bank of Bermuda, wrecks of Key West, the reef edges and holes of the Keys are typical of warm water areas that can, with knowledge, be productively fished. They show their excitement and readiness by the darkening of their coloration, excitement transmitted to the fisherman.

Small dead and live fish are successful chum, as are chunks of bigger fish and squid. Chumming generates one of the great sights of saltwater angling as the brown-and-gold torpedoes come up and splash and bump one another in their feeding frenzy. One thing is certain: they are just as exciting and tough in their Atlantic Caribbean homes as in the Indo-Pacific, from Panama to tropical Australia and on to Africa.

Chumming has brought amberjack into the category of a fish for all tackle, instead of just heavy tackle, as was previously believed.

Amberjack are important ingredients in another challenging saltwater fishery. This is for mako and tiger sharks. Fishermen, particularly in Florida and Hawaii, take advantage of these sharks' liking for amberjack.

Anglers fish for amberjack either to keep or to release, then if the big predatory sharks react to the vibration of the fighting amberjack by biting and chopping into them, the anglers become shark fishermen. They rig what is left of the mutilated amberjacks or live or dead previously caught fish as bait for the sharks. The benefits of this are twofold; the presence of sharks in the area has been proven, even if the sharks have not been seen, and they are in a feeding pattern ready for more amberjack flesh.

Amberjack are tough opponents that should be fought standing up with a hard brake on the reel. They should be played smoothly and without jerking bumps that will annoy or wake the fish up to more activity. These fish will take big live baits, even those slow-trolled for billfish. The big baits inhibit the fighting capability of the amberjacks, but they give the benefit of going deep to the depths where the jacks are marauding and terrorizing the bait schools. Another way of getting down to amberjack-preferred depth around reefs and wrecks is with deep trollers controlling the depth of the trolled bait or lures.

Even though amberjack appear in schools and seem an unlimited resource, in some areas they are affected by fishing pressure. Apart from those wanted for food or some other purpose they should be released as tired and wiser fish to give enjoyment and a tussle for other anglers.

Amberjack and yellowtail share the characteristic of taking big baits intended for billfish. Photo: Peter Goadby.

YELLOWTAIL

Yellowtail have an original and valued association with the sport and history of saltwater gamefishing. The anglers who came to fish for yellowtail, who honed their saltwater skills on these gold-striped hoodlums, were the same anglers who explored further offshore and discovered how, where and when to fish for billfish and other open-water gamefish.

Yellowtail, without doubt, deserve a special position in the saltwater Fish Hall of Fame as they established saltwater sport in many long-known fishing areas.

Yellowtail were one of the key species that attracted land-locked fishermen to Avalon, Santa Catalina, before and during the expansion offshore that led to the first-time landings of striped marlin and broadbill. New Zealand saw a similar trend when an angler named Campbell, who had come from Scotland to sample the thrill of yellowtail fishing in the Bay of Islands, landed the first striped marlin. So once again the humble yellowtail was the catalyst for world class gamefishing.

Similarly in Australia, it was no coincidence that the first black and striped marlin captures were made by anglers fishing yellowtail areas. Yellowtail are also important as gamefish in South Africa and Japan.

Wherever they are found they are great opponents—fast, tricky and untiring. When found away from line-breaking reefs and obstacles they are super opponents on light tackle. Their habit of zooming down to the obstacles immediately on hook-up necessitates the use of medium and even heavy tackle for the big bruisers.

In many cases the power and cunning of big yellowtail ensures loss to the fishermen even on heavy tackle. Some frustrated anglers swear that they can hear the marauders giving a big belly laugh as they snatch yet another bait and cut or smash the line. It is easy to visualize those pioneering anglers standing there with reel handles spinning backwards in a blur, barking knuckles, burning thumbs and then *pow!* another broken line and re-rig to try again. All yellowtail dive to obstacles instantly, but the power of the big greenbacks gives them more chances at escape as they vary the reverse rocket down with surface runs.

The biggest yellowtail in all areas are usually taken with live baits on the drift. This technique, often combined with chunking and surface chum, gives the angler a chance for a yellowtail to take a bait with minimum brake on the line. Once one or more baits are taken, the boat can be put into gear to gradually move away from obstacles of rock and kelp to open water before putting brake to strike and fighting the fish. Even then many of the big fish are lost on all weights of tackle.

Trolling for yellowtail is thrilling, as some of the school zero in on a bait with five or six fish bumping one another as they come in for the kill. The multiple

Yellowtail are welcome as both fighting and food fish, particularly those from cooler waters. Photo: L.N.E. Harris.

strikes from the school can work against the fishermen as free-swimming fish bump the leader and line. Yellowtail can be teased right up to the stern of the boat following the hooked fish for more hook-ups or cast jigged or trolled lures.

Experienced fishermen cash in on that first strike by jigging with rod tip and reel to maintain interest and get multiple hook-ups.

Trolling does not often give the angler a chance at the big ones, as the younger, less experienced members of the yellowtail gang usually rush in before the wiser heads of the big fish. This is one reason why live bait fishing on the drift or slow troll accounts for many record fish. The use of big live baits tends to screen out the smaller fish, although it is not unusual to see yellowtail harassing and trying to swallow a bait of almost the same size.

Use of big baits up to 2–3 kg (5–7 lb) has other benefits, in that they allow use of bigger hooks up to 10/0 or 12/0. The bigger bait seems to inhibit the fight of the yellowtail as they lodge in gill rakers. Another advantage of bigger baits is that they swim and give vibration actively while pulling strongly down deep.

Experienced anglers try to think and analyze just what the fish is doing. If it is heading towards the boat, they pump smoothly and fast to keep line tight and minimize the chance of again sounding. Sometimes they

In the Indo-Pacific, yellowtail maraud in schools to harass the bait species. Photo: Ron and Valerie Taylor.

ease the drag if it is sounding fast back to its reefy home to try to fool the fish that it is free. At other times they lock up and attack with short, quick pumps. Attack is

usually not as effective as smooth pumps while leading the deep fighter to better water.

Tag recoveries in Australia have shown that while there is movement along the coast and to deeper water in juvenile and medium-sized fish, some do move long distances travelling from Australia's east coast to New Zealand or vice versa.

This species can be taken from the rocks by high-speed spinning and live baits. The capture of heavyweight yellowtail from the rocks is a special challenge, even on live bait, as the take is right near the natural obstructions that they use to their benefit. Rock fishermen know the same thrill as those from boats, in that the fish or a school of them are often seen behind lures or bait.

Even in this age of super tackle and electronic fishermen in the quest for super fish, the ubiquitous yellowtail in their five or more Indo-Pacific populations remain one of the most popular and valuable gamefish. Anglers successful with yellowtail are invariably successful with other, bigger fish.

It is important for recreational anglers as well as commercial fishermen to remember that even though the schools of these fish seem vast, they are subject to fishing pressure. Populations can be drastically reduced to the point of concern for breeding stock, so even in cool waters where they have top edible qualities, anglers should take only what they need and release all others, big or small.

BONEFISH

His Highness and Shyness, the Grey Ghost, the Silver Bullet: possibly no other fish has so many respectful nicknames. Once believed by scientists to be one world-wide species, according to the latest research there may be at least five species of bonefish. However, whether one or five, the descriptive names and respect are universal. Bonefish are traditionally considered fish of the flats, and they amaze with their acceleration and speed. Those fast runs which literally strip line from spool in a blur are probably as fast or faster over 100 metres or yards than any other gamefish. The shallow water of less than a metre has the effect of magnifying this acceleration; speed, the thrill of seeing the fish in clear shallow water, plus their timidity and readiness to flee add to their charisma and challenge.

Fly fishing master and author, A. J. McClane, summed up their shyness when he wrote: 'This is probably the only fly fishing game in which the angler can scare a hundred fish with one bad cast.' Perhaps even more than tarpon, the bonefish moved fly fishing from fresh to saltwater.

Despite their well-documented shyness, bonefish show varying tolerance to fishermen. They sometimes

take a bait or lure as it is about to be lifted clear of the water right alongside the boat.

The charisma of fly fishing for these fish is so great that experienced guides comment that many of their clients would catch more and bigger fish by use of spin fishing rather than fly. Spinning tackle gives greater range and in windy conditions better accuracy to land the lure in its best potential position.

Thankfully bonefish are not always extremely shy and give anglers good chances on fly and spinning tackle. This was one of the fish that attracted Zane Grey to the Florida Keys and the fishing camp and characters at Long Key. Zane Grey describes, as only he could, the speed and challenge of these fish. It is interesting to realize that the tackle used in his day was linen line that even in six thread should have alerted every bonefish on the flats. His writings on bonefish in *Tales of Fishes* show humor and ability to tease himself and others of the 'Bonefish Bugs' in their quest for fish. In those days fishing was from small boats or from wading.

The bonefish is one of the few fish in the world for which special boats have evolved. The flat skiffs are not only practical in performance, but powerful so they can get to the chosen locations fast in the very shallow waters of flats and the banks. These specialized skiffs with poling platform, obstruction-free casting areas, live bait wells and exciting design and construction, are practical to travel in as well as to fish.

The bonefish was also the favourite of Van Campen Heilner who writes in his classic *Salt Water Fishing*, 'Of all the fish which I have had the pleasure and sport of pursuing, and this includes a lifetime of angling for everything from Brook Trout to Swordfish, my favorite is the Bonefish. From my personal experience I can say he is the gamest fish for which I ever wet a line.' He too was a bonefish 'nut'.

Bait fishing is also successful in taking bonefish, particularly when used with chumming. Shrimp and crabs are commonly used as baits, while shrimp or conch is used for chum. The bait or lure should be cast in front of the fish as they head into the tide. It should be cast to land about 1.1 m (4 ft) past the fish and about a metre or three feet in front of them. Some guides believe the angler should hold his cast until the bonefish are heading into the tide so the offering seems additionally natural. If shrimp are the bait, they are threaded on to the hook tail first. The rays on the tail should be removed so the bait moves cleanly through the water.

Flat, lightweight leaded jigs that are designed to move with the hook-up are effective for bonefish, particularly in shrimp colors. This lure or plastic worm type is not retrieved at constant fast speed. An effective retrieve is to move it a couple of times then wait and twitch it

again. Success in seeking bonefish, as in other inshore fishing, comes from recognizing when to fish, on rising or falling tide, and where to fish. Spinning is successful in 0.8–1.2 m (2–4 feet) depth and fly in 0.8 m (2 ft).

Some areas should be fished on the running tide, others on the same flats at the ebb. Some produce best on the big tides (the springs), others on the small tides (the neaps). If anglers are not familiar with a locality or fishing with someone who is familiar, they should save valuable time and money by seeking expert advice or a guide, at least until they have local knowledge.

The modern light tackle used for flats fishing is designed and built to cope with the speed of the fish with 200-metre (or yard) runs and repeats of the runs and a high speed circumnavigation of the boat. Once a fish is hooked on the flats it is important to hold the rod high so the line clears the natural obstructions on the bottom. Guides have tried, tested and proven tackle, but understand if clients wish to use personal tackle. The guide's advice on lures will be invaluable, as is his experience in spotting and pinpointing fish from up on his poling platform that otherwise may not be spotted by his anglers, even with top-quality polarizing glasses, at deck level. The guide takes great care in poling the skiff, being careful not to hit the boat or lift the poles clear of the surface to create noisy drips. The angler must be careful not to drop anything in the boat. The thump of tackle box lid or clunk of a dropped lead jig could ruin the hoped-for action at that locality.

Fly fishermen should be aware of the flies, lures and

Jim Allen about to release a Christmas Island bonefish. Photo: Tim Simpson.

Not all bonefish are silver. Many show darker blotches along the back. Photo: Al Pfleuger.

Boat Handling Tactics
for Small Fish

With a hook-up near an obstruction, use the boat to move the fish clear of the obstruction and try to position the boat so it is between the obstruction and the fish.

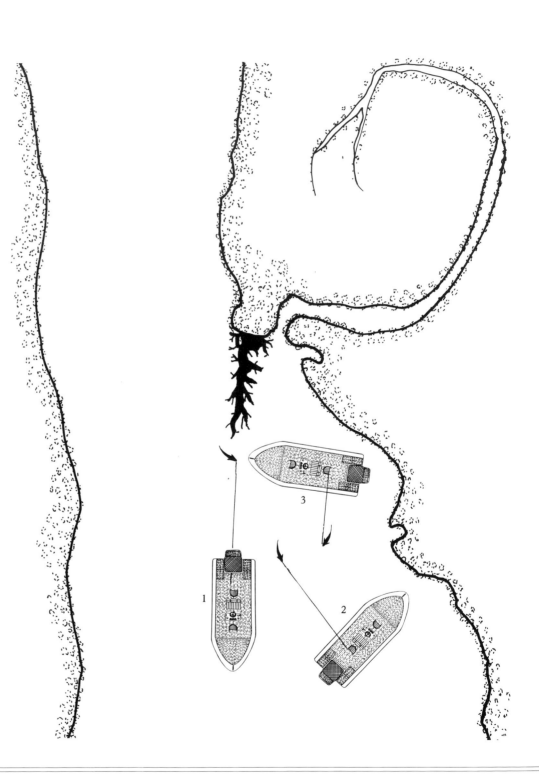

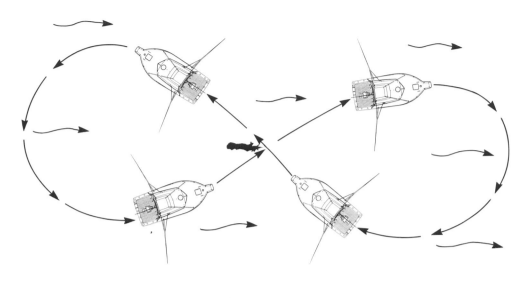

A productive trolling pattern around a log or weed mat—a figure of eight going with the current, not across it.

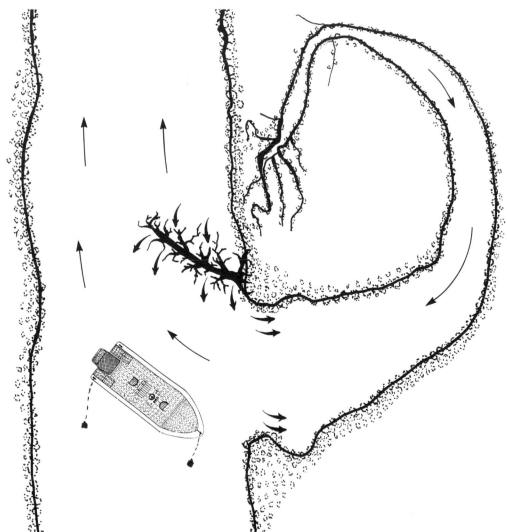

Anchor and position boat to allow right-handed casting and fishing as often as possible.

WHERE TO FIND SMALL FISH

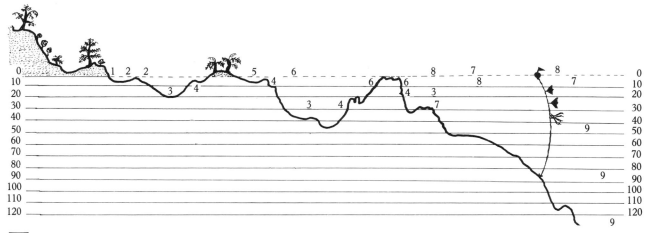

The depths at which the various gamefish are found:

1. Snook, tarpon, barramundi, threadfin salmon;
2. Bonefish, barracuda, permit, small sharks, trevally, jacks;
3. Requiem (whaler) sharks, tiger sharks;
4. King mackerel, tanguigue, spotted mackerels, queenfish;
5. Bonefish, permit, barracuda;
6. Sailfish, king mackerel, tanguigue, small black marlin, small tuna, cobia;
7. Big marlin, wahoo, barracuda, tuna;
8. Tuna, wahoo, mahi mahi, yellowfin, marlin, pelagic sharks;
9. Broadbill, big-eye, thresher sharks.

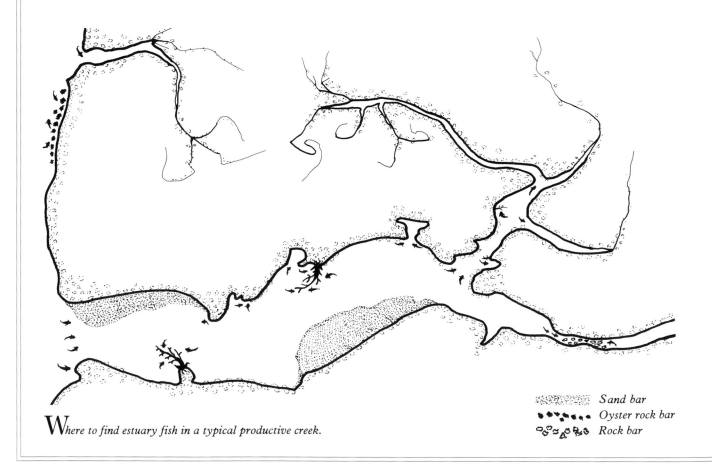

Where to find estuary fish in a typical productive creek.

	Sand bar
	Oyster rock bar
	Rock bar

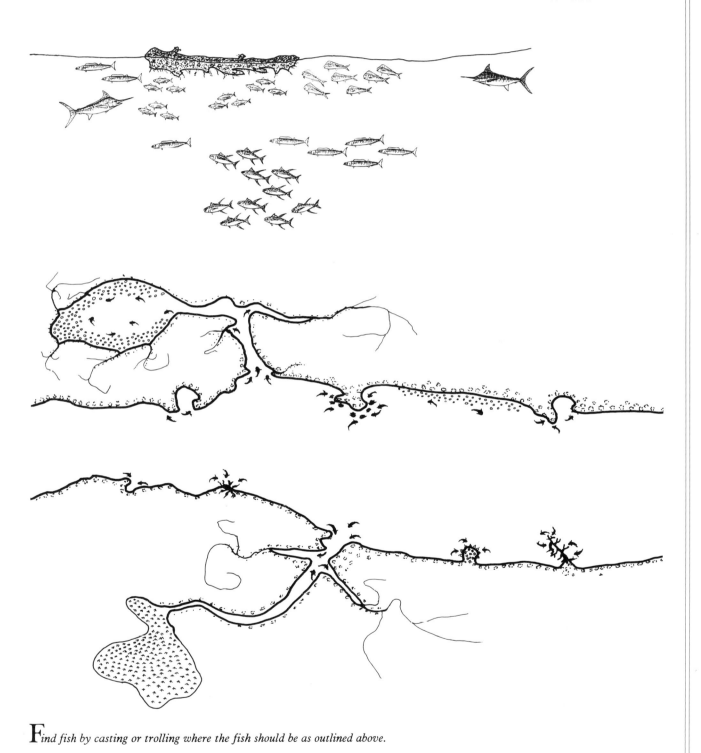

Floating logs and even small pieces of flotsam attract bait and gamefish very quickly in the warm currents.

Find fish by casting or trolling where the fish should be as outlined above.

Florida and Central America provide unrivalled river and estuary action on many light tackle species, including the super herring tarpon. Photo: IGFA—Joe Brooks collection.

quite unforgettable. Often in moments of quiet at sea as well as on land, memory goes back to what seemed like a bucket rising to the lure for a tarpon that Lefty Kreh and Captain Al Lipford found for me on a first trip to the Keys, a sight that ranks with the approach of a marlin, tuna or shark in heavy weights.

Many of the tarpon world records are held in western Africa, where they have long been regarded as food. Captures at Gabon have put European anglers within easier reach of the great sport offered by these fish.

Tarpon and bonefish have done much to popularize the modern angler's philosophy of conservation. Very few fish are kept; most are released to recover and continue their life cycle. The ethic of release of these gamefish has logically spread to other species, even popular ones that are highly regarded for their edible quality.

KING THREADFIN SALMON

Anglers who have not yet had the experience of tangling with Indo-Pacific king threadfin salmon have a treat in store for the future. They are yet to enjoy one of the great light tackle fish found in any waters in the world. Big threadfin seem to be most prevalent in northern tropical Australia and Papua New Guinea. Threadfin are in many ways mystery fish, appearing in river entrances or estuaries yet not in similar adjoining areas. They are usually present at specific times in estuaries while disappearing into the unknown, presumably further offshore, at other times. The long slender filaments that hang below the head, the unusual semi-transparent bulb nose, and the strong yet underslung jaw often distract angler attention away from one of its most important features, the powerful veed tail which has evolved to propel a powerful fish very fast. If bonefish are the 'grey ghosts', king threadfin are the 'golden ghosts', moving quietly and confidently, blending in with their estuarine environment.

The fighting capability of king threadfin is deservedly highly rated. They simply outperform, outrun and even outjump highly regarded, better known and more commonly found barramundi from the same waters. Once fishermen are aware of where and when threadfin will appear, the best chance of catching them will come at dawn or evening neap low tide in river and creek mouths running into deep water estuaries in true tropical water. For some reason the morning low is often more productive than afternoon. These neap low tides expose obstructions and snags and define the deep holes that have minimum water flow and maximum water clarity.

Threadfin are intriguing as well as tough, fast fighters that test angler reactions, reflexes and control to the maximum. The strike is usually different. First there is a tap perhaps from the strong, yet slender, thread filaments followed by a second tap that can become a hookup that strips line from the reel at blistering speed. Years of instinctive drop back with billfish has personally paid off with threadfin when lowering the rod tip then lifting it again on the second hump or tap gave a higher than usual hook-up rate while trolling. This technique seems to help sometimes with a non hook-up on the first bump by barramundi as well.

After the initial run, a long yellowish-silver shape with thread streamers flying will clear the surface before continuing the run in the original direction, or in a change of direction that may head it towards obstructions or back to the fishermen. At times the reel spool that was spinning in a blur or the line being retrieved will stop, so the slender line is limp without weight. The angler has a sickening feeling that the line has broken off or been cut off. Spirits lift as the line is again tight and the slender rod arches in a bow and it is obvious the golden ghost is still there. Sometimes in a flash the fish that jumped and was peeling line as it ran behind the stern of the dinghy will suddenly be jumping ahead of the boat, or on the other side, a nerve wracking maneuver that tests guide, boat operator and angler.

These fish maneuvers will be repeated many times before the threadfin is tired and ready for capture or tag and release. Boat handling and co-operation and understanding between angler and boat operator are important ingredients for success. The positioning of the boat between prominent snags, and maintaining position using the power of the motor against the tide that will carry fish and boat towards snags, is often most helpful. Threadfin are highly prized for both edible qualities and fishing qualities. Very experienced tropical angler/writers Col Roberts and Alex Julius rate threadfin well above all other estuary fish as excitement and challenge generators.

Fishing is a sport of memories, one in which anglers and everyone else remember one of the great fish or a particular fight, and threadfin create unforgettable fishing. Scientific records list that king threadfin grow to around 45 kg (100 lb) so lucky anglers will have great threadfin experiences in store, whether of this size or around the more usual 9 kg (20 lb). Very slow trolling with small swimming minnow middle-water lures is productive, as is casting these same type lures and bait fishing from boat or shore at estuary entrances. Careful fishing with minimum noise and vibration give the chance of the tap hook-up routine continuing until the fish are gone as suddenly as their appearance was revealed.

When these fish can be sighted there is excellent opportunity for spin or fly casting. This adds another

In Australia, giant threadfin salmon provide an even greater challenge than the better known barramundi of the same environment. Mrs Lorrie Fay is standing with line class records for both species at Bathurst Island. Photo: Peter Goadby.

dimension to fishing for these exciting big estuary fish where their water environment favours the fish. King threadfin are exciting fish that give anglers reason to return to try and try again as well as vivid memories of really great fish.

PERMIT

The term his 'highness and shyness' is used for the highly regarded bonefish, yet on the same environment of flats and channels there is a fish that is lightning fast yet bigger, heavier and even more shy—that fish is the permit.

The deep body of the permit exudes power whilst the big forked tail indicates speed and marathon swimming. Added to these natural attributes are well-developed eyes and a prominent lateral line that receives every vibration. Here is a fish evolved for hunting and survival in shallow water where sunlight and sea bed coloration help its silver shade become almost invisible.

The difficulty in spotting permit and the speed of

its disappearance to safer depths is shown by the experiences of skilled guides and anglers who only realise that a permit was in their sight as it turns and speeds away. Its wariness dictates the use of light tackle whilst its power and doggedness ensure that there will be no short fights. Most permit fights extend from thirty minutes to beyond two hours. The difficulty of setting the hook gives added importance to continually maintaining tight line even when this big shield-shaped fish indulges in its trick of banging its jaws on the sea bed to try to dislodge the hook. Nature has endowed the permit with a tough lining in its mouth. This makes

Permit are regarded as the peak of fly fishing on the flats. Only a few are taken on fly with most taken on natural baits. Photo: Al Pfleuger.

hook-up, whether in shallow or deeper water, difficult even after five or six strikes as hard as the tackle will allow.

Permit are deep dogged fighters that don't ever give up. They do not spend energy and waste oxygen in splashy jumps that may excite anglers. Those who have caught the various worldwide smaller relatives of permit in tropical surf or calm water understand why skilled anglers seek permit and rate them so highly. The power and acceleration of those fish with the ability to use its deep body to slice through the water at an angle while using every wave and current to its advantage will know that permit, the biggest of the family, deserve their high rating.

Despite the extreme difficulty in hooking and capturing permit on fly tackle, it is fortunate for anglers that permit will more readily take crustacea baits, particularly live baits, cast in their range on spinning tackle. Sometimes wrecks are home to a school of permit that respond to chumming, giving exciting fishing and chances at big permit, big permit are usually loners although the middle sizes are often in small schools.

Closely related species inhabit the Indo-Pacific waters from the west coast of Central America to the eastern coast of Africa. Their chosen environments are similar to that of the Atlantic and Caribbean locales of shiny flats, coral marl, rubble on banks, shallow lagoons and fringing deeper channels. Occasionally, in the Indo-Pacific, they are hooked accidentally in the surf while fishing for local species.

The greater the care in walking, wading and in minimising noise and vibration from boat, the greater the chance of permit success. When walking on the flats the angler's feet should slide across the flats rather than being lifted and replaced as in usual walking. Skiff poles should not be lifted clear of the surface or bump the boat. They should be used very quietly. Movement must be at a minimum.

Familiarity with the taking of bonefish on fly and spinning tackle is beneficial when the chance comes to try for a permit. Even when shaking at the awareness that here at last is a chance, the fisherman must carefully present the fly or bait within 30 cm (12 in) in front of the head of the fish.

Careful research and fishing development may one day show other areas in other oceans that will give anglers a chance at this fish with its well-deserved reputation as the greatest challenge on the tropical flats, particularly in fly fishing.

SNOOK

The snook species of tropical American waters are continuing proof that fish do not have to be massive, bulky marauders to be exciting, charismatic and challenging to anglers.

It is unfortunate that, as with their Indo-Pacific relative, the barramundi, snook are top edible fish because commercial and sales demand puts great pressure on the stock.

Snook attraction and reputation ensures that snook anglers travel to fish for them not only to Florida but wherever they occur in the east and west coasts of Central America.

The reputation of these fish is based not only on the adrenalin pumping experience of the visiting anglers, but also of resident anglers. These are fish that fight with the exciting tricks of other fish, running and jumping. The gill flaring and gill rattling jumps are combined with incredible awareness of the position of snags and other obstacles.

Pugnacious snook of several species and sizes are found in the salt and brackish estuaries, rivers and creeks of Florida, and on the east and west tropical coasts of Central and South America. Their home waters are bounded by mangroves to give natural ambush cover of tree trunks as well as man-made structures such as bridges and beacons. They can at times be taken on the open beaches washed by gentle surf as well as estuaries, canals, rivers and creeks. Open ocean beaches of Costa Rica give anglers yet another chance at snook as well as those that abound in the tarpon rich rivers and creeks. Snook can occasionally be found away from obstructions where they have ganged up on bait fish and shrimp, or while migrating across the flats on their way to spawn in open water. Adult as well as juvenile fish later return to the creeks and rivers. It is sensible and well worthwhile for visiting anglers to fish with guides who know the movements and locality of snook at different times and tides even though advice can be sought from local fishermen to give day-long action as tide changes indicate changes to other fishing areas. The snook's pugnacious reputation, whether hooked or going about their natural activity, is reinforced by their appearance. The long powerful underslung jaw, razor sharp cutters on gills, long powerful body, strong veed tail and dominant eye combine to give a worthy tough cunning opponent. This fish is no wimp, neither is snook fishing success associated with wimps. These are tough fish that are sought and taken in tough country.

Another unusual and distinctive feature of snook is the prominent black lateral stripe along the back, right down to and across the tail. As with all fish, coloration will vary due to environment or whether found in clear or murky waters. Snook are fished for unsighted in the brown water of creeks and rivers, while those taken sight fishing in clearer waters are more silver and less bronze. They are taken trolling as well as casting. Swimming

Snook with their gill-rattling jumps are now protected by closed seasons and size regulations in Florida. The black lateral line shows why Vic Dunaway calls this fish 'old linesides'. Photo: Al Pfleuger.

*F*lorida sportfishermen regularly release snook beyond the conservation regulations. Photo: Al Pfleuger.

minnows are successful trolled as well as cast, as are pencil lures and mirror lures. Poppers and chuggers will trigger action when used head first or when used in reverse. Polarising glasses assist sight fishing and give the added thrill of seeing and presenting the lures or bait for action, or just seeing the fish, as all fish spotting movement more often shows the fish position rather than a clear outline in expected colours.

The pugnacious nature and speed at which snook pounce and turn their head with a snap of jaw make those who have seen this feeding activity pleased that they are not the mullet, shrimp, crab or other natural food sought by the predators. Occasionally big snook are taken in shallow water or unexpectedly on the flats while fishing for other species.

The commercial demand and edible quality of snook plus recognition of their value as a recreational species has influenced the Florida fisheries managers to impose a two-way management plan of non-retention of certain sizes plus a closed season. They make every effort to work towards the survival and increased stock of this top inshore gamefish. In addition to the management plan, they are a species that have long been released by sport fishermen despite their fine edible quality.

There are several closely related species of snook, but wherever they are taken and of whichever species, they richly deserve their reputation as one of tropical America's big four of the inshore waters along with tarpon, bonefish and permit.

BARRAMUNDI

The tropical salt and brackish water environment around the world is inhabited by a fish of such power, savagery and fighting activity that improvements have been imperative in the casting outfits and lures used in the angling quest. The fish-forced improvements have been necessary to give the angler using the various classes of casting tackle an equal chance.

Rods and reels are now stronger with maintenance and resistance to salt water more practical. Lures and hooks have been beefed up to withstand the pressure and twisting of hyperactive aggressive tropical fish. The barramundi of the Indo-Pacific tropics is one of the fish species that have forced the improvements. These mangrove maulers are the bare knuckle fighters, the gang bullies that use strength, jumping and every natural obstruction in their efforts to beat the angler. The name barramundi is of Australian Aboriginal origin. Their importance to Aboriginals goes far beyond their food value. They are totem fish, reproduced on bark paintings and rock carvings.

The big glowing eyes of barramundi help its

predations in the dark-coloured water in which it spends much of its life. This species, like its close relative of the tropical Americas, the snook, is catadromus, that is it spawns in the salt water. The babies and many of the adult fish move up the rivers and creeks, even though some become land-locked in lagoons and billabongs during the dry season.

IGFA list barramundi as freshwater species for world record purposes. Like their American relative species of the east and west coast they live in tiger country that abounds in natural obstructions—mangroves, oyster and rock bars, and deep holes where they swoop on passing bait fish, shrimps and other food. These obstructions are used for ambush and naturally to gain their escape. Barramundi are one of those fish that with one smashing strike turn a quiet uneventful fishing day into one of action. They clear the surface with gill-rattling, head-throwing jumps that may break line before the angler can put brain or concentration into gear. This surface mayhem mauls lures and distorts hooks before the barramundi settles down to sub-surface runs and further jumps.

Cast lures of various swimming minnow types are retrieved slowly. Some guides prefer those that sink below the surface before they are retrieved. Nilsmaster, Elliott, Mirrolures, Rapala and Killa lures are just a few of the wooden or plastic minnows that have high success rates. These lures are also successful when trolled around likely snags or rock bars at very slow speed. Many lures need a change to heavier hooks to withstand barramundi power even though this change may alter the action of the lure. Rattling lures are also effective when fish are sluggish because of lower water temperature. Rattle lures are cast and jigged around log obstructions and cover often after the radical action of the cover being bumped with the boat. Trolling in darkness at neap low tides is often most productive and can provide unbelieveable action and excitement with big barramundi far into the night.

Swimming soft plastic tail lures also produce action. Big barramundi, particularly late in the afternoon and at night, respond to poppers and chuggers rigged from front or rear. Live bait of mullet, shrimp or frogs is also productive for big barramundi when drifting or at anchor in the deep holes of creeks and rivers.

As with the snook of America, fishing for barramundi is thrilling when the water is clear enough for the anglers to sight the big lunkers lazily cruising around or hanging motionless and watchful around snags and obstructions of feeding on bait species washed over rock bars on ebb tide. When these times and tides are right barramundi will strike actively at the same trolled or cast swimming minnow lures that work in daylight. Cast poppers are also effective in the darkness.

Twenty-three kg (50 lb) or heavier is the mark eagerly sought by barramundi fishermen. Col Cordingly who has caught several over this weight and Cairns tackle maestro, Jack Erskine, often troll identical lures in color and action one behind the other. Col's theory is that the first lure may not excite or cause a strike, but the sudden appearance of a similar critter in its home territory will trigger an explosive aggressive reaction.

Baitcasting outfits are generally used for trolling and casting. It is intriguing to see big men who are world class heavy tackle blue water anglers such as Arch Livingstone, John Johnston, Gus Fay as well as top charter skippers, Laurie Woodbridge, Dennis Wallace, and Frank Thompson equally dedicated and involved in the quest for barramundi. Most barramundi are now tagged and released after being lifted inboard for measuring and recording before being swum gently to aid resuscitation. Spinning tackle and saltwater fly is growing in use for the challenge of barramundi, particularly where sight fishing is practical in the clearer waters as well as in the game of chance, casting blind in turbid waters. Whatever tackle is used, it will be thoroughly tested by barramundi power.

Barramundi show their close relationship to the snook of the Americas with an active gill-flaring, jumping performance. Photo: Peter Goadby.

THE FISHING BOAT

THE SPORTFISHING BOAT

At ports right around the world, boats, particularly fishing boats, are magnets that draw people to the docks, wharves and marinas. Similarly, at every boat show, those who come to look and dream far outnumber those who actually own boats.

The boats that excite the greatest interest are fishing boats, boats with a purpose. The big fishing boats are dreamed of, transferred by thought out to the lonely blue of the warm currents—the fisherman, a boat, scattered birds, and the restless sea and fish. Some of the smaller boats, those under seven metres (about 22 feet), are dreamed of as fully equipped, and they are equally visualized far out to sea or fishing around the shore and the estuaries, the homes of the fighting species.

It takes more than dreams to turn a boat of any size into a fishing boat. Some stock boats can become good fishing boats, although they were not designed or built specifically for this purpose. Despite manufacturers' claims, there are boats that, notwithstanding the addition of all the good fishing equipment, still cannot become

The modern gamefishing boat is the quarter horse of the open ocean. Photo: Peter Goadby.

good fishing boats. They *look* like fishing boats, but do not perform perfectly to fishing's special demands. Then there are the proven custom-built or semi-stock boats of various sizes designed and built for fishermen. These proven boats have a special feel as well as performance; they can be easily maintained to keep on fishing. Boats such as Merritt, Rybovich, G & S, Norseman, Woodnutt, Plaisier, Whiticar, Monterey, Davis, and Daytona are built to fish and there are always keen fishermen who appreciate and need them. These are then fully equipped to become fishing machines. To these magic names can be added the top production builders, whose boats can be equipped to also become top sportfishing boats—Bertram, Hatteras, Blackfin, Savage, Striker, Ocean, Pacifica, Innovator, Topaz, Uniflite, Post, Pacemaker, Huckins, Sea Ray, Mako, Maverick, Viking, O'Brien and Salthouse.

There are the other boats, sometimes one-offs, built for fishing. They sometimes have specialist hulls, such as Hawaii's famous Haole Sampan. If prospective buyers are serious about fishing, they will find it more practical, more pleasant, less frustrating and safer to look at proven custom-built boats, the boats in which experience, purpose and tradition are directed at the search for and

The prowess and pioneering of Captain George Bransford made the name Sea Baby *justly famous. Here* Sea Baby II, *skippered by Captain Laurie Woodbridge, runs back after a day at No. 10 Ribbon. Photo: Peter Goadby.*

handling of fish. This applies to boats of any size. There is nothing worse than fishing in a boat in which the design and build resist, rather than help, fishing. The addition of outriggers, chair and electronic equipment does not create or miraculously transform a boat into a sportfishing boat that is easily and safely worked. A great fishing boat is logically built around fishing needs, rather than the fishing needs being added on by addition or alteration. Naturally, cost is a consideration, but so too are performance, safety and fishability and knowing that when fish are found, the boat will perform when it should.

The features that make a good fishing boat are:

• Design and construction that allow running fast in tough conditions when going forward, and a similar performance backing up in boats where propellers and rudders are under the hull. Boats with outboards and outdrives are naturally just not able to go as well backwards as forward, but despite this they have advantages and are practical propulsion in many smaller fishing craft.

• A hull design that, in addition to performing safely in tough conditions when going forward or backing up, has necessary strength without unnecessary weight to give range dictated by fishing needs.

• A practical working cockpit that facilitates safe and practical handling of fish and rigging baits and lures.

• The necessary electronic fish finders, navigation and communication equipment.

• Good visibility.

• Comfort for angler, skipper and crew.

The logical way of ensuring these features is:

• Check out and if possible actually ride a similar boat in fishing conditions, preferably when fish are being caught. Other sea trials often do not have true relevance to what shows in actual fishing conditions.

• Check the speed and fuel performance and range under operating load to ensure that the needed performance can be achieved.

• Check visibility particularly for the skipper, and generally while under way.

• Check that the boat will run fairly dry and the hull lays spray down as much as possible. There is nothing more frustrating, annoying and damaging to the necessary electronic equipment, fishing gear and tempers than boats that are wet from water thrown for the breeze to catch.

• Check that backing up is true and straight. Some boats will not track straight, others generate so much vibration that the boat appears to be, and may in fact be, damaging itself.

• Make sure that cockpit or fishing area is free of leader-catching obstructions. Trim tabs on the boat should be foldable flat against the transom for backing up and so that leader can be taken, wire pulled and released with minimum chance of tangling and jamming on obstructions.

• If the boat has a transom door, make sure this is practical, that it will allow the entry of big fish. The bottom of the transom door should be very close, around 25 cm (10 in) above the water line when the boat is at rest. A transom door is often a compromise. Those who work the cockpit prefer one that opens out, so the water pressure in backing up keeps it naturally pushed closed. Inwards-opening doors have water pressure trying to force them open. Transom doors that are not cut through the transom coverboard, i.e., that open only through the transom, are best for fishing, as this eliminates cuts or slots in the coverboard to catch and jam the leader when the fish is alongside for gaffing or tagging. There are natural advantages in loading and unloading with transom doors that open through the transom coverboard, so this is a matter of decision by use and practicality. If the transom door is through the coverboard, the height of the door opening is automatically determined. If through the transom but not the coverboard, in boats over ten metres (30 feet), the transom door to take most fish would be 1 m × 66 cm (3 ft × 2 ft), depending on the width of the transom and its shape.

- In positioning the fighting chair, the stanchion should be 1.2 m (4 ft) from the inside of the coverboard. This allows room for the crew to work aft of the chair, even with footrest extended for a tall angler. The rod tip when bent should clear cockpit corners; big boats may benefit from a gooseneck stanchion.

The cockpit and transom coverboard height for easy working of fish and safety should be between 65 and 75 cm (26 in–32 in). Shallower than 65 cm can increase danger; deeper than 75 cm makes it difficult to reach water and fish.

The height of the seat of the chair should be 5–7 cm (2–3 in) lower than that of the transom, although some skippers and anglers prefer the height of the chair level or even above the coverboard to give maximum height on pumps and help in clearing the corner of the cockpit. The seat of the chair is thus about 60 cm–70 cm (24–30 in) above the cockpit deck.

- The cockpit should have room for the fighting chair if heavy tackle is fished.

- The coverboards should be clear of line- or leader-catching obstructions. Cleats for gaff and mooring ropes should be immovably firmly fixed, not just screwed in position. They should allow room for more than one strong gaff rope and be readily accessible and workable.

- In addition to the cleats aft for moorings and gaff rope tying off, there is great benefit from the installation of a cleat or half cleat at the forward end of the cockpit. This allows for the holding of a fish close to the boatside, with head and body held forward after the first gaff is in position to allow placing of additional gaffs, if necessary, and a tail rope.

- The cockpit should have either a through-the-bottom (under the cockpit deck) live bait tank, or a tank with circulated water in the cockpit, bait boxes, bait-rigging bench with drawers for knives and needles and threads, files and other terminal tackle and needed equipment below the work area.

- Deck hose for washing away fish slime or cooling the decks.

- The bait rigging work area should be under the flying bridge overhang, for protection from the sun and spray and preferably clear of the obstruction of the cockpit bridge ladder. The placing of the ladder is always a problem as it takes valuable space and must facilitate quick transfer from bridge to cockpit. An upright ladder at or near the middle of the cockpit is generally a practical compromise. Safety rails on the rear and unprotected area of the side of the flying bridge are necessary for safety and for rod holders for fishing and stowage during a fight. Some boats have the bridge ladder recessed into the flying bridge, others have entry through a hatch.

- The flying bridge should be dry when the boat is running—even in fishing areas with high winds. Wet (spray-throwing) hull designs and conditions make

Bill Hoey's lovingly maintained 37 ft (12 m) Merritt is great for marlin at Kona, Hawaii, as well as the giant tuna for which it was designed. Photo: Peter Goadby.

Ted Naftzger's Rybovich spends many hours at sea off southern California singlemindedly scouring the seas for broadbill swordfish. Photo: Greg Edwards.

- In boats of all sizes, the walked-on surfaces should be non-slip. Teak is an ideal cockpit, side and transom coverboard material. High gloss varnishes, paints and gel coats that can cause slipping are a big no-no on fishing boats. If the cockpit deck or forward decks are painted, sand or some other non-slip material should be added to the paint surface.

  The tuna tower with full controls, which is a Rybovich refinement (as well as the balanced fighting chair and transom door adopted in other custom and production game boats) is of benefit not only in spotting fish and water color changes and other surface indication, but in safe navigating in reef waters. Visibility is greatly enhanced from a tower. Despite the bouncy conditions on Australia's Great Barrier Reef, captains such as Peter Wright and Dennis Wallace spend most of their fishing day in their lonely perch high above the water.

- The cockpit and transom coverboard should have more than enough rod holders, with two on the fighting chair (if one is installed), to allow all methods of fishing. Rod holders on side and bow rails are useful in fishing from anchor or on the drift and in walk-around fishing.

- Many boats are equipped with a row of rocket launchers at the rear of the flying bridge to hold extra rods and reels. These should be spaced to prevent contact and rubbing of the tackle.

- Outriggers are now generally built from aluminum or fiberglass.

The winter surf on Oahu, Hawaii's north shore, dramatically shows the need for care and seamanship as Marion B returns to Haleiwai. Photo: Jim Witten.

THE ELECTRONIC FISHERMAN

Modern offshore sportfishing boats are equipped with so much electronic fish finding and positioning equipment that perhaps the flying bridge should be renamed the flight deck. The miracles of miniaturization, of the silicon chip and practical waterproofing, mean that even small open boats can be equipped with low-voltage, low-drain navigating, positioning and fish-finding equipment to give results that only a few short years ago were available only on the biggest, most complete commercial fishing boats. Electronic equipment prices that once were a major investment are now most reasonable, allowing boats to be equipped with a complete wardrobe of electronics for less than the cost of just one a few years ago.

Modern equipment gives visual reading in color, in clearly read LCD digital, and on recording paper. Much of the equipment has built-in audio alarms to warn of shallow water, temperature changes and pre-set times. Some of the electronic aids to fishing are beneficial in safety at sea. Boats working offshore need and should be equipped at least with:

- Echo sounder—color, black and white, paper recording, flashing light, LCD digital, or combinations of these.

- Sea water thermometer.

- Two-way radios with bands and frequency to suit the operating area.

To these can be added for efficiency, time-saving and simply better and more productive fishing:

- Bottom-scanning sonar that gives a much wider coverage of the sea bed than with echo sounder or fathometer.

- Color sounder. Fishermen derive untold benefit once they are familiar with reading the unit of color sounders. Modern sounders will automatically adjust the depth scale and gain. Manufacturers are already preparing GPS (Global Positioning Systems) additions that will facilitate return to a previous fishing area.

- GPS satellite navigation equipment gives the position of the boat, the distance covered, the distance to be covered, the real boat speed, the effect of current plus the ability to return the boat to any desired position (even that of previous fishing), as well as continuous positioning.

- Electronic charts will benefit fishermen with chart plotters that will give clear data on screen at the control station instead of from paper charts. Loran is positive in positioning where Loran transmission is available. The same situation applies to Decca. Neither system is available worldwide. GPS in its present and future development will give benefits of Loran, Decca and SatNav (Satellite Navigation or Transit System) with added benefits worldwide of operation and simplicity of use.

- Color and daylight scanning radar have now replaced the early radar. Radar is available at long range, depending on model and height above the water. 16–32-nautical-mile range is sufficient for most boats in side scanning and parabola profile.

- Modern radar GPS navigators, Loran and depth sounders can be interphased to provide a tremendous range of practical navigation and fishing data. These capabilities can be enhanced by split screen and zoom features. Seawater temperature is given at surface and depth.

- Radios with multiple frequencies are necessary for offshore boats of every size. Ship-to-ship and ship-to-shore tranceivers with a range of frequencies and range from SSB to hand-held and telephone give fishermen every possible choice. An operating radio is a must for safety at sea. VHF is widely used.

- GPS with readout is already available in hand-held size that operates on AA alkaline dry batteries or a boat power supply to give:
  50 waypoints
  Latitude/longitude
  Range and bearing to destination
  Speed and course over ground
  Time to go and ETA
  Cross-track error
  Velocity and distance made good

Modern equipment and screens combine many functions previously provided by much other electronic equipment. Some equipment now gives course plotter, multiple course origin, destination and present position at the press of buttons. Other equipment gives depth, speed, elapsed distance, sea temperature, elapsed time, plus a three-dimensional view of the sea bed. Multiple-purpose split screens of dual frequency in a range of functions and zoom capability for closer definitions from a menu of eight possible functions are available in some equipment.

- Automatic pilots continue to be improved in positive simplicity as well as being more 'sea-kindly'.

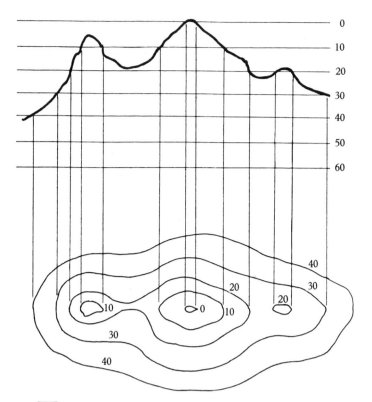

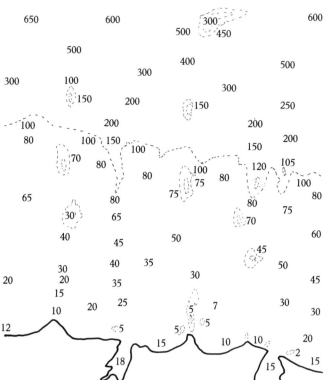

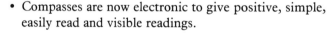

T o understand where fish should be, translate the soundings on a chart to vertical profile. Join up soundings of equal depth to establish contours.

T ypical reefs and canyons where the fish should be.

- Compasses are now electronic to give positive, simple, easily read and visible readings.

- Big boats now have options for on-board fax, weather fax and telex.

- Boat thermometers give not only surface temperature, but give temperature readings for below the surface for drift fishing to give the thermoclines and sub-surface temperatures where the fish should be. Modern equipment works at higher boat speeds.

It is obvious that to have any practical and safety benefit, this equipment must be in accurate operating condition. It is imperative that boat owners or operators know where and when to obtain regular and emergency service since it is particularly frustrating to need the benefits of a piece of equipment, only to be denied its use. Electronic equipment that is not in working condition is worthless junk that can create rather than assist problems. It is patently absurd and dangerous to overload the electrical capacity of a boat by installing electrical equipment without assessing whether the system and installation will cope. It is equally important to remember that, whether waterproofed or not, the electronic equipment should be protected from heat and water while still being in a practical position where it is is easily readable and operated.

The problem of exposure is naturally greater on small boats than big boats, so the wise buyer chooses equipment, keeping in mind where it is to be used. It is safer and more sensible to spend a few more dollars to obtain top-quality equipment, designed and manufactured for the small- or big-boat environment in which it will operate.

The best equipment, properly serviced, needs one other factor to perform as it should. That factor is the operator. It is imperative that the owner/operator understand what the equipment should and will provide. To do this he must know how it operates. Unfortunately, much equipment on boats is not used simply because of insufficient training or practice or not reading the manuals on service and operation.

One of the great benefits is that boat electronics can be interfaced with one another as long as there are interface outlets. Split-screen echo sounders can be interfaced with navigation electronics and will show the color picture of fish, bait and structures, water temperature and position with SatNav, GPS or Loran to give location for a future return to the fish's position. Radar can be combined with other electronics to show land, other boats, buoys and openings. Screens should be as big as practical so they can be easily and quickly scanned to gain the needed data. There is a growing trend to equipment that has several uses. It is particularly beneficial to have the boat track plotter visible on the same split screen showing depth. Other settings give depth, speed, temperature, bearing, way points, distance travelled and distance to travel to destination.

The development of electronics is already shown by one piece of equipment—eight-color screen, depth in feet/fathoms/metres, zoom, navigation mode, A scope, plotter, tracer, four full screens, eleven split screens, temperature drifting, temperature graph, boat speed, four alarms, and reducer and Navaid inputs.

EPIRBs, the emergency beacon that should always be carried offshore is now received by satellites as well as aircraft and emergency services.

MOTHER SHIPS AND LONG-RANGE BOATS

The concept of living aboard boats that are too big and unmaneuverable for gamefishing and then fishing from boats that are too small to travel long distances and to live aboard, has long been part of the sportfishing scene in salt water. Much of the pioneering exploratory fishing of the 1920s and 1930s was made possible by the combination of the big boat and small boat.

California angler Keith Spalding and his wife (who is part of fishing history, with the classic photograph of the petite woman and massive swordfish—the first by a woman angler, and a record Pacific sailfish) regularly visited Mexico with Keith Hancock, J. J. Hole and others in their yachts and fishing boats. Zane Grey and his magnificent *Fisherman* yachts and Geo. Thomas II and III showed the practicality and benefits of mother ships.

Michael and Helen Lerner used the mother ship concept in their successful broadbill expedition at Louisburg, Nova Scotia. Crews on the Nova Scotia schooner with control wheel high up on the mast spotted the broadbill that the Lerners successfully caught from dories skippered by Tommy Gifford. Zane Grey and his brother and sons explored not only the waters of Mexico and the Galapagos Islands but travelled across the Pacific to New Zealand and Tahiti. The *Fisherman* yachts carried the Greys' fishing boats. The mother ship concept was used in the Caribbean where Dinny Phipps and Jim Kimberly fished their Merritt sportfisherman while travelling and living on yachts.

Mother ships came to the fore again on the Great Barrier Reef where motor yachts, sailing yachts, cruise catamarans and specially designed catamarans became floating motels and fuel docks for specialized gamefishing boats. These mobile bases moved along the anchorages of the reef to enable game boats to fish off the reefs and openings where the marlin were active, instead of being limited to island or shore base while the marlin

Hooker *is carried on its mother ship's deck* (The Madam) *in a floating pull-on cradle. Photo: Jacquie Acheson.*

T*he long range Californian vessels that fish Baja and the offshore islands of Clarion, Roca Partida, Soccorro and San Benedicto, are also used for day trips. Photo: Peter Goadby.*

might be out of day range. These mother ships were serviced by fuel and supply barges with passenger transit by sea plane.

Humor has long been evident in the choice of mother ship names. The two-masted schooner used by Geo. Thomas III and his father Geo. Thomas II in their Mexican exploration trips in the 1920s was called *Radio* and the name of the 6-m (22-ft) whaleboat carried on board and used for fishing was *Static*.

English author and angler J. Mitchell-Henry, who carried on a running verbal and fishing battle with Zane Grey, used the mother ship as well as automatic chum benefit to travel 100–130 km (60–80 miles) into the North Sea on a herring trawler, then to dory fish for tuna raised by the herring in the net.

Three modern mother ship fishing boat operations have captured fishermen's imaginations and envy with their long-distance operations. Jim Jenks' 26-m (87-ft) *Ocean Pacific* and 10-m (31-ft) *Innovator* were both specially built as a combination. Jim Edminton's 30-m (95-ft) *El Zorro* was a Californian long-range boat and her game boat *El Zorro II* is a specially modified 10-m (32-ft) open gamefishing boat complete with tower. Jerry Dunaway, the owner of the most successful G & S 13-m (43-ft) game boat *Hooker* chose a 25-m (110-ft) oilfield work and crew boat as his mother ship. He continued and surpassed the Thomases' humor in combination names by naming his mother ship *The Madam*. These three combinations all carry the fishing boat on board, as does the 70-m (220-ft) *Kisula* with her 10-m (32-ft) *Hatteras*.

Other mother ships tow the fishing machines—Paul Caughlan's *Mustique/Kanahoee* combination on the Great Barrier Reef and western Pacific opt for the towing option. Extra surveillance day and night is provided by closed circuit television, also used for the engine room watch.

The success of these operations and their skilled skippers and crew is demonstrated by the capture and release records, including at least one grander black marlin on the GBR for each combination. *Hooker*, skippered by Skip Smith, has run up an incredible tally of men's and women's IGFA world records, the most by any boat in angling history.

A look into the crystal ball indicates that the next shift may be back to the Zane Grey *Fisherman* concept of carrying more than one fishing boat so that more water and more likely fishing areas are covered in any day's fishing. There is no doubt that the success of mother ships, proved in fishing history as well as today, will ensure that they continue to be part of the world scene.

Long-range live-aboard boats of 30–40 m (90–120 ft) have also made important and highly visible contributions to the sportfishing scene from southern California to Mexico's spectacular offshore islands and sometimes to the Galapagos. These boats are the live-aboard platforms for spectacular wahoo and yellowfin fishing in particular. Fish are caught in standing-up fishing; during the daytime, anglers must be practised in the 'Tuna Two Step' or 'Wahoo Waltz' to avoid line breaking, crossovers and tangles.

The night-time fishing in the lee of the islands produces the biggest yellowfin—superb fish in excess of 135 kg (300 lb). The boats with sufficient capacity for live baits and live chum take groups of anglers in comfort to action fishing. Fishing from long-range boats has influenced tackle developments in reels, rods, harnesses and rod belts in this hand-to-hand fishing. This is the fishery of the 'backup' rig, where the angler will clip a second line onto his first rod and reel as the first reel is spooled and almost empty. Ideally and usually, this rod and reel is recovered safely as the tuna is played out and circles the boat, so the fight can be resumed on the first outfit used on the hookup. Occasionally a second backup rig is needed, making the fish especially valuable, in every sense.

The trend to bigger boats is generally evident in modern offshore fishing. Gamefishing cruisers of 17 m (53 ft) were once regarded as around the biggest practical fighting chair gamefishing boats. Some of the recent boats, both stock and custom built, are in excess of 21 m (70 ft), a length once considered long enough and big enough to carry and service smaller boats from which to fish. The size and characteristics of boats change with the needs of modern fishing.

S M A L L   B O A T S

In the mini-battle wagons, boats under 7 m (21 ft), there are the same needs, but achievement is even more difficult. Despite the problem of size, small boats can provide incredible captures and fishing offshore as well as inshore. Many of these boats show the benefit of experience, ingenuity and thoughtful building with minimum unnecessary weight and maximum fishability, strength and performance.

The capacity to carry fuel, chum (berley), equipment, tackle and people is of course limited, but despite this they fish most successfully and enjoyably in competition with bigger boats. Techniques have been developed by the small boat fishermen that make them competitive with bigger boats and in some ways they have benefits rather than disadvantages in actual fishing.

Obvious benefits are that even on light tackle the small boat is a float that is a drag on the fish and can be towed by it. This minimizes the chance of shock line breakage. These boats are maneuverable and, with centre console and stand-up fishing, anglers can move around with the fish and have minimal chance of transom corner and hitting the hull problems.

Outboard and outdrive motors can be a problem when the fish is close and at gaff, or when trying to back up. Despite this they are very practical, and small boat skippers take advantage of their quick maneuvering capability to spin and run the fish in a manner forgotten or not used, although of great benefit in bigger boats.

To be equipped for hard fishing within the limitation of range, small boats should have:

- Radio, depth sounder, as well as the mandatory safety equipment of flares, EPIRB, life jackets, safety sheet anchor and long anchor line, plus as much fuel as can be safely carried for the day's planned fishing, and some in reserve.

- Drinking water.
- Spare propeller shear pin.
- Understanding of motor and regular service. The modern outboard is a dependable, sophisticated machine, but it needs regular service and checks. Many small boat skippers no longer carry small auxiliary motors. They prefer to maintain and be consciously dependent on the performance of their main power plant.
- Along with the necessary legal running and mooring light, small boats should have emergency lights and a powerful flashlight and battery lantern, if fishing happens to continue into the night.
- Gaffing and gaff rope attachment can cause problems and thought in small boat operations. Gaff ropes and gaff handles can be shorter than those used and needed on bigger boats. Cleats and other mooring line holders fixed in position have sufficient strength. However, care and thought must be given to the 'how' on handling big fish in small boats.
- Many small boats now have aluminum rocket launchers over the windshield to hold rigged rods. Others have rod storers at the rear of the helmsman's seat, fish or ice box.
- Small boats are practical with the centre console configuration that gives the benefit of full walk around fishing and a forward area for fly, spin or bait rod casting.
- Short towers are often beneficial and useful on boats about 7 m (21 ft) in length.
- Carrying of live bait and necessary circulated or aerated seawater can be a problem. Some boats have a live bait tank and fish box extending from the back of the hull or hulls, with the motor between these projections.

T*win and triple hulls are popular and successful. Practical and stable, these smaller size multi-hulls can be taken to fishing areas by trailer before heading to sea, as off Moreton Island, Australia. Photo: Jeff Webster.*

- Chum or berley cans on small boats should be attached in such a way that, if grabbed by a big shark, the shaking and rolling will not endanger the boat or crew, but could be torn free just in case.
- Plastic fish boxes are ideal for stowage of the necessary ropes, gaff heads, floats, tackle boxes, lures, baits and bait rigging equipment.
- Outriggers may be installed and are practical, but good fishing with angled rod holders is possible.
- Small boat fishing not only has benefits, particularly in light tackle fishing, but gives great enjoyment and, in common with big boats, yields many happy memories.

One of the benefits of small boats is that they can be towed, that is, moved by road from port to port instead of the chore and expense of travel by sea.

South African anglers, with their ski boats that are launched in the surf, have taken small boat fishing to an exciting and practical level.

Modern high-speed gamefishing boats are now as long as 24 m (80 ft) although 11 m to 16 m (36 ft to 53 ft) is still the most usual range of size.

There are also important sportfishing areas where small boats are a must. Fishing the flats and shallow channels in Florida forced the evolution of a whole new generation of specialized fishing machines for bonefish and tarpon. Powerful outboard motors drive these shallow draft stable boats at high speed through shallow water. Fishing needs and practicality have seen the integration within hulls of live bait tanks, obstruction-free casting areas, hulls that can be easily poled, poling–spotting platforms over the motor, plus the holders to safely carry tackle.

The next-size generation of boats are also well thought out with equipment dictated by practical fishing needs including centre consoles, forward mounted fishing chairs and a lightweight range of electronic equipment to pinpoint the sea bed. Fishing features are incorporated in fast, safe, sea-kindly hulls. The boats catch big fish

Florida is renowned for its well rigged and fully equipped smaller boat fleet as well as its powerful big gameboats. Photo: Peter Goadby.

Fishermen in small boats often equip them with top of the range reels and rods. Photo: Peter Goadby.

as well as the light tackle species for which they were conceived.

Multihulls—twin catamaran hulls and the range of tri hulls—come into their own in small boats under 7 m (25 ft). These hulls can be driven hard into rough water, handle rough seas and bars safely and are stable fishing platforms trolling, drifting and at anchor. Another big advantage of multihulls is that they give great fishing area and load-carrying space.

Small boats are maneuvered so the fish is fought with the boat going forward, so 'backing up' is not the necessary consideration that it is on big boats. Small boats in their own way are often more practical and successful than the bigger boats, but one thing is certain; boats are part of the fishing team, and they and their designers, constructors and operators contribute much to the enjoyment and success of fishermen, whatever fish they seek.

Anglers at Baja California, Mexico, catch billfish as well as roosterfish, yellowtail and dolphin fish in these traditional Mexican panga. Photo: Peter Goadby.

SMALL BOATS

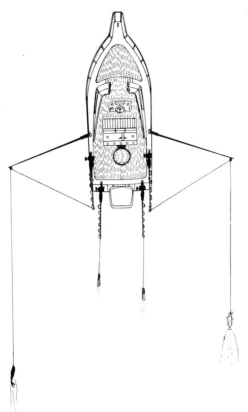

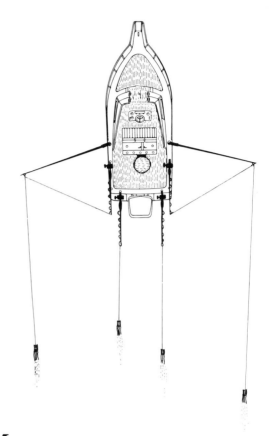

Lures and baits can be fished together from small boats. Small live bait tanks are practical in many small boats.

Modern small open boats are practical for trolling as well as jigging and casting.

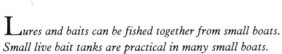

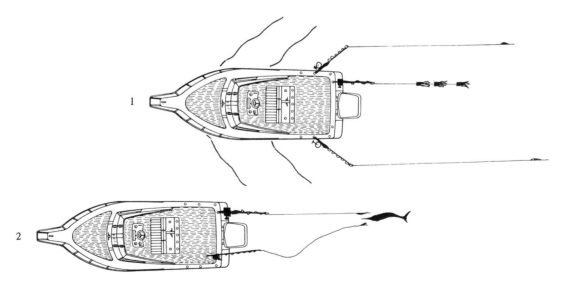

For saltwater flyfishing: 1. Billfish can be raised by trolling Panama strips or other hookless baits teased; 2. Boat must be stationary not under way while fly is cast.

EQUIPPING THE BOAT

OUTRIGGERS

In the beginning, when sportsmen first fished offshore, there were no outriggers, no drags on the reels, no harnesses, no chairs, and yet fishermen and big fish were locked in struggle with many of the early fishermen the winners. The sport began in 1898: when Dr Holder and Colonel Morehouse fought tuna and caught them, the Tuna Club at Avalon came into being and saltwater gamefishing was born.

About fifteen years after this beginning the silk kite took anglers' baits clear of the boat's wake and in front of the fish. These California kites were later joined on the boats by bamboo outriggers. These early outriggers pulled teasers, but did not pull the baits, which were kept rigged in the boats until the marlin or tuna attacked the teasers.

Harlan Major took the California kite to Florida and that great fisherman, thinker and innovator, Florida's Tommy Gifford, brought improved California outriggers back to Florida. Tommy had skippered William Bonnel's boat *Tarpon* in California, and *Tarpon* had California outriggers with teasers. Tommy not only devised strutting and braces so that his long outriggers on the small *Lady Grace* made boat and rig look like a grasshopper, but most importantly, thought of the clothespin line release that allowed the line to come free when the bait was struck. Tommy's innovation and concept on the line release led to outriggers being a symbol of a gamefishing boat as well as a practical fishing tool. The objective and thought behind the outrigger and the line release on strike were similar to those that George Farnsworth of Catalina devised with his kite. The bait was lifted, trolled clear of the wake and looked as natural as possible.

Just a few years after those first Gifford outriggers sprouted on the Florida east coast, they had migrated to Hawaii, possibly propagated by Harlan Major's visit to Kona, where he finally landed a blue marlin after much experimenting with bait. In Hawaii the bamboo poles of the outriggers were not as sophisticated as the developments on the east coast of the USA. In Hawaii, some outriggers were bound to the boat with cord and rope and they had a different objective. They were used to pull the feathers, the wooden tarporinos, and the wooden and bath towel rail lures with their flexible rubber tails that became the first trolling lures for big fish. In the modern age of plastic and color, those lures spawned the konahead and knucklehead in the many shapes and weights used right around the world.

IGFA founder Michael Lerner, guided by Bill Hatch, the dean of Florida's fishing captains, used those bamboo-type outriggers in New Zealand and Australia in 1939 to immediately and positively show their worth in trolling baits for billfish. Results spoke louder than words, so the use of outriggers became an integral part of the mix that makes for successful offshore fishing. Outriggers spread like wings on offshore boats right around the world. Today, nearly 100 years after their introduction, outriggers are not only accepted, but expected on gamefishing boats larger than five metres.

No one disputes that marlin and other pelagics can be and are caught on flat lines with bait and lures and that they are an integral part of many successful patterns, but the benefits of the outriggers are there for all to see, whether fishing bait, lures or both.

Outriggers ensure that baits or lures can be trolled in the chosen position relative to the wake, from right in the propeller wash to as wide as the outrigger spread and angles will allow. The riggers can be angled and set to give lift and position to skipping baits and depth and natural action to swimming baits. They are used to position and angle lures of various designs to where each works best and most effectively. With natural baits when generally only two or three are being trolled, they can carry the calculated drop back to assist the chance of a hook-up. With lures they give the pattern a wider spread of water to allow tangle-free trolling of four or five lures. They are practical and necessary.

Outriggers may be at right angles (90 degrees) to the hull of the boat, but most are at around 60 to 80 degrees. Outriggers that are angled back so the tips are at less than 60-degrees angle to the hull defeat one of the objectives, which is to move bait or lure out from the hull wash and propeller wash.

Outrigger angle to hull varies with different bases and different positions on deck or cabin side. The angle of the outrigger when actually fishing is changed by the pull of baits or lures and pulling the halyards tight.

Some of the early influential fishing writers and administrators of saltwater gamefishing decried their use and worried that outriggers gave gamefishermen unfair advantage over the fish. Some felt that outriggers, in giving an automatic dropback when combined with skillfully rigged baits, could give 100 per cent hook-ups, that the instinctive manual dropback and teasing by anglers (who had learned from experience) would be unnecessary, and that there could be an increase in deliberately deep-hooked fish.

Unlike marlin and tuna trolling boats in tropical waters, Canadian bluefin boats use light bamboos as outriggers, both drifting or trolling. However, most trolling on these boats is done directly from the rod tips. Photo: Peter Goadby.

Experience over the next fifty years has shown that neither of these concerns is valid. It is unfortunately true that on some potentially superb boats gamefishing outriggers have merely become extra flagpoles or status symbols on which to fly flags and pennants. These vary from the capture flags or tag-and-release pennants indicating a successful day, to the skunk or dead rat pennant that indicates what may diplomatically be called an unsuccessful day. For those boat owners who do fish but do not respond to the challenge of trolling for pelagic fish, the outriggers may be used only to place a drifting bait. Their use is not understood, and for those boats that rarely go to sea, their use may be simply for a pennant that says, 'Open bar—come and have one'.

In lure fishing, with or without outriggers, the consideration of 100 per cent hook-ups is not a problem, as many strikes are hit-and-miss on strike and very few lure-hooked fish are deep-hooked. This is a very sporting way to fish. The pioneering outrigger type in most fishing areas, including the exploratory days at Cairns, New Zealand, Hawaii and many other ports, has been the humble bamboo pole.

They are most successful if allowed to dry to minimize weight and maximize springiness. Bamboo poles, whether bound and wrapped between the nodules, painted or unpainted, are still ideal short-term outriggers, particularly on boats that are not completely equipped.

In this day and age of lightweight metals and plastics, the natural bamboo, spruce and oregon pole outriggers have been generally replaced by aluminum and fiberglass poles. The simple outrigger bases that allowed only pivoting in and out, and the later sail track that allowed a great multiplicity of positions and angles, have been replaced by brass and stainless outrigger bases that are easy to use and positive. In positioning they are combined with either guyed or strutted aluminum or uncluttered fiberglass poles. Both these outrigger types are available in two or more sections, and different weights and stiffness, to give a range of choices to suit boats of all lengths and purposes. Fiberglass outriggers allow positive use of the maximum length of the outrigger, whereas the unstrutted top section of the guyed and strutted aluminum outriggers may be bent after the load of the pull of a big bait or hard strike. For this reason on this type, many outrigger halyards are taken only to the furthest point of the guying and strutting.

Rough water, big baits and the hit of a striking fish put a heavy load on the working outrigger, so they must be rugged and practical in design, construction and installation. Outriggers can be swung from the deck, from the side of the wheelhouse, the top of the wheelhouse or from the side of the flying bridge. The areas to which they are attached must be strong and strengthened to take the load and shock without structural damage to the boat. A light cord from tip of outrigger to bow rail is a practical way to minimize whip and load.

Experience, skill and common sense are factors that help in getting the best results from the outrigger. There is an almost diametrically opposed use of outriggers employed mainly with lures. With baits, the objective and usual plan is to have one bait skip and splash with more of the same bait species rigged to swim and wriggle below the surface as realistically as possible. In natural bait fishing the outrigger clips are set just hard enough to hold the weight and pull of the bait, but light enough for the line to drop free once the bait is taken. The reel drag in natural bait fishing is set with just enough brake to prevent an overrun when the fish strikes the bait. If the angler prefers to control the dropback, the reel drag is set hard (around one-quarter to one-third the line class breaking strain) and the line dropback is trailed on the water with the plan that the length of dropback is ideally enough to allow the fish to turn and swallow the bait. With the long dropback and the drag set hard, skill, practice and a cool head are still required by the angler in backing off the drag while line is running out from a hooked fish, and transferring the rod and reel without overrun to chair gimbal or rod bucket. This can be a moment of truth, as an overrun can happen in a flash if the drag is eased too much and the rod and reel are difficult to take from chair holder or coverboard if the drag is left too hard.

Outriggers are rigged with outrigger clip or rubber band set to maximize hook setting and to minimize dropback in lure fishing. The plan is for the fish to pull against the reel brake, as well as the weight of line and spring of the rod, as quickly as possible. The hope is for an immediate hook setting following the strike. The use of a tag line has the effect of minimizing dropback, of changing the angle at which the lures are trolled, so that they are wider in the wake. The tag lines are rigged to assist in the controlled breaking of the rubber bands that may hold the line and provide the initial shock and impact to set the hook. Tag lines should be no longer than to reach from outrigger halyard pulley to the corner of the side and transom. If they are too long they may cause tangling of the tag line and fishing line.

In both lure and bait fishing some crews rig their outriggers with halyards of heavy mono of 272 kg to 364 kg (600 to 800 lb) test. Others use braided cord, which could give the advantage of less stretch under load on the strike than monofilament. Monofilament has longer life as it wears less in use. Heavy glass or metal rings are bound to the outrigger pole to hold the halyard or halyards close in alongside the pole to minimize halyard sag. Cleats or other devices are now rarely used to tie off the halyard. The modern practice is for the halyard to be pulled down tight to the coverboard so the halyard may be freely positioned along the outrigger and is held in place by the springiness of the outrigger pole or by

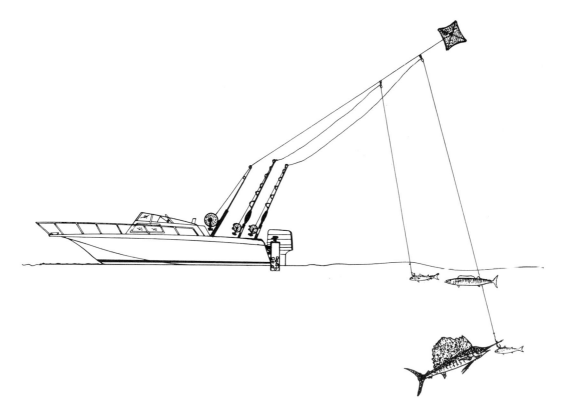

Kite fishing: two live baits can be fished from one kite. A lightweight outrigger clip, clothes peg and paper clip, or ring allow positioning of baits and quick release.

the use of a heavy shock rubber to keep the halyard taut. A twist at the bottom of the halyard is also useful to minimize slip. Two halyards are sometimes used; the main halyard runs the full length of the pole and another, shorter halyard runs about halfway up the pole. The second halyard gives the option of pulling a bait or lure that otherwise would be trolled from the rod tip or from some type of flat line, clip release or rubber band holder. The tag line or stinger should be long enough just to clear or reach the corner of the transom when it is hanging free. The tag line is often the same material as the outrigger halyard and many tag lines are clipped onto the halyard in the usual position of the outrigger release if lures and tag lines are to be fished. The rubber bands are used to hold the trolling line. Many crews around the world follow the common Hawaiian use of braided 59-kg (130-lb) class line at the free end of the tag line, while others use a strong coast lock or other small-diameter wire snap that minimizes the area on which the rubber band is pulling to assist the breaking of the band on strike.

There is a growing world trend to use metal or other heavy rings, or short tubes about 5 cm (2 inch) long as an automatic tag line return. Light cork balls about the size of table tennis balls are sometimes used on the end of the tag line to ensure quick recovery and to minimize tangling. The tag line return allows the tag line to pull from the halyard top when the boat is under way and the lure pulling. Not all lure-trolling fishermen use tag lines. Some experienced captains and crews prefer to use the usual roller-type outrigger clips, such as Aftco or Rupp, attached straight to the halyard, as for natural bait trolling. This outrigger release use is in line with the methods of successful lure fishermen, who believe that the fish hooks itself of its own impact and velocity as it takes the lure and closes the powerful lower jaw. In their opinion the very hard drags and gunning the boat to set the hook are unnecessary, and in fact the gunning of the boat may have only the benefit of running the hooked fish clear of the other lines and lures.

Fiberglass outriggers generally have more flexibility, whether built specifically as outriggers or from vaulting poles or windsurfer masts. Many boats have a short shotgun outrigger in the centre line of the boat from the flying bridge to run a shotgun lure way back in the centre of the trolling pattern. A support from the outrigger tip forward onto the bow rail minimizes whip and too much bend on the strike. Tangles not only cause frayed tempers but frayed lines and leaders. For this reason it is important to always run the outside lines into position first then the inner lines. When bringing lines back inboard, the reverse applies.

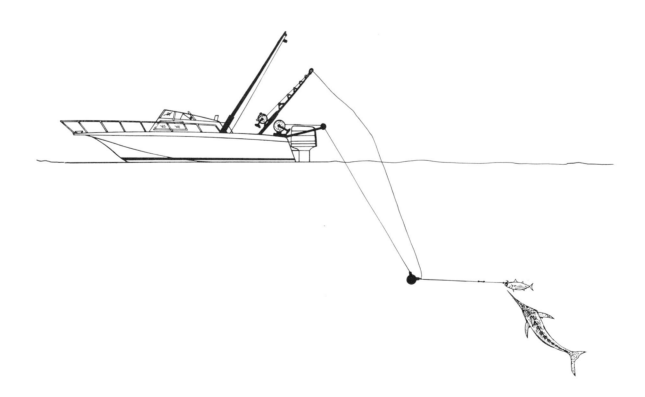

Deep trollers are productive with live bait and lures particularly where they can be worked around structures and bait schools.

POINTS TO REMEMBER FOR SUCCESS WITH OUTRIGGERS

- Troll one bait skipping on the surface and the other bait swimming deeper. Other baits can be trolled on flat lines direct from rod tip to give a different action and provide the fish with a choice.

- Troll baits outside and alongside the boat's wake and propeller turbulence.

- Troll baits or lures so that they are well apart and don't tangle. It is easy with outriggers to troll four or up to six rods if common sense is used in positioning baits and lures. The 'V' or 'W' pattern has been described earlier.

- Provide some or all of the dropback necessary in fishing for marlin and sailfish and yet still allow the hook-up of wahoo and other fast strikers.

- Allow the trolling of big baits without a constant holding strain on the rod and the angler.

- Allow the trolling of baits with only a light brake on the reel, just enough to prevent overrun.

- Keep the leader out of the water so that the bait can troll naturally, without the creation of bubbles that may frighten a shy fish.

- Keep a deep bait clear of the boat and other baits when fishing from anchor or on the drift.

- Improve the action of some lures, particularly of some of the big konaheads and vinyl squid replicas.

- When putting lures out put outside lines out first. When bringing lures inboard retrieve the center lines first to avoid tangles.

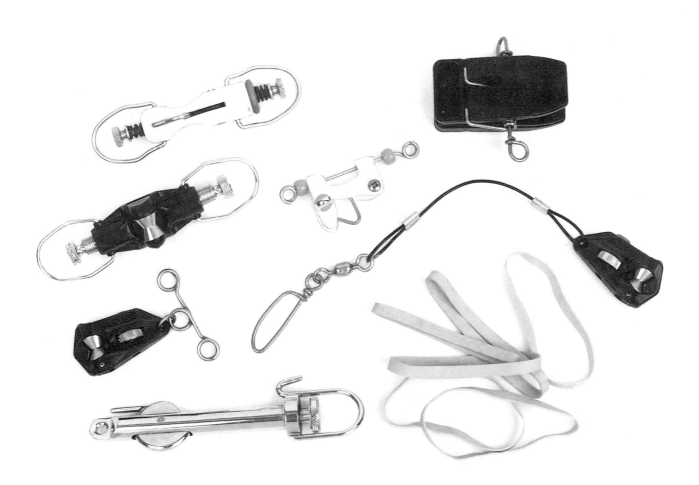

Outrigger clips and line releases range from the simple rubber band to sophisticated light and heavy tackle models. Photo: David Rogers.

*T*his fighting chair swings over the live bait tank to maximize available cockpit space. Photo: Peter Goadby.

*T*he rocket launcher developed by great angler Jo-Jo Del Guercio and the Staros Brothers brings light tackle to the heavy tackle chair fitting. Photo: Peter Goadby.

or coverboard. This configuration does not allow the leg drive and power advantage from curved butts and seat harnesses.

Thousand-pound black marlin and giant tuna and massive sharks have all been caught with straight butt rods, shoulder and kidney harnesses and fishing rather than the fighting chairs that are now almost standard wherever big fish are sought. Human ingenuity and need for efficient performance to combat the power and activity of giant fish have triggered the development of modern fighting tackle.

This chair development is indirectly a tribute not only to the fish but to the pioneering fishermen who caught the fish with simple tackle and equipment.

SKIPPER AND CREW

Gamefishing is true team sport. Consistent success comes to the angler, skipper and crew who understand this and always work as a team. Successful teams have understanding, communication and prior planning to eliminate as many as possible of the 'unexpected' occurrences that cause loss of fish or damage. Angler, skipper, crew, boat and tackle are the ingredients in the mix for success. These same factors apply to both team-skippered and crewed private boats and to professional skippers and crews.

Experience of professionals is one of the many reasons why anglers use charter boats, or employ skippers and crews on their own boats. All members of the fishing team must perform adequately for a consistent and safe result. Weaknesses, lack of experience and poor communication can cause not only loss of the fish but injury or accident to crew or angler, particularly when working with jumping billfish and big sharks.

Experience and practice in working together and understanding of what each is doing, or of what each is trying to do, shows not only in captures and safe fishing, but in enjoyment and team spirit. Communication, understanding and cool heads are the keys to success and pleasure for all involved. There is no need for upsetting, nerve-grating, raised voices and shouting during the fight. This should be saved only for a real emergency. Unnecessarily raised voices are annoying and put pressure on those who are already under pressure of performance.

It is important for all involved, even those who have great experience and who have fished together, to talk, to increase understanding of what each is trying to do, of what is expected of each other as soon as possible. Each facet of the day's fishing procedure in hooking and fighting fish must be understood. It is too late to establish complete rapport and understanding when the fish is right there. Communication must be established before the pressure builds and needs arise. The differences in methods, technique and experience make it imperative to quickly establish the plan, rapport, confidence and communication.

Without understanding, fish and opportunity are wasted. Fish are lost before being hooked on trolled baits and lures, unless both the skipper and angler know what each is trying to do.

A typical example of problems right in the beginning of hoped-for action is when either the skipper or the angler is trying for dropback before trying to hook-up, and the other is expecting a try for an instant gunning of the boat to assist hook-up.

THE CAPTAIN, SKIPPER OR GUIDE

This is the responsible and decision-making member of the team; decisions affecting the boat and safety are the captain's responsibility. The crew and experienced anglers are often involved before the final decisions are carried out. They make suggestions, request assistance with problems, but often such fast action is required that there is no time or opportunity for other than skipper advice as to what he is doing, what he wants—the responsibility is the captain's.

On many boats with experienced crews, one of the crew will be doing the talking to both angler and skipper. On many private boats the angler/owner skippers such as Ted Naftzger of California, the world's top broadbill angler with around fifty daylight fishing captures, and Australia's late Garrick Agnew with his many 452-kg (1000-lb) black marlin weighings, skipper their own boats to find the fish and to get the strike. Someone else then takes over the controls for the hook-up, the fight and boating of the fish. Naturally anglers ask their skippers and crews what they think, what they want, what they need during the fight, and the skipper will try to meet the request. This is part of communication. In the same way the skipper will make suggestions and tell the crew and angler what he is going to do, to back up, to run the fish, to circle, so those in the cockpit are balanced and ready. The skipper has the advantage of maximum visibility from his flying bridge and can generally see what is happening quicker than anyone else on the boat. The skipper will instinctively try to correct a problem or dangerous situation before it occurs.

An active marlin jumping at boatside or a shark rolling or diving under the boat does not allow time for a debate or committee meeting to reach consensus on what is to be done. At this time the skipper is the one who can take action; he must make his decisions instantaneously, and yet advise those in the cockpit of what he and the boat are doing.

It is important not only to understand what each is trying to achieve, but how best each can assist the other. Those involved must keep in their mind the power and potential for damage with each big fish, particularly when the leader is at or in hand. It is imperative as well as sensible for the captain always to maneuver the boat to give maximum assistance to those in the cockpit. Many

*C*aptain Bart Miller maneuvers Black Bart to aid his crew and angler. Photo: Peter Goadby.

steel wool in that shark's frenzy to escape. The mako did not attack me, although I landed almost on top of it. I was able to scramble back aboard with the memory of a magnificent grey-blue shape, angry black eyes and long, white, powerful teeth.

There are differing problems from different line and leader materials and the fish themselves. There is no doubt of the dangers created by big active fish at the boat. Crews must understand and practice how they will take and hold the wire, do their wraps, pull leader, how and when they will release if necessary. From the angler's viewpoint there is nothing more disappointing and annoying than to realize that at crisis time the crew can't safely carry out their function of bringing the fish into range of gaff or tag pole. Good skippers and crews know what the angler is trying to achieve with the rod and reel, without the need to continually yell instructions. They realize the benefit of quiet suggestions. Similarly, good anglers know and understand what skipper and crew are trying to do, and reciprocate by keeping cool.

The skipper is fish finder, navigator, electronic whiz, boat handler, engineer, meteorologist, bait watcher, decision maker and diplomat. The crew are important in always working with their skipper and assisting his responsibilities and working to success each day. Crew responsibility starts with having gear ready, the drags, lines and knots checked, in bait catching, in bait and lure rigging, hook sharpening, leader taking, gaffing, chair directing, drink carrying, diplomacy and communications, while being happy in the job. An ability to entertain and reminisce is also a real bonus.

Part of the pleasure of big gamefishing is to watch or be part of top crew work, when the skipper uses the boat like a quarterhorse, backing-up, running the fish and making it easy for the angler, while the crew are ready and competent at all stages, particularly in their moment of truth on leader, gaff or tag pole, to complete the fight. Crews must be familiar with the tackle being used. The five types of leader material used have their characteristics and problems in being taken, wrapped and put back overboard as it is recovered. Leader material is usually:

- Single-strand (piano-type) wire, or carbon or stainless steel
- Two twisted single-strand stainless wire to join a single carbon steel wire
- Multi-strand cable of stainless or galvanized wires
- Plastic-covered cable
- Monofilament plastic material such as nylon.

Chain of various types is also used in short lengths on some heavy and light tackle leaders down at the hook end.

The taking of the leader by an experienced leader man looks easy, but there are many potential problems to be avoided. The wrapping of the leader around the gloved hands is a major part, the key to success, in leader handling. Whoever is to take and pull leader should practice making the wraps, pulling leader and releasing, until completely familiar with procedures.

The leader man should be ready to take the leader immediately it is within range. Once the leader is taken,

The position of this gaff in the yellowfin tuna ensures minimum damage to the flesh as well as a firm hold. Photo: Gil Keech.

the angler must ease the reel drag, put on the click or ratchet, wind the swivel to the rod tip, then lower the rod tip. The angler must be ready to move the rod clear of the wire man and be ready with left hand to prevent an overrun or backlash if the leader man has to release the leader.

The reason for winding the swivel right to rod tip, and the rod tip being lowered, is to minimize any possibility of the leader tangling around neck, limbs or clothing of those in the cockpit, particularly the leader man as he moves and uses the cockpit space.

Some crew use the snap swivel to give a grip. Use of the swivel this way, however, gives the possibility that glove pressure may undo the snap. If the snap is unclipped, and it does happen, the leader man is faced with hanging on and not releasing the leader, and often this is impossible. If it is recovered with snap undone, the snap can be closed or the wire held strongly.

Of course it is possible for another person to do up the clip if time and leader distance allow. Great care must be taken to avoid a rule breach and disqualification or line break by touching line rather than leader. It is allowable under the IGFA fishing rules for more than one person to pull leader, but the line must not be touched by anyone but the angler. If more than one person is pulling leader, each must be aware of what the other, or the others, is doing, to work together. They must be extremely safety-conscious and not let go without the knowledge and awareness of the others involved. The taking and pulling of leader is a time of ultimate team effort and responsibility.

The leader man when taking the leader should come up from under the leader with his hand, positively, with the wire lying between his thumb and forefinger. (Some leader men crew come down from above with right hand and from under with left hand.) They turn their hand so the leader is wrapped around the palm of the hand. A single wrap will still slip under pressure, but even one wrap is better and more definite than any other way of pulling leader. A second wrap, the double wrap, is necessary to prevent slip. The wraps are repeated on each hand and a fish can be played by the leader man, keeping hands high and turning the body to assist as a shock absorber while recovering leader. The leader man moves about the cockpit—he is not immovable and flat-footed. It is his stage and he performs with the leader and moves to allow the gaff or tag man into position for his shot and completion of the catch.

There are times when the leader must be released: to prevent break of leader, or prevent a man being pulled overboard. If a fish jumps away from the boat, or dives down like a rocket for the deep, skill, determination and cool confidence are necessary ingredients in top leader men. They know to maintain weight and pressure on the leader even when the gaff is in place. This continuing pull on the hook helps to keep the fish under control at boatside.

*P*atrick Bowen, wire man on Captain Bristow's Avalon, experienced first hand the dangers of wiring when a 181 kg (400 lb) black marlin took off as he wrapped the wire to bring it close for tagging. The second photograph shows Patrick on his way overboard unless the wire frees. The third shows Patrick in the water holding with his left hand the marlin still jumping. He returned to the boat and was assisted back on by the other crew Jay Reiber. Angler Alan Cordan brought the wire back in reach as Patrick again wired, Jay tagged and the marlin was released. Patrick became another member of the informal 'Underwater Wireman's Club' with several other eligible wiremen, including the author. Photos: Captain Bill Harrison.

To tag or gaff? The crew hold a 200 kg (450 lb) blue marlin caught by Ralph Christiansen Jnr on Pescador at St Thomas, Virgin Islands. Photo: Captain Bill Harrison.

An Australian black marlin swims back to its cruising depth. Photo: Greg Edwards.

This is particularly necessary when taking choked or stunned fish or quick captures. Release or easing of hook pressure can result in an explosion of power that can pull off balance those holding the fish and create danger with a fresh green fish. A capture is usually completed with a second gaff or tail rope.

Many top gaff and tag men prefer to place the gaff or tag in the fish before its back breaks the surface of the water. It is then less panicky than when the back is above the water.

The same basic procedure is followed in tag and release. Whenever possible the fish is brought right to boatside for safe removal of the hooks before release. If the fish is increasingly active and could be damaged by further pulling the leader, it should be cut to allow the fish to swim free, even though the hooks are still in place. The fish, if it appears to be stressed or exhausted, or even dead, can be revived and resuscitated by being swum through the water for re-oxygenation until the glowing colors return. A length of heavy fishing line or light cord can be wrapped around the bill of a marlin or sailfish to allow safe towing and easy release of the fish when its color and activity show recovery. Scientific tracking has shown that fish recover from the trauma of a fight very quickly.

The leader is sometimes brought in by easy pulling without the need for wraps. Sometimes boat and fish are already leading together for gaff or tagging. Sometimes there is a protracted tough battle; the minutes tick by in the hand-to-hand fight between leader man and super fish in a heart-stopping drama. The ability to battle a big jumping fish or a determined deep-swimming dogging fish by a skilled leader man is a critical as well as dramatic segment of the fight. Naturally all involved hope the leader can and will be held the first time it comes into reach. Sometimes this is impossible and the fight returns to the angler. It is for this reason that a second man must be ready for gaffing or tagging. Skipper and crew are ready to resume the fight, particularly with big fish. On smaller fish, either skipper or angler can safely perform the gaffing or tagging function at the moment of truth.

It is hard to be sure which performance grabs the watchers' or anglers' imagination more—the skipper on his quarterhorse in command on the flying bridge at one with the boat and the fish, or the leader man in the cockpit face to face with his opponent.

All leader materials can be wrapped and pulled in the same way. Single-strand wire is easier than any of the other materials to free from gloves. The softer, more flexible materials tend to lie into the gloves and be more difficult to discard and free. For this reason extra care must be taken with the wraps to prevent overlap and ensure that it is possible to get rid of the leader. Strong men can break most leader used, but just hanging on is not necessarily the best way of ensuring success. Top leader men resist the opportunity to bullock and may consciously choose to apply only the same weight or pressure as that previously exerted on the line by the angler. At other times they work to their maximum, their weight and strength.

Experienced skippers help the leader man by maneuvering the boat during this close-quarters encounter. Fishing movies and videos sometimes show footage of the leader man standing apparently casually with one hand on the leader or in a wrap as the skipper backs the boat after a jumping fish—ready instantly for the opportunity to regain leader when the fish stops jumping and running.

In fights at close quarters, the skipper has the responsibility, the controls and power to assist the crew and maintain safety. It is a time for quick thought, instant reflexes, and responsive boats, as well as understanding. Communication is always of top priority with fish and boat close together.

The skipper's visibility is much better from the bridge than that of the crew at deck level. At this stage many crew are working without their polarizing sunglasses to minimize loss of vision from spray from flaying tails or wave tops. The removal of the glasses also eliminates another possible hazard—entangling in glasses or holding cord although some wear them protectively.

Crew should wear non-slip deck shoes while taking leader and gaffing; bare feet add to the possibility of slip. On boats with twin motors some skippers will have the motor near the fish idling in neutral and will maneuver with the other.

Some boats have covered foam padding around the cockpit edge, but my preference is for shaped teak that allows a firm surface for your body to work into. It is not slippery when wet, and does not cut with gaff points or other sharp implements.

Some leader men crouch to lock themselves against the coverboard, others stand upright balanced against it. They pull the wire high and swivel their shoulders and arms as shock absorbers against the active fish, ready to pull and wrap leader at every opportunity.

The leader should be held clear of the coverboard, gunwales and hull. The extra angle and pull over a hard surface could cause leader damage or a jam on high spots such as rod holders or other deck fittings.

Additional problems can be created by transom doors that are cut to open through the coverboard as well as the transom. These types of door give benefit when boarding and disembarking, when loading and unloading, but they can be a problem with big fish on the leader. If the leader slips or is pulled into the door opening, a leader can break or pull the wire man's hand down and off balance to jam against the immovable wood, fiberglass or aluminum of the transom. The trend for building transom doors that open in the transom coverboard as well as through the transom is increasing as longer and bigger boats are built. Skippers and crews are aware of this potential problem and try to maneuver

the boat and position the leader man away from the problem area as much as possible, as they have to with the other problem projections created by trim tabs, outdrives, outboard motors, chum pots and even underwater propellers and rudders.

Other factors necessitate that the leader be pulled and held as high and clear as possible. Hands and leader should be kept clear and above the level of the cockpit coverboard to minimize problems.

All on board should know early who is to gaff and wire or tag. This prior decision ensures minimal confusion at the critical end of the fight. Sometimes the skipper will gaff, sometimes the angler, if there is no second deckhand. Sometimes with a team or more than one angler, one of these will be considered of sufficient skill to gaff or tag.

Even if there is second crew, skippers are ready to leave their control station to assist and place a second gaff, meat hook or tail rope. Naturally many skippers and crew prefer the angler and non-crew to keep clear of cockpit involvement at this stage. Once again, this decision must be made early and clearly understood well before crisis time. This decision is predicated by safety and consideration, the experience and ability of the angler and the fishing team members or guests, and the

*S*harks are often gaffed in the mouth so the addition of wire leader linking gaff hook to gaff rope is obviously beneficial. *Photo: Tim Simpson.*

acceptance of their competence by skipper and crew. Well-meaning but inexperienced or unskillful contributions can create rather than assist potentially dangerous situations and loss of fish.

The necessary clearing of the cockpit after the strike and hook-up can be assisted by others on board if this is accepted by skipper and crew. There is much to be done. The angler must get to the chair, the fish must be struck, set, harness clips attached to reel lugs either before or after the strike, and the fish fought. The other outfits must be quickly brought in, clear of the cockpit, and safety lines and leaders removed and placed so the leader cannot be washed back through the scuppers. Gaffs and tag pole and ropes must be readied, gaff points sharpened if necessary, gaff ropes cleated off securely and all potential obstructions removed from the cockpit working area. Crew should wear and others know where additional cutting pliers are placed for emergency use.

Camera persons must know and understand that they must keep clear of those working, as they can inhibit vision as well as create other possibly dangerous close-quarter encounters for themselves and others.

The skipper is responsible for:

- Safety of the boat and all on board.

- Maneuvering the boat for maximum benefit to angler and crew at all times during the fight and at boatside.

- Ensuring that the objective of gaffing and boating or tagging and releasing the fish in good condition is achieved.

The crew is responsible for:

- Clearing the cockpit of rods and reels not involved in the fight, once the angler is in the chair.

- Assisting the angler into the harness ready for striking the fish or after striking the fish.

- Ensuring gaffs and ropes are ready and securely attached; blunt gaffs should be sharpened.

- Outrigger halyards should be unclipped clear of the coverboard and lifted to bridge level in case of boatside jumps from the fish.

- Gloves readied and non-slip deck shoes worn.

- Pliers and cutters should be checked and ready.

- Ensuring that tag and tag pole are ready.

- If a meat hook is to be used, this should be readied with a safety rope.

- Take, wrap and pull leader when in reach and hold until fish is safely gaffed and tail roped, or tagged and leader cut.

- Decide where and when to cut leader on release.

- Have tackle and baits or lures ready to quickly resume fishing.

- Clear cockpit of gaffs and ropes.

POINTS TO REMEMBER FOR ANGLER AND CREW

- Talk quietly on the boat, avoid shouts or yells, particularly when fish are seen or are believed to be in the vicinity.

- Arms should not be moved around in violent gestures that can easily be seen by a shy fish. Pointing emphatically at a fish can cause it to turn away.

- The boat should be kept going ahead until the hook is properly set, then the forward way is eased off and the motors left in neutral, or the boat can be backed up to recover line. It is important for the angler to concentrate on setting the hook before he settles down to recover line. The two actions should be separate. After shortening up on line in the water, the boat should be backed up or maneuvered to one side of the fish to help the angler try to break any fighting pattern dictated by the fish.

- It is often safe to back up to initially recover line until the position of the fish can be judged. The big belly of line created by a long run and possible course of the boat may cause the hook to tear out or break off.

- If a billfish strikes slowly and shyly, the angler should allow the fish more time and line than he may believe could possibly be needed for it to swallow the bait.

- Anglers should, if possible, have previously checked reel drags against scales and thus know where to set the brake for a striking drag and then for the desired fighting strain. The pull against the scales must be made with the line running through all guides to give a true indication of the brake against the fish or the scale.

- One of the many benefits of lever quadrant reels is that the brake can be moved and reset to the desired position. The brake can be reapplied to any previous pressure. On reels with star wheels, it is difficult to take advantage of pre-setting against scales. In all cases the angler should get the feel of the rod and desired brake to the greatest extent possible before a fish strikes.

- The striking drag should be about one-quarter to one-third the breaking strain of the line, and this may have to be eased back as the fish runs fast or jumps to the wide blue yonder. The maximum drag exerted is usually about half the breaking strain of the line until the double is on the reel, then the drag can be increased or thumb pressure can be used to take advantage of the doubled line. One-quarter strike is often chosen on light tackle and one-third on heavy tackle.

Darrell Jones brings a new dimension and feeling of being there with his photographs of fish at the boat. Photo: Darrell Jones.

FIGHTING THE FISH

Saltwater gamefishing is a team sport in which success comes from concentration, co-operation, communication and experience. Much of angler enjoyment and success comes with understanding of what the other members of the team, the equipment, and the fish are doing. In most fights between angler and big fish, there are times when heat and hurt force the angler to query if it is all worth it. At times, the power and endurance of gamefish and sharks show why they are great predators. There are times when, despite the comfort of easing up, the angler must remember that the next fish may be just as tough, just as dogged, so similar effort and hurt will be expended and endured to fight the next fish to a similar stage.

Nature itself, the sun and sea, combine to aid the fish and inconvenience the fisherman. On boats the glossy white of paint or gelcoat and scrubbed wood, plus the reflections from stainless steel, chrome and polished aluminum combine to multiply the glitter already present on the sea surface. On shore, equally there is no relief. The sun is there to add surface glare, heat and pressure on the angler who must fish in open space.

There are two particularly critical times when fish can be lost, with or without angler error. These periods are on the hook-up and first run, then when the fish is close to capture. Of course fish may be lost, hooks thrown, lines broken or the fisherman may endure any of the other factors that cause loss, when whatever can go wrong does go wrong between the critical times.

The problem on the first run, with and without jumps, is when the maximum dynamic power of the fish not only causes an adrenalin lift to the fisherman, but is a potential time for line break or overrun birds' nests. Generally on this run, the angler must remember that as the length of line reduces on the reel spool, the diameter of spooled line is smaller, so the reel brake on the line automatically increases. The high fish loss close to capture is caused by increase in the size of the hole made by the hook, the change in angle of pull on the hook, the chance of line break as line with minimum stretch leads straight from rod to fish.

US angler and author Harlan Major demonstrated in the classic *Salt Water Fishing Tackle* that a reel spool of 15 cm (6 in) set up with reel brake of 14 kg (30 lb) will increase to 21 kg (45 lb) when the line spool diameter has reduced to 10 cm (4 in), and 42 kg (90 lb) when the diameter has reduced to 5 cm (2 in). He also showed a diagram of the result of pulling the then linen line through water. He found that 300 yards (or metres) of 10-kg (20-lb) test would break at 15 knots, even without

The angler stands up to fight a black marlin on light tackle on Hooker. *Photo: Jacquie Acheson.*

THE FISHING BOAT

2 1 6

reel brake or fish, and that 400 yards of 15-kg (30-lb) line would break at 12 knots.

This automatic brake increase on the line makes a clear impossibility of the often-made statement that, 'I had the brake set on full drag on strike and the fish peeled off all the line, spooled me'. All this proves is that the brake was not set high to start with as, rather than being spooled, the line must have broken with less than one-third of the line from the spool.

Modern strike drags are generally set at one-quarter on light tackle to one-third on heavy tackle of the line class used on balanced tackle. Listed below are four brake recommendations that have proved successful over the years and through the tackle changes. Experienced fishermen often work well above the fighting brake outlined here when the fish and fight allow.

It is a revelation to work with aggressive anglers such as Ted Naftzger, a master on all line classes, as he uses his brake, working harness unclipped, while recovering line on 24 kg and upwards, using the harness when the fish is fighting deep. Ted's experience goes back to days with Tommy Gifford and experience of all the great ocean gamefish. He often fishes 24 kg (50 lb) and 15 kg (30 lb) and lighter on marlin, even giant blacks, while his expertise on 60 kg (130 lb) twice resulted in wins for his US team in the International Tuna Cup matches. IGFA vice-president Jack Anderson, on the other hand, when fishing on 60 kg (130 lb) for giant black marlin sets the strike brake at 25 kg (55 lb) and keeps the brake in this position, fully aware of the automatic increase in drag as line reduces on the reel spool. Both of these master anglers will move to sunset to full drag, when the double line is on the reel, while being ready to instantly ease back if the double leaves the reel. On light tackle with a big jumping fish, particularly one that changes direction, Ted will instantly ease the brake almost back to free spool.

Gar Wood Jr of Florida was not only accomplished with speedboats, but with fishing reels as a design engineer and constructor. He was of the school of fishermen in Florida and Bahamas who believed fish should be worked hard. Much of his experience was back when lines were linen and breaking strains and forgiveness much less than current synthetic lines.

Tackle class	Striking drag	Fighting drag
12 lb (6 kg)	4 lb (1.8 kg)	7 lb (3.1 kg)
20 lb (10 kg)	6–7 lb (2.7–3.1 kg)	12 lb (5.4 kg)
30 lb (15 kg)	8–9 lb (3.6–4.09 kg)	15 lb (6.8 kg)
50 lb (24 kg)	12–13 lb (5.4–5.9 kg)	25 lb (11.3 kg)
80 lb (37 kg)	15–16 lb (6.8–7.2 kg)	40 lb (18.1 kg)
130 lb (60 kg)	20–21 lb (9.09–9.5 kg)	50 lb (22.7 kg)

The name Estaban Bird is synonymous with the development of the fabulous blue marlin fishing off his home, San Juan, Puerto Rico. His recommendations suggested a decrease between strike brake and fishing

Yellowfin anglers often have multiple hook-ups and can land the multiples if they keep cool and ease brakes and pressure when lines are close to touching. Photo: Tim Simpson.

brake. The recommended schedule of this most successful Caribbean angler reflects not only the actual brake applied at the reel, but drag of the line through the water and line friction. Line friction is an interesting study in itself, in that it varies between monofilament and braided line.

Tackle class	Striking drag	Fighting drag
12 lb (6 kg)	3 lb (1.3 kg)	Less than 3 lb (1.3 kg)
20 lb (10 kg)	5 lb (2.2 kg)	3–4 lb (1.3–1.8 kg)
30 lb (15 kg)	9 lb (4.09 kg)	7 lb (3.1 kg)
50 lb (24 kg)	15 lb (6.8 kg)	9–13 lb (4.09–5.9 kg)
80 lb (37 kg)	24 lb (10.9 kg)	16–20 lb (7.2–9.09 kg)
130 lb (60 kg)	50 lb (22.7 kg)	24–30 lb (10.9–13.6 kg)

Frank Moss, a former Atlantic charter boat captain, magazine editor and author of two excellent books on gamefishing and tackle, published a schedule of striking drags that varied with species. This schedule reflects the difference between major species, with a lighter drag for the jumping marlin species.

*S*tand-up fishing as boat backs up off Baja California, Mexico. Photo: Peter Goadby.

Species	Tackle class	Striking drag
Mako	12 lb (6 kg)	2 lb (0.9 kg)
	20 lb (10 kg)	4 lb (1.8 kg)
	30 lb (15 kg)	7 lb (3.1 kg)
	50 lb (24 kg)	15 lb (6.8 kg)
	80 lb (37 kg)	20 lb (9.09 kg)
Swordfish	130 lb (60 kg)	30 lb (13.6 kg)
Bluefin Tuna	12 lb (6 kg)	3 lb (1.3 kg)
	20 lb (10 kg)	5 lb (2.2 kg)
	30 lb (15 kg)	8 lb (3.6 kg)
	50 lb (24 kg)	17 lb (7.7 kg)
	80 lb (37 kg)	25 lb (11.3 kg)
	130 lb (60 kg)	40 lb (18.1 kg)
Marlin	12 lb (6 kg)	1½ lb (0.68 kg)
	20 lb (10 kg)	3 lb (1.3 kg)
	30 lb (15 kg)	6 lb (2.7 kg)
	50 lb (24 kg)	12 lb (5.4 kg)
	80 lb (37 kg)	18 lb (8.1 kg)
	130 lb (60 kg)	28 lb (12.7 kg)

Modern tackle development techniques and balanced tackle generally use stiffer and more powerful rods, particularly in the tackle classes from 10 kg (22 lb) upwards. Associated with this is the modern philosophy of working the fish hard in attacking to burn the fish out. The philosophy is more towards 'pop or stop' rather than sitting or standing there with a big drag line in the water, hoping the fish will tire dragging this bag of line through the water.

In all these strike and fighting schedules, consideration must be given to the speed, position and activity of the fish. Common sense as well as experience dictates that there are times when it is imperative to ease up a little on the fighting drag. At times there is no need to pump at all, simply a need to wind as fast as humanly possible to lay line evenly on the reel. When pumping, short, rocking pumps are most effective. They keep the fish moving, ideally up and towards the boat.

It is important to think about what the fish is doing. Tuna and most other fish swim in circles through different levels. While the fish is on the up-swim of its circling,

IGFA LINE CLASS US customary lb	Line class		Safe strike drag		Fighting drag	
	Actual lb	kg	lb	kg	lb	kg
2	2.2	1	⅓	.15	⅓–½	.25
4	4.4	2	¾	.34	¾–1	.5
8	8.88	4	1½	.68	1½–1¾	.75
12	13.22	6	2¾	1.25	2¾–3	1–1.5
16	17.63	8	3¾	1.7	3⅗–4¼	1.75–2
20	22.04	10	5	2.27	5–6	2.25–2.75
30	33.06	15	7½	3.4	7½–8¼	3.25–3.75
50	52.91	24	13	6	13–16	6–8
80	81.57	37	22	10	22–27	11–13
130	133.27	60	45–55	20–25	55–80	25–36.5

line is gained. On the down-swim of its circling, line is lost.

Anglers who understand what the fish is doing take advantage of the fish circling to pressure—to pump and recover on the up circle and hold hard and evenly on the down. The position of maximum disadvantage to the fisherman is when the fish is down straight under the boat. Planing the fish is the best way to beat this and other Mexican stand-offs.

Two basic angling philosophies are used in bringing fish to gaff. One way is by attack. Attacking fishermen use a quick action of the rod, a quick lift and line recovery, even though some jerkiness or whip is transmitted to the fish. This technique is often used with soft and slow-action rods. Anglers of the other fishing philosophy tend to the 'leading' rather than the 'driving' method. They employ a constant smooth action of lift and recovery. The smooth technique suits quick-taper quick-action rods that will lift a fish. Though the pressure is even and constant, the pumping can still be in quick and short sweeps. Kip Farrington wrote that short pumps bothered and beat a fish more than the long ones.

The tempo of the fight should be controlled and dictated by the angler. The fish gets more benefit from a pause than the angler—its rate of recovery from fatigue is much faster. So keep the pressure on the fish.

Fishermen who lead and control their fish try to keep to one side of it, so that it is swimming with the muscles on one side working harder than on the other. When the fish changes direction the boat should be maneuvered so that the angle of pull stays the same. The constant pull away at one side tires the fish speedily. Fast 'backing up' is used often for quick marlin captures.

Many successful captains and anglers believe in keeping close to a hooked fish so that there is only a short length of line on which it can maneuver, sound or jump. Long lengths of line in the water give the fish a chance to jump against a bag of line or cross over the line, cut it and break free. Synthetic lines do not exert the same drag and friction as were given by the old linen lines, so there is less advantage now in having a long length of line in the water.

The fisherman, with the help of the skipper, tries to avoid the stand-off, a stalemate between the opponents with neither gaining or losing line nor changing relative positions. This situation, in fact, quickly wins an advantage for the fish, for the constant wear and tear of the fight carried on along a short length of line gradually and then quickly causes wear and eventually a breakoff. To change this losing pattern, a vigorous attacking technique, such as planing the fish to shallower level or circling against the fish, may be necessary. Line is lost from the reel spool initially during these maneuvers but the angle of fighting, of lift, gradually becomes more favorable to the fisherman. When a stubborn fighter is forced from where it wants to stay, the advantage is to the fisherman, but the lifting pressure must be maintained. The planing or circling maneuver often has to be repeated time after time until the fish finally gives in. Repeated circling or reverse circling by the boat, indeed, is often the only way to success against the deep fighters such as giant trevally, cobia and amberjack, and this circling pressure also helps to beat big tiger sharks and deep-fighting billfish and tuna.

In prolific waters, sharks present an added hazard by attacking and mutilating hooked fish, so every minute the fight continues is another minute during which mutilation becomes likely. It is nothing short of amazing how sharks shadow and wait on a tiring fish, the strong wolves of the sea waiting on weakening marine giants.

The fighting chair on Vici *is used to advantage by Ken Brown as he fights a 181 kg (400 lb) blue marlin on 23 kg (50 lb) test at Kona, Hawaii. Photo: Peter Goadby.*

*W*alking the fish:
tuna and sharks
usually circle anti-
clockwise.

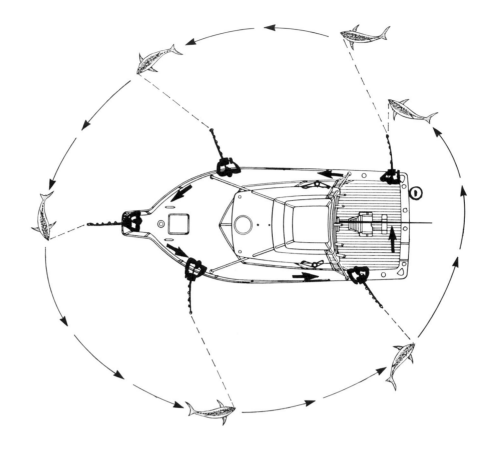

*T*he boat,
particularly those
equipped with twin
motors, can turn inside
the circling fish as it is
brought close. The fish
is usually closest to the
surface on the left side
of the circle.

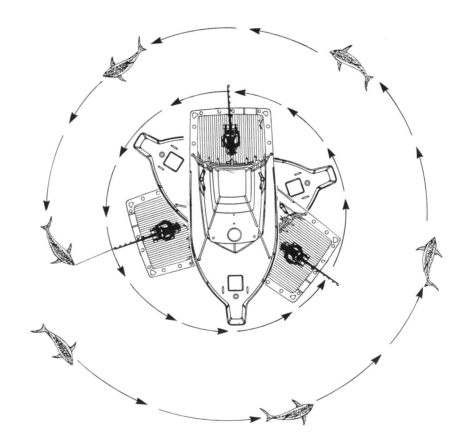

to run out at less than the breaking strain. Extra braking power on light tackle can be exerted by use of left thumb to press the line down against the rod foregrip. If the fish runs strongly, the thumb can be lifted instantly. Some successful heavy-tackle fishermen use the left hand to press against the side of the reel spool to apply extra resistance. Others have been known to hold the line high from the rod with a firm grip of the left hand and almost pull the line back onto the spool.

When the line is being wound in, the fisherman's left hand should lay it evenly along the spool to prevent a bunch-up. The pump is repeated again and again, dozens or hundreds of times, during a long tough fight. With the extra brake exerted by the downward pressure of the thumb the fisherman lifts the rod smoothly, usually to the vertical position, then it is dropped down quickly, almost horizontally, and at the same time the line regained by the lift is quickly reeled on to the spool. Sometimes only a few centimetres are recovered, sometimes metres; and once the fish weakens, more line can be recovered with each pump. With shoulder harnesses, pumping action tends to be longer and more sweeping. This is one of the reasons why shoulder harnesses are generally used on light tackle where lifting is combined with holding pressure while the fish runs against the lightly set brake.

A harness assists on all tackle from 6 kg (12 lb) upwards, and is particularly helpful in long fights against strong fish. Harness may not be needed for small fish, but if fish are to be 'walked' on a drifting or anchored boat, the harness makes the work easier and safer.

Harness allows the weight of fishing gear and fish to be taken evenly on the fisherman's back muscles. It eliminates the need for a deathlike cramping grip with the lifting hand and arm. Also harness makes it become more natural and balanced because unless the line is laid on evenly, it will bunch up and then collapse, or may jam against the reel seat or bars on the reel. Sometimes it seems as if the ideal angler should have four hands to do everything: to pump, to prevent sideways twist, to wind, to adjust brake as line-spool diameter alters and to lay the line evenly. The harness is also a must in team-fishing with yellowfin tuna, etc. When all team members have a fish on, the only way that hands and arms are made free to gaff or take a leader is when the tackle and fish are supported by harness; one hand can then be freed.

If maximum braking power is to be maintained, the experienced angler will occasionally alter the brake by using the star drag or lever; but novice anglers should set the brake and then leave it alone. Practice on boat and on shore will help the novice to gain the smooth technique of polished fishermen. The best way to learn how much weight is being applied at the hook is to pull with balanced tackle against spring scales with rod bent, as it is with fish on.

People often talk of luck in fishing. Sure, there is luck. Fish often act out of character, make mistakes—and these are often the record fish. But usually luck evens out, particularly with those who fish over a long period of years.

My personal assessment of the ingredients in consistent successful fishing is: thirty percent complete preparation by anglers, captain and crew, on gear, boat and fishing plan; twenty percent balanced tackle so that angler and crew have a visual indication of the fish's actions; twenty percent skill of captain and crew in rigging baits, fighting and landing fish; twenty percent skill of angler in handling his tackle and working in with the other team members; ten percent luck. Experience comes into the first four categories. Experienced fishermen and crews know almost instinctively what they should be doing and what the fish is doing.

The setting of strike drag against a spring scale is important, not only for strike, but for fighting. Setting the drag with rod in the angle that it will bend during the fight is logical although many pull straight from reel.

Despite this setting against the scale, common sense must also be applied; the brake plates will heat up as the temperature of the day increases. Regular checking, pulling line against brake, will ensure that the brake is practical in that position for the line class.

It is important to hold the rod firmly down in the rod holder with one hand while pulling with the other so the pull against the spool does not lift the rod from the holder and overboard. This applies when drifting or trolling, as a sticky drag can lift a rod clear of the rod holder in a twinkling of an eye, even though the drag is theoretically set just hard enough to prevent an overrun on a fast strike from the fish.

When pumping, keep the rod tip up as the rod is designed to be a spring as well as a lever. In stand-up fishing, whether the rod tip is short as in the 'short stroker' or of conventional length, positive results come from short, quick attacking pumps. Stand-up fishing is growing in popularity with both length rod tips.

It is important for each angler to find and to practice a style that suits individual build, strength and experience. One of the benefits of stand-up fishing is that it facilitates playing more than one fish at a time.

In the event of multiple hook-ups, anglers must keep thinking to analyse if their fish are circling and swimming anti-clockwise, as do most tuna and sharks. They must be ready not only to show their skill in the 'tuna two-step' as they move around boat and cockpit. They must be ready to back the brake right off to prevent crossed line cutting and then calmly pass one round the other with only the anglers touching their tackle so the fights can be resumed with fish separated.

Stand-up fishing requires a high level of fitness. Many anglers, even when fishing with 15-kg tackle, quickly appreciate the assistance of fighting or fishing chairs.

Serious advocates of fishing with short stroker rods, such as Marsha Bierman, often have an exercise regime to maintain maximum fitness for their fishing. The ultimate benefit of fighting with the short rods generally is associated with much practice and fitness exercising. Some anglers believe the short rod tips are of benefit with line classes up to 15 kg (30 lb). Others believe they benefit on lines of 24 kg (50 lb) and 37 kg (80 lb). Even the most experienced fishermen benefit from pumping practice on shore to ready themselves for their hoped-for offshore activity.

The mouths of most fish are hard, so consideration must be given to the all-important strike to try to set the hook. On trolling and even bait casting and spinning tackle, the hook-up can be made by increasing the drag and lifting the rod tip up and to the side two or three times. On fly tackle the strike is often made by the angler pulling the line rather than lifting the flexible rod tip. Care must be taken to prevent breakoffs with jumping fish. Lowering the rod tip, bowing to the fish, easing the drag, all assist in preventing the sickening sensation of broken line.

The technique of pumping to control the fish, to lift the fish, to recover line, is perhaps carried to the ultimate by experienced heavy tackle anglers in fighting chairs.

With heavy tackle, pumping is a combination of a rowing, sliding action. The angler slides forward or is pulled forward by the fish and may even lower the rod tip a little, then drives back with the power of legs and back while the left hand lays the line recovered by the winding of his right on to the spool. Often the only way to hold, to stop the fish, to recover line, is with the angler pulled to his feet high from the chair seat. The power, body weight and leg drive of the fisherman take effect and the harnessed body is back on the chair seat. Experienced, fit heavy-tackle fishermen often fight repeatedly in this position with left hand pressing down

hard on the reel frame and spool. Sometimes the right hand is used on the rod holder frame or armrest to steady on these lifts. This tactic often makes anglers wish that the rod butt were pinned to the gimbal or for a safety line to ensure they could not be completely lifted from the chair and overboard if the reel brake grabs or is set too hard. It is at this time and when taking the rod and reel from rod holder without assistance, while the line is running out fast and the fish jumping and hooked, that the angler must be most careful—ready to ease the brake if necessary, but conscious always of the danger and problem of an overrun. On light tackle an overrun and line jam is expensive and annoying; on heavy tackle it is dangerous, and more expensive.

Line friction, line drag caused by long lengths of line and loops in the water, is a problem of lines of all weights. The heavier the breaking strain, the greater the friction, but also the less chance of breakoff even with big loops in the water. With light line class, there is much more possibility of this causing breakoff, even without the action of fish or boat. Milton D. Shedd of AFTCO expanded and confirmed Harlan Major's work on reel brake increase with reduction of line of spool, and his reports on line friction and speed, although Harlan Major's reports dealt with linen lines. Milton Shedd's data provided information and further thought-starters on the need to back off as line disappears from the spool and to minimize bag of line in the water and the shape of the loops. The position of boat and fish, and the line breaking effect, he described as 'side-cutting' friction. The complications come from multiple loops in the water and the habit of fish, particularly marlin, changing direction and depth in their activity. The rod tip is a visual indicator as well as a lever and a spring, so experienced anglers use this indicator as well as experience and gut feel.

IMPORTANT FACTORS IN FIGHTING A FISH

- Ability to move safely on rolling boat.

- Knowledge of all the gear that is used. Check drag and deflection.

- Know from the bend of the rod whether more or less brake should be applied.

- Check drag against scales for strike and fighting positions.

- Drop the rod tip down when fish jumps or lunges but minimize slack line.

- Ease off drag when the line sings in breeze.

- Most anglers increase drag once fish settles down after first run.

- Remember as line shortens and fish is closer, there is less line to stretch and act as shock absorber. Be ready to ease as fish or sea dictate.

- Ease drag to give a hooked fish a chance to escape a shark, or if fish takes a long run.

- If doubled line is used, the drag can be increased once the double is on the spool. Ease drag if the fish pulls the double off again.

- On light tackle 'standing up' fighting, it is often easier to fight and land the fish from the bow, if this is safe and low enough for gaffing.

- When two or more fish are being fought at the same time, anglers must be ready to ease drags immediately if lines cross to facilitate uncrossing and prevent cutoffs—the 'tuna two-step'.
- Angler and captain must be in agreement on tactics to be used—communicate.
- Be prepared to vary tactics.
- Watch position of boat to fish.
- Skipper and angler should try to minimize bags or loops in line.
- Exercise for fitness and practice for tackle used—heavy, light, sitting down or standup with short or long rods.
- Have harness and if necessary rod belt to suit tackle used.
- Be alert to ease pressure on jumping fish.
- Keep concentrating.

Fighting activity will vary with the following factors:

- Angler familiarity with tackle to be used.
- The fish itself, whether it is male or female; its condition (healthy, ready to spawn, at its peak or rundown, having recently spawned), its mood (fighting mad, hungry or unaware that it is in trouble).
- Where and how the fish is hooked—shallow, deep, or foul.
- The angler: his condition (fit or tired), his mood (fighting mad or placid), his mental attitude (bright, 'on the ball', determined to win, or with his mind on other things besides landing the fish).
- The boat, gear and crew—good, bad or indifferent.
- Weather and sea conditions.
- Water depth and currents, reef obstacles.

- The shark problem, the possibility of mutilated fish.
- The presence of other fish that might cut the line.
- The time of day. A hook-up early in the day leaves plenty of time in daylight; a hook-up late in the day puts pressure on the angler.
- Mistakes on the part of the fish; luck or a choked fish.

In ultra-light fishing for big fish:

- Bow to the jumping fish, i.e., lean body and tackle towards the fish as it jumps to ease the strain on the fragile line.
- Regularly check leaders for cuts or rubs from coral or other obstructions, particularly after landing each fish.
- Hold rod and reel high overhead to help the line clear bottom obstructions while the fish is being played.
- Cast lures in front of fish or work across in front of its likely track. Do not cast behind and pull forward.
- The shock tippet of Sevalon or heavy monofilament helps cutoffs from sharp teeth or gill covers.
- Retrieve flies or lures slowly, unless the fish that is selected and hunted is swimming very fast. Some species, such as mackerel, move fast and fast retrieval and jigging is most effective. Cast to one fish, not the whole school.
- The fish must be worked hard and as evenly as possible on ultra-light, just as on other tackle categories.
- Maneuver boat so it is between fish and obstruction.
- The strip retrieve for line is used in saltwater fly fishing until hook-up. The line is dropped to the bottom of the boat or casting platform on the bow and dropped on the water when casting and wading.
- Noise must be kept to a minimum and the lure should be brought in very close before being lifted clear of the water for the next cast.

POINTS FOR SUCCESSFUL DRIFT AND ANCHOR FISHING

- Sharp hooks.
- Baits must be regularly checked for damage.
- Some lines may need weights or sinkers to get baits to a wished-for level.
- Always look for fins or fish working on or near the surface.
- Check drags often so that they are not set too hard.
- Use click as warning and overrun preventer.
- Replace live baits.
- Throw over live unhooked and discarded bait fish occasionally.

- Make sure lines have not tangled.
- Cover all water levels from within two metres of bottom on reef to surface with live or dead baits.
- A dan buoy (float) should be attached to the anchor line so that it can be slipped if a hooked fish has to be chased.
- If fish are sighted but not striking baits, try decreasing hook and leader size.
- If shifting position, keep chum trail unbroken.
- Always chum regularly to keep trail unbroken.

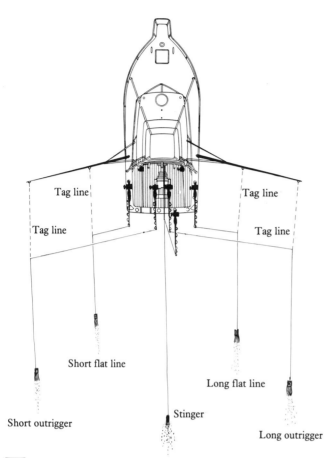

Tag line

Tag line

Tag line

Tag line

Short flat line

Long flat line

Short outrigger

Stinger

Long outrigger

Short short

Short flat

Long flat

Short outrigger

Long outrigger

The 'W' trolling pattern with tag lines. The inner lines could also be trolled flat from the rod tip.

The 'V' pattern. The short lines could be run from rod tip instead of from the clip or line release down on transom.

POINTS FOR SUCCESSFUL

BAIT TROLLING

- Sharp hooks.

- Make sure the line will come free from the outrigger with minimum weight related to bait and sea.

- The angler should be ready to take the strike, to tease or to drop back to the following fish.

- Baits should be changed if not working properly, or if stale.

- Baits should be supple and not waterlogged.

- Troll baits in a pattern so the boat can be maneuvered without tangles.

- A variety of bait species should be used in the fishing pattern.

- If a fish takes the bait, be ready to feed line, so that a shy fish will swallow the bait, not drop it.

- Harness and gloves should be close by, in known positions, ready to use.

- If a billfish drops a bait after striking, jig the bait to tease the fish back to strike.

- Binoculars are useful for spotting tailing billfish and bird activities.

- A soft vinyl psychotail over the head of a natural bait makes it last longer in trolling, and allows it to be trolled faster, particularly on light tackle.

- Skipper and angler must be agreed on the method each favors, and reach firm agreement on how the fish is to be hooked and fought before any action takes place.

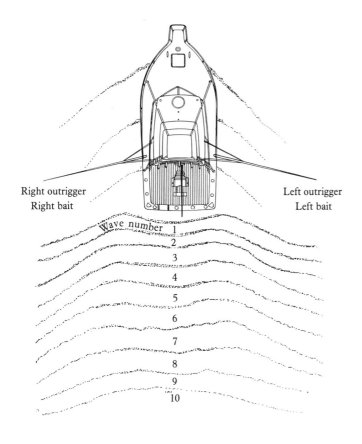

Right outrigger
Right bait

Left outrigger
Left bait

Wave number 1
2
3
4
5
6
7
8
9
10

Lure trolling—waves right and left.

Efficient trolling is practical even without outriggers particularly if one set of the side coverboard rod holders is slightly angled out.

POINTS FOR SUCCESSFUL
LURE TROLLING

- Sharp hooks.
- Experiment with a new lure in a proven pattern of successful lures.
- Troll the lures to cover a range of depth, some on the surface, some below the surface.
- Troll the variety in a non-tangling V or W pattern.
- The angler should always be ready for action.
- Choose lures with action and color to suit the day. Change lures as the day progresses, if success has not come on the first pattern used.
- The angler should be ready to tease a following marlin or to free spool back into the marlin's mouth if it is following with mouth open but not striking.
- Be ready to speed up to add to the excitement of following fish.

- Gun the boat to set the hook, then ease the drag once the hook is driven in so that the angler can take the rod from the holder to the chair, in accordance with IGFA rules.
- Troll each lure where it is known to be most effective.
- If two hooks are to be used, make sure this is done in accordance with the IGFA rule which prohibits the use of a dangling or swinging hook.
- Skipper, crew and angler must all be agreed on the methods favored, and reach agreement on how the fish is to be hooked and fought, before any action takes place.
- The angler and crew should be aware in a two-hook rig of the angles planned in the hook position.

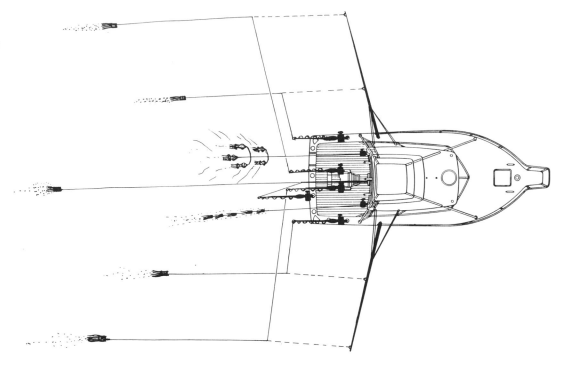

One or two teasers of various types can be trolled in a lure or bait pattern, particularly in low wind, calm water areas. They can be trolled with baits or lures.

CHARTER BOATS

There is a vast difference between fishing from a home port, where everything is available and familiar, and fishing far away. In addition to the problem of distance, there is the simple problem of limitations of what to take and carry. If charter boats are to be used at the destinations, other factors need to be considered.

The following recommendations are made from long and sometimes uncomfortable experience. They are intended to reduce the stress and problems of fishing away from home. Saltwater gamefishing should be a pleasurable challenge with no measures of disappointment, misunderstanding, and above all, no confrontation with anything but fish. Information, planning and elimination of possible problem areas are the key to a happy and successful trip with memories and a record of the trip.

Communication, confidence in all segments of the team, and understanding of problems (ideally before they arise) are all important. Remember too, that not all skippers and mates are familiar with your language, even if this is English; remember, too, that there is *your* English and English as it is spoken and understood by others.

In these days of many fish having high market values and, in the case of big tuna, almost astronomical dollars, the ownership of fish caught has to be established right in the beginning. There is often a chance of tension and argument when money in four or five figures is suddenly a factor.

A classic case of this is where a group of visiting friends and business associates charter a boat for a day's fun fishing. They have no knowledge of rules, records or the potential of the waters in which their charter boat's lures are innocently smoking and popping. Suddenly a lure disappears, the other outfits are brought in as a marlin's head wags from side to side, clear of the surface. All charterers take part of the action and pump with varying degrees of skill and results; finally the charter captain himself recovers the last few yards and gaffs the fish.

At boatside this is shown to be clearly a dream fish, huge. The marlin is too big for the regular scales and special arrangements are made to weigh it. The magnificent fish dominates its surroundings and an entrepreneur is quick to offer the charter captain a very high price for the fish if he can have it for mounting and exhibition.

The captain explains that his conditions of charter are that the fish belonged to his charterers. As the hubbub from the weighing and photographs dies away, and the boat is cleaned up, the skipper asks for his charter fee. Payment is refused by the charter group because they say the captain should have known their fish might have been a record and, despite their decision to all enjoy the action on the rod, he should have made sure that only one of them did. The captain adds that if they will not pay the charter, what would they like him to do with the fish? The suggestions are uncomplimentary as well as impossible, but in essence are that it is his to dispose of. The captain smiles and accepts this, and a quick call to an entrepreneur ensures that the great fish is preserved as a reminder of what can be found from that port.

I learned a hard-won and lasting lesson in communication with charter crews. The story is worthy of retelling as it exemplifies the problems that can arise from lack of communication.

Our charter boat, skipper and crew were new to us, but had a good reputation, although perhaps a little lacking in experience. The day started perfectly; we caught light tackle gamefish, mackerel, wahoo, some tuna, plenty for food and bait. Then we trolled for heavier tackle fish—we wanted billfish, particularly black marlin, striped marlin and sailfish. We had cobalt water, baits and lures that worked perfectly across the warm water. The swells creamed and broke opal against the rocky headlands and golden beaches. It was a day when fins and tails could be easily seen and a bait trolled perfectly across in front of the cruising billfish's bill, a perfect day to fight. Yes, this was to be one of the days.

Trolling records turned into minutes, minutes into hours; Portuguese men-o'-war, vellella, violet snails, all confirmed what the thermometer told us—the water was right, yet still the only fins or tails were in our tiring imaginations.

Then there was a fin, blue, moving confidently, slicing the dark blue surface. Not a billfish but a mako, a big one, a certain world record on the lines we were trolling. It seemed no one else had seen it, but that didn't matter as mako course and boat course were coinciding perfectly. No need for drama of pointing, of shouted instructions; it was all going to happen without any yelling or pointing to claim what was going to be my record mako. Now the mako could be clearly seen, and the ripples and wavelets from his dorsal increased as he saw the bait crossing in front of his pointed nose as he sped up and water slicked faster off his white snaggle teeth. *Now* . . . but now never happened. A crash of explosions nearly lifted me off the deck as the mako submerged away from the bullets that peppered the surface near that muscular body. Gone, disappeared. The bait trolled on, untouched, its chance for fishing immortality gone. The crewman of the boat turned with a wisp of smoke still coiling lazily from the muzzle of a rifle we didn't even know was aboard. Now he yelled, 'Did you see that shark? He nearly got your bait!'

Our fault, my fault, not the deckhand's. We'd talked of billfish and gamefish to the skipper and mate, but hadn't mentioned sharks, hadn't even thought of them on a perfect trolling day in the warm current. Our crew did not know or care it was a mako, that it would have been a record. To him it was vermin, a shark unwanted, a bait mutilator. He did what he thought was right, just what he did for other charterers, what he'd always done as a professional fisherman. When our tempers cooled down we realized it was our fault. From that day onwards we made someone fishing captain to make sure skipper and crew knew what the charterers wanted, to spend time building rapport to maximize concentration.

Another time we checked the gaffs, but not the handles. Then there was the boat that hadn't been finished—there were no cleats, the boat with no chair (we used a wooden fruit case), the boat with insufficient fuel, the boat on which the skipper thought we were providing rods, reels and lures, while we thought the boat was complete with them, the boat without a working head and a woman angler or guest on board, and the time both parties thought the other party was providing the bait.

Make sure in the various locations that the words used, even in English, mean the same to everyone. This was a lesson learned at Palmilla Hotel, Cabo San Lucas, Mexico, where all the charter boats were booked. An English angler wanted to fish at any cost as the marlin were thick. He declined a visiting US skipper's offer of a full day on his owner's yacht, preferring to fish an open Mexican Panga. Imagine his chagrin when the US skipper gave him a cheery wave as he headed for the Gordo Bank. The yacht was a Hatteras 53, fully rigged. To the Englishman, a yacht was a sailing vessel, quite unsuited to fishing for anything. To the Californians it is a big game cruiser in Mexico.

It is important to clarify possible areas of concern before confirming the bookings, and then again if there is any uncertainty. It is more peaceful and productive to arrive at agreement in the cool of the morning, not at the end of a hot tiring day whether successful or not.

Tipping and the rate of tipping if it is practiced is another area of possible concern. If tipping is practiced for a particular port or fishery, seek guidance from other anglers on the rate they give for successful and unsuccessful days and for the skipper and crews that work really hard and co-operatively.

Other points are:

- Cost of charter. Does cost include food, drink, fuel, crew payment? Is payment to be made before or after the day's fishing?
- Length of fishing day, departure and return times. Anglers sometimes become upset at boats leaving port

*S*kip Smith *backs* Hooker *hard as his angler fights on light tackle. Photo: Jacquie Acheson.*

and returning at a set time, just like a bus service that can't be varied, say 7 am out and back at 5 pm, without regard to sea or tides or the fishing unless there is a fish being fought. Charter boatmen, on the other hand, naturally wish to keep regular hours because they have to do this work all day every day, and regular hours help their health and home life.

- Ownership of fish caught. Anglers sometimes get upset when they find that captured fish are accepted as belonging to the crew who may sell the fish, so the anglers may have to buy back their capture for mounting. Sometimes too, anglers wish to use salable fish for bait. So get this worked out before leaving.

- Who is to provide lunch for anglers, skipper and crew? There is nothing much worse than anglers or crew going hungry while the others are eating.

- Make sure skipper and crew know what sort of fish the anglers particularly want to try to catch.

- Determine what weight of tackle anglers prefer to use. Is this on the boat, and does its use balance with the boat and crew?

- Make sure whose gear is to be used—boat's or angler's.

- Make sure that the angler will hook his own fish in accordance with IGFA rules, even if he misses hooking up through inexperience. Make sure that IGFA rules are followed at all times and that the crew understands the angler's wish to fish within the rules, including transfer of rod and reel from holder to chair gimbal,

and the rules relating to live bait and cast baits.

- Be sure the crew understand whether the capture of one big fish or a bag of small fish is the main object.

- Everyone must understand the position of the photographer or photographic crew if there is to be one on board; whether it is more important to land fish as they are hooked or to allow photographers to take good action photographs close up, or into the sun or against the sun, or under the water, or anything else they may want.

- Anglers should check length of doubles, leaders and method of rigging on leaders personally, so they can't complain later. If these are not within the rules it is the angler who loses the record.

- Make sure gaffs and tail ropes are OK and within rules.

- Check on local superstitions so captain and crew are not unintentionally upset.

- Anglers who fish with a woman companion should make sure that the boat, fish and conditions are suitable for her.

- If tipping is customary, check to find out the standard percentage, so that visiting anglers are not too far above or below the accepted level and do not upset the local customs and economy.

- Make sure that the anglers will fit comfortably in the fighting chair, that the footrest or a makeshift equivalent can be adjusted to suit the angler.

- If you are carrying your own harness, make sure it will fit the harness lugs of the reels you are going to use.
- Ascertain whether the skipper prefers to be left alone on the bridge or whether he appreciates conversation and company.
- Anglers should take every opportunity to learn as much as possible from the experiences of skipper and crew.
- Remember that charter crews are as keen as, often keener than the anglers to land and bring in big fish. Their livelihood and their pride depend on success.

- If anglers wish to use their own gear, it is advisable to make sure before leaving port that the rod butts will fit into rod holders and fighting chair gimbals.
- If there is difficulty in understanding between angler and crew because of language, try to find some way of overcoming this before going to sea. An interpreter may be necessary.
- Reach agreement as to policy on tag and release, or release, or if any fish are to be taken, what size is to be kept.
- Check local laws, closures and bag limits.

FIRST AID AND ACCIDENT PREVENTION

Many boats that fish offshore will carry first aid emergency kits and many skippers or crew have knowledge of emergency medical procedures. Despite this, experience has shown the benefits of the travelling fisherman carrying some simple and necessary personal medical supplies and equipment.

The sun is the old and continuing enemy of saltwater fishermen. Excessive exposure to the sun can cause headaches, heat exhaustion and the need for eye protection. The fisherman who carries his own supply of analgesics such as aspirin or other compatible medication with codeine can offset the effects of sun glare headaches. If heat exhaustion is likely to be a problem, salt tablets will assist in treatment and prevention.

Sunburn effects can be minimized by use of a hat or cap with a brim, polarizing glasses, proven UV filter suncream or liquid, UV filter lip salve, light shirt, if necessary with long sleeves, and long trousers.

Exposure to the sun, despite these precautions, should be graduated from short spells, perhaps twenty to thirty minutes, to longer times. Of course fish will change all this with a hook-up, with fish heading into the sun on the very first day. The great number of UV water-resisting sun screens and lip salves will save later pain and blistering. Vaseline Intensive Sunscreen, Johnson & Johnson and Roche, as well as other reputable manufacturers, all have effective water-resistant products. The SPF (Sun Protection Factor) should be 15 or higher.

A liquid or cream antiseptic is beneficial for nightly application to hands or other damaged areas to minimize the infection that can quickly arise from spines of fish or bait and line or knife cuts.

Fishermen should also carry in their kits a mixture of Bandaids, sharp scissors, tweezers or sharp knife and Lomotil. The last is useful for minimizing diarrhoea caused by the changes in drinking water.

The fishermen's *bête noire*, seasickness, need no longer be a problem for most who wish to go to sea. Proven tablets such as Dramamine, Bonamine, Travacalm and Marzine are regularly available, often without the need of a prescription. There is benefit in taking a tablet the night before heading to sea, then another or a half dose in the morning. The effects usually last through a day's fishing. It is worthwhile experimenting to see which brand and dose are most effective; some can cause extra drowsiness.

Another product is a scopolamine patch, which lasts several days, worn behind the ear. Some fishermen benefit from the use of wrist bands that exert pressure at key pressure locations on the wrist pulse.

The debilitating effects of seasickness and the efficiency lost because of it are unfortunate, so it is worth planning ahead to find out which is the most beneficial tablet or patch. It is too late when miles out to sea and concentration and performance are necessary for success.

A personal container of insect repellent is always worth having. Everyone going to sea should have some knowledge of mouth-to-mouth and cardiopulmonary resuscitation. This is readily available in brochures and other publications that are easily carried, although ideally skippers, guides or crew will be skilled in this, just in case.

Travelling fishermen should also carry a supply of personal medications for their trip away from home.

TACKLE

CHOICE AND MAINTENANCE OF MODERN TACKLE

Close examination of weigh-in photographs shows that only the fish have remained unchanged since that classic photograph of Dr Holder's first big tuna. Angler clothing has changed from suits and ties for men or neck to ankle-length long-sleeved dresses for women to shorts and golf shorts, or even swimsuits. The most important difference evident in the photographs is in the tackle. The photographs show some of the development changes—reels without brakes, rods with ring guides, linen line. Later photographs show roller tips and star drags, then full rollers on the rods and lever drags on the reels. Many changes have been made in the name of progress. Some have died after a short life, others have continued in evolution to the super tackle of today, in a change from natural materials—wood, linen, simple metals to space-age lightweight materials that are super-strong.

It is perhaps ironic that the evolution of modern tackle has coincided with a powerful trend towards catching the saltwater gamefish on tackle other than the trolling tackle specifically developed for these big fish.

Fly rod enthusiasts appreciate the fighting quality of sailfish. *Photo: Darrell Jones.*

The willow wand of fly casting outfits, the short bait-casting outfits and spinning outfits once expected to be seen and fished in freshwater streams and lakes are now familiar fishing tools in salt water.

Anglers used to this tackle in home fishing appreciate not only the attributes but the extra challenge and fun factor to now fish routinely with these light-tackle outfits. New space-age materials and engineering skills make this tackle tough, dependable and practical.

The new materials are synonymous with strength, light weight, ease of maintenance, resistance to exposure, balance and power.

Today's anglers now have an unprecedented choice of manufacturers for whatever equipment they need. The competition of the market place has not only triggered the proliferation of improvements, modifications and new concepts, but ensured that prices remain competitive and in real terms lower than ever. There are still a few further developments in the flood of technological advances that now seem to be nearing their peak, particularly in reels, that will benefit anglers.

Reel manufacturers now seem to understand that brake materials should allow the spool to roll smoothly under pressure of the brake material, that reels should weigh as little as possible yet be super-strong, that reel spools must not burst or distort under line pressure, that the spool should have sufficient capacity.

The perceived need for reels a size bigger than maker's recommendations or numbering varies in different fisheries, even in the same country. Skilled anglers who use a reel the size bigger are conscious of these benefits:

- Smoother drag with line pulling from high on the spool.
- Increased line capacity to cope with long run of fish and boat maneuvering.
- Adequate line length after line is shortened to remove abrasion, rubs or sun exposure.
- Cooler brake temperature from bigger brake area.
- Faster line recovery with bigger spool diameter.
- More comfortable fast winding.

Those who balance the reel size and manufacturers' line recommendation believe they will not need a longer length of line. They appreciate the lighter weight and perceived maneuverability of the smaller reels. Stand-up fishermen often use the smaller reels for their chosen line classes. The extreme variability of chosen line classes for a particular reel size makes it difficult for manufacturers to produce reels with a brake range to suit all needs.

There is now an increasing range from manufacturers of reels with two or even three gear-speed selections. The multi-gear variable speed reels have positive gear changes that give the double benefit of fast recovery or low gear ratio of 1.1 to gradually lift and force the deep-swimming or tail-wrapped fish back towards the surface.

The benefit of new materials in brakes, spools and frames are evidenced in smooth casting and hard fishing. The new reinforced plastics and lightweight metals are featured in bait casting, trolling, spinning and fly reels. Even some of the lightweight bait-casters offer the benefit of two gear ratios. Revolving-spool casting reels for surf fishing, deep jigging and high-speed lure fishing are available with gear construction materials and ratio designed for this demanding performance fishing.

Manufacturers of the fixed-spool spinning reel have turned this reel design, once considered mainly for its convenience of non-line twisting and non overrunning when casting with lures of all weights, into a practical fishing tool. The top-of-the-range spinning reels now meet the needs and demands of fishing for saltwater gamefish. Spinning reels that stand up to the rigors and perform well for line classes up to 10-kg (20-lb) class are available in several brands with line rollers of non-grooving metal that roll readily as line is retrieved or stripped by the fish. Spinning reels are ideal and used extensively for casting live baits to sailfish and other lighter-weight billfish.

Fly reels are another category of critically used, high-performance, balanced tackle where performance is imperative. Saltwater gamefish are unrelenting opponents that quickly and frustratingly find any weakness in tackle. Once again several manufacturers offer dependable fly reels with sufficient line back-up capacity, balanced casting in light weight, with smooth braking capabilities and all necessary features to overcome saltwater species in this fast-growing fishing described by its devotees as the ultimate fishing experience.

Rods for all fishing categories—fly, spinning, bait casting, jigging, high-speed spinning, live bait casting, stand-up trolling and conventional trolling—are built from modern materials to give the desired performance.

Rod blank design, handle and butt design, all reflect the benefit of skill of rod blank designers and manufacturers who are aware that rods have to perform several functions. If used for casting, they have to deliver the lures the required distance in addition to acting as springs against the power and jolts of the fish, and be a lever to lift in line retrieval.

Trolling rods are the simplest in performance functions, with saltwater fly rods the most diverse. Trolling rods are now finished with improved roller guides; other rods have efficient, cool, non-grooving ring guides, also used on some light trolling rods.

New materials, new shapes and recognition of how rods are used against fish power and deep sounding are shown in butt design, with straight and curved aluminum butts for trolling rods of all tip lengths. Slightly offset trigger grip bait casting rod handles, instead of the once-mandatory pistol grips, are growing in availability and popularity. These longer, almost straight butts are comfortable and effective in casting, while giving tremendous benefit for fighting, with butt along and under the holding arm or with butt comfortably on the chest.

In every fighting category modern materials provide performance in all facets of use. Rods that are light in the tip to deliver the fly, the lure or the small live bait, but which have maximum lifting and holding power, are readily available.

Lines have always been critically important, and naturally the break point in saltwater gamefishing. Again, manufacturers consider the characteristics they and the customers want in their product. Stretch and elasticity make the line more forgiving. Stiff lines may wear longer but not sit tightly on the reel spool. Soft limp lines cast well, but some do not wear well. Some fishermen prefer thin-diameter lines that allow greater yardage on the spool, while others look for thicker-diameter lines because they believe this minimizes line wear.

Color of line is another factor that generates debate among fishermen. They want the line to be of minimum visibility up to the time the fish is hooked, then want and need maximum visibility for skipper, guide and angler following the hooked fish.

Some fishermen choose fluorescent colors, others prefer clear or very soft pink, blue-grey or green or white. Others prefer dark shades in these colors, or even black.

Color available in fly lines ranges from white, through bright visible colors, to black.

Trolling lines are another product area of diverging opinions. Advocates of braided line recognize the benefit of minimum stretch, while the advocates of monofilament line believe its benefits of long wear, ability to withstand abrasion and nicks outweigh the disadvantage of stretch, feel and the difficult characteristic of bags of line in the water. It is possible to combine the best characteristics of braided and monofilament lines by using the low-stretch braided line with hard-wearing monofilament line for the last 50 metres (or yards).

GENERAL POINTS FOR TACKLE SELECTION AND MAINTENANCE

- Rod should suit personal choice and be of top quality.
- Spinning reel rollers must roll freely and not be grooved.
- Check line-bearing surfaces for nicks and grooves.
- Rods should be within IGFA published specifications.
- Regular maintenance and inspection of guides, both rollers and ring guides, is necessary in case of wear.
- Pulling against a spring scale with rod will show the poundage that can be exerted on the fish.
- Choose the best reels you can afford. Poor reels make the landing of record fish difficult.
- Regular maintenance and cleaning.
- Use reel a size larger than the maker's recommendation.
- Drag must be smooth, not jerky.
- Handle should be lightly oiled to turn freely.
- Line should be laid on evenly.

- Check drag often while waiting for a strike in case the brake has increased with the heat of the day, has been accidentally altered while sitting in the rod holder or has been affected by flying spray or vibration.
- Make sure the reel is tight on the reel seat.
- Replace worn or aged section of lines, particularly near terminal tackle.
- Use double line if conditions allow and to gain maximum knot strength.
- Pull all knots and plaits tight and even after lubrication.
- Make sure knots and plaits will pass through guides.
- Use dental floss to over-bind and prevent slip.
- Make sure double line is even before and after swivel is attached.
- Test lines for breaking strain before using.

CHARACTERISTICS OF MATERIAL USED FOR FISHING LINE

ADVANTAGES

Braided Dacron
- Minimum stretch.
- Can be joined by proven splices or plaits.
- Line readily visible to skipper and crew.
- Packs well onto reel spool under angler and fish pressure.

DISADVANTAGES

- Individual fine strands are easily cut or abraded to appreciably reduce breaking strain.
- Subject to wear in outrigger clips.
- Breaking strain reduces from exposure to sun.
- More visible to fish.
- Can be burnt if wound on carelessly too fast with a dry glove.

ADVANTAGES

Monofilament nylon
- Minimum visibility to fish.
- Can be joined with proven knots and plaits.
- Generally more resistant to abrasion, and high breaking strain maintained despite surface cuts.
- Visibility can be improved with fluorescent color.

DISADVANTAGES

- More stretch than braided line.
- Greater diameter than braided lines of equivalent nominal and starting breaking strain.
- Knots are likely to slip, and care must be taken to slide knots together by wetting or wax.
- Slip can be minimized by completing knots with 60-second super glue or rubber adhesive.

Discussions about the characteristics wanted or tolerable in a line are logically influenced by rod characteristics. Rod blanks with exotic material such as boron, graphite, kevlar and S-glass have inherent lifting power that offsets line stretch. All factors of use must be considered, as there are many line products on the market. It is a basic premise that good line does not cost, it saves. Fishermen in tropical areas, in particular, must consider the damaging effect of ultra-violet rays from the sun. Some line brands and colors are more quickly affected by the sun and salt than others.

Some brands of line consistently test higher or lower than the test labelled line class to cause lost fish or, equally frustrating, lost records. Careful fishermen, those who seek and hope for records, use known and pre-tested line and re-test their purchase before filling reels.

Hook makers offer a wise choice of designs to give fishermen the product to suit their intended fishing. Hooks are available in different shapes, thickness and type of steel. Hooks that are not kirbed or offset are used with trolled soft or hard head lures and baits. Offset hooks are used to improve the odds of a firm hook-up in drifting baits. Short shank offset or non-offset hooks are used in live baiting yellowfin tuna or sailfish or small marlin, where minimizing visibility is a major consideration.

Hooks must always be re-sharpened and touched up before use. No hook is sharp enough out of the box. Hook points must be sharp and strong, otherwise they will not penetrate. They must be sharpened and re-sharpened without removing so much metal that they bend or break. There is wide divergence of opinion of the advantages and disadvantages of hook designs and shapes, but when it comes to stainless or non-stainless some fishermen swear by one or the other. Others swear about them. Consideration is also given to which metal is best for the fish once released. The Norwegian hook maker Mustad has now released a hook that will corrode quickly in released fish. This company make trolling hooks of various designs as well as hooks for drifted and live baits. The excellent trolling designs and other hooks of the French company VMC are also popular, as are the live bait and other trolling hooks of US-made Wright McGill Eagle Claw hooks.

The points of double and treble hooks used on lures must also be sharpened before and between use. Files, sharpening stones and electric hook sharpeners are all effective, with once again many opinions as to which is best.

Visibility to the fish is always a factor to be considered. Black finish swivels minimize the chance of non-strike by the sought-after fish as well as the possibility of cutoff by unwanted razor-gang wahoo, mackerels and barracuda attracted by shine and movement. Ball-bearing swivels with coast lock snap are usually chosen for lure trolling, and crane swivels, again with coast lock snap, in other fishing where swivels are useful.

Gaff hook points should also be kept sharp to ease penetration. The choice of gaff lies between fixed head gaffs and flying gaffs. Flying gaffs are used on marlin and sharks over 100 kg (220 lb). Fixed-head gaffs are successfully used on gamefish and sharks under these

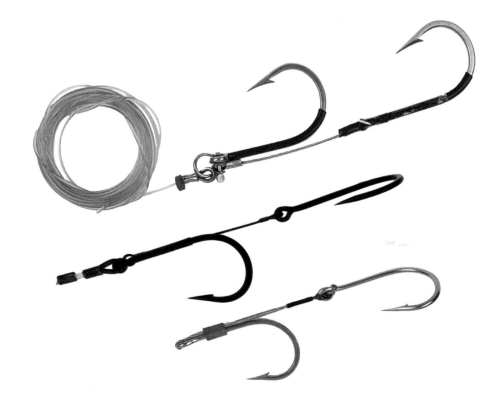

Two hook rigs used in billfish trolling have the hooks at angles from 0°-180°. Lure makers often have two hook rigs ready for their lures. The makers of the hooks shown (from top to bottom: Pakula with red shrink plastic to add rigidity; Doornob Lip-Latch with black teflon coating, and Comstock), as well as Murray Bros, Moldcraft, and C & H, all offer rigged hooks. Pakula and some other riggers use a small stainless shackle to join hooks to an eye on the leader. The Lip-Latch rig is teflon coated.
Photo: David Rogers.

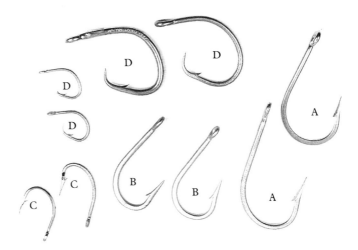

*T*rolling hook designs from Mustad come in stainless as well as corrosion-resistant plating (A); carbon steel V.M.C. trolling hooks have a special corrosion-resistant coating (B); offshore live bait hook from Mustad and Eagle Claw has short shanks (C); Polynesian and Japanese shape hooks work effectively on a range of fish from bonefish on the small sizes to broadbill and tuna on the bigger hooks (D). Photo: David Rogers.

weights, as well as on tuna. Fixed-head gaffs are easier to use than flyers with which some find problems in holding both rope and handle and retrieving the handle.

Heavy cane, as used in furniture, is ideal for gaff handles. It combines flexibility with sufficient rigidity. The fish-holding ability of fixed-head gaffs can be improved by attaching a light rope from around the gaff hook and along the handle. A loop on this rope assists crew holding on to an active fish. Release gaffs, fixed-head short-handled and fixed-head gaffs are placed through the fish's lower jaw to hold it while the fly or lure is removed.

The increasing use of curved-butt trolling rods has polarized the choice of harness designs. Seat and kidney type harnesses are needed to maximize the benefits of curved butts, while shoulder and combined shoulder and kidney harnesses are used with straight butts and in stand-up fishing.

Rod belts are a necessity for comfort and performance in stand-up fishing. Several designs take the length of rod butt and tip into consideration, as well as giving necessary protection and practicality while pumping and fighting the fish.

It is difficult for today's anglers to visualize the high degree of maintenance needed by past tackle. Natural material lines that had to be wound off and dried after fishing and wet before use for maximum breaking strain, guides that could chip, fracture or groove, rods that could delaminate under pressure, reels that required almost daily stripping and service, brakes that became so hot that brake materials bonded and choked up, fly lines that required regular applications for desired performance, rod finishes that deteriorated in the sun and needed touchups on chips or fractures that allowed water into the cane or wood, wooden butts that also needed treatment to exclude damaging water, and wire leaders that had to be checked for corrosion or crystallization and discarded before fishing were some of the maintenance problems now mainly in the past.

Even though today's tackle no longer necessitates the high rate of maintenance of the past, there is need for regular attention, as follows:

- Rods benefit from a daily wiping with fresh water.
- Roller guides should be checked and if necessary lubricated with lubricant to ensure that the rollers roll; older-type rollers should be checked for screws that are loose. If necessary, locking screws can be ensured by application of nail polish.
- Reel brakes should be checked for smoothness, particularly after a fight or after heavy wetting from spray.
- Reels should be wiped with fresh water, not hosed or dunked, then wiped with an oiled cloth.
- Lines should be checked for wear and nicks particularly where held in outrigger releases or rubber bands.
- Lines should be run out for at least 45 metres (50 yards) behind the boat at speed to remove twist from the day's trolling.
- Monofilament leaders should be checked for wear, tooth marks and rubs.
- Wire leaders including the short length of wire in two-hook rigs should be checked for fracture and crystallization.
- Knots and plaits should be checked.
- Double lines and the top length of line should be checked and replaced regularly with a new line 'top shot' of monofilament or braided line.

Apart from line addition or replacement or reel strip to clean and smooth the reel brake, none of this routine maintenance is major or time-consuming.

The short time spent in common sense maintenance each day is beneficial in a subsequent successful enjoyable capture or tag and release. Preparation and maintenance ensures happy and successful fishermen expending perspiration with minimum worries and problems.

HOOK TYPES

KIRBED OFFSET POINT HOOKS

- Whole drifting baits, where hook is embedded in the side of bait.
- Live baits trolled slowly for short distance.
- Drifting strips.
- Bay of Islands rig.
- All live baits and whole fish or fish cut for use when drifting or at anchor.
- Double rigs where only point and barbs are projecting.

STRAIGHT HOOKS

- Whole trolled fish baits where bait swims and hook is not embedded or is embedded in throat.
- Trolled lures.
- Whole fish bait in Panama-Bimini live-bait style with hook on top of head.
- Trolling baits on bridle.
- Live baits trolled for long distance.
- Trolling fish or squid baits with hook embedded.
- Strip baits

General points to remember:
- Keep hooks sharp.
- Do not file or grind hooks so far that the point is weakened and it may break instead of driving home.
- Remove rust, but do not discard hooks just because the cadmium or zinc plating has worn off—brown hooks can be effective, particularly with shy fish.
- Check the eye of the hook where leader wire will cause wear.
- If fish are shy, use smaller, lighter hooks.
- Paint or color live bait hooks so they are minimally visible.
- Keep points free of baits or lures so that they do not choke back in the bait or tangle in the skirt.

GAFFS

Gaffs should always be kept sharp. Points can be protected by a cork or a few centimetres of hose or plastic tube. Heavy gaffs should be reinforced with a second welded rod to minimize chances of straightening on big powerful fish. Gaffs in various sizes should be carried on board ready for instant use. The perfect gaff complement is two flying gaffs, from 30 cm (12 in) down to 20 cm (8 in); plus two fixed gaffs, with 12.5–15 cm (5–6 in) bite; plus two small fixed gaffs, about 7.5–10 cm (3–4 in) bite. A large 60-cm (24-in) diameter landing net is a great help in landing small gamefish that are to be kept alive and undamaged. Small jumping jacks such as dolphin and queenfish are more easily handled in a landing net than with a gaff. Strong spring clips are ideal for holding gaffs in position, ready for instant use, on cockpit sides or upright from cockpit deck to flying bridge. Large-size shark hooks, with or without barb, make satisfactory gaff hooks. The kirb or offset in the shark hook should be bent back so that point and shank are in line. These are for smaller gamefish.

The gin pole on the Hatteras' Duchess is another way of bringing fish inboard. Captain Tommy Gifford preferred a pivoting 'A' frame. Gaffs ready for action often hang alongside the gin pole. Photo: Peter Goadby.

ADVANTAGES	DISADVANTAGES	ADVANTAGES	DISADVANTAGES
Stainless		**Carbon steel**	
• Clean, corrosion-resistant	• Can be bent, twisted and straightened more easily than carbon steel	• Maximum strength for diameter	• Rusts and corrodes
• Medium strength for diameter	• Point subject to bending	• Can be sharpened to excellent points and cutting edges	• Some carbon steel of high strength may break rather than bend or flex
• Can be sharpened to excellent points and cutting edges		• Holds edges and points	

TACKLE FOR FLY FISHING

This is a fast-growing method of fishing, combining the thrill of hunting and sight fishing with the skill and technique of casting, hooking and fighting the fish on slender rod and fragile line class tippets. The shock tippet allowed by IGFA rules is 30.48 cm (12 in), and the tippet breaking strain classes are 1 kg (2 lb), 2 kg (4 lb), 4 kg (8 lb), 6 kg (12 lb), 8 kg (16 lb) and 10 kg (20 lb). Class tippets must be at least 38.10 cm (15 in) inside the knots.

Rods range from those that would be used for trout with No 8 line to powerful fish tamers used with No 12 line. Reels are single-action, carrying 275 m (300 yd) of braided Dacron backing and 31 m (100 feet) of monofilament backing. Saltwater fly fishing is a difficult challenge given the allowable length of shock tippet, and use of only fixed-head gaffs, two of the tackle regulations that add to the degree of difficulty in catching big fish on fly. The fly fisherman needs to be instinctively and completely familiar with a selection of knots, which will be made quickly and safely.

The saltwater fly fisherman utilizes skill in all aspects. This shows in the need for various types of knots used in leaders. The thinking fly fisherman carries spare leaders, ready for replacement, as well as the selection of flies. As with all fishing, the hooks must be needle-sharp. It is always difficult to set hooks in the tough mouths of fish, but with the willow wands of fly rods designed to cast flies, the problem is increased. Those seeking billfish on fly also know that the short length of shock or rub-resistant leader is often the vulnerable link in the chain between angler and fish, particularly billfish—a letdown after the work and skill in finding and teasing the fish, offshore, or being in the right place at the right tide with tarpon. The drag and brakes and capacity on the modern saltwater fly reels give anglers a chance at heavy fish.

*J*ohn Donnell carefully applies maximum pressure to his Costa Rican sailfish ready for a flurry of jumping. Photo: Darrell Jones.

The design and materials of modern fly rods allow the angler to fight big fish aggressively. Some of the saltwater species such as tarpon and bonefish, despite their jumping and speed, are ideally sought on the fly. Master fly fisherman Lefty Kreh stresses the need for all aspects of preparation, familiarity with knots, a tight loop to offset the effect of the wind, the need to hold the rod high so the line will clear rough patches on the sea bottom, great care with jumping fish, bowing, dropping the rod tip with jumping fish or those changing direction fast on the surface. He stresses the need for practice in casting and fishing to gain instinctive and complete familiarity with the tackle once the fish are found.

Buck fever is a natural problem for all fishermen; however, with fly fishing the margins for mistake are minimal even with wire or heavy monofilament shock leaders. Nylon-covered wire is popular for shock leaders.

BAIT CASTING TACKLE

The bait casting outfit is an intriguing combination of the ability to cast light line and light lures, often in restricted fishing areas, with the lifting and stopping attributes of a mini-game outfit. These reels are the oldest overhead and multiplying reels. First made in England before 1770, they were improved by Kentucky watchmaker George Snyder and other watchmakers from that state far from the sea. Jonathan Meek is credited with the sliding button to operate the click ratchet.

It was from these reels that modern overhead surf reels and trolling reels of all sizes have evolved and been refined. The current bait casters look fragile, but in fact are generally rugged pieces of machinery, finely constructed of most suitable materials.

Skiffs evolved for Florida flats fishing are as specialized and practical as the big battle wagons of the blue water. Photo: Al Pfleuger.

The use of bait casting reels in salt water highlights the necessity for regular wipe down and wipe over with light oil or silicone to minimize and avoid the corrosive effect of salt water. The bait casting rod and reel is ideal tackle to use when trolling from dinghies and small boats, as well as when casting. The tackle not only gives every sporting chance and challenge on active and jumping fish up to 10 kg (20 lb) and 6 kg (12 lb) line classes but gives superb fights and captures or releases of active fish, two, three or even four times that weight.

On heavy fish and when trolling, a longer rod handle is of benefit for better control during the fight, although the usual short pistol grip handle has casting benefits.

As with fly and spinning tackle, practice and familiarity increase casting and fishing pleasure. A well-placed cast gives satisfaction even if no strike results. With regular usage, the bait casting rod becomes an extension of the arm and the decision to place the lure exactly where it should excite a strike. Many reels have magnetic and other cast controls as well as efficient brakes and long-wearing level winds. The saltwater bait caster fisherman has benefited from the demand created by volume and usage of the freshwater bass fisherman.

Line wear can be offset by use of top-quality heat-dissipating ring guides. Roller guides are not practical even on the tip guide, as casting as well as fish catching requirements are necessary factors. The development of these reels has taken in LCD electronics indicators. The usual preference for salt and brackish water usage is towards ruggedness and dependability, practicality combined with reasonable self-maintenance and ready availability of parts.

Many saltwater species have razor-sharp cutting teeth that dictate the use of a short leader of around 45 cm (18 in) to resist teeth and abrasive gill covers. In estuarine

waters away from the high density of toothy critturs such as the mackerels and barracudas, 24-kg (50-lb) monofilament leader is ideal, except with the fanged fighters, in which case plastic-covered multi-strand wire can be joined to monofilament leader or to a double line with an Albright, Uniknot or improved Albright knot, so the leader can be wound through the guides. Some anglers attach a small snap swivel. Many prefer the leader attached with Albright or Uniknot to the double; they then cut the leader to replace lures with the free-swinging Homer Rhode Knot. Brass or aluminum sleeves can be used on leaders, but most bait-casting fishermen prefer the familiar knot connections on this light terminal tackle. They use the Spider knot, braid or plait to make the double line. Sixty-second glue or rubber cement makes an additional safety factor on knots used on this tackle, particularly the Albright knot, as it does with fly and spinning tackle that has to be wound right through the guides.

Some species traditionally taken on bait casters are listed as freshwater species, even though commonly taken in estuaries or inshore waters, as well as freshwater rivers and lagoons. Barramundi and the salmons, even when taken in salt water, are listed as freshwater species by IGFA.

The tackle regulations for freshwater species allow a maximum leader length of 1.82 m (6 ft) with a maximum similar length for double line. On species listed as saltwater species, the saltwater line class limits apply, allowing up to 6.1 m (20 ft) of combined leader and double with a maximum of 4.7 m (15 ft) allowable in either.

Bait casting outfits with short rod length are ideal in the confined spaces of fishing and casting from dinghies.

SPINNING TACKLE

It is doubtful whether the innovative thinkers and engineers who invented today's spinning reel ever thought that it would be used for billfish, tuna and most offshore gamefish species. This has become versatile and practical fishing equipment used alike by tyros and master anglers.

Spinning tackle, based on the ubiquitous egg beater, ranges from ultra-lightweight balanced outfits for small and lightweight species, right through to the heavy outfits designed to cast lures and live baits and to battle billfish and tuna. They are also used in jigging.

A double line and leader combination meeting IGFA saltwater or freshwater tackle regulations, combined with a wide range of lure types and weights, ensures the popularity of these multi-purpose outfits. As with other tackle, fish teeth dictate use of wire, with practiced use

of monofilament in other species. Double line is of benefit in knots and in saltwater species may be wound on the reel spool to aid at this stage of the fight. In many areas spinning reels have replaced the overhead casting reels for surf fishing.

Reels are now made in tough long-lasting construction to withstand the needs of rugged fishing. Naturally, as with other reel types, the more practical fishing tools are more expensive than those of lower cost and often similar appearance.

Jigging: Jigging can be considered as vertical lure retrieval. High speed reels and powerful rods give lift and stopping power. Most lure fishing is synonymous with surface action but in jigging the strikes are usually far from the surface, down deep near the sea bed, unseen by angler and crew. Jig rods are around the length of standard trolling rods. Some are finished with a roller tip and ring guides, others have ring guides along the length of the blank. Power and lift are built into the butt section, even though the tip section may have more flex to give better action to the jigs.

Onshore Gamefishing: Rods used for live bait rock fishing for billfish, tuna and other oceanic gamefish are a compromise between a surf or spinning rod and a trolling rod. The reels are top-quality big-fish trolling reels that have to give the same standard of performance, or even better, on land as they do on boats. The roller guide rods have the same basic characteristics of length action and tip as overlength trolling rods of around 2.4 m (8 ft). The extra length, although giving the fish extra mechanical advantage, is helpful in keeping line clear of the rocks. Live baits are cast out by hand or by the rod to a position where wash and current will take bait and float out in deeper water. Small sliding breakaway floats or sometimes a balloon are practical floats for the live baits.

High-speed overhead casting or in some locations spinning reels give active fishermen a chance at pelagic species as the gamefish move close to rocky shores, sometimes singly or in small schools, sometimes in big active schools. Conventional surf rods are satisfactory in combination with the high-speed-retrieval reels. This fishing gives a new dimension to action. Long gaffs and great care and watchfulness are also necessary for the capture of pelagic gamefish from the immovable rocks.

TROLLING AND GEAR-CHANGING REELS

The power and dogged fight of saltwater gamefish have forced a constant improvement in saltwater trolling reels. A few years ago only Fin Nor in their 12/0 size manufactured a gear-changing trolling reel, although manufacturers had tried in the 1930s. The gear-changing feature gives anglers the benefit of 2:1 ratio for fighting fish near the surface as well as for fast line recovery and 1:1 for turning and lifting and changing direction of deep stubborn fish. Fin Nor now have gear-changing reels to suit light as well as heavy tackle, plus a special model 12/0 with three gear options.

Penn Reels and Shimano also have a range of gear-

Reels in gold and black: (A) Penn, (B) Shimano and (C) Fin-Nor gear-change trolling reels come in a range of sizes to cover most line classes, stranded and wide. Photo: David Rogers.

changing trolling reels. Lever drag reels with large smooth brake areas are available in these three brands plus those of Daiwa, Abu, Mitchell, Everol, Gladiator, Olympic, Hardy and others.

Penn were the first with wide spools to meet the need in some fishing situations for extra line capacity. Anglers also meet the need for increased line length by using a reel a size bigger than that designed by the maker.

The pre-set feature on the lever drag trolling reels gives anglers the chance to set the drag or brake to the desired poundages before starting fishing by pulling against a spring scale either straight from the spool or through the rod. Adjustment by the pre-set allows the necessary brake or strike and full drag positions. The lever brake design allows the angler to return the brake to a previously selected position after being backed off or increased as necessary.

With fly bait casting and spin fishing, practice is necessary to improve casting accuracy and lure presentation as well as line recovery. On trolling reels practice is beneficial for maximum familiarization of pre-set, brake, winding and pumping action. If fishing charter boats have unfamiliar reels, then a familiarization session with the tackle is a top priority.

LURES

The quest for saltwater gamefish on man's artificial creations, on lures instead of natural or live baits, is as old as fishing itself.

The space-age synthetic material development of the last fifty years, plus the knowledge of the where, how and why of successful lure fishing has brought it to its peak of universal acceptance. Today's and tomorrow's world of plastics, of colors, of non-corrosive metals has opened a Pandora's box for those who fish with lures.

Modern adequately stocked tackle stores, as well as specialist stores, offer the angler an apparently bewildering collection of lures, some of which are designed to attract fishermen as well as fish. Fishermen are attracted to lures like iron filings to a magnet. We keep on acquiring lures, making them, buying them, using them. We fishermen hope that maybe, just maybe, here at last is the lure that is the one, the lure that is irresistible to the fish.

Most ingredients for success with lures are exactly the same as for success with natural baits. The where and when of saltwater fishing are first and second in importance, rating with 'how' in research, preparation and experience. Simply fishing with proven lures is not a substitute, or a panacea for lack of preparation and knowledge. Success with lures comes from fishing where the fish should be, knowing which species to seek, how big they should be and when action is most likely.

Lures are fished in all levels of the water column from surface to bottom. Lure fishing can be trolling, casting, jigging, sight fishing in shallow water, or raising fish unseen from the deep. Lures by many names range through those presented on slender fly tackle to the stump pullers on 60-kg (130-lb) class trolling tackle. The tackle range and type meets the size and power of fish of most species and weight. In fact, a bigger spectrum, a wider potential of species and habitat is possible than exists in bait fishing.

Saltwater lure fishing on all tackle gives the additional satisfaction that the great gamefish are responding to manmade rather than natural creations. To this must be added the satisfaction that comes in fishing with lures, which give the fish every chance, not only because of the reduced hook-up rate but by throwing the lure, to beat man once again. The growth and refinements of all tackle have been part of the lure fishing explosion. On fly, bait casting, spinning, jigging and trolling tackle, lures have accompanied the move for anglers to use much of the same types of tackle they are familiar with in their freshwater fishing.

Florida and Hawaii have long been the universities and trendsetters of successful lure fishing. Each is a leader in certain techniques: Florida in light tackle of all kinds, particularly fly, jigging, bait casting and spinning, the basic tackle designed and evolved for freshwater use. The rigors and demands of saltwater fishing have forced the evolution of beefed-up tackle so fishermen have a chance with the fish. These developments give more fishermen the chance to enjoy the challenge of saltwater fishing and the pleasure that comes from skillful use of lures, tackle and line that by their lightness and lack of bulk give action and activity for anglers, even those who suffer disabilities. Satisfaction is derived from finding the fish and getting action not only where the angler or the captain figured the fish would be, but in seeing the fish and getting strike.

Judicious use of chum and natural and artificial teasing is part of modern lure fishing, particularly saltwater fly and bait casting and spinning. The challenge of tuna, billfish and other big saltwater species has brought much of the world together in accepting trolling tackle in boats offshore.

The thrill of tarpon on lures adds to the excitement of the smashing leaps of the silver king after it has struck and hooked up on something artificial. Fly tackle is

LURES

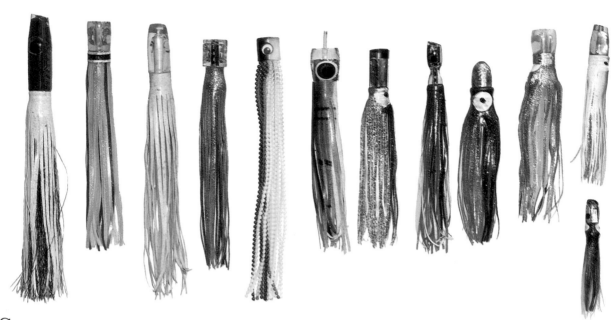

Smaller plastic trolling lures work well on sailfish and tunas as well as marlin. The Sadu Frehm lure on the left uses stranded material with a molded outside skirt in a successful marlin lure. The others by Pakula, Sevenstrand, C & H, Moldcraft, R & S, Marlin Magic, Doornob, Gary Eoff, Top Gun and other makers around the world are ideal for sailfish. Tuna take bullet nose lures rigged with a single hook at times when they are not taking those that dive. Photo: David Rogers.

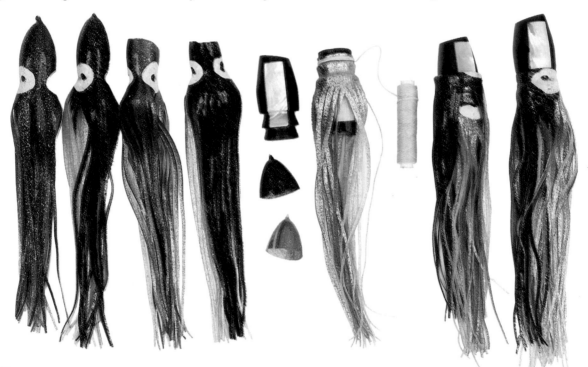

Hard plastic trolling lure heads have either parallel or almost parallel sides to which skirts may be glued or, as in the popular Hawaiian makes, two tapered ridges to which the skirts may be slipped inside out and tied in position. Both types of cast heads allow for skirt replacement after mangling by toothy critters. Photo: David Rogers.

Lures that pop and splash are sometimes effective when quieter lures fail. Spools from Hopkins Drone and other manufacturers are successful at slower speeds. Lures for jigging come in a variety of metal with or without color tails of nylon, bucktail or feather. Photo: David Rogers.

Lures that swim and wiggle come from Finland, USA, Hawaii, England and Australia. The bibless lures such as bottom right can be trolled fast to be successful on many tropical offshore and inshore species. The lures with bibs or soft tails are cast or trolled at slower species. Photo: David Rogers.

particularly suited to the quest for bonefish and the blunt-headed permit, as well as the gill-rattling jumpers—snook in their home waters in the Americas and barramundi in the western and Asiatic Pacific. To these estuary and flats champions can be added barracuda, cobia, threadfin salmon, amberjack, rooster fish, the jacks, trevallies and permit, and the ultimate, the billfish and tunas.

Hawaii is to offshore lure trolling the equivalent of Florida, the Caribbean and Central America in casting lures. The development of lures as a deliberate first choice rather than a poor cousin to baits for the oceanic pelagics has been centered in Hawaii. From these jewels of the ocean, lure trolling has spread into the skilled live bait areas of the world—the Caribbean hot spots of Bimini, Walker's Cay, Puerto Rico, St Thomas and Venezuela. It is popular from California and Baja California and other Mexican areas to Australia, New Zealand, Tahiti and Fiji in the Pacific, and Mauritius in the Indian Ocean. The offshore world is now a world of lures.

The names associated with saltwater lures are often those of the captains who developed and used them.

Zane Grey, a master angler in all waters, was a skilled fly caster; he recognized the value of flashy action and teasing in salt water. He combined some of the benefits of lures in his teasers which were lures without hooks; his hooks were in carefully rigged natural baits. It was interesting and informative and thought-provoking to discuss this with Zane Grey's fishing sons, Dr Loren Grey and Romer Grey, with the realization of the fine line between modern and pioneering anglers, between innovation and traditionalist. Perhaps the availability of modern plastics might have finally ensured Zane Grey's transition from hookless teaser to lures with hooks.

Casting and trolling lures for light gamefish and for use with bait-casting and spinning tackle are metal spoons and minnows that travel below the surface, usually at low speeds or surface poppers and chuggers.

Some spoons, such as Drone 3½, can be trolled fast. Wooden or plastic minnow types and popper lures are very effective for most of the saltwater gamefish. Minnows with bibs and high-speed minnows (without bibs) cover a range of trolling and retrieve speeds.

The bibless high-speed lures can be trolled at up to 20 knots. Both types of minnow are available in a range of sizes.

Although designed as a casting lure, poppers can be trolled. They are particularly successful with jacks and trevallies and queenfish.

Other types of casting and trolling lures are:

- Saltwater flies: although designed for fly casting, these are also successful with small tuna when trolled.

- Lead head jigs: used for deep water jigging, available in a range of weights.

- Candy bars/irons: casting and jigging lures popular in California and Mexico.

- Bonefish jigs: triangular lead head jigs that travel with hook up.

- Feather lures: some now have plastic tails. The old standby as a trolling lure or when used in front of a strip bait or trolled small fish.

- Surgical tube: casting lure made from surgical tube.

- Lead head: worm and swimming tail jigs are also effective casting for some species of light gamefish.

- Weighted plastic squid and fish: replicas, as with feather lures, can be trolled or jigged as a lure or added to a trolled bait.

Both trolling and casting lures come in a big range of colors, so local advice should be sought for best results.

The blue water churns opal and white as the boat hull creates a propeller wash that gradually disappears back into the rest of the ocean. The propeller wash and turbulence are flanked by four or five white lines of bubbles. The boat seems to be just travelling because of its speed of 8 to 10 knots. But this boat is fishing, marlin fishing, not travelling. Those bubble trails stream from flashing lures, lures that attract and trigger action in marlin and tuna.

The locality of this scene, once synonymous primarily with Hawaii, could now be at any of the world's proven marlin fishing grounds. The boat and lures could of course be fishing Hawaii, but could also be off southern Queensland and New South Wales in Australia, off New Zealand, Tahiti, Cabo San Lucas, Mexico, Mauritius or anywhere in the Indian and Pacific Oceans' warm waters. The same scene is repeated day after day at Walker's Cay and Bimini in the Bahamas and on the east coast of the US from Florida to New York, in the Azores and the Ivory Coast of Africa.

The 1980s saw the spread of artificial trolling lures from Hawaii to fishing grounds wherever anglers seek marlin. There have been surprising benefits from the change from natural baits to artificial lures, the 'fantastic plastics'. The world comes to fish the tournaments of the Hawaiian International Billfish Association. Fishermen know that they will learn more about lures and lure fishing and gain knowledge that will help them in their home fishing. The benefits of lure fishing have become evident as anglers and crews change from natural to artificial baits. The benefits show in the number and size of the marlin tagged and released, or verified on the weigh station.

Here are some of the positive results.

- Increase in fishing time, no wasted time in catching and rigging baits. Just run out pre-rigged lures when water temperature and sea bed configuration indicate worthwhile fishing. Prior to this the boat can travel as fast as practical until natural indications say 'fish'. Even at high speed, two or three high-speed bullet-shaped lures can be run to give hook-ups at 20 knots or more.

- Increase in length of season. Results from lure fishing boats have proved that good fishing is available for longer than before, and indicated that the chance to take marlin, particularly striped and big blues, is there on a year-long basis.

- Easier rigging. It has been shown that more people can adequately and competently choose and rig proven lures than could skillfully rig baits. Lures last longer and do not fall to pieces while trolling (although of course lures as well as baits are vulnerable to the cutting choppers of the marine razor gang).

- Lures add variety in speed, color and action. Enjoy the excitement and visual action of marlin following, to strike and strike again.

- Lure fishing gives an immediate chance for repeat action, as the successful lure pattern can be quickly formed again.

- From the beginning, teasers were an integral ingredient in raising marlin to the baits. Lures retain those benefits —they are teasers with hooks. The challenge of teasing a fish into striking, of being part of the hook-up, remains with the alert angler, just as it does in bait fishing.

- There is every probability that a marlin hooked on a lure will be in better condition for release than one that has swallowed natural bait.

- Tag and release can be carried out as effectively on lure-hooked marlin as on those of natural bait hook-ups.

- Lure fishing in many areas produces heavier fish than those taken on bait. Cairns is of course an exception at this stage, but here too more marlin are taken and released on lures each year.

- Finally there is the benefit that the greater speed at which lures are trolled allows more territory to be covered, more potential attractants trolled and presented to more marlin.

Offshore fishermen are fortunate that they have ready opportunity of acquiring and using proven lures made locally or those imported from successful lure makers to give the very best action and color combinations available. Many tackle store staff are knowledgeable and experienced in recommending what is working and suitable for various boats and in rigging.

Theoretically, skilled lure makers could reproduce the same lure to give the same results in endless repetition. Unfortunately this is not the case as, despite every care in the manufacturing process of heads and skirts, there is slight variation in the combination. The changes could come in the curing rate that affects the final shape of the lure, in position of the tube insert, and in thickness and length of the skirts. Then of course, there is possible difference in the rigging of hooks. For all these reasons successful fishermen zealously guard their 'hot' lures— those that attract fish and action.

IGFA Vice President Dudley Lewis long recognized these factors with decades of successful lure fishing in his home waters of Hawaii. Once he found a lure that worked in a particular position on his boat *Leimalia*, that lure was used on the same rod and reel and went back to that proven position day after day.

History shows that this paid off as that one lure was successful each day on the same rod and old Penn Senator reel to win the prestigious Hawaiian International Billfish Tournament for his team. That lure, a Joe Yee salt and pepper (ground shell on black) straight runner, took all their tournament fish. The lure was lost eventually to a monster marlin and, despite trying other lure heads that appeared identical in every way, Dudley did not find another that was as dependable and hot.

Many fishermen have recorded similar experiences. They go through the sickening trauma of their special lure being lost through a mistake, carelessness, or just to fish that were too big or broke away for some reason.

Some fishermen run a variety of colors and head shapes every day. They fish darker-colored lures on dark cloudy days and lighter colors on bright, sunny days. Some change their colors in changing light or, if not getting action, hoping for a jackpot. Others stick to their proven positions and colors.

Brookes Morris, the fighter pilot who became a thinking fisherman and lure maker with his radical-shaped Doornob lures, fished both the KHBT and the HIBT in 1987. His team were defending HIBT champions from 1986 and they realized that it was all or nothing on the last day if they were to retain their HIBT crown. Fishing from big fish captain Freddy Rice's *Ihu Nui*, they gambled on the color combination that had produced most fish for them in these tournaments. To win or place they needed several average marlin on those lures or one really big lunker that with the bonus points for heaviest of the day, heaviest of the tournament, plus bonus points for a 24-kg test (50-lb), would top the 742-pounder (337 kg) already landed by the great Hawaiian lure maker, Joe Yee on 24-kg (50-lb) tackle.

It all happened for the team on *Ihu Nui* when a giant blue grabbed one of those five identical lures and took off into the air like a loaded jet airliner. This marlin was big enough, but perhaps too big for the 24-kg (50-lb) tackle. Angler Gil Kraemer, skipper, crew and team worked in copybook fashion for the capture. The spontaneous applause from the spectators at the weigh station told the story that here was a really big fish. It weighed in at 481.94 kg (1062.5 lb), the heaviest of the tournament, and scored not only the necessary tournament points but a still-standing world record— who says the great ocean marauders do not eat plastic? Here again was a marlin that for whatever reason found the color, the action, the sound, the vibration, the fizzing bubbles irresistible.

Bubbles, the smoke trail, are one of the features of lure action that fishermen look for. Many choose lures that pop the surface about every thirty seconds, that run fairly straight and produce the smoke trail. Many shapes and color combinations regularly produce. Some heads are scooped (to create dart and dive), some are angled (straight runners), some are straight cut (pushers), some have jet holes, some have bullet noses, some are weighted, some are unweighted. Success comes from using well-rigged lures and running them in a pattern to suit that boat. Eyes in the lure head or on the skirt are regarded as worthwhile. Some riggers even skirt their lures with skirts that have eyes, even though the lure head already has eyes on the insert or the insert is all eyes.

It is interesting that generally in the Atlantic the lure riggers and successful lure fishermen use the heavier, stiffer-type skirts similar to those made by Moldcraft and Newell, whereas in the Pacific and Indian Ocean fisheries the softer Sevenstrand and Japanese Yamashita and Yozuri skirts are most popular. There is of course much mixing of preference for lure skirts, and some mix both types and upholstery materials. The length of the skirt once on the lure also varies with personal preference and the action sought. Tangling of the skirt on the barb of the second hook can be avoided by cutting the tails so that they clear the point of the second hook.

Australians are fortunate to have several proven and skilled lure makers scattered around the coast to provide top fish takers. Pakula, Top Gun and Pacific brands as well as many copyists of these successful local and overseas designs, give plenty of choice.

Even though to be successful lures must first attract the fishermen to gain water time, the Australian-made lures as well as the Joe Yee, Guzman, Sadu, Black Bart, C&H, R&S, Schneider, Moldcraft, Lock Nut, Gary Eoff, Marlin Magic, Doornob, Sevenstrand and Braid give an almost bewildering selection of quality products from which the fisherman can choose.

Successful color combination can vary, depending on light conditions and sea conditions, the boat wave pattern and position of the windows (the smooth unbroken surface in the boat wave pattern and propeller suds). So it may not be productive to run a white or basically light-colored lure where the propeller surface wash is dominant, while a dark lure may be effective.

Color combinations are in some ways like the fashion business, with changes each season. Some of the established fish-taking combinations resemble basic fish colors, green over yellow (dolphinfish), blue over white, light blue over pink, blue or lime green over silver (many bait fish), brown over blue or pink fleck (squid). There are, however, productive skirt colors that do not seem to relate to nature: black over green, purple, orange, red or pink, red over yellow, blue-silver over green-gold, or yellow-orange and green in combination. Silver or gold fleck seems to improve attraction, certainly for the fisherman, as do skirts that are darker on one half than the other. Head colors range all the way from black to pearl white and colors in between. Black seems logically to be successful with other dark colors in heads and skirts, as they are readily silhouetted against the light. Light colors, particularly blue and green with reflective inserts, add flash and excitement, the panic action of bait fish. Despite the results with natural look-alike lures, many believe lures work in both hard plastic and soft heads because they attract the fish who attack something 'strange'. Whatever the reason for their working successfully, the tournament competition results and record books tell the story of lures. The age of plastic is here and now.

GENERAL POINTS IN THE HOOK-UP FOR LURE FISHING

Action of Fish	Action of Fisherman	Action of Fish	Action of Fisherman
• Attracted to boat and lures.	• Reel alarm click ratchet is 'on'. • Strike drags are set as hard as possible within line breaking strain around ¼ of the line class to ⅓ on heavy tackle.	• Runs away because of hooking, line drag and forward way of boat.	• Once a big fish is hooked, all other outfits must be brought in; if a small fish is hooked, the other lures may be worked to try to hook others from the school, so rod can be taken to chair gimbal.
• May look at and just follow lures. • May strike at lure.	• The fish may be teased into striking. • Boat can be sped up or lures jigged to increase attraction and help set hooks.	• Jumps, runs away hard or sounds.	• Drag can be eased a little. Boat can be backed up or, when the fish slows down, it can be chased or run to recover line.
• Pulls stretch/spring resistance out of line and rod and hooks up against drag of reel.	• Angler should be careful to avoid overruns or excess drag.		

RODS

Bait casting tackle and spinning tackle can be used for trolling but most effective trolling is carried out on tackle purpose built for trolling lures and baits from a boat. This tackle is equally effective on trolling live or dead baits, or when used on the drift or at anchor.

Trolling tackle comes in all tackle classes with roller guides used from 4-kg (8-lb) class up to 60-kg (130-lb) class. Some anglers prefer the short rods with short tips around 122 cm (48 in), while others prefer standard length rods with rod tips around 165 cm (65 in).

Butts also come in a range of lengths, both straight and curved. A few heavy-tackle rods with long tips to clear wide transom corners, have been built with straight butts, the length of which can be varied to suit angler or chair gimbal; the angle of the rod tip can be adjusted with a locked curve above the reel. With this rod a handle is fixed to the reel to assist balance and lift.

Under IGFA rules the rod tip must be a *minimum* of 101.6 cm (40 in) and the butt cannot exceed a *maximum* 68.58 cm (27 in). These measurements are both taken from a point directly below the centre of the reel. These limitations do not apply to surf rods. The minimum tip length covers all rods, not just trolling rods. Short trolling rods have been around for many years with advantages as well as disadvantages. Some believe they are of benefit basically for lighter lines up to and including the 15-kg (30-lb) category. Others believe they are of benefit from 15 kg and heavier, i.e., 15 kg, 24 kg and 37 kg. The short stand-up rods are used with straight or curved

butts. Short stand-up rods around 185 cm (5 ft 2 in) overall with tip length close to the minimum allowed under IGFA rules (101.6 cm (40 in)) with a butt length sometimes close to the maximum allowed 68.58 cm (27 in), are popular in some fisheries.

Lift and power are important design characteristics of trolling rods, while the features of rods used for casting as well as fighting are not needed. Trolling rods walk the fine line between the need for lift and power (using 25 per cent to 33.3 per cent of line class during the fight, more if the double is to be of benefit) and the need for flexibility in the tip section to act as a spring shock absorber.

The tips of some of the custom-built modern 24-kg (50-lb), 37-kg (80-lb), and 60-kg (130-lb) line class rods are deliberately made longer to assist in clearing the transom and side coverboards on the bigger boats.

Trolling rods are the most specialized of all rods, as they are there primarily to do one job—catch the fish. Good anglers take advantage of the design characteristics by varying their pumping action, depending on circumstances, during the fight. The value of short pumping, of recovering even a few centimetres at a time, of attacking the fish, of keeping line tight at every opportunity, is now widely understood and practised. Modern trolling rod blanks are now available in a variety of exotic materials—graphite, boron, kevlar, S-glass as well as other types of fiberglass. Most are built on hollow blanks but some economical and adequate rods are built on solid glass.

RIGS AND RIGGING

The big fish, the fish the angler had been seeking, praying for, was close to the boat. The leader was almost in reach, the great head again cleared the surface, throwing water and spray. This fish was easily a potential record, a 'dream fish'. Now the fish was leading, heading tiredly towards the slowly moving boat. The leader man nervously tugged at his shorts, the gaff men were ready, tense. They knew what they had to do to complete the catch. From his bridge, the skipper watched, ready to keep the fish clear of propellers and rudders, working to keep that tired fish coming to the boat, helping his angler.

The leader man reached for the wire, took his first wraps, then suddenly cursed: 'She's gone'. The gaff men replaced their unnecessary gaffs. The leader was pulled in board so all could see what happened; strangely, its

full length of leader seemed to be there. All on board were quiet as the last length was pulled aboard. All the wire was there, only the hook was gone, gone with that huge fish. Inspection of that leader end mutely told the story. It had been rigged without enough twists in the haywire and had pulled free. A record lost irretrievably for the sake of just a few minutes at most in rigging—a few more necessary wraps to ensure the leader could not unroll.

There have been similar happenings with sleeves and knots that have caused problems that resulted in lost fish: fish that would have been records, the culmination of anglers' dreams.

Careful rigging is one of the keys that open the door to success in fishing. It is no coincidence that those who

Great Barrier Reef trolling baits for black marlin. Those with a hook out of the throat are rigged to swim. Photo: Peter Goadby.

know and understand and are skilled in how to rig, whether for fishing with baits or lures, consistently bring in the fish and the tag and release cards. It is satisfying for everybody on board to know that everything possible that could be done to bring about a successful conclusion had been done.

It is easy to make mistakes in this most critical section of every day's fishing. Crimps, sleeves and knots that have not been completed properly can and will slip on the fish that matters.

Ties in wire that are loose or have been done short with insufficient twists will let go on big fish with hard pulls. It is much better to use more twists than the believed maximum, to rig again properly, than to take a chance.

Conscientious crews will discard single-strand wires, whether of stainless or pre-straightened galvanised-type wires, once the bait is chopped, swum out or no longer usable, or has taken a fish, even a small fish. They know it is safer to replace the leader than to have it break through a kink or flexing crystallization just when it matters. They have learned from bitter experience that discarding used wire will help ensure the capture of the fish, the big ones they seek. They also take great care to ensure that with swimming baits and those where the hook eye and leader loop are not visible, the leader wire has actually passed through the eye of the hook, not just alongside it. One of the most embarrassing and frustrating moments in fishing comes when that carefully rigged bait is taken by a big fish or any fish, then the line becomes tight, but there is no hook, no action, and inspection reveals a perfect complete loop. This disappointment has happened with many top bait riggers; after that they check carefully that the hook eye and leader loop are safely connected.

Riggers need to think and decide just what is needed for each type of leader material—to over-rig to be on the side of safety and elimination of error, rather than taking a chance. Many top crews on heavy gauge .035, .040, .045 single-strand wire, will use as many as twenty to twenty-two haywire twists before the barrel wraps. They know from bitter experience that fewer wraps may hold, but this number will hold on heavy wire, even though fifteen wraps may be sufficient on medium-weight wire and eight to ten on light-gauge wire. Crews who choose monofilaments for their leader quickly learn the need, whether using one or two sleeves, to crimp them evenly and tight. They learn not to crimp the outer edges into the mono, and to turn the leader back through the sleeve and to burn the end of the mono to create a blob that will minimize chance of slip. It is beneficial to crimp with press or pliers that suit the sleeves used. Sevenstrand, Hi Seas, Nico Press and Jinkai crimpers give dependable results with the sleeves made for them.

Care must always be exercised with knots.

Speed in replacing baits or lures is part of the success pattern of top crews. They coil each leader the same way, coiled from hook end to loop for attachment to snap. Leaders should be coiled right to left, the coils should be even—about 30 cm (12 in) in circumference. The leader loop end should be left free about 45 cm to 60 cm (18–24 in) and then looped three times around the coils. This coiling is used by most professional crews as well as on angler-crewed boats for speed and uniformity. Use of the plastic-covered wire twists manufactured for garden or kitchen bag use provide a satisfactory holding material, even for leaders pre-rigged with bait or lure.

It is important to use leader materials matched to the maximum size fish expected. Heavier-than-necessary

RIGGING MATERIALS

Braided line pulled tight with bound ends

Monofilament line slipped inside opened braided line

Opened braided line

Braided line

Tapered monofilament

The top shot: it is possible to join monofilament to braided line by opening out the end of the braided line and tapering and roughing up the monofilament. The braided line overlaps the monofilament by the longest possible margin (30 cm, 12 inches or more) as it pulls tight over the mono. The ends are bound with dental tape or waxed nylon to further strengthen the join. Super Glue (60 second) or rubber glue can further minimize the chance of slip at each end.

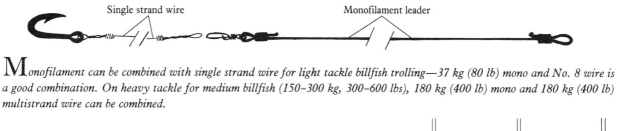

Single strand wire   Monofilament leader

Monofilament can be combined with single strand wire for light tackle billfish trolling—37 kg (80 lb) mono and No. 8 wire is a good combination. On heavy tackle for medium billfish (150–300 kg, 300–600 lbs), 180 kg (400 lb) mono and 180 kg (400 lb) multistrand wire can be combined.

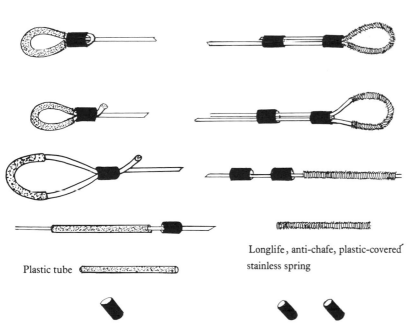

Plastic tube

Longlife, anti-chafe, plastic-covered stainless spring

Using one sleeve on each end

Using two sleeves on each end

Single or double sleeve leader eyes: on monofilament leader, slip can be prevented by burning the end of the monofilament leader or by using a bigger size sleeve so the leader can be passed back. Wear on monofilament leaders can be minimized by a sleeve of plastic or a section of longline, abrasion-resistant plastic covered stainless wire spring. Always crimp tightly and evenly.

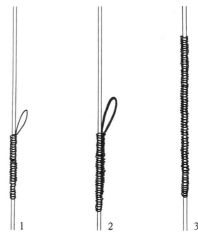

1   2   3

For rigging:
1. Dental tape, dental floss and other waxed threads can be looped or bound in tightly around the fishing line with half hitches to give loop for outrigger slip with pin or clothes peg type.
2. Heavy dacron or monofilament can be bound on and locked onto fishing line so it does not rub on outrigger clip.
3. The main fishing line can be whipped with waxed thread for protection when trolling.

In these baits the wire is twisted up tight when lead is added to the rig whilst the loop is loose to allow the bait to turn inside the loop when no lead is used. Photo: Peter Goadby.

leader adds a safety factor but has the real disadvantage of restricting the desired action of baits and lures and adding to the problem of visibility.

The choice of hooks is important. Baits and lures for trolling should be rigged with straight, i.e., not offset or kirbed, hooks. Trolling offset, kirbed hooks increases the probability of bait or lure spinning. Apart from the problems created for line and leader by twisting, this action is not wanted on the baits and lures, as it is not generally attractive or strike-inducing to fish.

Hooks used for bait trolling are not kirbed or offset. Hooks used for live, dead and cut bait, fishing at anchor or on the drift are kirbed or offset. Short shank are popular live bait hooks. These have point and shank in line. Some anglers choose hooks that are kirbed or bend the hook to give this effect. Long-line and Polynesian-style full circle hooks are also popular with live bait. Hooks are available in a variety of finishes. Mustad are usually cadmium-plated, while VMC have another non-corrosive finish. Mustad also make a range of stainless steel hooks.

Most lures are rigged with treble hooks from Mustad, VMC or Eagle Claw. Bronze-finish hooks rust quickly in saltwater use, whereas stainless last indefinitely.

The use of non-corrosive stainless hooks raises a question in the minds of some fishermen and conservation organizations who feel hooks that will corrode away after release or break away have benefits.

To be effective, hooks must be made sharp and kept sharp: the sharper the better. Some prefer the hook points to be round needles, as made by VMC, others prefer triangulation and others four edges from the point. Some conservationally-minded anglers depress or remove the barbs on their hooks, as they intend not only to give the fish more than an even chance in the fight, but to release most of their fish.

The choice of leader material is also important. If sharks are the intended or probable antagonists, use of wire leaders of various types is imperative.

All types of leader have benefits and disadvantages. The weight and diameter of the leader is governed by the benefits and need for minimum visibility, strength, abrasion resistance, flexibility and resistance to crystallization fracture. Australian shark fishermen in some areas are convinced of the benefits of plastic-covered wire, even though the necessary wire strength, plus the plastic coating, makes for a thick leader. These heavy-looking leaders would logically seem to be highly visible. Experience has shown that even the blue, clear or green plastic over the multi-strand wire increases diameter but improves fish taking.

Bait and hooks rigged on the plastic-covered wire have a higher strike rate than on smaller diameter uncoated wires. The teeth and abrasive dermal denticles of shark skin often shred the plastic cover from the wire to force either discarding the leader or shortening to remove damage. Use of this big-diameter wire on light tackle for sharks looks incongruous, but its practicality and strike rate are undoubted. Plastic-covered wires can be pulled and wrapped by the leader man in the same way as other leader, despite its bulk and tendency to slightly adhere to gloves. One disadvantage of coated wire is that the wires, whether stainless or galvanized, can corrode under the plastic coating once subjected to salt water.

Leaders to be used for drifting or at anchor are usually rigged with a single hook. Two hooks were popular for shark fishing until fishermen realized that two-hook usage increases the possibility of hooks being broken or straightened when one or both are hooked externally on the body and subjected to the wriggling, powerful, body-twisting, swimming action of the shark. A two-hook rig is rated by many to be of benefit in lure fishing for bill-fish, and in trolling natural bait and lures where wahoo and other giant toothy mackerels are active in the razor gang and in some natural baits intended for mackerels, barracuda and cobia and other light gamefish species.

Trolling lures specifically intended for tuna are generally rigged with one hook. Leaders to be used for natural baits are rigged to be free-swinging. Free-swinging hooks minimize metal fatigue and chance of crystallization fractures.

Some lure fishermen believe there is benefit for their billfish lures in rigging so the hooks are rigid or as stiff as possible to maximize the odds on hook-ups.

Rigging for trolling lure fishing has created added awareness of the benefits and problems associated with hooks and leaders overall. The knowledge can be applied to other fishing techniques. Lure fishing is the fastest-growing recreational fishing style right around the world, so it is beneficial to review lure trolling in great detail.

Most offshore lure fishermen rig for billfish with two hooks, usually of the same size and type, although some do mix designs and sizes. Lures directed at tuna are usually rigged with one hook. Hook types are usually Mustad 7731, 7691, 7754 or similar designs in VMC. Some riggers choose similar Mustad shapes in stainless nos 7732 and 76915. When rigging with two hooks, care must be taken to make sure that the minimum length between the eyes of the hooks is the shank's length of the longer of the two hooks. Some part of both hooks must be within the lure skirt; the eyes of the hooks must be not more than 30 cm (12 in) apart.

Rigging with a minnow-type lure that can be trolled or cast forces a choice and decision in leader materials: Tarpon, snook, barramundi, threadfin, jacks and trevallies and many other brackish-water species are fished for with monofilament nylon leader to give minimum visibility and maximum action and natural flexibility for the lure action.

Supple 49-strand wire is the best compromise for trolling action lures such as minnow-type, high-speed bibless and spoons. This wire is made in various breaking strains from 60 kg (135 lb) to 370 kg (800 lb). The lighter breaking strains are ideal for high-speed action trolling. Single-strand wires in either stainless or galvanized wires of seven strands and plastic-covered wires of seven or other low number of strands, are less supple than 49 wires. The penalty fishermen pay for the advantage of suppleness on the 49-strand wire is that each wire strand is very fine and thus easily cut, and so weakens the wire overall.

Single-strand wire also has inherent problems, particularly crystallization associated with flexing. Each leader material has its benefits and its disadvantages. It is up to the lure or bait rigger to know and understand the characteristics and benefits of each material.

The following basics cover rigging for successful offshore trolling for marlin.

Leaders: Monofilament leaders are used, except where and when toothy critturs regularly cause problems. Supple stainless wire leader made from 49-strand wire is then used instead of monofilament to minimize or prevent cutoffs. To prevent monofilament leader wear at snaps and hooks, plastic tube or coiled plastic-coated stainless steel coils are used. Riggers often prefer to use

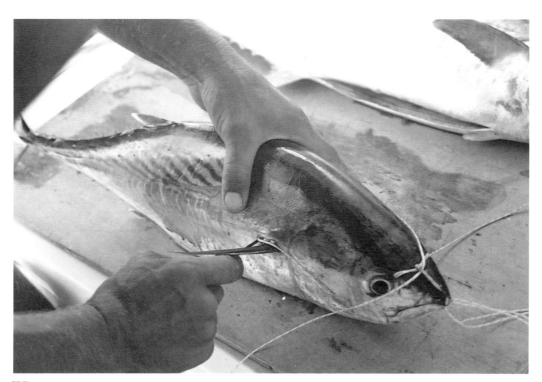

*K*awa kawa and other heavy baits are rigged to ensure the bait holds together. *Photo: Peter Goadby.*

plastic tube to minimize bubbles at the snap and the plastic stainless coil at the hooks. One or two sleeves can be crimped to form the loops at each extremity of the leader. For extra non-slip security, the end of the leader before crimping can be heated to create a bulb with match or light flame (keeping the flame and melted mono well clear of the other leader material). When this bulb or knob cools, the leader is pulled against the sleeve or top sleeve and the sleeves crimped tightly and evenly.

Experienced riggers, because of stretch and elasticity, keep well within the maximum allowable lengths of leader and double and the combined length. These are:

Line class up to and including 10 kg	Leader maximum—4.57 m (15 ft) Double maximum—4.57 m (15 ft) Combined leader and double—6.1 m (20 ft)
Line class 15 kg and above ...	Leader maximum—9.14 m (30 ft) Double maximum—9.14 m (30 ft) Combined leader and double—12.19 m (40 ft)
Barramundi and salmon when caught in salt water are still included in the freshwater categories. The maximum length of leader and double line for freshwater species is:	Leader maximum—1.82 m (6 ft) Double maximum—1.82 m (6 ft) Combined leader and double—3.04 m (10 ft)

Fly fishing class tippet must be at least 38.1 cm (15 in) long measured inside the connecting knots. With knotless leaders the last 38.1 cm (15 in) will be the class tippet.

A big fish and an active fight apply forces to the leader and double that not only cause stretch, but can change the shape of loops in mono and wire so as to affect compliance with the rules and tackle regulations when submitted after a capture. Rig well inside the limit.

Choice of leader materials: Monofilament of a hard type in 100-kg (220-lb) to 275-kg (600-lb) test is ideal for the main length of trolling leader. The heavier leader material is chosen where big marlin are expected.

Wire, that is, 49-strand or two or more twisted strands of heavy single-strand wire (around .040), or other cable wire, is used for the leader linking first and second hooks. Wire from coat hangers is sometimes used by those who strive for extreme rigidity in their two-hook rigging. Some two-hook rigs use monofilament nylon, but most use a wire of some type on the second hook for protection from abrasion and cutting. To give the desired action and 'smoke' trail, it is important that the lure swims on a supple leader. Two-piece leaders are sometimes used. These are 1–1.5 m (3–5 ft) of 49-strand wire used at the lure, and this is joined by a snap to a longer trace of monofilament or nylon-covered wire to bring it to the desired overall length allowed by the rules. The coastlock or Hawaiian corkscrew type and the McMahon snaps are all satisfactory for this purpose. Two-part leaders also give the benefit of the lure not sliding right up near the monofilament line.

*A*tlantic herring rigged for a tuna daisy chain in Nova Scotia. Photo: Nova Scotia News and Information.

ADVANTAGES

Single strand stainless steel
- Thin diameter
- Moderately high strength for diameter
- Low visibility, particularly in brown color
- Minimum trolling bubbles
- Maximum resistance to tooth-cutting gamefish and sharks

DISADVANTAGES

- Stiffness
- Breakage and lowering of breaking strain by flexing and vibration of active lures
- Electrolysis
- Wire will coil after strike

Single strand galvanized carbon steel
- Thin diameter
- High strength for diameter
- Initial medium visibility then loses shine
- Minimum trolling bubbles
- High resistance to tooth cutting from gamefish and sharks

- Lowering of breaking strain if kinked
- Rust
- Breakage and lowering of breaking strain by flexing and vibration on active lures
- Wire will coil after strike

Single strand rigged by Haywire twist, sometimes with Flemish Eye
- Low breaking strain if kinked

Low number of multiple strand galvanized wires
- Medium diameter
- Visibility reduces as wires oxidize
- High strength for diameter
- Medium visibility until oxidized
- High resistance to tooth cutting from gamefish and sharks
- Less subject to kinking
- Rigged by crimping sleeves

- Stiff for breaking strain
- Breakage and lowering of breaking strain from flexing and vibration
- More bubbles and interference than single strand wires
- Rust

High number of multiple strand stainless e.g., 49 strand
- Medium diameter
- Medium strength for diameter
- Medium visibility in brown color
- Medium resistance to tooth cutting and fish rolling
- Resistance to kinking
- Suppleness and flexibility allow maximum lure performance
- Rigged by crimping sleeve

- Breakage and lowering of breaking strain from flexing and vibration
- Can be cut and broken by big sharks rolling
- More bubbles and interference than single strand wires
- Electrolysis

ADVANTAGES

Multiple-strand medium-diameter galvanized carbon steel
- Medium visibility once strands oxidize
- Resistant to kinking
- Highly resistant to tooth cutting and body rolling
- Rigged by crimping sleeves or wire and solder

DISADVANTAGES

- Those with fibre centre more liable to corrosion from inside than those with wire core
- Not supple or flexible, liable to crystallization from flexing and vibration
- Rust

Plastic-covered wires in stainless or galvanized
- Apparently medium visibility even in big diameters
- Resistant to kinking
- Medium breaking strain
- Reflects diameter and type of wire insert
- Minimum electrolysis or electrical field for reception by sharks' ampullae of Lorenzini

- Will corrode or rust under plastic covering, so should be discarded if discoloration is present
- Large diameter makes slightly more difficult to pull leader, but wraps can be taken
- Plastic coating makes a more slippery surface when recovering leader

Monofilament nylon or similar material
- Maximum flexibility
- Minimum visibility
- Resistant to kinking
- No electrolysis or rusting
- Rigged by crimping sleeves

- Bigger diameter than wires of equivalent breaking strain
- Can be easily cut and abraded by teeth or rough skin or by touching or rubbing on boat
- Stretches under weight of fish and recovering leader

A *fixed loop from the hook eye to where the hook shank is tied to the head of the tanguigue prevents slippage while trolling and at the strike. The thread harness through head and shoulder keeps bait intact when attacked by a marlin. Photo: Peter Goadby.*

Hooks: Cadmium-plated and stainless-steel hook types are successful and practical. They should be made very sharp and checked often and resharpened, if blunted or bent by a strike or after coming into contact with hard hull or deck. Hook points should not be sharpened to the stage that they are too thin and thus subject to bending or breaking. Most riggers in their sharpening leave plenty of metal for strength, even though the point down to the barb is in fact very sharp in a round, triangular or even four-sided configuration. If hooks are sharpened by filing, most use the file so it is stroked from barb to point, not from point to barb. Final smooth honing can be obtained by use of sharpening or oil stones of various types. Razor-sharp hooks are a key factor in hook-ups and fish at boat. Hooks must be sharpened and checked for sharpness each time they are brought in, particularly after a strike.

Care of lures: Care must be exercised when bringing lures inboard or readying them for trolling. It must be remembered that the polyester plastic used in konaheads and indeed the finish on most lures can be easily damaged and chipped by careless handling against the boat or cockpit. Once inboard, the leader should be coiled and the lure placed where it is safe from going overboard and available when needed. Do not leave lures and hooks on the cockpit deck. Rusting of hooks occurs after the cadmium plating or galvanizing has worn away as a result of electrolytic action between the aluminum or brass sleeves, stainless wire, hook plating and metal of hook or hooks.

Use of trolling or other beads is helpful in ensuring that the hooks are pulled evenly against the rear of the lure head. Several beads can be used to regulate the positioning of a single hook in the skirt, or in high-speed lures to give body.

Swivels: Most correctly balanced and rigged lures do not spin. Despite this, it is beneficial to use top-quality, ball-bearing Sampo snap swivels with snaps of Coastlock, McMahon or Hawaiian corkscrew types. If ball bearing swivels are not used, a top-quality crane swivel and snap is often satisfactory. Swivels must always be of dependable quality.

Some fishermen minimize the number of hook rigs needed for their lure stocks by using a stainless thimble at the lure end of the leaders, in combination with a small shackle. Hooks can be thus easily transferred from one leader and lure rig to another by undoing the shackle and attaching it to another leader-rigged lure.

Bill marks and unavoidable rubbing, chafing and wear or possible leader nicks and cuts on monofilament leader or expected crystallizing of wire by action at the lure head dictate the necessity for regular leader inspection, particularly where it goes through the lure tube. If mono leader is used, wear can be minimized by use of plastic tube over the leader and down into the lure head. Some fishermen prevent their lure sliding up the leader by using a crimped sleeve or wedging a match, toothpick or skewer in the tube or by binding the leader above the tube with dental tape. Many believe that a lure that has slipped up to the swivel gives the increased possibility of a chopoff from wahoo or other fish when it is travelling at high speed through the water behind a hooked fish. Others prefer to take this chance and feel that if the lure is free to slide up the leader, it helps keep the hooks in an active fish. Lures that do not slide up the leader slightly increase the difficulty of lure recovery in tagging and release.

Experimenting: Because of the variations on boats, in lures and sea conditions, it sometimes takes time to put together the right combination for a particular boat to fine tune for best results. Experimenting continues to take place once knowledge is gained and new lures are tried or old lures lost. The keeping of a log is most helpful for this, as for many other reasons.

Most success falls to skippers, crews and anglers who maintain concentration and a constant watch on lures and what is happening in and on the sea. The factors that aid success in bait fishing are equally important with lures.

To avoid tangling when putting lures out or bringing them in, follow this suggested procedure. When putting them out, the outside and far back lures are placed in position first, then the short or inside lures. When bringing them in, reverse this procedure. Bring in the inside and short-positioned lures first. The one rule in lure fishing technique, as in all fishing, is that there isn't just *one* way or the *only* way. There may be a best way or personal preference, but there are lots of different ways, and even more opinions and interesting alternatives. You pay your money and you make your choice and take your chances.

Here is a small sample of frequently heard opinions:

Skirts
- Stiff skirts
- Soft flexible skirts
- The old red rubber sheet and upholstery material combination (particularly with silver)
- A mixture of soft and stiff materials
- Skirt ends cut evenly
- Skirt ends tapered
- Glued skirts (to lure head)
- Tied skirts (to lure head)

Tag lines
- Great—they minimize drop back and improve hook-up from rod tip
- Never use them, prefer to use roller releases

Hooks
- Use only galvanized or cadmium-plated steel, never stainless
- Only stainless

Hook position in trolling
- Both in line
- At 180 degrees to one another
- At 90 degrees to one another
- At 60 degrees to one another
- At any angle
- Place them so hook points out towards boat wake
- Place them so hook points in from boat wake

Hook or hooks
- Use two hooks
- Use one hook

Second hook rigging
- Mono
- Flexible wire
- Very stiff wire
- Hooks free-swinging
- Hook made rigid as possible by binding with dental tape, plastic insulating tape or rubber band, or with sliding surgical rubber tube or shrink tube

First hook position
- As close to flush at rear of lure
- Lure recessed so hook is partly inside head

Second hook position
- As close to first hook as rules allow
- As far from first hook as rules allow

*P*lastic skirts and a small lure are added to some small natural fish baits to aid attraction, change the action, and prolong the trolling life of the bait. Photo: Peter Goadby.

Molded squid type skirts come in a wide range of colors and sizes from Yamashita, Sevenstrand and Yozuri. The heavier sheet type molded skirts from Newell, Moldcraft come in a triangular and beaded finish. This material is tough and slightly stiffer than the molded squid types. The squid type skirts should be cut so they are shorter than the eye of the second hook to avoid chance of tangling. Photo: David Rogers.

Hook size
- As big as lure will carry and work
- As small as pull from line class dictates

Hook points
- Round
- Triangular
- Rectangular, with top and cutting edge

Hook colors
- Shiny silver
- Black tape or paint
- Red
- Yellow
- Orange with tape or paint
- Green

Hook shapes
- 7731 type point out, hopefully for more hook-ups (perhaps easier for fish to throw)
- 7690 type point turn in (so hook harder to throw, but perhaps fewer hook-ups)

Lure eyes
- In or on lure head only towards rear
- In or on lure head towards front (particularly with fish shape inserts)
- In head and on skirt
- Only in head
- Only on skirt

Angle of lure head
- Scooped and angled
- Bullet
- At 90 degrees hollow on pusher
- Cut at other angles such as 150 degrees
- Sharp edges on cut
- Rounded edges on cut

Body taper on lure
- Even
- Even to a ridge then a slight reduction in diameter
- Even to a ridge then parallel
- Bubble bulge in centre or rear third of head
- Barrel-shaped tapering from front to rear

Tube in lure
- Brass
- Aluminum
- Teflon
- No tube
- Positioned in centre
- Positioned in top or bottom third

Lure head colors
- Clear
- Light blue
- Light green
- Purple
- Dark blue
- Red
- Yellow
- Color stripes top or bottom
- Swirl mixture of colors
- Colored mother-of-pearl effect

Lure material
- Hard, to give clarity and flash
- Soft, to encourage return strikes

Inserts
- To look like fish or squid
- Rectangular reflective
- Thick reflective or color
- Thin reflective or color

Action
- To smoke without breaking surface more often than every 60 seconds
- To dive and wriggle before resurfacing
- To stay on top and splash
- To revolve around an axis
- To pop about every sixty seconds or more often—then dive
- To run straight

Weight
- Weighted inside lure with around 75–100 grams
- No weight

Lures and bait
- Run lures when trolling live or dead baits
- Lures only with lures; bait only with bait

Acceptance
- Some swear by their lures
- Others swear at and about the thought of them

Trolling speed
- 7–10 knots—most shapes include soft fish replicas and squid
- 4–7 knots—knuckleheads and minnow types
- 12–20 knots—high-speed metal head and jet lures

Bird teaser and other flashing teaser
- Some like to use them
- Others prefer interest and action to be only on the lures with hooks in them

Changing lures if no action
- Change often as light changes—a new one might work to bring a strike
- Don't change once successful pattern and colors are established

TEASERS

The use of teasers in successful billfishing goes back to the start of fishing for marlin. The world's first rod and reel marlin, a striped of 92 kg (203 lb) was taken by E. Llewellyn of Santa Catalina in 1903.

The pioneering Catalina method was to troll flying fish rigged without hooks until the marlin were sighted and following, then to replace the hookless flyers with those complete with hooks. Some of these southern Californian boats trolled their teasers from poles. These no doubt gave Atlantic captain Tommy Gifford the idea for the outriggers he built and developed on his return to Florida after a season skippering in southern California.

After using Tarporenos for king mackerel, barracuda, cobia and amberjack in the Florida Keys, Zane Grey realized that the darting, diving action and flashing colors were attractive to billfish as well as to toothy reef dwellers. The big wooden or hollow metal teasers he used in his exploratory fishing were oversized Tarporenos trolled

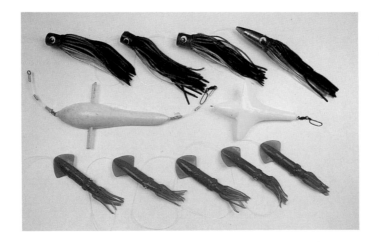

Birds (yellow) of various shapes work as teasers when trolled ahead of a lure. Molded plastic squid (red) can be rigged as a teaser in a daisy chain or coat hanger spreader rig. Captain Skip Smith of Hooker combined Moldcraft pusher lures (black) with a final lure in a bullet shape for a most successful combination. Photo: David Rogers.

without hooks in conjunction with rigged natural baits. Zane Grey and anglers of that period experienced the thrill and satisfaction of seeing billfish raised by the teasers and transferred the killing strikes from unnatural hookless teaser to hooked natural bait.

Coincidentally the scooped head and towing angle of the Tarporeno and the teaser was adapted with the addition of feathers and other early skirt materials to the first trolling plugs that became konaheads in Hawaii. These early trolling lures, with heads of brightly painted wood scooped or angled, were developed with heads made from chromed towel rail with wooden inserts. The skirts were feather, rubber sheeting in red and black and other simple available materials. Later plastic upholstery material and silver-coated plastic and clear plastic cast heads opened up a whole new world of teasers—teasers with hooks, ready for a hook-up.

The use of outriggers and the benefit of combining outriggers and flat lines with natural baits led to a reduction in interest in teasers although daisy chains, a combination teaser and hooked bait, remain an important and integral rig for giant bluefin in the Atlantic. The development of soft rubber and then plastic fish and squid replicas opened up a resurgence in teasers. The skilled fishermen in Florida trolled these replica combination teasers in conjunction with natural baits or lures. Later developments combined soft head pusher and straight cut heads in combination as teaser or daisy chain, with hooked lure behind the hookless teaser rigged on the leader or on a coathanger rig.

The teasers were beneficial, particularly on sailfish and white marlin in the Atlantic and Caribbean.

The teaser rebirth with soft plastic squid and fish replicas and soft and hard plastic-headed lures, sometimes with final hooked lure, has again spread worldwide. The value of teasers with or without the final hooked lure has been taken to its optimum development by Captain Skip Smith and his crew on the *Hooker*. The multiple world-record angler-owner captures by Jerry Dunaway and fellow record-breaking angler Debra Maddux have given teasers a new boost. The pattern of teasers trolled in *Hooker* raises the billfish, then after a skilled assessment of size, weight and potential record, a bait or lure complete with hook is presented to the billfish raised by the teaser.

One of the techniques used on *Hooker* in their string of record breaking is to research what records are possible in the area, particularly billfish, and to have outfits in the possible line classes ready to use. The sighted and estimated fish is offered a bait on a line class that could turn the fish from another unknown opponent to be tagged and released into a record claim fight balanced to the tackle.

Teasers with their unbroken links to fishing, the start of modern sportfishing, will continue to be part of the fishermen's armory in their quest for the big fish; so, too, will teasing with natural bait species.

In all fishing methods, trolling and fishing at anchor or drifting, it is important for the angler to know how and when to tease, to excite a shadowy, unexcited predator into explosive action. Often this is done by experienced crews before the angler is aware of the need. There is, however, a special exhilaration and satisfaction for anglers where they have created the trigger from a following fish to action on the baits or lures.

This teasing is sometimes carried out by sharply retrieving line by hand, sometimes by cranking the reel. The daisy chain rig with giant tuna, as sometimes happens with other rigs and lures, will often be taken with the leader in hand right at the boat. Teasing with lures or baits or part of baits is effective after an initial strike as well as with shadowing, casually interested predator species. Sometimes it is necessary to work and tease the big fish several times before obtaining the hoped-for strike. Changing to a live or more lively bait will also often trigger a strike from a sighted but non-feeding, non-killing fish. This form of teasing, which may entail the extra activity of two or three released unrigged live fish, or removal of part of a tail or other fins to give the bait an unusual or wounded action, may be beneficial. Spare rigged baits, lures and live baits should be ready just in case.

Water jets and sprays are integral in the successful pole fishery for tuna. This form of teaser would also appear to have potential for sportfishing for tuna at drift and anchor or trolling. It could also be of benefit trolling for tuna and marlin with both bait and lures despite the possible annoyance of wind-blown spray to anglers on the deck.

RIGGING BAITS—TROLLING, DRIFTING, CASTING

Successful offshore trolling is now often regarded as fishing with lures or live bait. Despite the popularity and success rate with those two methods, there are times and places where fishing with dead natural baits is still, and always will be, important and productive. Modern fishermen should be competent in all methods. Success goes hand in hand with learning and using the methods of today.

Natural baits are logical and effective, particularly in established fisheries where local bait schools, sea bed configuration, currents and usual hunting areas are well known.

It is a pity that the numbers of skilled bait riggers have reduced as lure and live bait fishing has increased. There is still and always will be a need for natural baits rigged to troll, in association with live baits, for small marlin and sailfish and to troll in proven areas for giants of the species. There is pleasure in watching and learning as skilled bait riggers practice their art and skills in making a dead fish act naturally to entice the peak predator fish of the ocean. Knowledge of how to rig baits is still important in this plastic age. Knowledge of when and where to use bait and how to rig baits well can determine whether a fishing trip is a monument or merely a milestone.

The benefits and results from trolling at least one dead bait in conjunction with live bait are well proven. So, too, is the strike and capture rate associated in trolling for big or light game species. Knowledge gained from professional crews can be successfully applied in angler-skippered and crewed boats of all sizes.

Natural baits rigged for anchor or drift are usually rigged to hang head down, although some rig whole fish tail down so they are pulled head first in the current and drift. Neatness is an integral factor in successful bait rigging. Gamefish and sharks swallow baits head first so trolling baits must be rigged so the baits can be turned to swallow. The baits must troll head first as in the New Zealand rig and have light ties that will break when the

marlin strikes so it will be turned to be swallowed head first.

The other trolling rigs must turn either about the hook or loop in the leader wire at the hook. Ties on drifting and anchor baits must be strong so the hook is firmly held.

The point of the hook must be kept clear of the bait so that when the fish is struck the point will be driven into the fish, not back into the bait.

Bait must be fresh or preserved by lightly brining or salting body cavities or applying formalin formaldehyde to the bait in storage.

Trolling baits should not be stiff. Stiff fish will spin when trolled, so the backbone should be removed for part or the whole of its length, or broken and stretched by 'working' (flexing) the bait.

Baits should be of a size to suit the fish sought, even if this means missing out on larger or smaller species for which the baits and hook sizes are unsuitable. The size of fish used for baits to attract even one species of fish can vary widely, but even if the bait is small the hook still needs to be of sensibly large size. Long, easily trolled barred mackerel and wahoo up to and over 10 kg (22 lb) may be used for the jumbo black marlin at Cairns, where these big baits take 68–90-kg (150–200-lb) specimens; but small 120 to 240-gram chub mackerel, goggle eye (yellowtail scad), mullet and balao (garfish) are used for small marlin and sailfish.

It is important to ascertain where natural bait can be obtained, whether it is to be used alive or dead.

Countless arrow squid school for mating each year off Santa Catalina, California. Photo: Peter Goadby.

When using whole or cut baits it is of prime importance to tie the fish or the cut bait firmly to the hook to prevent any slip with the consequent bunching and choking of the point of the hook. Drifting baits should be attached firmly particularly at the eye of the hook.

Variations in rigging methods and types of baits give the gamefish a choice. One bait rig may interest and attract while others are ignored. A range of baits rigged in different ways gives more chances. As with lure trolling, the pattern—i.e, the positioning—of the baits is important. Each rig works best in some given position on outriggers or flat lines.

Baits for big marlin are usually trolled from outriggers so there is one skipping, surface splashing bait, trolled sometimes from only halfway up the outrigger. The other, a swimming bait, is trolled from the full length of the rigger. The skip bait is usually a tuna or bonito or some species of toothy mackerel, queenfish or rainbow runner; kahawai are popular in New Zealand, as are flying fish in California and Mexico. The swimming baits are rigged from smaller toothed mackerels, scad (double-lined mackerel), small queenfish, mullet, kahawai and bonefish. Mahi mahi and barracuda are sometimes used.

Mullet rigged to swim are top bait for giant bluefin in the Bahamas, while herring and chub mackerel are used for trolling in daisy chains in cooler waters. Menhaden, whiting or other fish are used for bluefin baits at anchor and on drift.

Baits for smaller billfish are rigged from small mullet, ballyhoo (garfish), chub mackerel, goggle eye (yellowtail scad), blue runner and squid. Small eels are attractive to Atlantic white marlin. These species can be rigged for both outriggers and flat line trolling.

Strip baits cut from side fillets and belly strips are also productive trolling baits. The whole fish and strip baits for small billfish are often run in combination with plastic skirts, plastic squid, feather lures or hexheads.

Drifting bait species include tuna, bonito, mullet, toothy mackerels, yellowtail, amberjack, trevally, jacks and squid. Pilchards, sardines and anchovies are top light-tackle small-hook baits.

Squid are the best bait for swordfish, both in daylight fishing and drifting at night.

Excitement in the action of the bait often means success; so does apparent competition, if bait fish appear to be chased or escaping from another fish, all the baits seem to be chased and struck.

Successful baits are easy for a hunting fish to find by sight, scent, vibrations, or the combination of all three. The success of the Cuban deep-drifting combination of a cluster of big and small fish, lifting, moving and catching all available light, takes full advantage of these requirements—sight, smell and vibration.

Any pelagic or fish caught from the sea bed, surface or in between can be used for live bait. Tuna, bonito, yellowtail, amberjack, trevally and rainbow runner are popular big fish live baits and chub mackerel, goggle eye (yellowtail scad), mullet, ballyhoo, blue runner, sardines, anchovies and fresh-caught reef fish are prime baits for smaller billfish and tuna.

Those listed above are established baits. To these can be added caught-on-the-spot species for both live and dead baits. The peak predator species are opportunistic feeders that take a great variety of fish and other marine life.

Surprisingly successful results have been obtained

With a burst of power this black marlin surges out of the blue depths. Photo: Mike Kenyon.

TROLLING BAITS

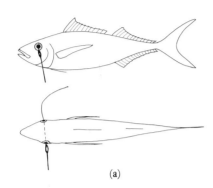

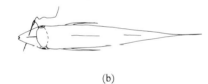

(a)

(a)

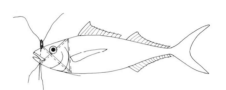

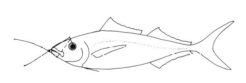

(b)

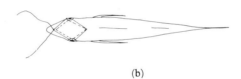

(b)

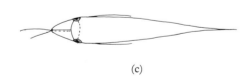

(c)

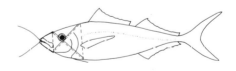

(c)

BRIDLE RIG FOR TROLLING DEAD BAITS

(a) Thread through top of eyes.

(b) Knot ends over eyes. Push thread down through head, top to bottom. Cut groove in lip.

(c) Tie with surgeon's knot. Closed mouth gives two threads for towing bridle and for tying close to mouth.

HALTER RIG FOR BAITS WITH HOOK IN FRONT OF NOSE

(a) Double cord through needle eye. Push needle down through back with two equal lengths. This gives four ends.

(b) Take two lines and knot over eye, then push needle through from top of head. There are now two threads at top of head, two at lower.

(c) Knot over mouth ready for half-hitches onto hook.

TROLLING BAITS
CONTINUED

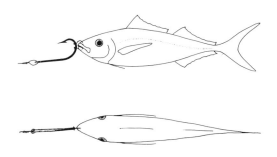

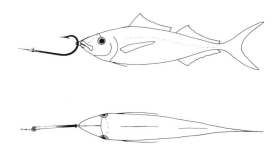

RIG FOR LIVE OR (USUALLY) DEAD TROLLING
If live leave mouth open with slack 3 cm (1 in) to 1.5 cm (½ in) bridle. For a 'quickie' rig, the hook could be placed through jaw as in Catalina rig.

OLD BAY OF ISLANDS TROLLING RIG
Trolling dead fish with 3 cm (1 in) to 4.5 cm (1½ in) bridle through mouth and eyes.

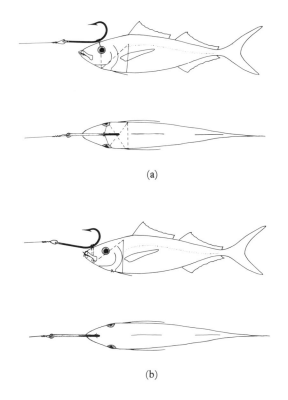

(a)

(b)

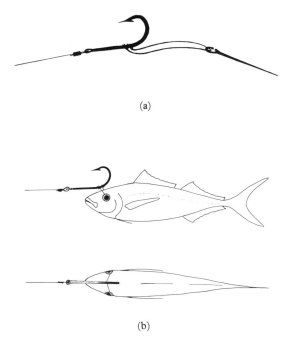

(a)

(b)

SIMILAR RIG FOR DEAD BAITS
(a) Mouth sewn closed.
(b) Hook tied on nose instead of eye (Cairns variation). These can also be rigged with second hook towards tail.

BIMINI OR PANAMA TROLLING RIG FOR LIVE BAIT
(a) Needle with slot eye ready on hook for live bait trolling.
(b) Live bait trolling—open mouth. Dead bait trolling— mouth closed. Bridle 1.5 cm (½ in) to 3 cm (1 in).

TROLLING BAITS
CONTINUED

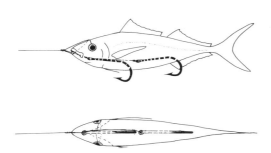

CABO BLANCO TROLLING RIG
Two-hook trolling rig with hooks in belly. Sometimes the backbone is removed.

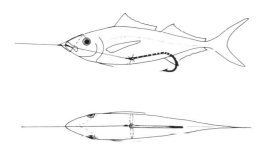

BLUE MARLIN TROLLING RIG
The single hook rig, sometimes with backbone removed. Bridle through body as well as mouth is an aid on bigger size baits.

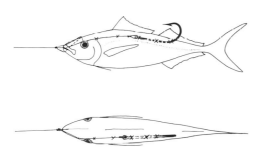

TROPICAL MARLIN TROLLING RIG
To allow a short drop-back which may be beneficial when trolling dead fish (where the gamefish may take the baits from the rear and swallow quickly), the leader can be bound with dental tape to facilitate non-slip tying of towing bridle. The dental tape stops slip and makes sure the pull is on the head. A practical rig where wahoo and other razor gang fish mutilate marlin baits.

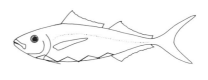

HOW TO CLOSE INCISIONS IN TROLLING RIGS
Herringbone stitching is used to sew up cut belly or back. Care must be taken to allow space around hook to allow natural movement without hook being sewn tight. The gills as well as the mouth of the bait should be sewn tightly closed to restrict water entry.

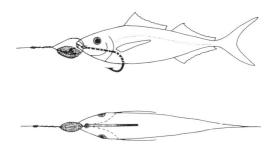

SWIMMING RIG WITH HEAD SINKER (TROLLING)
Rigged as shown. Trolling a dead fish, with the backbone removed or broken. Leader is passed through the eye of the hook. In this rig an oval sinker is used to make the bait run deeper and to vary the action.

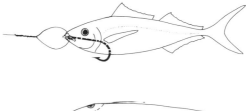

SWIMMING DEAD FISH
The leader is passed through the eye of the hook. Mouth is sewn shut and leader has a big loop to enable the bait to be turned. The backbone can be completely removed and the body, including tail, split.

TROLLING BAITS
CONTINUED

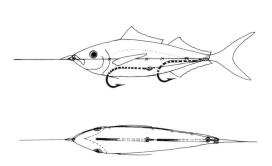

TUKER'S DOUBLE HOOK BROADBILL TROLLING RIG
A successful bait for big broadbill. The backbone is often removed for flexibility. Use on skipjack and other small tuna.

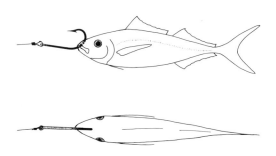

CATALINA TROLLING RIG
The hook goes through the nose of the bait (as shown), or may be used in reverse position through the lower jaw. Used also with hook across the nose. A good quick rig for small dead bait.

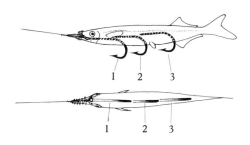

SINGLE HOOK BALLYHOO (GARFISH) TROLLING RIG
The hook can be below or from the side in any of the three positions shown. Hook position depends on size of bait and type of fish sought. Break the bill off short and bind leader to stump of bill to hold and close mouth.

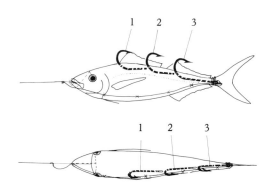

MAYOR ISLAND TROLLING RIG
Can be rigged with hook in positions 1, 2 or 3. When towing the bait the pull must be on the light bridle not on the leader along the body. The ties on the leader where it runs along the body must be light. Thread tied at the tail and eye of hook must be strong.

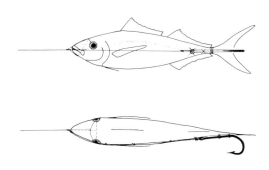

PORT STEPHENS TROLLING RIG
Trolling dead fish for big yellowtail kingfish or other fish that follow and swallow tail first. Can be used slow trolling in conjunction with chum.

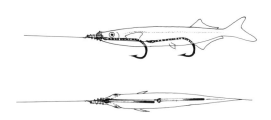

BALLYHOO (GARFISH) TWO-HOOK TROLLING RIG
Break the bill off short. Hooks can be:
(a) one up, one down; (b) both in from side; (c) two down.

TROLLING BAITS
CONTINUED

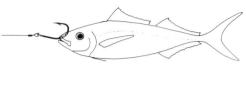

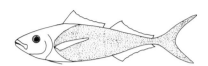

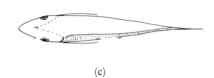

(c)

LIVE BAIT TROLLING
Hook through nose. A short bridle in same position helps the bait to swim actively and last longer.

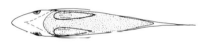

(d)

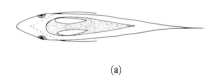

(a)

(e)

TYPICAL STRIP BAITS FOR TROLLING
(a) Belly strip (short) for trolling.
(b) Belly strip (long) for trolling, with swimming tail to vary action.
(c) Side strip bait from mullet or other small fish.
(d) Panama strip—top edges are sewn together in position.
(e) Strip bait held with safety pin in wire.

(b)

DRIFTING
AND ANCHOR BAITS
CONTINUED

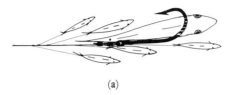

(a)

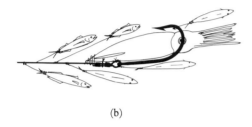

(b)

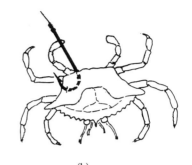

(b)

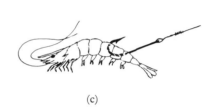

(c)

CUBAN DRIFTING RIGS
(a) *Fish rigged tail up. The bait fish can also be rigged head up if desired.*
(b) *Squid and fish combination.*

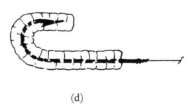

(d)

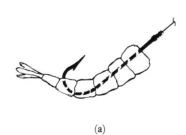

(a)

BAITS FOR INSHORE SPECIES
(a) *Dead shrimp (prawn); (b) live or dead crab; (c) live shrimp; (d) worm.*

*C*aptain Bill Edwards backs up Tainui *working with angler Ted Naftzger on a giant black marlin. Photo: Peter Goadby.*

with live bait caught on the spot; reef dropoff trevally are successful live baits on the Great Barrier Reef. A local reef fish, the nannygai or red fish, is a prime live bait for big yellowfin tuna at Bermagui in southern New South Wales, yet is not so successful on the yellowfin grounds further north.

Live and dead natural baits of local species of fish, prawns, shrimps, crabs and squid have proven to be a natural and prolific way to take gamefish inshore, in estuaries and into rivers. Mullet are also universally popular live or cut baits.

The effectiveness of dead whole fish drifting baits can be increased by partly filleting the bait fish to allow free escape of blood and oils, while still retaining some of the silvery skin to contrast with dark red flesh.

Dead bait fish or the tail portions of big fish rigged as baits for use at anchor or on the drift will often spin like tops in tide or current, twisting and damaging the line. The best way to prevent this is to cut the tail lobes right in short so that there is no natural propeller to catch the moving water.

The edges of strip baits should be trimmed and bevelled off so that the strip trolls flat. The edge of the Panama strip can be left at the natural belly thickness or bevelled before it is sewn up, as the bait rigger wishes.

It is often helpful with strip baits to sew the eye of the hook to the strip and the front of the strip to the leader to give extra support for long trolling periods.

The hole through which the hook sits in strip baits should be long enough to allow the bait to flap and flash on the surface. The hook is anchored by the leader through the eye of the hook in the swimming mullet rig—the mullet 'swims' freely around the slit in the belly where entrails and backbone were removed. This slit is not sewn up the full length, if at all; one or two stitches behind the shank of the hook will suffice.

A safe way to work billfish with cast lures, or live bait on a ball of baitfish, when more than one or two boats are involved.

LIVE BAIT FISHING

Many species of bait fish and crustaceans are used as live baits as it is logical for the predator gamefish and sharks to feed on the species they hunt naturally. The attractiveness of the baits is related to the fisherman's understanding of the need to exercise care in handling the baits so they stay lively and active.

Chub mackerel, green mackerels, goggle eye and yellowtail scad can be caught on light line and then transferred to live bait tanks without being handled. The schools can be chummed up then caught on bait on small hooks or Joes. The bait fish will drop clear of the hook into the bait tank if the hook is turned upside down, or the wriggling fish touched against the side of the tank. Skipjack tuna, other small tunas, amberjack and yellowtail often benefit from being lifted inboard with a landing net. The bait fish should be held upside down while the hook on which it is caught is removed and the big fish hook put in place. Often they are held with a wet towel to protect body slime.

Small bait fish kept alive with circulating and aerated water in the tank can be carried long distances. They can be released if not wanted at the end of the fishing day or kept in holding traps. Skipjack and the other live bait species can be kept alive for a short time by running a deck hose into the mouth of the ram ventilators.

One of the keys to successful fishing with live bait is to have the leaders ready for instant use. Leaders for skipjack and other big bait species should have hooks sharpened, the dacron or other bridle fixed on the shank of the hook and the rigging needle in place. The needle passes the loop of the towing thread through the opening sinus above the bait's eyes. The loop which held the

Charlie Davis has his live bait tank equipped with rod holders for quick access to live bait and rods and reels. Photo: Peter Goadby.

needle is quickly passed over the point and barb of the hook two or three times before the bait is slid overboard to swim at its chosen depth. It is sensible to have the live bait and leader already attached to the line to be fished before the bait is rigged and the bait and leader placed overboard. Care must also be taken to ensure the snap is safely done up.

The positioning of the short, sharp hooks varies with both the current and whether the bait will be trolled or fished on drift or at anchor. Baits to be trolled and fished in a fast current have the hook placed through the nose, those fished at anchor or drift are rigged in one of several locations on the back. If kirbed (offset) hooks are used they should be positioned from one side or the other so that the point will pull clear not back into the bait. It is important to remember the importance of the lateral line and back bone so care must be taken to ensure that the hook is clear of these important areas.

BAIT RIGGING

The tools needed for bait rigging are 1 large and 1 small diameter deboner; rigging pliers in sheath; stiff, short-bladed knife; long, thin-bladed filleting knife; ice pick for making hole in heads of bait; light, medium and heavy cotton or linen rigging thread; light and heavy waxed nylon thread; leader materials; lead sinkers, preferably egg or oval for swimming baits; short and long bait needles (at least one with slotted eye); hooks; crimping sleeves; crimping pliers; files; sharpening stones or sharpening tool; and wire cutters.

'Split-tail' Charley Hayden, who can rig mullet and other baits so they call up gamefish, recommends several methods of trolling mullet. These are wedge and debone; deboned swimming mullet; split tail; split back and cut back.

To wedge and debone: Cut out and remove a diamond-shaped wedge from the red spot on head to first dorsal. Debone through wedge. Make a short slit in the belly to insert the hook. Use ice pick through head red spot to make a clean hole for the leader wire. Slide leader wire through head and hook. Twist the leader wire together with haywire twist to give a wide loop so the bait can be turned by the marlin. Use needle to take thread from one side of head to the other above the hook. Tie around head two or three times. Sew mouth closed.

Deboned mullet: Bend mullet at throat. Debone through throat, cut anus, cut another short slit near pelvic fins for hook insertion. Use ice pick through head red spot to make a clean hole for leader wire. Slide leader through head and hook. Twist leader together with haywire twist to give a wide loop. Sew mouth closed.

Split back mullet: Backbone is removed from top of back after cutting along both sides of backbone and breaking near tail. Use ice pick through head red spot to make a clean hole for leader wire. Twist wire tight on lips.

Split tail mullet: Start diamond wedge closer to nose than red spot. Wedge is cut almost back to dorsal. Wedge

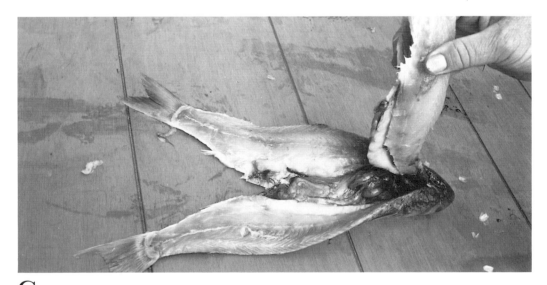

C*harlie Hayden has cut his split tail bait so the backbone can be removed in one piece. Photo: Peter Goadby.*

Deck hoses and a plastic fish box combine as a successful and practical live bait tank. Photo: Peter Goadby.

Cut back mullet: Cut along top of back, including dorsal fins. Cut down both sides of back bone so it can be removed with gut. Use ice pick to make a clean hole for leader wire. Thread wire with sinker through head and hook in place on underside of body. Twist the wire tightly against lead.

Ballyhoo (garfish): Prepare leader wire. Haywire twist leader onto hook and make an upright pin of about 1.25 cm (0.5 in). Twist 15 cm (6 in) of soft copper wire around head of bait. Flex the body of ballyhoo. Break bill about halfway and use it to pull skin from under rest of bill. Measure where hook will be positioned, bend body of bait and slide hook into place. Push pin through head and wrap copper wire around mouth and down bill so that the leader wire sits in the groove made by the skin removal. Pull leader and if necessary enlarge slit around hook. This rig can also be used with two hooks, the second of which has point up, the first point down.

Big skip and swimming baits: Gills and gut should have been previously removed from bait fish.

Big skip baits: Sew mouth shut. Sew belly slit closed with herringbone stitch. Tie strong thread or cord five or six times around the shank of the hook so it cannot move. Leave two lengths of about 60 cm (2 ft). Each of these threads or cord is pulled on a needle one at a time through head and throat and tied off firmly. The threads are then pulled through belly sides and shoulder to make a strong towing halter, using the strength of head and shoulders. Check to make sure that the point of the hook will not dig into the shoulder of the bait

is cut with short stiff knife. With longer fillet knife, cut along body and split the tail from anus back. Use head cut to free backbone. Turn over and make a similar cut on other side. Backbone and gut can then be lifted clear. Gills are also removed without damaging the throat latch. This bait works well with a weight under the chin. Place sinker on leader wire and slide leader through hook that can face upwards in wedge cut. Make haywire twist tight against lead (about thirteen twists). Tie thread two or three times around wedge area. This bait is used for giant bluefin as well as billfish and whatever takes it.

A small black marlin almost jumps into the boat and shows the tuna bait swallowed head first. Photo: Peter Goadby.

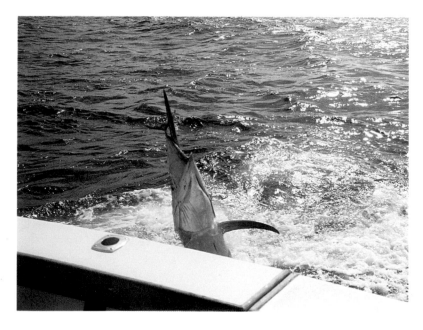

The cockpit space on the Bertram Blowout *is used practically. The live bait tank has a viewing port and is of a height that allows storage and quick availability of fishing tackle. Photo: Peter Goadby.*

when the bait is turned by the marlin for swallowing head first. If a piano or galvanized wire leader, it is attached to eye of hook with twenty to twenty-two twists and five to six barrel rolls.

Big swimming baits: Sew mouth shut. Use ice pick to make clean hole for leader. Slide leader through hole in head and through the eye of hook. The hook should be in the body cavity behind the pelvic fins. A loop of leader about 5–7.5 cm (2–3 in) is made so the leader wire is twisted and barrel rolled. This loop will ensure that the bait can be turned for swallowing by a marlin. As with the big skipping baits, the wire should be twisted

evenly twenty to twenty-two times with five to six barrel rolls. Care must be taken to ensure that the wire twists are tight and even and twisting and wrapping does not heat the wire. The fish's belly is then sewn with herring-bone stitches about 2.5–5 cm (1–2 in) apart. Some riggers take this stitching over the backbone for extra strength.

These brief descriptions refer to single-strand piano or galvanized wire. Other leader materials—monofilament nylon, plastic-covered cable, or two strands twisted of stainless single-strand wire either singly or in conjunction with others—can be used, e.g., short, single-strand wire is joined with a snap swivel to monofilament leader.

POINTS TO REMEMBER

- Do not break throat latch of any baits.

- Keep hook and wire in centre of body and head width.

- For light tackle, single-strand wire should be twisted evenly and tightly 6–8 twists and finished with 3–4 wraps then broken flush by bending the wire into a right-angled crank.

- On heavy tackle, single-strand wire should be twisted evenly and tightly 20–22 twists and finished with 5–6 wraps before breaking wire flush with right-angled crank.

- When making knots, make an extra overlap in a surgeon's knot so the thread will hold as knot is completed.

- Rig baits neatly.

- Leader material should be chosen carefully. All have some advantages and disadvantages.

- If hooks cannot be removed in a tag and release, cut the leader behind the wire man if fish are to be released when he requests the cut. He knows when he wants it cut, when it is safe to do so and then when to release.

- Examine all leaders after use and discard if there is the slightest doubt. Many crews discard single-strand galvanized wire after one use so they are working with maximum-length leaders in the best possible starting condition.

- Store baits and leaders in refrigerator or ice boxes so they will not tangle.

One way to ice the bait—Charlie Hayden stands on an iceberg. Giant bluefin were caught where these icebergs drifted in Newfoundland. Photo: Gil Keech.

KNOTS, PLAITS AND JOINS

Human error is usually the reason for the frustration of a fish loss. Hours of work and effort may be negated by a few seconds of carelessness or hurry in the preparation of critical knots, plaits or other joins in single and double line.

Double line, even though the allowable length has been reduced in IGFA regulations, is still important in rigging, though it is less useful at the final stages of the fight. The maximum allowable length of double line and double line/leader combination if maximum length leaders are required means that double lines are short, or in many cases are not used at all, even on heavy tackle. One of the great benefits of double line under the present regulations is increased knot strength in all lines.

It is important to know how to make the Bimini roll, the plait or braid, or spider hitch to create a double line. It is important to know how to safely join and replace the top length of line, and worn line without replacing the full length. Practical knowledge of knots is integral to success for fly fishing and light tackle. Fly fishermen use more knots in number and variety than in any other kind of fishing.

Faulty ties are often associated with trying to work quickly or while unbalanced by the motion of the boat. Knots should be checked regularly; even if they have not come undone they may have moved and be ready to finally come apart.

Knots and joins reduce the breaking strain of line to varying degrees. It is therefore important to know which knots are strongest, most dependable and easiest to tie. Anglers who fish from charter boats often depend on guide, captain or crew to tie the necessary knots. Despite this, every angler should be proficient in the necessary knots and carry in his kit the few necessary

tools, pliers, knife, dental tape, dental thread, 60-second glue or rubber glue.

One of the reasons fishermen carry pliers on their belts is to assist in holding the loose end and pulling tight. Monofilament weakens quickly as it is pulled over itself, so lubrication with saliva, water or beeswax on the line before the knot is made and pulled down tight keeps the monofilament cool and able to move smoothly.

Knots used in joining lines particularly benefit from application of a few drops of 60-second glue or rubber-type contact cement to give added security, as well as smoothing the passage of line and knots through the guides. If dissatisfied with the knot or not sure if the standing and loose ends are in correct positions, cut the knot and do it again. Some fishermen find a combination of the knots they need in Vic Dunaway's Uniknot system. Others choose to use an improved clinch, an Albright or Uniknot joining knot plus the Buffer or Homer Rhode Loop.

Dependability in knots comes from practice, familiarity and repeated use. It is important to know the loss in breaking strain in the various knots. Knot strength can be checked against line testers or scales. It is important to know the advantages and disadvantages of the various knots.

Some knots are ideal on light lines, but not on heavy. The Spider hitch is satisfactory on light line classes if carefully and evenly tied. Many fishermen have reservations regarding its use on line classes above the 15-kg (30-lb) class.

Crimps and sleeves are now commonly used on heavier line classes, monofilament leaders, in place of knots. The sleeve loops are dependable as well as being smaller in bulk and bubble-producing bulk.

Knots and their Uses

IMPROVED CLINCH KNOT
To attach hook to leader. Wet knot as it is pulled up tight.

JANSIK KNOT
A strong, quick way to attach hook to leader.

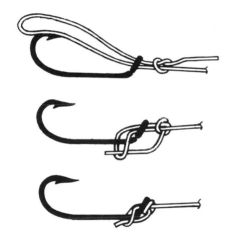

BAIT HOOK KNOT
To attach hook to leader.

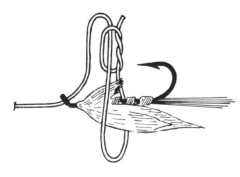

TURTLE KNOT
To attach hook to leader.

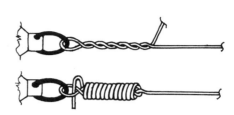

ROLL KNOT
Similar to roll for double. A popular knot to attach by single or double line to swivel or ring.

RETURN KNOT
To attach leader to hook.

DOUBLE CLINCH KNOT
Wet the knots as they are pulled up tight.

PIANO WIRE TWIST WITH SAFETY CLIP
For strip bait.

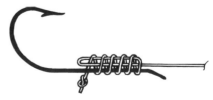

AUSTRALIAN CLINCH KNOT
To attach hook with or without eye to leader.

Knots and their Uses

FISHERMAN'S KNOT OR DOUBLE O KNOT
Used for tying line to swivel.

DROP LOOP
To attach lure to leader.

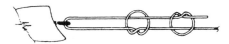

BUFFER LOOP
To attach lure to leader to give loop for lure to work.

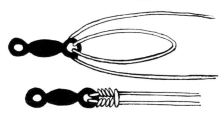

BIMINI HITCH
Turn swivel inside loop of line four to six times, then slide up tight.

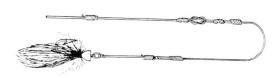

FLY LEADER

1

2

3

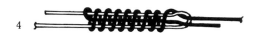

4

Tube nail

NAIL KNOTS
1. Nail knot. 2. Offset nail knot. 3. Double nail knot.
4. Nail knot with tube.

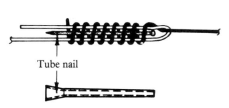

TO JOIN SEVALON TO MONOFILAMENT WITHOUT SWIVEL OR RING.

BLOOD KNOT

STU APTE IMPROVED BLOOD KNOT
For joining leader to line. The improved knot uses the double strand of the lighter line in tapered leaders or tippets. Used to join shock leader to nylon.

KNOTS AND THEIR USES
CONTINUED

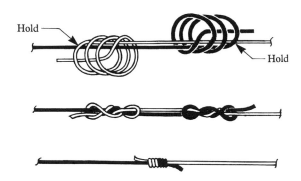

Hold

Hold

LEADER KNOT
To join leader.

Hook

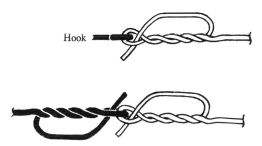

HALF BARREL KNOT
To join to hook and for joining lines of similar diameter.

ALBRIGHT KNOT
To attach long leaders to fly line.

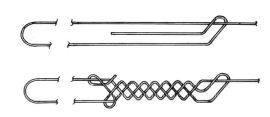

DOUBLE LINE PLAIT
A strong safe way for double line. Plait must be tight and even. Also used to join two lines of equal size.

GEORGE PARKER'S PLAIT JOIN
Solid line indicates extra line to act as a buffer and to form the third line for the plait.

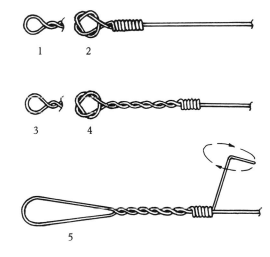

BIMINI TWIST (DOUBLE LINE)
To form a double line finished with a half hitch on each strand. A similar knot can be used to attach double line to swivel.

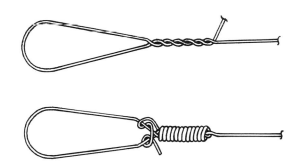

1   2

3   4

5

1. ROUND EYE SINGLE LOOP. 2. ROUND EYE WITH FLEMISH EYE. 3. PIANO TWIST SINGLE LOOP. 4. PIANO TWIST WITH FLEMISH EYE. 5. HAYWIRE TWIST WITH SINGLE LOOP.
Always finish single strand wire with wire twist. The 'crank' finishes the twist without a cutting edge. Pliers and other cutting tools leave a sharp edge to damage hand or line. Single loops are often used rather than eyes to reduce bubble.

SURGEON'S KNOT
To join line to monofilament leader or lines of different diameters. Always wet knot as it is pulled up tight.

SPIDER HITCH
To make a quick double line for lines up to 10 kg (20 lb) class.

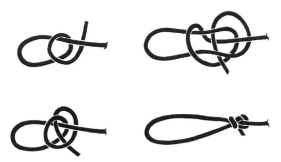

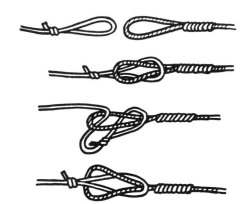

PERFECTION KNOT
To make a strong loop.

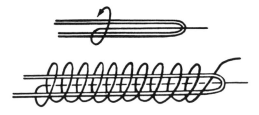

TO JOIN LEADER TO FLY LINE

VIC DUNAWAY UNIKNOT
The basic Vic Dunaway uniknot with six turns can be used for many joins. A uniknot must be pulled evenly and tightly. A uniknot tied with each line can be used to join lines.

IMPROVED ALBRIGHT KNOT

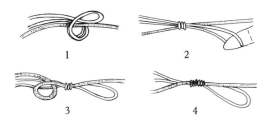

1   2

3   4

JOINING LEADER TO DOUBLE LINE
1. The uniknot can be used to join leader of up to four times the breaking strain of leader to line.
2. The uniknot is tied three times with double line around the leader.
3. The leader with uniknot three times around double line.
4. Wet knots and pull together hard and evenly.

JAM KNOT
To join leader to line without swivel or ring.

KNOTS

- Make all plaits, joins and hitches longer than really necessary. For example, plait for 5 cm (2 in) instead of the 2.5 cm (1 in) that satisfactorily holds on double line.
- Tie off with two tight half-hitches instead of one at the finish of the plaits, roll-knots or any other knots finishing with hitches.
- Burn the end of the free line into a knob—melt the end of the line with a match or cigarette lighter.
- Plait in one or more strands of dental floss, dental tape or waxed thread on line joins and doubles to minimize slip in plait or braid.

- On heavy lines, bind over the loose ends as an extra precaution.
- Make sure all knots and plaits are pulled tight at all stages and that the strands are running straight—make sure there are no weakening half-hitches or loose lengths in the main line.
- Splice braided line. Splice hollow braided line with the special splicing needle supplied or fine piano wire through hollow centre of braid. Some ease it once or twice through outside line. Bind both ends.
- Join monofilament to braid by tapering monofilament and sliding up centre of braid. Bind ends.

LEADERS

- Slide one or two sleeves or crimps over the leader.
- When attaching the hook, make an overhand loop in the leader after sliding on plastic anti-rub tubing or coil spring tube, as made for long lines.
- Continue with a second overhand loop to form the Flemish Eye at swivel on shark leaders.
- A single loop with plastic anti-rub is neat and effective for lure leader loop at swivel end.
- Bring short end of loop down through the sleeves and pull in tight.
- Crimp sleeves with crimping pliers; select sleeves for neat and tight fit.
- Cut off any protruding length of wire flush with sleeve.
- If only one sleeve is used, the free end of the wire or monofilament can be tucked back under the sleeve before it is crimped. In this instance, sleeves should be big enough to take the third strand. Always crimp sleeves tightly and burn the ends of the monofilament or nylon-covered wires into a globule to guard against possible slipping.

- Use 2.4–3-m (8–10-ft) light-tackle leaders on stand-up fishing so that the fish can be gaffed without the leader being handled. On heavy tackle with chair, use maximum length allowed by the rules and common sense for stretch.
- Continually check leaders for wear and kinks.
- Fine leaders and monofilament garner more strikes than heavy, more visible leaders.
- Make sure no corrosion or crystallization shows beneath used nylon-covered wire. If corroded discard it.
- Make sure the wire is twisted, trimmed or cut to eliminate cutting edges.
- On shark leaders twist the two wires together for 45 cm (18 in) after making a Flemish eye for the hook attachment.
- Keep leaders coiled, neatly bound with Scotch tape or plastic-covered copper wire or garden twist, or in plastic bags or Zip-Loc bags ready for instant action.

SWIVELS

- Use swivels as small as the line breaking strain dictates. If strength is unknown, check against scales.
- Black swivels and snaps are less visible.
- Inspect swivels to make sure they are not damaged by wear.
- Make sure swivels will turn.

- In areas where striking fish cause cutoffs, rig with the swivel into the middle of the leader and join double to leader with a neat knot.
- Use snaps of a proven, dependable type.
- Bind over knots of line to swivel to minimize bubbles.

COMPETITIVE FISHING

THE FISHING CLUB

The fishing club is the logical and visible extension of the bonds and companionship of fishermen. It is the link between the master angler and the novice, the distributor of information, and the catalyst that makes possible maximum enjoyment of fishing as a sport and recreation for most people. Coincidentally a well-run club is a public relations vehicle for those who fish, and a contact point for government and scientific dialogue. Recreational fishing is, in fact, an organized sport with rules, ethics, competitions, and national and international affiliations and structures.

The reasons for fishing clubs' existence are as varied as their sizes and structures. Their purposes may include organizing fishing competitions, increasing fishing knowledge and skills, family and youth participation, creating something of importance in the community, or just plain getting together to shoot the breeze.

Clubs reflect the interests of their members, from those whose fishing equipment is the lightest of tackle to those who favor matching muscle power and 'stump-

A sight to gladden tournament Chairman Peter Fithian's heart, a grander, a world record 483 kg (1062.5 lb) blue marlin on 24 kg (50 lb) line in the HIBT. Photo: Peter Goadby.

pulling' equipment in combat with ocean giants. All are fishermen, all derive benefit from clubs.

The contrast in fishing equipment is reflected equally in the emphasis that clubs and members attach to competition. To some, competition is all-important; to others it merely interferes with fellowship and spoils their recreation. Clubs cater to their members' interests, which may range from the patience, quiet and specialization of European match fishing to the explosive power and sought-for action of the mighty fish that rip blue water into white.

Many benefits make the effort of establishing a fishing club worthwhile. These flow to members and the community in general.

Those running a club are usually found among the dedicated fishing 'nuts' who are prepared to give their time, their experience, their expertise, and often part of their finances so that the majority of members and the community itself can benefit. These people, as IGFA says, 'help make the world a better place to fish in'.

Clubs should not forget that surveys reveal that the principal reason people go fishing is to catch fish to eat—the other benefits are secondary.

The needs that lead to the effort of club organization vary from area to area, from group to group. Once a need is recognized and partially defined, a fishing club usually begins with a particularly enthusiastic person who calls a meeting, with a few other enthusiasts. These people meet to discuss the possibility, the advantages and the problems involved in the formation and management of a club. It is often worthwhile to give even such a preliminary meeting widespread notice.

Mutually agreed upon and well-defined objectives give the club a firm establishment base; they should be printed and circulated to all foundation and prospective members. In this way the club gets off to a planned start with everyone who is interested understanding what the club is and what it is trying to accomplish.

Understanding of the club's objectives simplifies the next step—drafting the constitution. This is usually best done by a small sub-committee. It is beneficial if some members of the sub-committee have legal, accounting, and, perhaps most importantly, club administrative experience. The drafted constitution should then be submitted to a meeting of other interested and prospective members for final ratification, amendment and agreement.

The club constitution should spell out such matters as the office bearers, club dues, management of the club (whether this is to be handled by the executive committee or overall general meeting of members), provision for calling extraordinary meetings, replacement of office bearers, number of meetings, eligibility for membership, different categories of member, and so on. Legal requirements and constitutional requirements vary from country to country, sometimes even from state to state. Local legal and financial advice is recommended when drawing up a constitution.

The constitution, like the objectives, should be printed and given to all members and should be available for perusal by prospective members. The constitution should, of course, have provision for amendments as required and provisions for by-laws, which are executive or general meeting decisions affecting the operation of the club.

Once agreement is reached on the objectives and the constitution, the club becomes a reality, an operating entity. When properly constituted and operated, a club is in effect a corporation or firm. Large clubs are often incorporated because of the legal burden on individual members. Most smaller clubs do not take this step. But whether or not the club is incorporated, it is important that it protect itself and its members from legal claims.

There are many legal reasons why incorporation benefits members, particularly in regard to liability of clubs whose activities bring them into contact with the public. Clubs should carry public risk insurance. Wording absolving the club from liability is often a part of membership application forms and notices of various club activities.

Some clubs, whether incorporated or not, make major contributions to the community, apart from adoption of a charity or contributions to education.

They maintain regular schedules and liaisons with police, rangers, coastguards, and other rescue and safety organizations. All this activity increases the need for active and able administration.

Clubs operate with a structure of at least a president, a secretary/treasurer and committee (or board of trustees). Most of the workload and responsibility for planning and achieving fall onto the president and secretary. In small clubs the secretary may be completely unpaid or receive expenses and a small honorarium, hence the term 'honorary secretary' or 'honorary treasurer', as distinct from a secretary and treasurer who are paid.

The executive structure of small clubs may spread in large clubs to the following: president, meeting chairman, vice-presidents (one of whom may be executive vice-president), secretary, fishing captain, honorary legal adviser, publicity officer, club manager, tournament organizer, outings officer, honorary scientific adviser, education officer, newsletter editor, boat safety officer, entertainment chairman, premises chairman, charity chairman (where the club supports a community charity), co-ordinator of fishing or tournament activity, rules chairman, membership committee chairman, keeper of records, weighmaster, tour organizer, official photographer and purchasing officer.

It is interesting to note how many of the world's most skilled and successful competitive anglers respond to the even greater challenge of administration—in leading and in giving their time, organizational ability, expertise and experience to helping others. The realization comes that, in fact, there is something more important than personal fishing and competition, as they dedicate their time and leadership to helping others enjoy and understand their own beloved recreation and environment.

One clause that should always be listed in the club objectives and constitution is in relation to conservation and scientific study of fish to increase members' overall knowledge and understanding. Conservation, an understanding of the environment, the preservation and management of fish and maintenance of the ecological balance are part of our generation's responsibilities to future generations. Emphasis on science and conservation ensures that instead of taking and using selfishly and thoughtlessly, we leave something worthwhile behind.

There are two published policies on gamefishing that are followed by today's anglers. The first is the long-standing words from the Tuna Club of Avalon, Santa Catalina, California, the world's first gamefishing club:

'The underlying spirit of angling is that the skill of the angler is pitted against the instinct and strength of the fish and that the latter is entitled to an even chance for his life.'

The other and more modern policy is the Conservation Policy of the International Game Fish Association (IGFA), which leads in conservation as well as records, rules and ethics:

'1. *Encourage each recreational fisherman never to be wasteful of the fishery resources, conserve where appropriate, and be mindful of the sensitivities of habitat and environment.*
2. *Encourage and support compliance with the angling rules and regulations as an indication of fishing in a manner that lends itself to proper conservation and management of the fishery resources.*
3. *Encourage and support the obtaining and interchanging of knowledge and information on recreational fisheries, the species and their environment to aid in proper conservation and management of the fishery resources, and for the benefit of these principles.*
4. *Encourage and support efforts to conserve and manage each species for the benefit of all recreational fishermen on a continuing basis.*
5. *Encourage and support recognition of the value of recreational fishing to the areas fished and economics supported or enhanced thereby.*
6. *Encourage and support recognition of the responsibility of those managing or responsible for fishery resources to provide for a healthy and continuing recreational fishery.'*

Knowledge is virtually useless unless it is available to others and so built upon. A club newsletter as well as talks by experts are two important ways of increasing members' knowledge, and holding their interest and enthusiasm.

Tradition and local fishing methods often dictate and mould the ethics for fishing in an area. The use of chum, the quick taking of fish, fishing manners and courtesy in association with other boats, other anglers and commercial fishermen, and availability of forage and gamefish species all influence ethics in any given area.

There are many known 'dos' and 'don'ts' that cannot be covered, even by international rules. A club that helps educate and direct its members on how not to pollute or annoy or adversely affect other users of nature and ecology is performing a prime function.

Clubs need projects to take their members outside their own narrow field of interest. Activities with wives and children of members, support of a charity, restocking lakes or ponds, scientific projects and rescue operations all serve to strengthen the club and expand its scope. Individuals can do a lot, but clubs, through organized participation, can make major contributions. The many successful and worthwhile tag-and-release programs throughout the world are examples of this. Bluefin tuna, black marlin, bluefish, bass and salmon are just some of the species now showing the benefit of club tag-and-release participation.

Club members usually take pride in identifying with their clubs. Many clubs have distinctive and tasteful stationery, pennants, capture flags, T-shirts, decals, lapel badges, and (particularly) patches for jackets and caps. Club members fishing in tournaments are identified and respected as representatives of their club by their patches and uniform shirts or jackets and caps. The sale of patches, flags and badges at a profit is also a worthwhile way of raising funds over and beyond regular dues and entrance fees.

Social events are other club features that serve the multi-purposes of companionship, entertainment, relaxation and fund-raising. The club and its finances, of course, should be run as a business with full and proper books of account, audited annually to the complete satisfaction of members and statutory requirements.

One social function that is of major importance is the annual award banquet or dinner. Even though fishermen gain much of their personal satisfaction in competing against themselves, continually improving their own standards, there is still real satisfaction in proving skill in competition with other fishermen. The award dinner or trophy award evening is a chance for the fisherman's family and friends to share in the public acknowledgment of his skill and/or luck.

Trophies, particularly perpetual trophies and awards, quickly help a club establish identity and tradition. This gives a club pride and encourages it to strive to maintain and improve its standards. Many trophies are beautiful works of art, sustaining the memory of a capture or a release. It is important to so recognize a great fish and record it for posterity and memory.

The banquet can assist club finances as well. Income can also be derived from raffles, lectures, tournaments, films, tackle auctions, fish fries, and other functions of a social nature. These extra funds may be used for charity, as a means of doing something for other sections of the community and to help dispel any selfish or predatory image of fishing clubs often projected to non-fishermen.

Two examples of great and worthwhile clubs are the Tuna Club of Avalon, Santa Catalina, California, and the Rod and Reel Club of Miami, Florida. The Tuna Club is one of the world's first offshore fishing clubs, and its traditions and rules, ethics and leadership have continued unabated for more than seventy-five years. The Rod and Reel Club has had a great influence on light and ultra-light saltwater sportfishing around the world. These clubs maintain a complete history of their activities and development. Their trophies, records and awards of merit have become models for much of the saltwater fishing world. In a similar way, the trout and salmon angling clubs of England and Scotland have provided the tradition and history of freshwater angling.

The proper keeping of fishing statistics and records

by clubs cannot be overemphasized. Clubs are the types of established organizations to which government departments, scientists, and legislators go for advice, information and data on fish and fishing as well as policies affecting the sport, the environment, people and ecology. The experiences and records of clubs and their members are also sought on government fishery committees directly involved in decision-making processes.

Publicity, whether for an individual or a club, is an activity that must be carefully handled and directed. Publicity sought by individuals can divide and split a club; individuals should not appear publicly to be more important than the club or the sport itself. The best way to avoid this problem is to appoint a club official as a publicity officer responsible to the executive committee. Sometimes publicity of the wrong kind, stressing quantities of fish taken rather than skill and recreation, can adversely affect community relations. Clubs should consciously direct their activities towards improving skill, improving knowledge, and leading in conservation, management, and education of children, rather than exerting most of their efforts toward improving the size of the catch.

Recreational fishing is the world's greatest and most popular sport. The best way to keep it growing and maintain its popularity and leadership is through the orderly, planned organization and activities of the fishing club.

TOURNAMENTS

For some fishermen, fishing a tournament is just going fishing, for others it is a highly competitive sport that requires even more effort, more planning, more thought, more of everything than usual—including, ideally, more fish. The worldwide trend towards tag and release has affected tournament tactics to some extent, as many tag-and-release point scores award the same points for each fish of the target species, irrespective of estimated weight.

Tag-and-release tournaments therefore often direct team thought and effort to where they should find the most billfish or other point-scoring species, whereas in take tournaments the effort is directed at where the biggest fish should be. The world's number one billfish tournament, the Hawaiian International Billfish Tournament, is a blend from its carefully planned and researched point score of tag and release and take. The bonuses for marlin over 220 kg (500 lb), the heaviest of the day, the heaviest of the tournament, ensures that those who catch the big fish as well as those who tag and release a number of marlin irrespective of weight, or recover a tagged billfish, have a chance of winning the distinctive wooden billfish trophies.

One of the most important tactics in a tournament, particularly when leading or in contention, is whether

Costa Rica hosts a successful annual saltwater fly billfish tournament. Photo: Darrell Jones.

The open transom door shows the value of this simple safe way to bring fish inboard for Hank Onishi and his Japanese Game Fish Association team in the HIBT. Photo: Peter Goadby.

Another consideration that affects choice or change of tackle category on the last day is that on this day, because of trophy awards that evening, fish or tag cards must be presented for point awards by a certain time cut-off. In tournaments without this cut-off, this is not a consideration.

Successful tournament anglers confer and take advantage of the knowledge and experience of skipper and crew. Teams using charter boats must make every effort to build co-operation and confidence among and in the charter members of the team.

Recognition of charter effort at the end of each day's fishing also helps in co-operation with other boats in the draw if boats are changed each day. It is important also for the team and professional crew to decide beforehand whether the team is to take part in the gaffing or tagging activity.

The regular radio reporting schedules are used by hard-working teams not only for information on the other teams, particularly the teams in contention, but to dissect information on strikes, size and type of fish and areas of activity. It is important to have assessed by prior research what is most productive and when most strikes are likely—top or bottom of the tide, or whenever.

Once a fish is hooked and for those who are to take the strike, concentration and alertness are important. Most teams have, by drawn straws or nomination or team decision, decided who is to take the strike. Teams usually have those who are to take strike ready in the cockpit while other team members are resting in the shade. Strikes are often rotated on an hour-on, hour-off basis, often combined with thirty minutes ready for strikes on rods on one side of the boat, changing to move and readiness for strikes on the other side when trolling. In drifting or at anchor, strikes may be taken strictly on the time basis, or again rods on left or right side of the boat in the interest of fairness and equality in the team. Of course some teams have decided that because of experience or pressure one angler will take the strikes deliberately.

to back one's own experience and knowledge to go to fish the chosen area and method, or whether to cover the leading teams.

In tournaments that fish multiple line classes a critical decision that affects each day's fishing for the team, particularly as the days go on, is which class or classes to fish, light or heavy. It is important for success to evaluate points, what is needed to win. Early in the tournament it is logical to fish the lighter line classes for maximum points for each capture, then if the fish are running big or the leading points are low, to go for quick certain points on smaller fish, plus the maximum chance of holding on to a big fish if one strikes and hooks up on the heavier classes.

In a coming together of beautiful fishing islands, the colorful hard fishing team from Club Nautico de San Juan, head to sea in the classic Hawaiian Sampan skippered by Captain Butch Chee and crewed by his brother, Joe Chee, sons of the legendary Hawaiian Captain Henry Chee. Photo: Peter Goadby.

ESTABLISHING AND ENFORCING FISHING TOURNAMENT RULES

Two common problems face tournament organizers. The first is deciding on the rules and regulations to be used during the tournament, and the other is ensuring that the competitors fish to and observe these rules.

What rules should govern the event?

The aim should be to use rules that fit the specific needs of a tournament. Primarily the tournament committee must ensure that the rules make the competition as fair as possible to all the competitors and to the fish. The rules should also ensure that competitors face a challenge to their ability and that the tournament in its final result gives sporting achievement and fulfillment.

Tournament regulations can be divided into two major categories: the angling and equipment regulations that will govern the event, and the rules devised for the specific tournament, such as fishing times and areas, scoring systems, tackle limitations and eligible species.

ANGLING AND EQUIPMENT REGULATIONS

Most tournaments throughout the world fish according to International Game Fish Association equipment and angling regulations, which have been many years in the making and are continually updated to take into account new fishing equipment and techniques.

Intended 'to establish uniform regulations for the compilation of world gamefish records, and to provide basic guidelines for use in fishing tournaments and other group angling activities', these regulations not only establish criteria for types of tackle and equipment used, but deal with the process of angling from hook-up to gaff. For example, leader lengths, hook arrangements, and the treatment of multiple strikes are among the items covered.

There are many reasons why it is logical as well as easy for tournament committees to incorporate the current IGFA rules. One of the principal reasons is that these are the rules with which most anglers and tournament officials are familiar in their day-to-day fishing activity. Another prime motive is the possibility of a tournament angler boating a world record catch.

Now that IGFA has included freshwater angling in its fishing rules and established a separate set of rules for fly fishing, no doubt they will become the backbone of tournaments which fall into freshwater and fly fishing categories, just as the saltwater rules have become the standard for offshore and saltwater tournaments generally.

TOURNAMENT RULES

It is imperative that IGFA angling rules be supplemented by specific tournament regulations. These are what make a tournament work. The rules should designate such facts as the start and finish times, the line classes that can be used, the weighing location and even hearing of protests and appeals.

Some of the items that should be defined and published for all participants include:

Eligibility: Is the tournament open or by invitation only? Who may participate, the number of members required for a team, who has the final say on eligibility, etc.

Scoring system: There is no simple standard for establishing a scoring system as it greatly depends on the emphasis of the tournament; for example, whether it is a release event or whether points are given for fish weighed in. In any case, species for which points will be awarded should be defined, and if the tournament committee has established specific tackle that must be used, such as 24-kg (50-lb) and 37-kg (80-lb) test line only, a system might be devised where bonus points are given for fish taken on the lighter line. Many tournaments also establish a minimum weight for eligible species, thus requiring that smaller specimens be released.

Fishing times and areas: Fishing days and hours must be spelled out as well as the waters which can be fished, if applicable. Some tournaments provide maps or grid charts to define fishing areas. Most tournaments allow that a fish hooked before the closing signal each day can be fought to the finish, no matter how long it takes. However, a fish hooked even five minutes after the closing time would not be counted in the tournament tally. It is also wise to establish rules to accommodate bad weather days, a shortage of boats, and any other unforeseen circumstances.

Tackle classification: Most tournament committees specify line classes that may be fished during an event, based on the size and fighting characteristics of the species sought. For world record purposes, IGFA designates a maximum line class category for each species listed and it would be wise to check this list before establishing tournament tackle rules. For example, if someone caught a trophy-sized bluefish on 37-kg (80-lb) line, it would not qualify for an IGFA line class record as the association does not accept line class applications for this species on tackle exceeding 24 kg (50 lb).

Weighing and judging: The location of the official scale and procedures for weighing should be defined. Some tournament committees require that the angler fill out a form before weigh-in stating tackle used, date and time of catch, boat and skipper, witnesses, etc. It should also be stated how, where and when any protests concerning the validity of any catch should be filed and with whom the final decision rests. The objective of the judges is to ensure that the tournament is fair to all competitors.

Perhaps the best advice to someone compiling tournament regulations for the first time is to obtain published rules from other tournaments, particularly those run in a similar manner and with similar objectives. By examining regulations compiled by tried and true events, the tournament committee may avoid many unforeseen dilemmas.

PUBLICIZING AND ENFORCING THE RULES

While IGFA makes its angling and equipment regulations available for tournament use, this in no way means that the association backs, supports, or is involved in the tournament or its decisions. Enforcement of the rules is up to the tournament committee and officials only, and they have sole responsibility for any final judgments or rulings made within the scope of the tournament.

Sometimes when world record claims are received from tournament competitors, it is embarrassing for all concerned when those applications cannot be granted because of non-compliance with IGFA tackle regulations or other infringements. Often these disqualified claims have occurred for fish that not only won individual trophies, but also contributed to team or club placings. Sometimes an overlap or a two-hook rig has caused the disqualification, sometimes an overlength leader or double line or combination of the two. If such errors were noticed at the time of weighing, the capture could have been disallowed right there. This, in turn, would save the subsequent embarrassment of tournament officials and the annoyance of other competitors who, because a record is not issued, become aware of having been beaten by a disallowed catch. Inspection and measurement at the time of weighing avoids many subsequent problems. Sometimes it is felt that tournament officials who don't measure tackle can breathe a sigh of relief when a tournament is completed without record claims.

Records notwithstanding, it is imperative that tournament regulations be clearly understood, publicized and strictly enforced to give every participant an equal chance. Judging on fishing rules can be difficult because of the wide-ranging effects of the decisions, and the involvement of money in jackpot tournaments and calcuttas raises even more problems and pressures. Many such events have ended with lawsuits, and more and more tournament committees involved in money events are hiring lawyers to help formulate their rules and procedures.

For the traditional fishing tournament, however, where healthy competition, fun and fellowship are the major rewards, there are ways of minimizing disqualifications and rule breaches and maintaining the festive atmosphere of the event.

Te Ariki Nui, *with its special demountable tower, is a true long distance fishing wanderer, for multiple record holder and successful tournament fisherman Bill Hall of New Zealand, having travelled twice to Australia and once to Tonga. Photo: Peter Goadby.*

The first move is to publish all regulations and make them available before the start of the tournament, preferably well before the time of entry. Another aid is for a page with simple drawings to accompany the rules. The drawings could show both legal and illegal hook arrangements, as well as indicating how equipment such as double lines and leaders are measured to help clarify the printed word.

Next, a tournament briefing should be held for team members and boat crews where new and changed rules or interpretations are highlighted, as well as known problem areas from previous experience. The briefing must give an opportunity for frank questions and answers. Because some people are reticent about publicly asking questions, further opportunity should be given after the briefing and throughout the tournament for judges and officials to answer questions. If the questions and answers or interpretations are important to the tournament overall, they should be made known to all competitors.

Despite all the printed material, the review of the rules at the briefing, the questions and answers, the interpretations and methods used to measure, mistakes will occur. The next step is then for the tournament committee to, in fact, check and enforce the rules.

The Hawaiian International Billfish Tournament (HIBT), held at Kailua-Kona each year, is one in which the Board of Governors attempt to cover all eventualities and give maximum assistance to all competitors and charter crews. The tournament rules and fishing and equipment regulations are printed and accompanied by explanatory drawings. The rules are also covered at the team briefing with time allowed for questions and answers. In addition, the judges make random waterborne visits to watch competitors in action, and when a fish is brought in for weighing, all tackle and equipment are checked and measured, and line samples are taken and

tested for breaking strength. The judges are experienced administrators for different countries and cover as wide a range of the countries participating as possible. The operating and staffing in smaller tournaments are streamlined by having the weighmaster or the tournament's committee adjudicate on the rules and tackle at time of weighing.

It must sometimes perturb charter crews and teams who have made successful captures, to know that their carefully prepared double line and other tackle may be taken as a sample. They know also that their great work in finding, fighting and capturing a fish could all be lost at the judges' stand instead of in combat between man and fish. Yet such is the good feeling common with anglers and charter crews that generally these annoyances are accepted in a most sporting manner. The anglers and crews sometimes learn the hard way that double lines and monofilament leaders can stretch and that loops, even on wire leaders, can tighten and so lengthen measurements. Even when using IGFA rules, angler errors can still occur.

The mistakes that the judges in the HIBT have found cause most disqualifications occur in five main areas: the length of the double line, the length of the leader, the hook arrangement if a two-hook rig is used, the position of the hooks (distance between them) and the position of the hook or hooks in a lure, if one is used. Occasionally there is also a problem with line breaking strength or on the overall length of the gaff. At sea, the main disqualifications come from rule breaches in assistance to the angler, with someone other than the angler striking the fish or setting the drag or transferring the tackle on which the fish was hooked from rod holder to chair.

The adherence to angling rules and equipment regulations in tournament, as in day-to-day fishing and record breaking, remain a matter of honor and honesty.

It is possible to deliberately break the rules, to cheat, but I think this is rare in traditional tournaments. In fact, I have seen anglers enforce the rules against themselves as a matter of sporting ethics. There is such a high standard of honesty that anglers often disqualify their captures themselves when they realize a breach has occurred, or those who may be a little unsure ask officials for a ruling on something they felt might have been an error.

For those very few who deliberately breach the rules, there is always the thought that the truth eventually will out. The pressure of being up to tournament wins or record breaking sometimes shows on anglers without the additional strain of cheating.

The degrees to which rules are enforced or observed can be a problem sometimes. The natural inclination of a judge is always to be helpful. He or she may feel that, well, it's only a little bit too long and that an inch or two or a few centimetres in 30 or 40 feet could not really make any difference to the capture. But once leeway is given, there is no end. What happens when the next angler's double line or leader is just a bit longer than the last overlength allowance?

Hard experience has shown that the best way, in fact the *only* way, to adjudicate is to strictly interpret the rules, to observe the printed words and the intent of the rules literally, and to allow no leeway. Officials and judges must be completely fair and work on the principle that either the capture and rule observance is right or it is wrong. There can be no such thing as just a little bit wrong, a little rule breach. Either a capture is in line with the rules and their intent, or it is not.

The question is often posed whether or not strict rule observance in a tournament is worth the effort. The answer to that is a resounding 'yes'. Without observance of the rules, the intent of the rules, and sporting ethics, recreational fishing would lose not only its reputation, its tradition and much of its sport and enjoyment, but its credibility as well. Some tournaments do not survive while others such as the annual Billfish Tournament of Club Nautico de San Juan in Puerto Rico, the world's oldest billfish tournament, go from strength to strength.

The marlin board lives up to its name as the world record Pacific blue marlin of 420 kg (916 lb) on 37 kg (80 lb) test is brought to the weigh station at Kona, Hawaii in the HIBT. Photo: Peter Goadby.

OFFICIALS: THE WEIGHMASTER

The weighmaster's responsibilities remain the same for day-to-day captures and recordings. Their duties have increased pressures and responsibilities in times of tournament.

Weighmasters should be ready and available at expected weigh-in times and at short notice when anglers may feel the need and benefit of weighing a fish as quickly as it can be brought to shore. IGFA rules for records spell out that only fish weighed on land on certified scales will be considered for record claims.

The weighmaster's responsibility starts before the first fish arrives for weighing. The scales must be checked to ensure that they are within test. Under IGFA and GFAA rules, scales must be certified every twelve months and must be checked to ascertain that they are correctly zeroed.

Tailropes should be examined to ensure they are in good condition and safe to use. Each should be weighed so that its weight can be deducted from the gross weight of fish and tail rope so that the mean weight of the fish can be determined. If there is a record claim, the scales must be photographed clearly and given with a copy of the certificate of test and date stamp. Fish should be weighed by the tail, although occasionally big fish need to be weighed in a sling because of their length.

If the needle of the scales lies between weight marks on the dial of the scale, the weight must be taken at the lower of the two weights even if the needle *almost* reaches the higher mark. This can make quite a difference as some types of spring scales are marked in 2-kg (4.4-lb) increments.

Each weighmaster should have for easy and quick reference an updated and current list of world, national, state and club records. Gross and net weights should be announced clearly and loudly by the weighmaster, and the angler or the boat captain should be given the opportunity to view and check the weight.

If the fish is a potential record capture, it must be photographed full length with fins fully extended. Another photograph of the fish on the scales showing the weight is most helpful. The rod and reel must also be photographed and the fish measured as provided on the record claim with overall length, body length and girth at the widest section of the body. If the capture is a shark, a photograph must be taken of the open mouth clearly showing the teeth. If the fish is photographed on the ground a photograph of the fish should include a measuring tape showing the length of the fish. If there is doubt about the identification of the species of fish in potential records, every effort should be made to

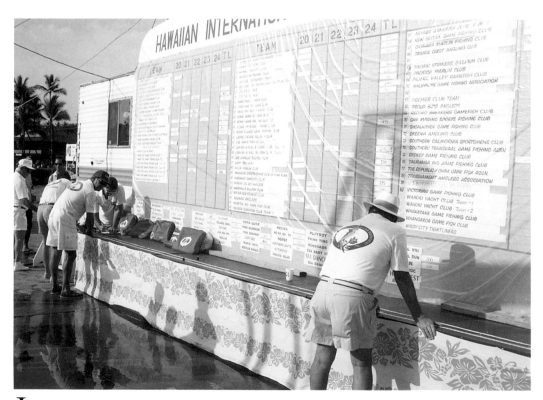

*J*udges at the HIBT measure tackle and test lines on each capture or tag and release as if it were a record.
Photo: Peter Goadby.

correctly identify the species. Clear photographs of the fish will assist ichthyologists or other experienced experts in correct identification.

If there is a potential record capture, the entire leader with hooks, plus the double line complete with snap and swivel or other method of attachment and 16 m (50 ft) of single line from where it is attached to the double line, must be taken and prepared for the record claim. In the case of two-hook rigs, these should be shown in a photograph or tracing, and this should be enclosed with the claim. In fly fishing records the entire tippet must be included.

The tackle used in the capture must be measured and be within the limits set out in the rules. The tackle to be measured includes rod tip length, rod butt length, gaff overall, gaff rope (if flying gaff), tail ropes. The published rules in words and illustrations show how the measurements must be taken.

The angler should be reminded of the *time limits* on lodging claims with the relevant body.

Records can be granted for tied weights or equalling of records if the net weight of the fish does not exceed the weight by the limits as published in the rules.

Records are kept in line classes 1, 2, 4, 6, 8, 10, 15, 24, 37 and 60 kg, and for male and female anglers. In Australia a junior angler is generally one who has not had his or her sixteenth birthday by the date of the capture and separate records are available.

If a catch is a record claim, the weight of the tail rope should be rechecked.

If the fish is mutilated or cut in any way, photographs of the damaged area should accompany any capture record or record claim.

IGFA record application forms are included in rule and record books issued by these bodies. The IGFA form must be used for IGFA claims. IGFA publish minimum

A *neat modern steelyard weighing a 49 kg (108 lb) Florida amberjack caught on plug casting tackle and 7 kg (15 lb) line for Jim Anson's entry in the Miami Metropolitan tournament. Photo: courtesy Jim Hardie, Miami Metropolitan.*

weights for vacant records. IGFA world records may be claimed by any angler.

The points for measuring fish and the checklist for record requirements are printed on the IGFA record application form.

Records can be claimed only on the line class used to make the capture. Care should be taken to establish that the tackle and line fit the class claimed by the angler.

RECORD BREAKING

Examination of the IGFA world record list shows that many anglers have more than one record, while a few have several. There are many facets to successful fishing for world records, but basically these fall into two categories—those who fish for records and those whose records are a serendipitous combination of the size of the fish and the line class to give the right weight and species on the right line caught in routine fishing.

These are perhaps the most satisfying and fun records. There is, however, a great satisfaction in planning, looking for and catching a record. Angler against great fish is always an exciting challenge. It is

the angler's name that appears in the record chart, on the record certificate with the fish, the weight and the line class, but record fish catching, like most fishing, is a team effort.

In planning for records, it is important to see which record categories are in reach. Some anglers and crews who seek records do not put bait in water until the fish is seen and its weight estimated so that the balanced tackle on the line class to provide a record is chosen in the hope of success.

Many other anglers work on the philosophy that to gain the maximum experience from their fishing, they greater research, planning, preparation, dedication and concentration than are normal in any successful fishing trip. Most fishermen have a philosophy that the objective of a successful fishing day is to catch fish and have action. The logical progression from this is the hope of big fish. For many anglers, skippers and crews it is vastly satisfying and somehow the top of the mountain to help others gain the record.

The planning and preparation in record chasing starts long before a bait or lure or teaser is put in the water. It is important to research and decide what fish can be expected at that time of the year in the current conditions.

Those seeking records will have ascertained:

- What records are potentially available.
- Where the fish of the record size are to be found.
- Where they are most prolific.
- If equipped boats with experienced crews are available. (Is it practical and possible to take a boat with skipper and crew to the area if satisfactory craft and experience are not available?)
- Expected weather conditions (rough seas add to the difficulty of record breaking, particularly on light line).

Alf Dean, fishing in South Australia, held world records for white sharks in the 1950s. Photo: courtesy Alf Dean.

should choose the tackle class for the size of fish they hope to catch. They know that a fish of a certain weight may be a record in one of the light line classes, but fish a line class in the hope of handling a really big fish if it takes a bait or lure. The smaller fish of lesser weight are planned to be released in any case, so the plan is for these fish to be brought to the boat with minimum trauma and tagged and released, or just released. This also allows maximum time in fishing and seeking a really big fish expected in that environment.

One of fishing's great satisfactions is when a fish of unexpected size takes a lure or bait on a line class— often one traditionally too light for that particular fish species and size—and is brought to the boat by teamwork plus a bit of luck. For some reason fish caught under difficulties, whether records or not, are sometimes longer remembered as important than those of the records.

If anglers, skippers and crews hope to make record captures, the best chance of success will come with even

Bob Dyer, fishing out from Brisbane, also held records for white sharks in the 1950s, including the all tackle records as heaviest rod and reel captures. Photo: courtesy Bob Miller.

The Japanese Game Fishing Association team bring in a blue marlin at the HIBT to add to their successful tournament record. The Japanese team have won this tournament and have been consistently placed in the first ten teams. Photo: Peter Goadby.

- Who can give personal data and share previous experiences.
- Check the IGFA fishing rules and tackle regulations to familiarize as to what will disqualify (check lengths of gaffs, ropes, leaders and terminal tackle).
- Tackle must be serviced; new, tested lines of the chosen category with plenty of spare lines wound on; leaders must be prepared and ready for action.
- Cameras must be checked and in working order.
- Availability of scales and weighing facilities should be checked and if necessary, planned and provided for.
- Bob and Dolly Dyer set and broke many world records, including shark records. Their preparation was thorough and complete. Bob planned one of his annual expeditions to Moreton Island to coincide with whaling—with the natural availability of oil and meat for chum—so as to try to take a white shark on 10 kg (22 lb) test tackle. The IGFA rules for this tackle allowed a maximum length leader of 4.5 m (15 ft). Experience spelled out the difficulties of this objective, so Bob's great skipper Charley Chambers rigged 100 leaders that length with the suitable hook for the record attempt. Charley knew which attempt on the great

white shark was successful because he answered my questions as to the number by saying fifty-six! When I asked why he was so definite, he said it was because once they got the white shark on that 10-kg test, he had 44 leaders left and unused. The white shark they finally landed that did not roll on leader or break that light line was a monster 494.44 kg (1068 lb). Any white shark a quarter that weight would have been OK for the record, but as it turned out the one that was finally caught was four times bigger than it needed to be, a record that may never be broken.

- The next step after preparation is for the captain and crew not only to be competent and capable of giving the angler every chance of success, but to understand that this is the objective, or one of the objectives, of the day or trip, so everyone is going to one goal.

- Daily preparation of line and the replacement of worn line or the lengths exposed to the ultra-violet rays of sunshine is most necessary each day or after each fish.

- Once the fish is found and hooked, every effort, all experience, all concentration, must go into capturing the fish.

- Every possible potential for loss must be eliminated and minimized: a cleared cockpit, sharp gaffs, gaffs tied off, understanding of procedure, the decision about who is to do what is most critical.
- Communication between the members of the team is crucial, not only for success in capture or release, but in safety of those in the firing line working in the cockpit.
- If the capture is made, the decision must be made whether to return to port and weighing scales, to maximize the weight of fish or to continue the day's fishing to try for more action.
- The fish must be kept wet, under sacks or other material, to retain maximum weight.
- Finally the line sample, terminal tackle and all necessary photographs, test certificates, measurements and paperwork must be completed to establish the claim.

Perhaps the greatest difference between dedicated day-to-day fishing, tournament fishing and deliberate record-breaking is that in record-breaking everything is planned, everything subjugated to the objective of the record and the prospective record-breaking angling.

*C*aptain Peter Wright, angler Mick McGrath and crew with the heaviest marlin so far weighed from the Great Barrier Reef, Queensland. Photo: John Pesch.

*C*anada (above) has dominated the bluefin tuna world records with catches at Prince Edward Island and Nova Scotia. Photo: IGFA.

COMPETITIVE FISHING

GAMEFISHING RECORDS

Alfred Glassell with his 709 kg (1560 lb) black marlin at Cabo Blanco. Photo: courtesy Alfred Glassell.

The most important gamefish, a bluefin tuna, ever caught on rod and reel was in June 1898.

The first yellowtail under fishing club rules was landed in 1898.

The first gamefish over 200 lb was a 251-lb (114-kg) bluefin tuna caught in 1899.

The first marlin, a striped of 125 lb (56.8 kg), was caught on rod and reel in 1903.

The first marlin over 300 lb, a striped marlin of 339 lb (154 kg), was caught in 1909.

The first yellowfin tuna on rod and reel was captured in 1904.

The first black marlin on rod and reel was landed in 1910.

The first giant bluefin in the Atlantic on rod and reel was landed in 1911.

The first broadbill swordfish was landed in 1913. It weighed in at 358 lb (162.7 kg).

The first record mako shark on rod and reel was landed in 1915.

The first tarpon on fly was landed in 1878.

The first big tarpon, 174 lb (79 kg), was also landed in 1878.

The first gamefish marlin over 400 lb (181.8 kg) was weighed in in 1916.

The first gamefish over 900 lb (409 kg), a black marlin, was weighed in in 1926.

The first blue marlin in the Bahamas was weighed in in 1933.

The first tiger shark over 1000 lb (454.5 kg) was weighed in in 1936.

The first shark over 1120 lb (509 kg), a tiger shark, was weighed in in 1938.

The first gamefish over 1000 lb (454.5 kg), a black marlin, was caught in 1952.

The first gamefish over 1500 lb (681.8 kg), a black marlin, was caught in 1953.

The first shark over 2000 lb (909 kg), a white shark, was caught on 9 January 1952.

The first shark over one British ton (it weighed 2250 lb or 1022.7 kg), a white shark, was caught on 6 April 1952.

The first gamefish on 80-lb (36.3-kg) line over 1000 lb (454.5 kg), a black marlin, was caught in 1966.

THE TRAVELLING FISHERMAN

It has always been part of the fisherman's temperament to wonder and want to find out what is beyond that far wave, what fish can be caught on that distant locale—are those rumors of super fish, super fishing, true?

Modern air travel has brought fish and fishermen closer together. It is integral to many fishing plans. The transport of the angler and his tackle is now familiar and welcome business to airlines that co-operate with the carriage of unwieldy rod tubes, heavy tackle boxes, camera cases and suitcases of clothing.

Some airlines are more appreciative than others of carrying anglers, yet even these are noticeably under-whelmed when angler passengers arrive with unnecessary baggage, baggage that becomes increasingly difficult to handle and keep track of as distance and time go by. It is important to carry only the minimum, to not carry unnecessary items and weight. The first step is to check

Bertram make boats of many lengths used for gamefishing. Big boats that travel south from California to Baja, Mexico are called yachts. Photo: Peter Goadby.

what services your charter boat, guide or lodge will provide. It is important also to know the quality of tackle, lures and terminal tackle and whether extra top-quality additions will be welcome.

Anglers, particularly light-tackle anglers, prefer to use the tackle with which they are familiar and that has proved itself. Despite this, a conscious decision must be made about what is needed and what will be unnecessary.

Still and video cameras are necessary for recording and later enjoying the fishing trip. Remember that airport terminals will use X-rays on hand luggage and often on other baggage, so carry unexposed film in those lead-lined bags or take other precautions such as hand carrying. Don't take more cameras and lenses than are needed, yet try to anticipate Murphy's Law. My personal choice is Nikon 801 in US No 8008 body with Nikon 35–135 zoom, Nikon 70–210 zoom and flash, instead of carrying lenses of each needed length. A second camera, waterproof to 9 m (30 ft), a Nikon AF AW, is carried to give a chance of shallow underwater photographs and those otherwise damaging wet cockpit shots backing up in a rough sea. Both lenses have a skylight filter for their own benefit and to protect the lens. Moderate-speed 200 ASA transparency film is used, although naturally many fishermen choose color print film. Always carry plenty of film to remote destinations and keep it protected from extreme temperatures and humidity. Boat and sea conditions are not environmentally friendly to camera lenses and film. These should be carried and kept in the mildest temperatures and in minimum humidity. Common sense care and maintenance are all needed to ensure a worthwhile record of your fishing trip and dependable survival of camera equipment.

Research, common sense and safety give positive leads of what clothes and footwear are sensible for fishing any locality. In fishing cold climates for bluefin tuna or salmon, the example of the Canadians should be followed.

It has proved to be better, warmer and more practical, when hooked up and working, to have several layers of clothing rather than fewer layers of heavier and difficult-to-remove coverings. Light waterproof boots are welcome and practical on boats. Cold feet not only prevent enjoy-ment of any day, but highlight the difficulty of fishing in the colder climes where the breeze cuts through and the sun appears to provide light rather than warmth. Make sure the soles of waterproof boots are non-slip. There are excellent soles used on waterproof boots designed for ocean-racing yachtsmen.

Waterproof jackets and pants should be dry and practical, preferably in non-sweating, condensation-absorbing materials. Like the boots, they should be easily removable in case of a slip overboard. The jacket in particular should be easily discarded as the angler heats up during the fight, particularly if spray is not flying inboard over the fisherman when the boat is backing up.

A change of clothing on the boat is advisable in any climate. It is much more pleasant to be as clean and dry as possible at all times.

Those with blond or reddish hair and light-colored skin may need long sleeves and slacks as well as suitable hats or Florida-type fishing caps with peak and back and earflaps. Hats, where they overlap face and eyes, and peaks of caps should be dark green or any other dark

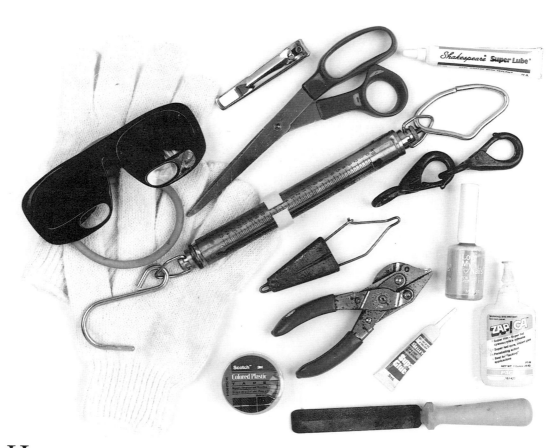

Handy bits and pieces for the travelling fisherman: fit all sizes cotton gloves; polarizing sun glasses; nail clippers to trim knots; scissors to trim skirts of lures or for tuning lures so they run correctly; scales to set drag; spare harness clips for harness on safety lines; lure retriever for snagged lures; nail polish for roller screws; pliers with cutter; 60-second glue for knots and skirts; plastic tape; and file. Because of aircraft regulations, knives should be purchased on arrival. Photo: David Rogers.

color not only to minimize the effects of reflection, but to enhance vision. Florida fishermen generally take advantage of the most practical clothing and footwear.

The type of clothing in warm climates for both men and women is the same—light, loose and practical with non-slip shoes or sneakers.

The great pioneer angler-writer S. Kip Farrington highlighted the need for comfortable fishing clothes when, during a long, hard fight with a broadbill, his tight binding shorts were, on his instructions, cut off despite the presence of women guests aboard. Kip successfully completed the fight faintly embarrassed in his jockstrap.

A light windproof water-resistant jacket is ideal for cool mornings and evenings. Some fishermen like to wear these jackets with club and tournament patches. Others fish in practical clothes, then change to dressier club outfits for weigh-ins; they prefer their photographic records of successful days to be as neat as possible. The demand for comfortable fishing clothing is now recognized. Tarpon and other companies now manufacture and market special tropical-weight fishing outfits. Golf shirts and T-shirts with superb Guy Harvey paintings, have established a new level of fishing attire with fishermen able to wear natural reproductions of their favorite fish species. Outdoor suppliers have long been established for practical cold-weather clothing. A collared shirt gives added protection from the sun while a pocket is helpful for holding glasses and other bits and pieces.

Quality polarizing glasses are a must in all fishing where vision, hunting and seeing the fish are part of success as well as pleasure. This applies to onshore fishing, as well as from boats. There are benefits in the choice of lens colors in polarizing sun glasses for various water colors fished—brown or amber enhances vision in inshore waters and shades of grey are better offshore. Experience shows what color and shapes suit individuals' eyes. Check that the glasses you choose are polarizing before you buy them.

Topsiders and similar type boat shoes with non-slip soles revolutionized the choice of practical footwear on boats. Their non-slip characteristic on wet decks have improved crew and angler confidence, performance and safety. Anglers who are on strike should be already wearing the shoes ready to take their strike.

The benefits and protection of good boat shoes at time of wiring, gaffing, tagging and bait catching are now generally understood. Many experienced anglers really worry when crews are working in bare feet at this critical time. Crews often go about their work in bare feet while watching, changing baits, cleaning up and doing all other jobs while readying for a strike. Once the strike comes and other rods, lures and cockpit are cleared away, the crew change into deck shoes ready for the most critical and dangerous time of all, taking the leader, gaffing or tag and releasing. Leather soles are not welcome on boats, firstly because they can be slippery, particularly when wet, and because leather and other dark soles can discolor white or light-colored decks or flying bridges. Boat shoes are also beneficial when fishing in skiffs and small boats used for inshore trolling and casting. They minimize chance of slip as well as providing protection against teeth, spines and slime.

Proven non-slip soles are equally important in fishing from shore, particularly on a rocky surface. Anglers who fish on rocky foreshores have shoes or sandals with special clips to give grip in the water or on wave-inundated and slimy weedy rock surfaces.

Hats and caps should be lightweight and comfortable, of a practical type that will not blow or lift in slipstream or wind. My personal preference is for the Florida-type peaked cap with ear and neck turndowns. The underside of hat brim or cap should be black or dark green to minimize reflection. If not manufactured this way it can be treated with a black or dark green marking pen. If this pen is not of the waterproof type the result can be different and not necessarily artistic on a wet or windy day. A length of heavy fishing line that goes under the chin and attaches to the restraining cord of the necessary polarizing glasses helps prevent lost time and lost cap or glasses.

SCIENCE
AND THE
FISHERMAN

TAG AND RELEASE

The greatest change in gamefishing in recent years has been the movement to tag and release instead of capture and kill. The trend to tag and release has been as a result of co-operation between fishermen and scientists. The species released include fish that are popular as food, but are tagged and released to assist the survival of the fish and knowledge of their wanderings and growth. This overrides the taking of fish for weighing and food.

There are many major tag-and-release programs around the world. Many of these are international, with fish tagged and released and then recaptured in different countries and high seas. Some anglers choose to simply release rather than to tag and release in the belief that information gained can work against their interests by providing information that benefits those who are already putting pressure on the gamefish and shark stocks. Similarly some domestic and international commercial fishermen do not return the tags they recover from caught

Jacquie Acheson catches the fleeting color changes of Jerry Dunaway's grander black. Jacquie Acheson.

fish because they believe knowledge gained can be used against them or benefit the country or area of origin.

This is unfortunate. It is now imperative that all fishermen and scientists co-operate in gaining factual data to assist sound management and survival of the fish for future generations. In the USA the tagging programs located at Woods Hole, La Jolla and Narragansett are world leaders in the gathering of knowledge of ocean gamefish through tagging and release and tag recovery.

Some tag-and-release programs have tag and releases by commercial and recreational fishermen and scientists, as well as tag return from these groups. In others the tag and releases and recoveries are mainly by the sport fishermen and scientists. It is generally true that the greater the number of fish tagged and released, the better the information and potential of the program. Where sport fishermen participate in commercial programs such as that on southern bluefin tuna, some of the information and important recoveries have been from releases by sport fishermen, giving further proof that fish survive the trauma of capture and release very successfully.

Not all the tag-and-release records of importance have entailed recovery after transoceanic crossings or a long time between release and recapture. Some of the very short times between capture and recapture are of scientific importance as well as great interest. The short-term records—as held by juvenile tuna and yellowtail with elapsed time between release and recapture of only one to three minutes and a lapse of only thirty minutes for marlin—add knowledge about recovery from capture and resumption of feeding cycle.

Tagging programs are based on all coasts of the US and in Hawaii, Canada, England, Ireland, Japan, Korea, Spain, Senegal, South Africa, New Caledonia, New Zealand and Australia. Tags and data from the programs, particularly from USA and Australia, are used in other countries that do not have domestic tagging programs. Much of the tagging effort and important data for management is directed at the pelagic species that are important both commercially and recreationally. Naturally these include the high-charisma pelagic species.

IGFA lists major sportfisherman involvement with the tagging programs of IATTC at La Jolla, California, USA; International Pacific Halibut Commission at Seattle, USA; CSIRO at Hobart, Australia; Northern Fisheries Research Centre, Cairns, Australia; Queensland DPI, Rockhampton, Australia; DPI, Darwin, Australia; Ministry of Agriculture, Lowestaff, Suffolk, England; Marine Sport Fish Tagging Program, Dublin, Ireland; JGFA, Tokyo, Japan; Marine Gamefish Tagging Program, Whangerei, New Zealand; Billfish Tagging, Durban, South Africa; National Tagging Program,

This blue marlin showed no signs of disability from its lack of bill. Photo: Peter Goadby.

Black marlin sometimes have deformed bills, lost fins or lobes of tails. Photo: Greg Finney.

Durban, South Africa; California Pelagic Shark Tagging Program, Long Beach, California, USA; NOAA, NMFS, Marine Gamefish Cooperative Tagging, La Jolla, California, USA; Cooperative NMFS Albacore Program, La Jolla, California, USA; NMFS Lemon Shark Program, Miami, Florida, USA; NOAA NMFS Coastal Pelagic Tagging, Panama City, Florida, USA; NOAA NMFS Cooperative Game Fish Tagging Program, Miami, Florida, USA; Small Marine Fish Tagging Programs, New Orleans, Louisiana, USA; American Littoral Society Fish Tagging Program, Sandy Hook, New Jersey; Striped Bass Tagging Program, Stony Brook, New York; NMFS Co-operative Shark Tagging Program, Narragansett, Rhode Island; Marine Game Fish Tagging Program, Charleston, South Carolina; Fish Trackers Inc., Corpus Christi, Texas; Dept of Fisheries and Oceans, Vancouver, British Columbia, Canada; Salmon Research Trust of Ireland, Mayo, Ireland; Oregon Department of Fish and Wild Life, Clackamas, Oregon; Stock Assessment of Anadromus Salmonids, Corvallis, Oregon; Ecology of Juvenile Salmonids, Corvallis, Oregon; NMFS, Portland, Oregon; and US Fish and Wildlife Service, Olympia, Washington.

These and other saltwater co-operative tag-and-release programs give sportfishermen (whatever their preferred fish and wherever they fish) the chance to help science, the fish, their future fishing and that of future generations. Scientists and fish managers do not have the opportunities of active fishermen who can observe and monitor the living marine world, so observation and reporting by fishermen helps fill in the unknown. There have been many instances where reports of happenings that are commonplace to fishermen are important and

Numbered plastic and stainless headed tags with similarly numbered information cards and applicators in tag poles are now an important part of equipment on most offshore sportfishing boats. Certificates (here from the New South Wales Fisheries) of both tag and release, and recovery of tagged fish, are secured with pride. Photo: Peter Goadby.

helpful to scientists and yet were previously unreported. Thankfully more and more anglers are using their video cameras and Nikons to record and pass on what they see to scientists.

Fishermen in all parts of the world proudly display tag and release and tag recovery certificates in their offices and homes. These fishermen are rightly proud of their contribution to knowledge.

There have been many examples of how tag and release information has been helpful to recreational fishermen and to the fish. It was scientist-fisherman and tagging leader Frank Mather of Woods Hole laboratory who noted the frightening decline of the Atlantic bluefin stocks as well as proving their trans-Atlantic crossings and possible populations.

Tag returns show that giant bluefin are in fact trans-Atlantic and Mediterranean travellers, so added commercial fishing pressure and kills in one locality affect potential breeding stock and numbers of fish in others.

Tag recoveries in black marlin released with tags supplied and co-ordinated by NOAA's La Jolla, California laboratory and NSW Fisheries of Sydney, Australia, have provided valuable information on this once mysterious marlin. Information from the tagging in the Great Barrier Reef fishery and other parts of the Australian coast was of assistance in the decision to close a large section of the waters off the northern Great Barrier Reef to local and international longlining. Data from the programs showed the importance and movements of this stock not only from Australia's east coast, but generally through the western and into the central Pacific.

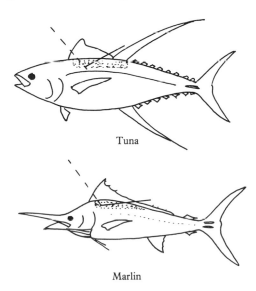

Tuna

Marlin

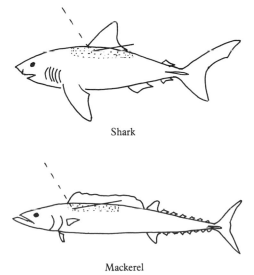

Shark

Mackerel

All fish species should be tagged near the dorsal fin, below the dorsal where there is sufficient muscle to hold the tag, but above the line of vertebrae and lateral lines.

The leader is cut down short on the hook. Photo: Peter Goadby.

The published papers from tag-and-release programs co-ordinated by NOAA's Jim Squire (which coincided with the start of the GBR giant black marlin fishery in 1968) and Dr Julian Pepperell of New South Wales Fisheries, Australia, cover 9008 black marlin tagged in the Cairns/Lizard Island area plus a further 2505 from other east coast ports from 1968 to 1986. Recovery of some of these black marlin showed that the fish were in the area near where they were tagged one, two and three years later, while others were recovered as far as 7000 km (4200 miles) from release well north of Tahiti.

Other important recaptures have been north of the Equator around Papua New Guinea, off New Zealand and at many points on the east coast of Australia. There have so far not been any tag returns through the Torres Strait or in the Indian Ocean.

There have been two important black marlin recoveries that indicate how far this species travels. One

was recovered between New Zealand and Australia, 5700 km (3420 miles) after release off Baja, California, an average of 9.4 km (6 miles) per day, while another tagged at Christmas Island south of Hawaii was recovered off the coast of New South Wales after 137 days. It had averaged 24.9 km (15 miles) per day for the 3411 km (2000 miles).

The speed of travel is difficult to define accurately as a straight division of distance and days. Black marlin have been recovered near where they were tagged as long as 36 days previously, while another was recovered only 14 km (9 miles) north-west from release point after 725 days. It would indeed be interesting to know its wanderings in those 725 days. Would it have travelled 3872 km (2322 miles) north in 172 days, or 4200 km (2520 miles) north-east in 210 days or 1415 km (850 miles) south in 75 days as have other black marlin?

Fish movements to the south are important for thousands of anglers off Australia and New Zealand. Two Great Barrier Reef black marlin have been recovered off New Zealand. The tag recoveries south of their northern Great Barrier Reef release area shows a heavy movement in that direction in various age groups. The recovery of New South Wales tagged marlin on course and back to the northern Great Barrier Reef area shows the two-way movement.

It is intriguing to think of the wanderings and activity of the tagged marlin between release and recapture: the time spent hunting, in fleeing from predators, the periods of stay where bait schools and other food are prolific. De Pepperell's paper shows regular recoveries back near the place of tagging after 330–410 days. This time period is repeated after two, three and four years in the Cairns/Lizard Island area.

Dr Pepperell's New South Wales Fisheries data and report on tag returns on Australia's east coast sailfish from Dunk Isle and Cape Bowling Green on the Great

Yellowfin are important tag and release species in New South Wales' waters whether on lures or natural baits. Photo: Tim Simpson.

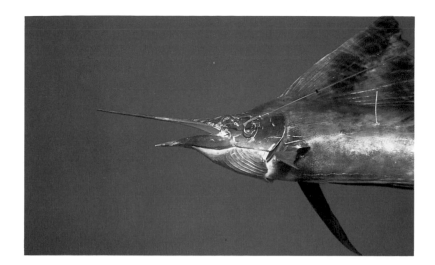

Barrier Reef and Moreton Bay in southern Queensland indicate a completely differing pattern from that of the wandering black marlin or the Atlantic sailfish. So far there is no indication of south/north or north/south or distance at all. The tag recoveries have been back at their area of release after varying times.

Tag returns on striped marlin in New South Wales showed they stayed in the same canyon area for at least two months before continuing their wandering. A tagged New Zealand marlin of this species headed north-east towards the Cook Islands after a long-distance recovery. Most of the striped marlin tagging has been off California and Baja, California, in the NOAA/NMFS tagging program co-ordinated by Jim Squire at La Jolla. Returns show that the striped marlin move south from California off Baja and other Mexican ports, while those tagged off Baja have continued to swim south and south-west with recoveries of 5500 km (3450 miles) and 3700 km (2300 miles) being two of the many.

The 1990 NOAA Billfish Program listed striped marlin tag recovery No 490, released on 26 October 1986, and recovered off Cabo San Lucas in March 1989.

Another tagged off Lanai, Hawaii was recaught off Wainae, Oahu, 35 days later, while another tagged off Kona, Hawaii was recaptured 92 days later north of Hawaii.

Captain Bobby Brown is the pioneering tag-and-release captain in Hawaii, with many tags and several recoveries of all three Pacific marlin in Hawaiian waters. The prestigious Hawaiian International Billfish Tournaments also moved to tag and release with recognition and acknowledgment of the tagging angler and team at the weighing station in the tournaments.

Kawa kawa and skipjack live baits are often speared by marlin before being swallowed. Photo: Peter Goadby.

Tagged and released mahi mahi (dolphin fish) rejoin their school and life cycle. Photo: Tim Simpson.

Blue marlin recoveries are important, as fewer have been tagged by sport fishermen than other species. At thirty minutes between release and hook-up and recapture, a Kona Hawaiian blue marlin probably holds the marlin record for the shortest time free. Tag returns already show that Pacific blue marlin tagged off Kona, Hawaii were recovered one and two years later in the same area. As in other parts of the world, Hawaiian recreational fishermen are responsible for a high percentage of tag returns. It is disappointing that many local and international commercial fishermen, those who kill the majority of billfish, tuna and other gamefish, do not return all the tags they recover.

Pacific tuna also move long distances across the oceans. Skipjack tuna have been tagged in commercial scientific programs to give information on their wanderings, both short and long distances. A skipjack travelled west from Baja, California to west of the Marshall Islands, a straight-line distance of 9500 km (5900 miles). Skipjack returns show journeys in all directions— north, south, east and west, including journeys across the Equator to, from and along land masses and high seas.

Albacore travel right across the northern Pacific east from Japan and west from California as well as from southern California north past Oregon. Pacific northern bluefin tuna (giant bluefin) are also recorded from the tag returns as northern Pacific crossings from California to Japan and Japan to California and Baja, California, with a tuna travelling 8530 km (5300 miles) at an average speed of 26 km (16 miles) per day. The related southern bluefin has long had scientific and commercial as well as sportfishing tagging that shows movement around southern Australia to New Zealand and beyond, with the bigger fish crossing the Roaring Forties west to and past South Africa and into the Atlantic.

Tagged yellowfin tuna in the Pacific have shown movements westward to Japan from open ocean and west/

*T*agged barramundi have yielded valuable migration and growth information. Photo: Arch Livingstone.

east and east/west travels as well as north/south and south/north travels between Mexico and South America across the Equator. Yellowfin in the Atlantic tagged off western Africa have been recovered in the West Indies. Most yellowfin recoveries have been less than 1600 km (1000 miles) from tag point in the eastern Pacific, although some have travelled 5149 km (3200 miles).

The giant bluefin's regular appearances at various localities in the Mediterranean were known in pre-Christian times. Tag returns from tuna fishing specialists Elwood Harry, Bill Carpenter and the other dedicated anglers confirmed that bluefin were trans-Atlantic voyagers. Tuna released off the Bahamas were recaptured off Norway and Brazil. Those tagged off north-east USA and Canada's maritime provinces crossed to Europe and

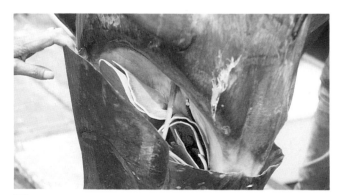

*P*acific blue marlin and other marlin species often have small marlin, broadbill and other billfish in their stomachs. This 273 kg (600 lb) blue marlin had the bill of a smaller marlin through its gills. Photo: Peter Goadby.

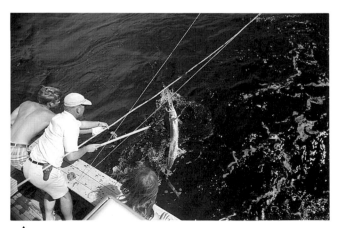

*A*tlantic white marlin about to be tagged by the Keeches fishing at Atlantic City. Photo: Gil Keech.

the Bay of Biscay, and fish tagged in that area have been recovered off the USA. Tag recoveries around Gibraltar, the guardian gate of the Mediterranean, were both North Sea- and US east coast-released. Atlantic bluefin have been recorded at 7773 km (4830 miles) in 119 days to average 65 km (40 miles) per day.

Atlantic blue marlin have been revealed to travel from the Virgin Islands in the Caribbean across to Africa's west coast. Atlantic big eye tuna tagged off central Africa have been recovered north to the Canary Islands and across the Atlantic to Brazil.

The tag recoveries of the Atlantic sailfish created information not only on their journeying off Florida to Venezuela, but that they lived far beyond the generally accepted seven- to eight-year term previously known in tag recoveries. An adult-sized sailfish estimated at the then life expectancy of seven years, tagged off Florida, was recovered ten years later off Venezuela to give a new and positive idea of life limits, while others have been free for five years. White marlin have been proved to wander from the east coast of the USA to the Gulf

*G*uide Wayne Ross swims a tagged barramundi by the lower lip to ensure its resuscitation. Photo: Peter Goadby.

of Mexico and further south to Venezuela and Brazil, while others have moved eastward out into the Atlantic to be recovered after ten and twelve years.

Yellowtail are regarded as species that generally reside around islands and reefs and that, particularly in the smaller sizes, do not travel long distances along the coast or out to sea. A small yellowtail (7 kg, 15 lb) tagged off Coffs Harbour, eastern Australia showed that the short migration theory was not always valid. This fish was recovered 651 days later off New Zealand's east coast Bay of Islands. A yellowtail tagged off Tauranga on New Zealand's east coast completed an east to west trans-Tasman crossing when recaptured at Bermagui, south-eastern Australia. A mako shark tagged at Port Macquarie, eastern Australia, made a west/east Tasman crossing to be recaptured near North Cape, New Zealand after 257

*T*he speedster wahoo (above), despite its top edible qualities, is regularly tagged and released. Photo: Darrell Jones.

A black marlin (left) at Cabo San Lucas about to be tagged with the new nylon tag of the Billfish Foundation for angler Jorge Redondo. Photo: Captain Bill Harrison.

Big rays often work with sailfish schools. Cobia in Florida often work with rays feeding on the seabed as they disturb the crabs and other food. Photo: Greg Edwards.

days. This further strengthened awareness of oceanic crossings. Most Australian mako recoveries showed that they moved along the coast seasonally.

Shark migration distances in the Atlantic are long, as are times out. Jack Casey's Narragansett-based NMFS program, with over 5000 sharks tagged, demonstrated the distance movements of some of the Atlantic sharks. Blue sharks released off north-east USA have been recovered after journeys north and east across the Atlantic to Canada and the European coast 6115 km (3800 miles) from tagging to recovery point.

Blue sharks tagged off north-west Africa and Gibraltar have been recaught northwards to the English Channel, north-west towards Venezuela and westwards to the Gulf of St Lawrence.

The Narragansett program shows an Atlantic mako travelling 2735 km (1700 miles) from off New York to the West Indies and from the Gulf of Mexico east to the Bahamas. A mako travelled 2414 km (1500 miles), averaging 28 km (17.6 miles) per day. The apparently slow-moving tiger shark is one of the species that moved from New York to Costa Rica. The requiem sandbar

shark, once regarded as a shallow water estuary dweller, moved from just south of New York to the Gulf of Mexico.

Anglers, skippers and crews can be truly proud of their release records and assistance to science. The billfish, tuna and other highly regarded species constitute not only a major contribution in time, in expenditure and experience, but often entail the possibility of human injury, particularly when fish are close to the boat for tagging or release with hook removal or leader cutting. There is sometimes a chance of hurt with billfish jumping or sharks rolling and thrashing at or near the boat.

The high degree of co-operation and understanding between anglers, skippers, crews and scientists was again demonstrated at the 1988 and 1989 Hawaiian International Billfish Tournaments, when co-operation far beyond that established in the previous 28 years of the tournament was experienced. Scientists Kim Holland and Richard Brill were conducting tracking experiments in 1985 on billfish and tuna with electronic tags. They had experienced success with yellowfin tuna, but billfish hook-ups from just one boat were more difficult. The scientists wondered if the tournament committee and the competitors, skippers and crews could help with marlin, even with the pressure of the tournament. Tournament boats were successful in bringing blue marlin to the boat so they could be tagged with the electronic tags by the scientists, who then tracked the marlin. In 1989, the experiments and need for participation were doubled.

Dr Frank Carey and Dr Barbara Block were engaged in telemetry electronic tagging and marlin-following experiments using even more sophisticated electronic tags. Again, competing boats were successful in contributing live blue marlin for electronic tagging for both project teams.

Preliminary general information from the telemetry programs showed the value of this angler/crew/ scientist co-operation. The initial information showed that marlin not only survive but quickly recover from the trauma of struggle and being brought to boat to resume their

The Pescador crew with a tagged Atlantic blue marlin for Ralph Christiansen Jnr at St Thomas. Photo: Captain Bill Harrison.

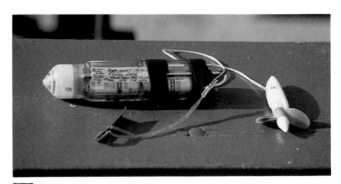

This is one of the types of sophisticated sonic tags used by the teams of Drs Carey and Block, and Drs Holland and Brill, in telemetric experiments on Hawaiian marlin. Photo: Peter Goadby.

daytime 51–91 metre (25-50 fathom) and shallower nighttime 0–10 metre (0-5 fathom) cruising and hunting along the ledges with the tuna schools, with depth relative to the upper layer of the thermocline.

Some of the releases moved north, some south, while others stayed near the FAD or ledge where first hooked, rising in the water levels with the tuna school.

Scientists at the HIBT have for over thirty years examined and recorded the stomach contents of the weighed fish. Those contents show that the marlin feed on bottom-dwelling fish species, as well as pelagic species and squid. One of the surprises has been in the occurrence of juvenile billfish found in the marlin stomachs. Baby marlin and broadbill appear in the stomach sacs along with the remains of bills and swords. One blue marlin had the sword of another marlin right through its gills.

The size and weight of tuna removed from marlin stomachs and throats has also been surprising. A 340-kg (748-lb) blue marlin taken on a lure right where boats had been slow trolling live baits all day had a 30-kg (62-lb) big eye tuna in its stomach. The contents of the big eye stomach were not recorded, but here was a clear example of the predator/prey life cycle. That marlin was taken by Dick Davis while fishing with Captain Bart Miller, a master bait fisherman who had baits positioned perfectly to give his angling team every chance, yet these and other baits were apparently ignored in favor of man's plastic creation. An 820-kg (1805-lb) blue marlin, also taken on a lure, had a 63-kg (140-lb) yellowfin in its stomach.

Scientists and fishermen from around the world are together for the Hawaiian International Billfish Tournament and the summer congregation of blue marlin in this year-round marlin fishery. Information on the spring structure of marlin backbone and the use of their narrow red and majority white muscle tissues give fishermen a better understanding of the marlin's explosive power and long-term swimming power. Marlin use that narrow band

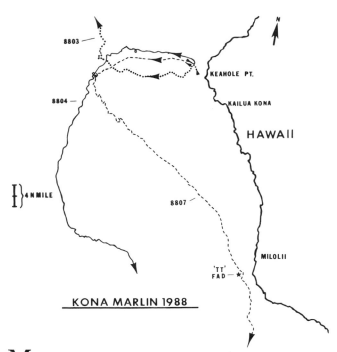

*M*igration of Drs Holland and Brill's sonic tagged marlin.

of red muscle to cruise and the white muscle when explosive power is needed in the kill, to avoid being killed in the chase and hunt, or to jump and escape. Fishermen now more clearly understand the benefits of attacking fishing to trigger and burn out the power of that white muscle. The marlin can cruise for hour after hour on their red muscle, so angler tactics have to ensure the fish uses and tires its white muscle.

A wag remarked after a presentation on billfish physiology at a billfish symposium that billfish are truly 'hot-headed' fish in the way they strike and jump, run and sound, charge and jump at boats, and strike at lures and baits time after time, particularly after teasing. The

*B*lack marlin are held after tagging and hook removal, or leader cutting by hand or with a line, until their color lights up to ensure resuscitation. Photo: Peter Goadby.

Even black and white film shows the glowing striped marlin with its lights turned on. Photo: IGFA— Lerner Expedition.

remark came after a presentation of a paper on 'brain heaters'. Scientists have established that marlin do have heaters in the brain and in the eye muscle that keep brain and eyes warmer than surrounding water. Billfish, tuna and the lamna sharks—whites, mako and porbeagle—have performance-enhancing heaters. Dr Barbara Block and Dr Frank Carey have shown in their papers that muscle tissue in the big tunas is up to 15°C (17°F) higher than ambient, that the makos, whites and porbeagle sharks' muscle tissue is up to 5°C (9°F) warmer, that marlin eyes and brain are 4°C (7°F) above ambient. Another scientist, C. C. Lindsay, has written that marlin muscle tissue is 2.5°C (4.5°F) warmer. Broadbill are another important gamefish with a brain warmer at 1.4°C (2.5°F) above ambient. New Zealand's Dr Peter Davie, a regular visiting scientist at the PORF laboratory at Kona, lists 142 papers relating to billfish anatomy and physiology in his book *Pacific Marlin Anatomy and Physiology*.

These papers and others on migration, stock and fishing pressure and billfish-related subjects show that billfish are indeed VIFs (Very Important Fish) to the scientists as well as to recreational fishermen. It is a pity that as much interest in their survival is not often shown by commercial fishermen of many nations and fisheries managers. Broadbill swordfish and marlin are shown in Japanese and other papers to be target species of the efficient longline industry, yet are repeatedly referred to by fisheries managers as incidental take in the tuna fisheries. This is yet another reason why sportfishermen should not only know more about the fish, but about the industries that are dramatically reducing stock. The

published papers from Billfish Symposiums I and II, held at Kona, Hawaii in 1972 and 1989, contain much of the world knowledge about billfish and fishing pressure.

Thinking fishermen are aware through observation and scientific information, plus the visual indications of good water, of where to fish for best potential. They know that the presence of surface life on the current is a clear indication of warm water favored by the gamefish. All fish have upper and lower temperature limits as well as preferred temperature isotherms where they may be concentrated.

The living current indicators are some of the most beautiful and intriguing marine animals that are carried by the warm current. They were recognized as warm current dwellers long before the availability of built-in seawater thermometers and thermisters.

These current indicators, like all life in the current, are associated with the killing of other animals. The best-known killer is the Portuguese man-o'-war, with its virulent stinging tentacles that can kill fish this stinging colony feeds on. A small electric-blue barred fish lives safely among the tentacles, immune to the stings, safe from fish that would feed on it, while it entices other fish into the killing tentacles. The apparently frail animals of the current all pack a punch that kill and paralyse other animals that become their food; the beautiful floating nudibranch glauca has a stinging capability in its gills inherited from the Portuguese man-o'-war (physalia), on which it preys. The innocent-appearing warm-current animals are classic examples of beauty and frailty; of the iron fist in a velvet glove.

Blue is the color of the warm current and its living creatures, and it is associated in fishermen's memories with lit-up striking gamefish. New Zealand's Dr Peter Davie has studied how marlin light up in those unforgettable glowing colors. He found that in the skin, in the epidermis, lie cells that are called melanophores. These give billfish their dark appearance. Spaces between these cells can produce the blue and silver. These iridiophore cells reflect the light like tiny mirrors to produce the bright colors. Withdrawal of the dark melanophore cells allows the light and brilliant colors of the iridiophores to show when stimulated.

The shades of the glowing electric blue and neon colors are produced by variations in the positioning of the cells with their reflective quality. It seems that the bright coloration that shows when a marlin is kept moist in a plastic sheath or hosed with fresh water has triggered the opening of the dark melanophore cells so the light colors show through. The results of further study will be interesting if they explain the lighting up of body stripes, the pectoral fins and tail that is sometimes seen when the whole body or sections of it light up.

The age of the fish and rate of growth are regular points of discussion wherever fishermen and scientists meet. Marlin, unlike many other fish, have only tiny otolith ear stones, yet under a powerful microscope, like the larger ear stones of other species, they show rings similar to the annular rings on wood or on the scales of some fish. Research on marlin has shown that both males and females live to about the same age, although the males do not grow much beyond 190 kg (418 lb), whereas females of the same age weigh over 455 kg (1000 lb). It seems logical that males do not grow to the massive weights and size of the females, as several males fertilize the millions of eggs produced by the female.

Tagging and release programs have now been combined with injection with tetracycline. This compound stains the otoliths and bones in the fins, so study of the time between injection, tagging and release and recapture, combined with the number of rings beyond the stained bone, will confirm whether the rings are annually laid down.

Learning from scientists, improving one's own knowledge of the fish and marine environment is one of the great pleasures as well as necessities and benefits of fishing for the great gamefish. Fishermen and scientists both have much to learn, much to study to ensure knowledge of the sea and its inhabitants. Contribution to scientific knowledge, conservation and management of the resources will ensure not only their survival but that they will be there for further generations of fishermen.

Fishermen and scientists have many joint interests including the history and recording of the gamefish. It is ironic that the broadbill swordfish, still difficult for fishermen, was familiar to the ancients. Greek and Roman writings recorded much that is known about broadbill—

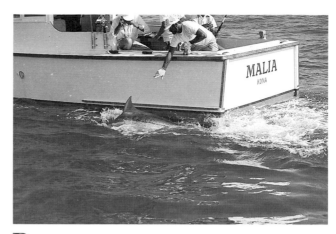

*P*acific blue marlin with glowing stripes and greenish tint show why they are highly regarded for their color as well as power. Photo: Jeff Webster

their migrations and life cycles, particularly in the Mediterranean. Bluefin tuna were also well recorded. The definitive information of most of the other gamefish had to wait until the eighteenth century, the era of explorers accompanied by scientists and artists.

The quest for first written references and illustrations of the gamefish often requires imagination and research as well as knowledge. There is also the problem of writings in different languages and mistakes in illustrations being repeated time after time as artists drew from previous illustrations. The classic hand-colored lithograph Marcus Bloch published in 1779 was reproduced many times, sometimes with the original mistake in the beautiful print in that the teeth and jaws were shown upside down.

A reference to a billfish that predates the flood of information from the late eighteenth century explorations is contained in William Dampier's book, *A Voyage to New Holland*, after his 1699 second visit to New Holland (Australia). In a bay he named Shark Bay for obvious reasons, he wrote, 'We saw a large garfish leap four times by us which seemed to be as big as a porpoise.' Shark Bay, Western Australia, in the late twentieth century became well known as the locality noted for the capture of Australian record sailfish. Were sailfish the 'large garfish' which seemed as big as porpoises, or were they marlin? Sailfish were also mentioned by explorers Renard and Valentjin in Indonesian waters in 1680 and 1720. The naming and illustration of the Indo-Pacific sailfish was by Shaw of the British Museum in 1804, and Valenciennes in 1831.

The first reference to Atlantic sailfish noted by Goode in his *Swordfishes* is Piso's *Historia Naturalis Brazillae*, published with illustrations and descriptions in 1648. In 1802, French naturalist Lacepède published a drawing of a chubby marlin washed up at La Rochelle on the Bay of Biscay in 1800. The length of this marlin was 330 cm (11 ft), and the weight 364 kg (800 lb). This

HISTORIC GAMEFISH
ILLUSTRATIONS

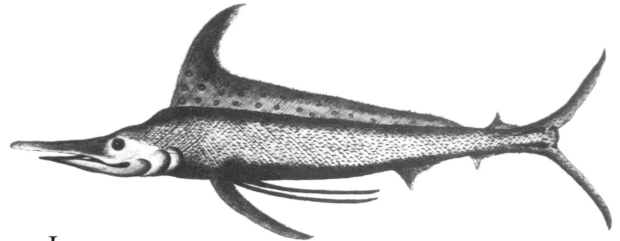

Illustration from 19 July 1787 of an 80 lb (36.3 kg) billfish taken on Lady Penryhn. *Photo: Peter Goadby.*

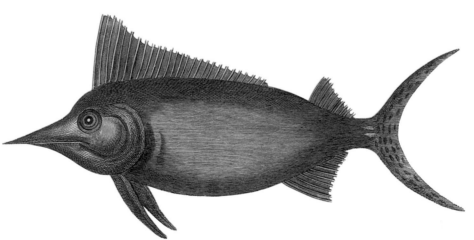

Lacapede's 1802 blue marlin illustration of a fish washed up at La Rochelle, France. It was reported to be 11 ft (330 cm) long and weighed 800 lb (364 kg). Photo: courtesy Bob Dunn.

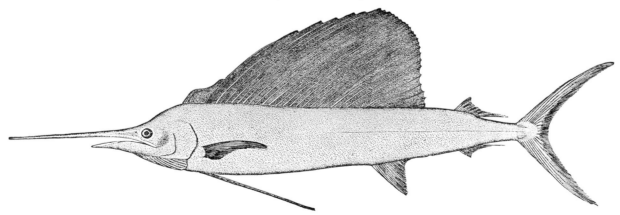

The 1880 illustration from Goode of the 'American Sailfish'. Photo: Peter Goadby.

drawing is now accepted as a blue marlin.

Strangely the settlement of Australia is involved in an even earlier illustration of an Atlantic marlin, a blue by the shape of the dorsal. Arthur Bowes Smyth, surgeon of the First Fleet ship *Lady Penrhyn*, one of the ships that brought the first settlers to Australia, caught this marlin after leaving St Helena in the Atlantic on the return voyage to England.

This journal has many natural history references and illustrations, including the first drawing by a European of an emu. Bowes Smyth was a keen observer with many references to sea birds and fish. There are many references to albacore, bonito, sharks, dolphin fish and fishing: 'The Women in general fish with a hook & Line the men strike them wt. a kind of spear. The Hook is made of the convoluted part of the Ear Shell, sharpen'd on a stone to a fine point.'

The journal also has a color drawing of a male dolphin fish (mahi mahi) caught by the steward Richard Young on 13 July 1789:
'A fine morng. & moderate breeze. Abt. 8 o'Clock this morng. the Steward caught a very fine Dolphin—As this Fish is Esteem'd the most beautiful of all others both in the Water as also whilst it is dying (wh. is in abt. 10 minutes after it is out of the water) for the variety & vividness of the Colours it exhibits. And as in general you very rarely see a Good Likeness of it painted, I think it will not be amis to subjoin a painting of it whilst dying taken by Richd. Young our Steward—in the best manner the time & Circumstances wd. admit of—'

Sunday 19 July was even more important: 'A Brisk breeze & quite fair. go 6 Ks—At 7 O'Clock this morng. the Steward caught a very curious Fish, it was taken just out of the water wt. the Line & held there till it was struck with the Grains—It was of the Xiphias (Sword Fish) Genus—'

It is a pity the journal does not have an illustration of the lures used to successfully take so many fish for the steward artist fisherman. Perhaps the lures were amongst the Tahitian goods traded for nails and beads when the ship reached Tahiti before continuing on to China on its return to England via St Helena. The journal gives a valuable clue to how the fish were caught:
'—Very large Shoals of Albarcore abt., wh., abt., 4 o'Clock p.m. began to take the bait & between that time & dark there were not less than 25 taken wt. the pearl fish hooks. & got safe on board, besides many that were hook'd but dropt off again. Upon an average they weigh'd 16 or 17 lb Each.' Perhaps they were using Tahitian pearl jigs to take their fish including the ultimate, the marlin.

There are similar valuable references in journals, logs and diaries of many of the exploring voyagers to all parts of the world for fishermen interested in fish and fishing and science.

Angler Raul Gutierrez and the Avalon *crew saw this 320 kg (705 lb) Great Barrier Reef black marlin light up like a Christmas tree. Sometimes stripes show even on the grander pluses. Photo: Captain Bill Harrison.*

NATIONAL MARINE FISHERIES SERVICE CATCH AND RELEASE QUICK REFERENCE CARD

Why release fish

1. A fish is too valuable a resource to be caught only once.
2. A personal commitment to conservation adds fun to fishing.
3. Size, season, and bag regulations make release mandatory.
4. Stressed fish populations need your help to recover.
5. The future of sportfishing is in your hands. Pass it on!

How to begin

1. Decide to release a fish as soon as it is hooked.
2. Land your quarry quickly, don't play it to exhaustion.
3. Set the hook immediately. Try to prevent a fish from swallowing the bait.
4. Work a fish out of deep water slowly, so it can adjust to the pressure change.
5. Use hooks that are barbless and made from metals that rust quickly.
6. Always keep release tools handy.

Handling your catch

1. Leave the fish in the water (if possible) and don't handle it. Use a tool to remove the hook or cut the leader.
2. Keep the fish from thrashing.
3. Net your catch **only** if you cannot control it any other way.
4. When you must handle a fish:
   - Use a wet glove or rag to hold it.
   - Turn a fish on its back or cover its eyes with a wet towel to calm it.
   - Don't put your fingers in the eyes or gills of your catch.
   - Larger fish can be kept in the water by holding the leader with a glove or by slipping a release gaff through the lower jaw.
   - Avoid removing mucous or scales.
   - Get the fish back in the water as quickly as possible.

5. Protect against personal injury by handling each species carefully and correctly.

Removing the hook

1. Cut the leader close to the mouth if a fish has been hooked deeply or if the hook can't be removed quickly.
2. Back the hook out the opposite way it went in.
3. Use needle-nose pliers, hemostats, or a hookout to work the hook and protect your hands.
4. For a larger fish in the water, slip a gaff around the leader and slide it down to the hook. Lift the gaff upward as the angler pulls downward on the leader.
5. Do not jerk or pop a leader to break it. This damages vital organs and kills the fish.

The final moments

1. Place the fish in the water gently, supporting its mid-section and tail until it swims away.
2. Resuscitate an exhausted fish by moving it back and forth or tow it alongside the boat to force water through its gills.
3. Use an ice pick, needle, or hook point to puncture the expanded air bladder on a fish taken from deep water.
4. Watch your quarry to make sure it swims away. If it doesn't, recover the fish and try again.
5. **REMEMBER, A RELEASED FISH HAS AN EXCELLENT CHANCE OF SURVIVAL WHEN HANDLED CAREFULLY AND CORRECTLY.**

Prepared and distributed by:
US Department of Commerce
National Oceanic and Atmospheric
   Administration
National Marine Fisheries Service
9450 Koger Boulevard
St Petersburg, Florida 33702
(813) 893-3141

FADS

The word 'fads' has several meanings for fishermen. For some, 'fads' describe the current trend of the month—the lure, the bait, the technique, the color, the secret that produces action. There are fads that do produce gamefish of all species. These fads are spelt FAD. The letters are the initials of Fish Aggregating Devices. Some fishermen think the initials are for Fish Attracting Devices. The attractant as part of FADs comes from the shelter that these manmade devices with their underwater structures give to the tiny forms of marine life, the fish crustacea and squid that are ceaselessly hunted by bigger predators that in turn are hunted and eaten by bigger predators right up to the peak predators, the sharks, billfish, tuna and other oceanic gamefish.

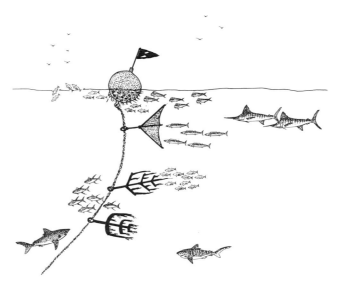

The effects of FADs—they concentrate passing fish and bait.

Weed lines, weed patches and kelp paddies are always worth trolling for mahi mahi, yellowtail and other species. Photo: Peter Goadby.

Manmade FADs recreate nature's FADs of drifting logs, weed lines and upwellings. A FAD has the effect of a floating reef, placed within range and visible to fishermen.

There is considerable debate wherever thinking fishermen, managers and scientists get together. They realize that manmade FADs help commercial and recreational fishermen by showing fishermen where the fish should be. Those who argue against the installation of FADs are aware that they do not increase the gamefish population; they simply make them more accessible to fishermen around the FADs instead of the grounds, ledges, peaks and natural upwellings that concentrate the food for the predators. They feel that these natural food congregators are known and found only by knowledgeable and experienced fishermen who have learned to decipher the riddles of finding offshore fish. Those against the

installation of FADs are concerned that the ease of finding the gamefish and the concentration may also place too great a pressure on existing stocks, as they only aggregate the population; they don't increase the gamefish population.

Despite the discussions and opinions of the pros and cons on manmade FADs, there is no doubt that they can make it possible for recreational fishermen to catch more fish and for more fishermen to find fish although the boat traffic will be heavy. McIntosh Marine of Fort Lauderdale, Florida, manufacture and market FADs that are easily assembled and moored.

Apart from the proven benefit for those seeking the peak predator species, FADs provide an ideal environment for catching suitable bait species to be fished near where they were caught or kept alive ready for a fast run to some nearby likely hot spot.

FADs give potential for all anglers to fish their favorite boat fishing methods. The areas around FADs are trolled with baits, with lures of proven successful speeds, slow trolling with live or dead baits, drifting with live bait, dead baits and strips, casting with spinning or bait casting tackle. Judicious use of chum and chunking will also add to activity around FADs even though sharks are logically included in the smorgasbord of big species attracted by the complete food chain activity in the area.

The FAD is an obstacle that will cause cut-off or break-off so thought and care must be exercised in boat positioning and maneuvering. Depending on position of boat and fish it is sound practice to restrain the impulse to lock up and fight hard until away from the buoy and its attendant underwater appendages.

NATURAL INDICATORS

OCEAN CURRENTS

Ocean currents are nature's highways and food chain providers of the high seas. The warm water Gulf Stream, sometimes 800 km or 500 miles wide and about 650 m or 350 fathoms deep, is perhaps the best known 'River in the Sea'. This current, which runs at 4–5 knots through the Florida Straits, moderates the temperature of the land masses on its course, as well as carrying the complete marine food chain and gamefish.

In offshore fishing, blue is beautiful, as this is often the color sought for big fish. In many places fishing is hot when the current is hot. Not all gamefish come from the blue water. At times for many reasons the action comes in green and brown water, but whatever the color, the dominating effect of the currents is known to successful fishermen. The current temperature and flow over the sea bed, coastal configurations, continental shelf and deeper canyons and dropoffs trigger the concentrations of microscopic plant and animal life that start the food chain.

Currents trigger upwellings of the deep ocean water with its concentration of nutrient-rich decaying and dead organisms brought to the surface. This concentration of minerals and salts stimulates the growth of plant plankton which is the start of the food chain that nurtures the

Wise fishermen keep an eye on changing cloud formations. Fish often bite freely at the approach of strong wind and weather changes. Photo: Peter Goadby.

microscopic animals that are the base of predatory life in the ocean. The current edges are most productive.

Cold water in the polar regions sinks and travels towards the tropics. The Humboldt Current of South America moves north along South America and is then deflected by the earth's rotation and shape of the South American west coast to warm in the tropics. Similarly the shape of Africa's west coast and the warm Guinea Current deflects the cool Benguela Current to the west. The west coast of Australia is unique in that it has a warm current instead of the cool currents that are generally present on west coasts of major land masses.

The currents and counter currents become ocean drifts as they weaken or are wind driven. All have names. Their direction is guided by that of the prevailing winds, the rotation of the earth and the shape of the coastline. Northern Hemisphere currents circle clockwise, Southern Hemisphere currents circle anti-clockwise. This 'coriolis' effect is popularly believed to show in the direction of bath water disappearing down the plug hole. Even though currents often appear to be streams running along the coast, in reality they meander in pools and eddies surrounded by the circling edge of the current.

These pools and eddies are important to offshore recreational and commercial fishermen, who look for current and temperature edges. The edges are a guide to where to fish and are clearly shown on photographs from cameras and remote sensing equipment on orbiting satellites. This information is of primary importance to weather forecasters who pinpoint and predict the El Nino

FISHING IN CURRENTS

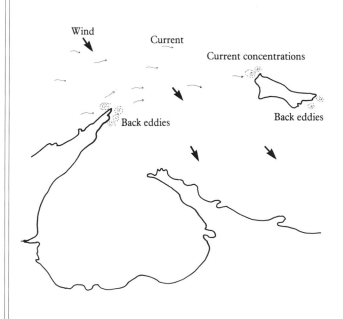

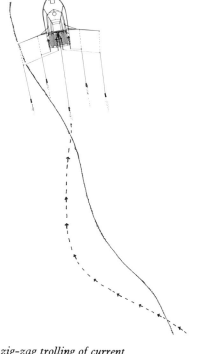

*S*hore formations attract big fish in warm currents to give action right inshore.

*P*roductive zig-zag trolling of current or temperature variations.

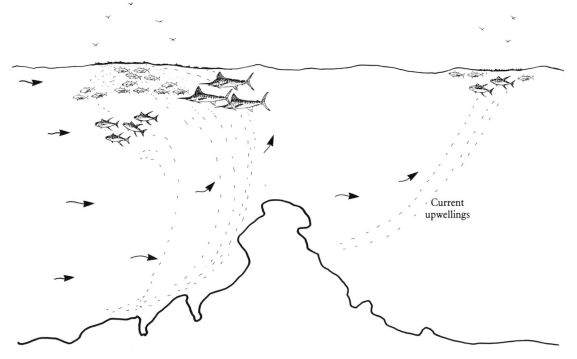

*F*ish should congregate upcurrent of higher bottom formations of reefs and peaks. In fast currents there are also fish congregations where the current returns to the surface downstream of bottom projections in a second upwelling.

Trevally feeding on surface plankton in Bay of Islands while the kahawai work deeper. Photo: Peter Goadby.

Trevally and kahawai explode through the surface as a black marlin marauds. Photo: Peter Goadby.

SEA SURFACE ISOTHERMS (°C)

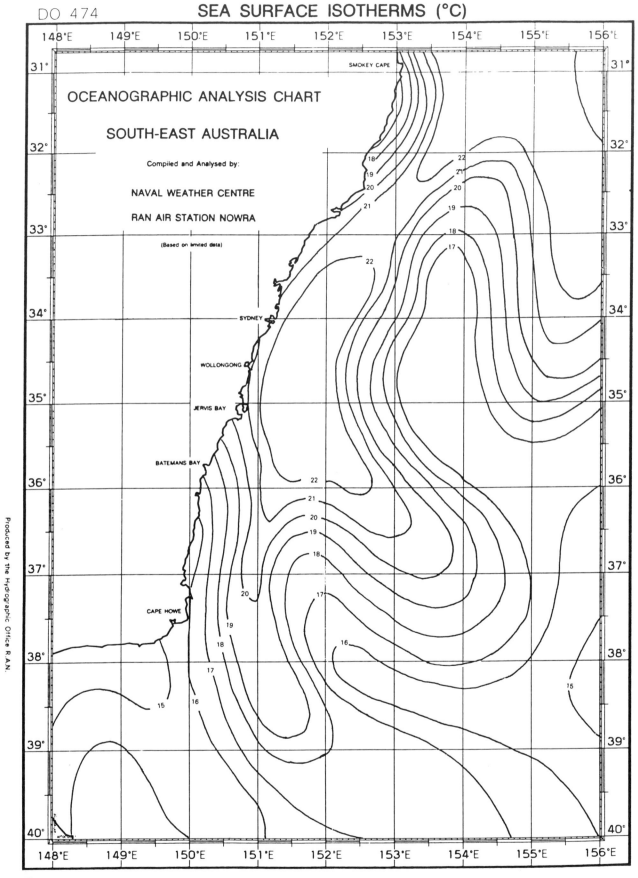

OCEANOGRAPHIC ANALYSIS CHART

SOUTH-EAST AUSTRALIA

Compiled and Analysed by:

NAVAL WEATHER CENTRE

RAN AIR STATION NOWRA

(Based on limited data)

Oceanographic analysis chart.

250m ISOTHERMS (°C)

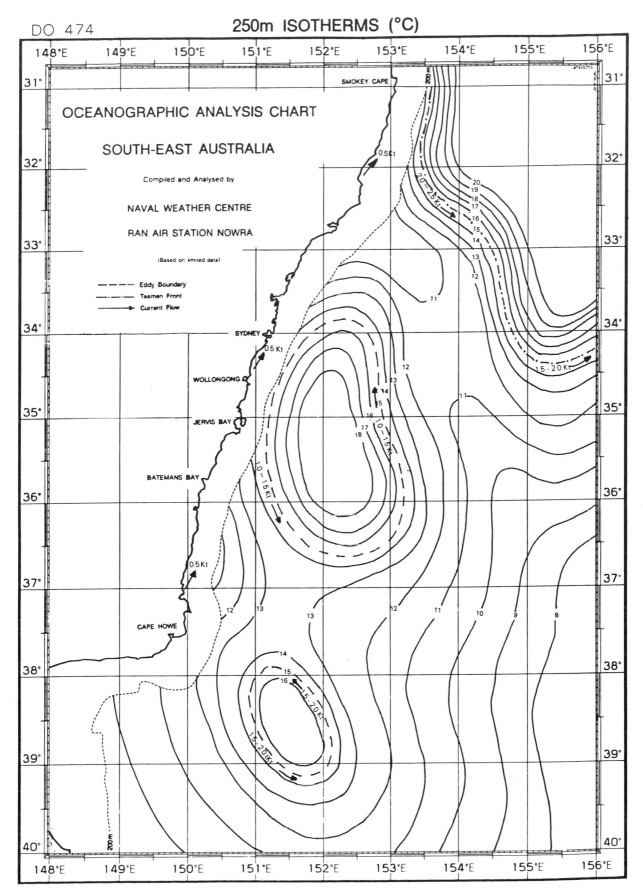

Oceanographic analysis chart.

The prolific school skipjack tuna are an important part of the food chain between plankton congregations in the upwellings and the peak predators—billfish, sharks and big tuna. Photo: Kim Holland, Honolulu.

and counter El Nino effects that affect fishing as well as climate.

Ocean current waters run down pressure from areas of high pressure to low pressure with movements caused by melting ice, heavy rainfall and evaporation by hot sun. Low temperatures make the ocean heavy and dense, while high temperatures make it lighter and less dense.

The currents are the hunting ground as well as the moving home of the gamefish, many of which wander within the currents rather than adhering to the defined migrations of other fish. Recording of tagged gamefish and sharks has shown that many species pass or congregate in the same area at approximately the same time and conditions each year. The Atlantic crossing of giant bluefin and blue sharks, the Pacific wandering and return of black marlin at Cairns, Australia, blue marlin off Hawaii and albacore off California provide information that can assist realistic management of these species.

The currents vary in temperature, velocity and direction from season to season and sometimes even from month to month. At some seasons, fingers of differing water temperature will push into the water along the coast. These fingers have the benefit of providing temperature edges but can have the disadvantage of pushing cool water in close to the coast and moving warm water further offshore out of range of sport fishermen.

The names of the transoceanic currents can be confusing as they make the passage between the continents. The current that has been named Gulf Stream off the east coast of the USA and Canada becomes the Gulf Stream Drift and the North Atlantic Drift, then the Portuguese Current, the North Equatorial Current, and the Antilles Current before again becoming the Gulf Stream. All stages of this North Atlantic current system are warm except the Portuguese Current.

The North Atlantic, South Atlantic, North Pacific, South Pacific and Indian Oceans have similar current systems where around three-quarters of the major transoceanic current is warm and the balance is cool. The winds that have most influence on these currents are the north-east trade winds in the Northern Hemisphere and the south-east trades in the Southern Hemisphere.

Not all gamefish and sharks are ocean wanderers over long distances. Some move only short distances and are subject even more to the effects of fishing pressures. Some species are associated with continental shelf habitat, while others are usually associated with the currents and drifts.

SEA BIRDS—THE FISHERMEN'S EYES IN THE SKY

Since man first hunted fish, birds have been some of the most important natural indicators of where fish and action should be. The world's great fishing grounds are naturally home to the birds whose fragile existence is dependent on the life of the sea. The best and most successful primitive fishermen were those who could read the pages of the ecological book revealed by the sea birds.

This has continued to modern times, despite the multitude of electronic devices that give today's fishermen even more visible indicators of fish and bait. The sea birds are more than natural guides. They have a unique beauty as well as purpose.

In some areas visiting and local people go to sea to watch and band sea birds. Man not only recognizes and respects these birds that survive the ruthless conditions of the water world, but realizes there is much to learn. Fishermen have a unique opportunity to watch and learn.

Visiting fishermen often notice the bird life more than locals. Nick Rutgers of Tahiti was fishing with us out from Sydney at the end of winter. Nick, a keen observer of nature, was amazed to see albatross of seven different species that day, as well as the confident way they sat in the chum trail at the boat. He was intrigued by the ungainly walking-on-water takeoff and landing that contrasted with their soaring grace once airborne. In contrast, we had been equally entranced by the number and range of birds that provided a living, wheeling, hovering backdrop to the prolific life in the passes that linked the Tahitian lagoons to the ocean depths. We learned the importance of the fluttering white terns and the high soaring frigate birds in Nick's home waters.

In Baja, visiting fishermen are intrigued by frigate birds and flocks working the other birds and bait as well as more familiarly soaring high in the blue, watching fish and birds, ready to swoop.

Sea birds link and bring together the marine world. The tropic birds with their graceful long twin tail feathers and powerful head and big eyes are there for those who know and recognize them. The long-tailed tropic birds ride high over the big fish, markers for marlin, tuna and mahi mahi. History and legend tell us that tropic birds had an important part to play in Christopher Columbus' discovery of the islands of the Caribbean, triggering the further exploration and settlement of the great land masses and riches of the Americas. The crew of Columbus' *Santa Maria*, after long days of sailing the boundless unmarked ocean had lost faith and demanded abandonment of the expedition and return to Spain, to their home waters, unsuccessful but safe. The sighting of tropic birds and other sea birds with a known offshore range of a maximum of 65 kilometres (40 miles) from shore provided the incentive to continue, to find the islands that led to the subsequent development of North America, with its attendant changes in the course of world history.

Fishing at Walker's Cay in the Bahamas is a reminder of the link between tropic birds, man and fish. This is also so at low-lying Christmas Island, Kiribati, which has its own subspecies of tropic bird, a variation of the widespread white tails. The white-tailed tropic bird occurs in all tropical oceans, while the striking red-tailed tropic bird is an Indo-Pacific species not found in the Atlantic.

The sea birds that are part of the ocean fishermen's life range from the tiny storm petrels that appear too

A *flock of frigate birds off Baja California. In other areas frigate birds are usually loners high in the sky. Photo: Al Tetzlaf.*

Pelicans around the world have the same massive bill, graceful flight and ungainly landing whether in Australia or the Caribbean. Photo: Peter Goadby.

fragile and surely lacking range and toughness to survive in their harsh environment, to the dark brown of the deep-diving, long-ranging shearwaters. These blend with either the blue or green of the oceans they traverse on their long migrations north and back to return to their homes in deep southern latitudes. A migrant from the cold southern waters to equally cold waters of the north, the worldwide sooty shearwater is just one of these travellers moving from southern islands north to the frozen waters bordering Alaska, Greenland and the Bering Sea, a similar north/south range to the Wilson's storm petrel.

It is ironic to realize that these small sea birds cover such a great north/south route, while the albatrosses with their massive wingspans travel mainly east and west. Their ocean wandering does not include equatorial crossings. Apart from their size, habits and attractive colors, the legend that killing them will lead to disaster (as in Coleridge's poem *The Rime of the Ancient Mariner*) makes them a source of wonder to fishermen.

Nine of the thirteen albatross species live and soar only in the southern oceans. Three, including the Laysan Albatross, occur in the warmer waters of the north Pacific, and the black-footed albatross in the northern tropical Pacific. Giant petrels, despite the distinctive double tube on top of their bill, can be confused with albatrosses as they glide and soar, skimming the surface of the ocean, using the wind, going into it, downwind and across. Albatross are also called mollyhawks.

The wandering albatross with its wingspan of up to 324 cm (130 in) is the biggest of the ocean wanderers, while Elliott's storm petrel with a wingspan of less than 15 cm (6 in) may be the smallest, although Mother Carey's chickens are equally small. The pintado, the most striking of the petrels with its shepherd's plaid pattern, also has two names, pintado and cape pigeon. It is seen in flocks in the Roaring 40s of the south and occasionally singly or in small numbers north to the Tropic of Capricorn.

Fishermen also become confused with the divebombers of the bird world. Various species are called gannets in the cold climates, and their almost identical relatives in the tropics are called boobies. These birds fly 15 to 30 m (50 to 100 ft) above the surface of the sea. Then when they sight their food they fold their wings and drop like arrows through the water surface and beyond.

Frigate birds, also called man-o'-war birds, are the pirates of the marine air waves. They soar and glide with their distinctively hooked wings, motionless. They ride over bait schools or big fish waiting for surface or bird action, poised to pick up small fish right on the surface or to harass other feeding birds into disgorging the food they have already taken. Frigate birds lack the natural oil on their feathers that enables other sea birds to set and live comfortably on the surface of the sea. Their marauding, harassing, aerial dogfight tactics force the other birds to disgorge the small fish, squid or crustacea they have swallowed, and the frigate birds pick it up before it hits and sinks below the surface. The piratical activities of these birds extend also to robbing chicks from the nests of other birds. The male frigate bird is very striking with its bright red balloon throat patel and glossy green-black feathers.

The eight pelican species of the world are perhaps the easiest of all birds to identify; no other bird has the massive bill and expandable pouch. All the pelicans, except the Chilean pelican of the Humboldt Current, range from inland to coast to provide interest and curiosity to the fishermen of bays and estuaries in particular. The Chilean pelican is the only known offshore species. Pelicans are graceful in flight and most efficient hunters. While travelling in flight they carry their neck tucked into the shoulder, then while fishing they fly with bill pointed down. When they sight their prey they suddenly stop as if shot, folding their wings as they drop to the surface with a resounding splash. At other times they paddle and hunt under the surface, picking up food from the muddy surface water and even from the shallow sea bed. If any efficient fish-hunting bird deserves the description 'cute', this is it.

Gulls and terns are the most numerous of the sea bird families. Gulls live and hunt mainly along the coast and inshore. The various terns hunt further to sea, although most of their activity is in shallow water. The tropical and sub-tropical world species, the brown winged tern, and the tropical world species sooty tern, range out into the deep water of the ocean far from the coast. Many of the terns have black caps on top of their heads, but the white tern with snowy white body, large dark eyes and dark bill exhibits an ethereal appearance of spirit from the tropical world of other sea bird species. The gulls are the other numerous and prolific family that in their adult plumage show how black, white and grey can be blended, merged and reversed in a bewildering range of species. The raucous cry of the gulls negates their attractive colorations, confidence and adaptation to modern changes in their environment.

Gulls always seem to have their bills open ready for food and squawking loudly. The bills and legs of some adult gulls are bright red, in contrast with their body coloration. Gulls and their look-alikes feed on the surface. The activity of gulls raises false hopes for fishermen as they work and circle on trash instead of the hoped for feeding fish.

Pelicans, shearwaters and cormorants are the deep divers of the sea birds. Of these three, the cormorant has the unwelcome reputation of feeding and reputedly affecting populations of immature fish that would grow to sporting size. The flexible snake-like neck of the cormorant darts underwater to unerringly allow the bill to grab and hold its prey before attempting to swallow. Chinese and other indigenous fishermen use cormorants

Albatross of several species are a source of interest to anglers in Southern Hemisphere, temperate waters. Photo: Peter Goadby.

with neck ring and line attached to a powerful paddling leg as a feathered fish gatherer. The fish caught by the cormorants become food for the humans instead of birds.

The sea eagles (fish hawks or ospreys), although they fish inshore, add majesty as well as a sensation of remoteness as they use the natural updrafts and air currents to soar without wing movement before plummeting to secure their food for themselves and their family. Their stick nests sitting on stark trees, boulders or manmade structures add to the charisma of these birds, even though the hunting activity is of no assistance to human fishermen.

The other sea birds add to the romance of the marine world and to fishing. They can see far into the water from high in the sky. They are living links between man and giant fish right around the world, as well as part of the moving tapestry of a day at sea.

The days with the greatest number of birds and most bird activity are, for those fishermen who know and recognize the messages they are giving, often the most successful and interesting fishing days.

ESTIMATING WEIGHT WITHOUT SCALES

IGFA rules provide that record claims shall be weighed on scales and that the fish must be weighed on land and not at sea. The travelling fisherman can still gain a fairly accurate assessment of the weight of his capture if it is too big for any available scales. A time-proven formula that fits most species of gamefish and sharks will give a weight that is remarkably close to correct, though of course calculated weights are not eligible for record claims. The girth of the fish is taken at its greatest part and converted to inches. The length of the body is taken from the tip of the lower jaw to the middle of the crotch of the tail and converted to inches. The width in inches is squared and multiplied by the length in inches. This total is divided by 800 and the answer is very close to the true weight in pounds; e.g., girth 3 ft 4 inches is equal to 40 inches; square of 40 is 1600; multiply by length of 8 ft 4 inches, which is inches = 100; final figure of 16,000 is divided by 800, which gives an approximate weight of 200 lbs.

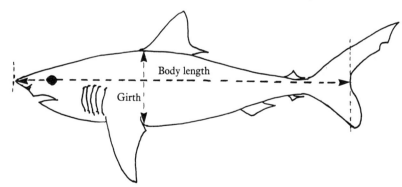

*W*eight calculated by measurement for sharks.

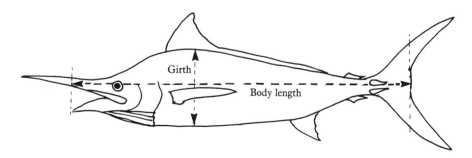

*W*eight calculated by measurement for billfish.

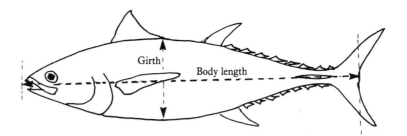

Weight calculated by measurement for tuna.

Blue marlin may be 10 per cent above the calculated weight.

Charter captains in the Great Barrier Reef black marlin fishery have ascertained that a circumference of 50 cm (20 inches) at the butt of the tail on a black marlin is a positive guide to whether it will exceed the magic 454 kg (1000 lb) mark.

All tackle used must be submitted at time of weighing. IGFA rules now say that at least 15.24 m (50 ft) of line plus the double, if one was used, in one piece and leader must be submitted with the completed record claim and photographs. IGFA each year issue their fishing rules with the current world record chart. IGFA address is 3000 E Las Olas Boulevard, Fort Lauderdale, Florida 33316, USA. Membership of IGFA is open to clubs and individual anglers who receive a news sheet and patches direct from the world body.

INDEX

PAGE NUMBERS IN *ITALICS* REFER TO ILLUSTRATIONS AND CAPTIONS.

Excitement-generating mahi mahi are active jumpers in all tropical waters. Photo: Captain Bill Harrison.